MASTERPIECES OF THE MODERN THEATRE

A NINE VOLUME SET EDITED BY ROBERT W. CORRIGAN

MASTERPIECES OF THE MODERN GERMAN THEATRE

Edited by ROBERT W. CORRIGAN

FIVE PLAYS

WOYZECK

MARIA MAGDALENA

THE WEAVERS

THE MARQUIS OF KEITH

THE CAUCASIAN CHALK CIRCLE

COLLIER BOOKS
A Division of Macmillan Publishing Co., Inc.
NEW YORK

Library of Congress Catalog Card Number: 66-23476

FIRST COLLIER BOOKS EDITION 1967

Fourth Printing 1975

Cover photo of Bertolt Brecht by Gerda Goedhardt

Macmillan Publishing Co., Inc.
866 Third Avenue, New York, N.Y. 10022

Printed in the United States of America

Grateful acknowledgment is hereby made to Macmillan Publishing Co., Inc., for permission to reprint material from *The Modern Theatre,* edited by Robert W. Corrigan. Copyright © by Robert W. Corrigan, 1964.

CONTENTS

THE FRONTIER SPIRIT OF MODERN
GERMAN DRAMA

By Robert W. Corrigan

UNLIKE OTHER IMPORTANT PERIODS in theatrical history, the
theatre of the past 150 years has been dominated by
neither a single dramatic form, nor one overpowering style
of production. Just as change has been the essential characteristic of modern life, so too in the theatre. The modern drama
has been mercurially eclectic, boldly experimental, and extremely volatile in spirit. And nowhere are these qualities
more clearly observable than in the German theatre. Since
the time of Kleist and Buechner, Germany has always had a
frontier theatre, and her playwrights have pioneered just
about every significant new dramatic movement that has
emerged since the turn of the nineteenth century.

Georg Buechner, that amazing undergraduate who wrote
three important plays before he died at a youthful twenty-
four, is still an avant garde playwright 130 years later. It is
well known that in Woyzeck, Buechner created the first lower-
class protagonist (Miller's Willy Loman is a syrupy parody
by comparison), but most people do not realize how revolutionary *Woyzeck* is in other ways. Today, especially because
of the efforts of Artaud and Brecht, we have once more been
made aware of the fact that the theatre is primarily a gestural
and not a literary art. But in *Woyzeck* language *is* gesture! In
the powerful, breathy rhythms of his dialogue, Buechner has
expressed the tragedy of language—man's inability to grasp
the words that will save him—in a manner which only Ionesco
has been able to equal since. However, more important than
Buechner's innovations in theme and theatrical language was
his use of essentially cinematic dramatic structures. The short,

staccato scenes (some only a few lines long) of *Woyzeck* were unheard of in the theatre anywhere on the continent in the nineteenth century. And even now, despite the profound influence the film has had on our new writers, few playwrights will attempt, at least not with any confidence, to use those techniques which Buechner had mastered at such a tender age. In theme, language and technique he was ahead of his time, and he still is in the vanguard.

When compared to Buechner, Hebbel seems hopelessly out of date. Fair enough. But we should not forget that Hebbel was in many ways Ibsen's spiritual father and that *Maria Magdalena* preceded *A Doll's House* by thirty-five years. Old Anton's "I don't understand the world any more!" heralds the revolutions of 1848, and as the curtain came down on the first performance of *Maria Magdalena* in 1844, naturalism and the middle-class drama had arrived. This play—as well as his essays on the theatre—had a profound effect on playwrights for the next fifty years and Ibsen, especially, was influenced by them. The Scandinavian giant described the nineteenth century in the theatre as "a war to the knife with the past." It was Freidrich Hebbel who put the knife in Ibsen's hand.

Gerhart Hauptmann and Frank Wedekind were pioneers in much the same way. Today when we think of Hauptmann, *The Weavers* invariably comes to mind. This is undoubtedly his best play and his decision to use a mob of weavers as a collective dramatic hero was in itself a major innovation. However, in his eclecticism Hauptmann may have made an even greater contribution to the modern theatre. When we examine the careers of Ibsen, Becque, Chekhov, Strindberg (at least until 1898), and the early Shaw, we are conscious of the evolution of a dramatic style. Each of these writers developed and changed, but their growth was organic and only in retrospect is it clearly discernible. Not so with Hauptmann. Each of his first thirteen plays, beginning with *Before Sunrise* (1889) through *Michael Kramer* (1900), was written in a markedly different style. Strindberg is more famous for this kind of eclecticism, but in point of fact Hauptmann was the first modern dramatist of major significance to employ variety as an artistic principle.

On the other hand, Wedekind, like Buechner, was and still is a vanguard dramatist. We usually think of him in terms of his early "Tragedies of Sex," but these seem to be relatively minor achievements when one examines the total body of his work. He was a bold experimenter and the father of dramatic expressionism, and yet he had moved on to new theatrical techniques long before that frantic style had spent its energies. *The Marquis of Keith*, with its cultural centers, beatniks, organization men, and smooth-operating entrepreneurs, is in many ways descriptive of the 1960's, and it comes as a shock to discover it was written before the turn of the century. Brecht, who was seldom guilty of exaggerations, probably best expresses the modern theatre's debt to his mentor in this tribute written at Wedekind's death: "It was the enormous vitality of this man, his energy, which enabled him to create—in spite of all the scorn and ridicule which was heaped upon him— his song of songs in honor of humanity, and which also gave him such personal charm. He did not seem mortal. . . . He was, together with Tolstoy and Strindberg, one of the great educators of the new Europe."

And then there was Bertolt Brecht, the prophet for the drama of a collective society. Brecht was the first playwright in the modern theatre to comprehend fully the effects of industrialization and collectivism upon our social structures, and he realized that the conflicts created by these forces were not being dealt with in the theatre. As early as 1925, he wrote: "When one sees that our world of today no longer fits into the drama, then it is merely that the drama no longer fits into the world." Brecht's epic theatre is an attempt to express the drama of a world that was gradually being transformed from a traditional community into a highly organized collective state. Thanks to the continuing activity of Brecht's own theatre, The Berliner Ensemble, we are just now coming to understand what he was up to. European playwrights openly acknowledge their debt to him, and here in America his influence is beginning to be felt in the work of several of our younger dramatists.

The German theatre has always been on the frontier, and it shows no sign of changing its role. If abstract expressionism ever catches on in the theatre, it will be largely due to the efforts of Günter Grass, Tankred Dorst, and Peter Weiss. The most significant experiments in documentary drama, the newest trend in continental theatre, have been made in Germany by Rolf Hochhuth (*The Deputy*) and Heiner Kippardt (*The Case of J. Robert Oppenheimer* and *The General's Dog*). And on it goes. The history of modern Germany is a chronicle of calumny and change, horror and holocaust, guilt and greed, complexity and contradiction; and through it all, her dramatists have been the theatre's most adventurous pioneers. In spite of their history, and because of it.

MASTERS OF THE MODERN THEATRE

By Robert W. Corrigan

AFTER VISITING the United States in 1835, Alexis de Tocqueville described the kind of literature he believed an industrialized democratic society would produce. "I am persuaded," he wrote in *Democracy in America*, "that in the end democracy diverts the imagination from all that is external to man and fixes it on man alone. . . . It may be foreseen in like manner that poets living in democratic times will prefer the delineation of passions and ideas to that of persons and achievements. The language, the dress, and the daily actions of men in democracies are repugnant to conceptions of the ideal. . . . This forces the poet constantly to search below the external surface which is palpable to the senses, in order to read the inner soul. . . . The destinies of mankind, man himself taken aloof from his country, and his age, and standing in the presence of Nature and of God, with his passions, his doubts, his rare prosperities and inconceivable wretchedness, will become the chief, if not the sole theme of poetry." Any examination of the arts of the past century would seem to indicate that de Tocqueville's prophecy has been fulfilled, and it is certainly clear that the theatre's general pattern of development during this time can be best described as a gradual but steady shift away from universal philosophical and social concerns toward the crises and conflicts of man's inner and private life. It is possible to discover foreshadowings of this change in direction and emphasis in the plays of the early nineteenth-century Romantics—Buechner, Hebbel, Kleist, Gogol, Musset—but it was not until Ibsen that the theatre's revolutionary break with the past became clearly discernible. In fact, Ibsen's career as a playwright to a large extent parallels both in form and in theme the modern drama's increasing tendency to be concerned more with the conflicts of the individual's interior world than with the significance of his public deeds.

The causes of any revolution are always as difficult to untangle as its consequences are to assess, and any attempt on the part of the critic to describe them will inevitably result in oversimplification. But it is possible to discover certain basic changes in attitude which had been evolving in Europe since the time of Luther and which had begun to crystallize in Continental thought by the second half of the nineteenth century. And the works of the revolutionary playwrights— Ibsen, Strindberg, Chekhov, Shaw, and Hauptmann—were the first to express in the theatre certain of these radical shifts in the way man had come to think of nature, society, and himself. What follows is an attempt to set forth briefly some of the more important aspects of this revolution in the drama which Ibsen referred to as "a war to the knife with the past."

One of the dominant ideas of the modern *Weltanschauung* is the belief that it is impossible to know what the world is really like. Beginning with Luther's refusal to accept that there was any intelligible relationship between faith and works, the sacramental view of experience gradually disappeared. In rejecting the phenomenal world as an outward and visible manifestation of man's spiritual condition, Luther began a revolution in thought which, because of the achievements of science and technology in the past two hundred years, now makes it impossible for man to attach any objective value to the observations of his senses. This insistence on such a clear-cut division between the physical and the spiritual aspects of reality had a profound effect on the modern dramatist. Inevitably, it made him increasingly distrustful of his sensory responses to the "outside" world, and at the same time it tended to negate whatever belief he might have had in the objective validity of his subjective feelings and sensations. The modern artist no longer holds a mirror up to nature, at least not with any confidence; he can only stare at his own image. He becomes a voyeur to his own existence.

Probably no force in the nineteenth century did more to destroy man's belief in an established norm of human nature, and hence begin this process of internalization in the theatre, than the advent of psychology as a systematized field of study. In his book *"Modernism" in the Modern Drama*, Joseph Wood Krutch argued that the basic issue confronting all the dramatists of the past hundred years was the problem of "modernism." Briefly, modernism involves both the conviction and the practice that to be modern is to be, in many important ways, different from anyone who lived before. This does not mean that man has changed; human nature is the same, but man's way of looking at himself has changed significantly. It is this new view of man that creates the problem for the dramatist.

Good examples of this changed perception can be found in Ibsen's *Hedda Gabler* (1890) and Strindberg's *Miss Julie* (1888). Hedda and Julie have the distinction of being the first fully and consciously developed neurotic heroines in dramatic literature. By neurotic we mean that they are neither logical nor insane (in the sense of being random and unaccountable) but that the aims and motives of each has a secret personal logic of their own. The significant thing about both characters is that they are motivated on the premise that there is a secret, and sometimes unconscious, world of aims and methods, a secret system of values which is more important in human experience than rational ones. This approach to character is not, however, the same as the Romantic attitude which affirms the superior validity of the nonrational. We need only read Strindberg's famous Preface to *Miss Julie* or Ibsen's working notes for *Hedda Gabler* to discover that they did not believe, as did the nineteenth-century Romantic poets, that the irrational was a supernatural and unknowable force; rather, in giving detailed account of why their heroines behaved as they did, Ibsen and Strindberg insisted that neurotic behavior and mysterious events are always explainable in terms of natural causes. The significant difference is that neither of these characters can be explained or judged by a common standard; the actions of each character (and by extension, of each human being) are explicable only in terms of that peculiar combination of forces, frustrations, and desires which is unique to himself.

For us living in the middle of the twentieth century there is nothing very new in these psychological ideas; but, coming when they did, they were quite revolutionary, and they have created problems for the playwright which have not yet been solved. By convincingly demonstrating that normal people are not as rational as they seem, and that abnormal people do not act in a random and unintelligible way, psychology has made it difficult, if not impossible, for the dramatist to present his characters in a direct way. In earlier times when it was believed that there was a sharp distinction between the sane and the insane, the irrational "aberrations" of human behavior were dramatically significant because they could be defined in terms of a commonly accepted standard of sane conduct. It seems clear, for instance, that Shakespeare believed Lear on the heath to be insane, while it is equally clear that Macbeth at the witches' cauldron was not. But for the modern dramatist deeds do not necessarily mean what they appear to mean, and in themselves they are not directly revelatory of the characters who commit them. Miss Julie, Hedda Gabler, and Kostya Treplev of Chekhov's *The Sea Gull* are all suicides; but, unlike Othello's suicide, the meaning of each of their deaths cannot be clearly ascertained from the actions that preceded it. The plight of the modern dramatist in this regard becomes apparent when we realize that without Strindberg's Preface or Ibsen's Notebook we could never know for certain what the significance of each heroine's death really was. And the ambiguity of almost every interpretation of *The Sea Gull* is largely due to the fact that Chekhov never made the meaning of Treplev's suicide explicit.

All drama of the past is based upon the axiom "By their deeds shall ye know them." The significance of the dramatic hero was revealed by his deeds, and there was a direct relationship between the hero's overt acts and his inner spiritual condition. The significance of Oedipus, for instance, is revealed by his deeds, not by some explanation that he is suffering from an Oedipus complex; and there is a direct relationship between the act of tearing out his own eyes and his solving the riddle of the Sphinx. Even when a charcater commits a dissembling deed, it is to deceive the other characters in the play, not the spectators. Certainly one of the chief functions of the soliloquy in Elizabethan drama was to keep the audience informed as to what was going on. Hamlet may put on an antic disposition, but not before he tells the audience he is going to do so. However, beginning in the nineteenth century, the drama began to reflect man's growing distrust in the ability of his senses to comprehend the true nature of reality. Appearances are no longer believed to be direct reflections of ideal reality, like the shadows on the wall of Plato's cave; rather they are thought of as a mask which hides or distorts reality. And by the time of Pirandello, particularly in such plays as *Right You Are, If You Think You Are* (1916), *Six Characters In Search of an Author* (1921), and *The Mock Emperor (Enrico IV)* (1922), appearances not only do not express reality, they contradict it, and the meaning of these plays is not to be found in appearance or reality but in the contradiction itself.

One of the great achievements of the Elizabethan dramatic form was its ability to express several levels of experience simultaneously. The world of Hamlet is both public and private, a world in which personal and familial relationships, fantasy and mystery, and political and psychological conflict coexist in a state of constant dramatic tension. One of the main reasons why the Elizabethan dramatic form works so successfully is that appearances can be taken at face value. But when the dramatist begins to distrust the validity of his sensory perceptions, it becomes difficult, if not impossible, for him to dramatize the complex totality of experience in a single form. Reality must be broken down into its component parts, and each part can be expressed only in a form peculiar to itself. Admitting individual differences in the works of each dramatist's writing of any given period, it is nonetheless possible to describe with some accuracy the dramatic form employed by the playwrights of the fifth-century Greek theatre, the Elizabethan and Restoration theatres of England, and the French neo-classic theatre of the seventeenth century. But in discussing the modern theatre we must always speak of forms, for there is no single, dominant form in the serious theatre of the past hundred years. It is for this reason that the evolution of the drama since the time of Shakespeare has been so aptly described as a process of fragmentation.

It is likely that every serious dramatist believes it his artistic duty to be true to his presuppositions about the real nature of the world in which he lives. However, once a playwright believes that the meaning of every human action is relative and intelligible only in terms of a unique and subsurface combination of forces, the dramatic events of the plot cease to have meaning in themselves, and they take on significance only as the secret motivations of the characters who participate in them are revealed. (The technique of earlier drama is just the reverse: the motivations of the characters are revealed by the events of the plot.) But how does the dramatist objectify the hidden and unconscious, and what happens to the theatre when he feels obligated to explain and

probe into his characters' hidden lives? Explanation is always
a dangerous business in the theatre (since the time of the
ancient Greeks, exposition has always been the dramatist's
most difficult problem), but the moment a playwright assumes
that if he explains his characters he has written a play, that
danger becomes mortal. All too often the writers of the modern theatre have forgotten that a dramatic situation requires
not that we *understand* a character but simply that we
believe in him. Dramatic action always leads to a judgment; it requires that something shall happen to and
through the characters; something that is embodied in the
events of which the characters are a part. Whenever the
personality of the character, rather than the action of which
the character should be a part, becomes the playwright's chief
concern, dramatic process dissolves into explanation, and
when that occurs, the range of the theatre is drastically reduced, if not unalterably damaged.

One has only to compare the plays of the mid-twentieth
century to those of Ibsen, Shaw, or Strindberg to realize just
how much the scope of the theatre has been narrowed. However, early evidence of the gradual loss of belief in dramatic
heroes, who needed no explaining, can be found in the sentimental bourgeois drama of the eighteenth century. For the
first time a character was no longer noble, responsible, or
morally significant, and therefore dramatically interesting just
because of his birth, position, power, or wealth. As a result,
the dramatist was obliged to justify both his choice of characters and the situations in which they are engaged. The Romantic drama of the eighteenth and nineteenth centuries
resisted a break with the past and attempted unsuccessfully
to perpetuate the forms and figures of earlier times. Certainly
the revolt of Ibsen and his contemporaries in the last quarter
of the nineteenth century was in some measure due to their
conviction that the dramatic conflicts of the Romantic drama
were inflated and without significance, and that the nobility
of its characters was artificial and contrived. In rejecting the
artificialities of Romanticism, the modernists changed the
theatre in many ways; but for all their dissatisfaction with
their predecessors they were unable to forestall disbelief in the
possibility of heroic characters who needed no explaining.

This was largely because as a literary movement nineteenth-century naturalism was so closely related to nineteenth-
century biology. Darwin's theories of evolution (*Origin of*

Species, 1859) and the discovery of new genetic laws had convinced many writers that man's existence, including his personality, was a phenomenon that could be explained in terms of scientific laws. As a result, increasingly, man's complex biological needs rather than his capacity to make moral choices were thought to be his most significant characteristic. Once such a view was accepted, however, the exceptional man, who because of his position and power had the greatest freedom of choice, ceased to be the fullest embodiment, and therefore the best representative, of those conflicts and choices that most clearly define the human condition. Instead, the lives of the poor—where the role of natural necessity is most readily observable—became the playwright's most suitable subjects. The drama of the common man, then, did not happen by accident, nor did it evolve because some dramatist or group of dramatists wanted it to. Given the problem of creating in a world in which all human actions tend to be explained in terms of psychological or sociological cause and effect, a world in which the possibility of deliberative and moral choice is doubted if not rejected outright, it is difficult, if not impossible, for the playwright to fashion a character of traditional heroic stature.

There is an old saw about no man being a hero to his valet. Neither is he one to his psychoanalyst. Nor can he be one to a playwright who views his actions as behavioral phenomena explicable in terms of some kind of laws—scientific or otherwise. Oedipus, for example, remains a hero of great stature so long as he is not suffering from an Oedipus complex. But once we learn to explain him in terms of repressed hopes and fears, traumatic childhood experience, or a vitamin deficiency in infancy, although he may remain interesting —in fact he may gain a new kind of interest, as Cocteau's *The Infernal Machine* attests—he loses stature. Even if we are able, temporarily to accept the Elizabethan attitude toward heroes, which of us can understand a Hamlet or a Lear? And which of us can forgive an Othello or a Macbeth? But it is precisely because they seem mysteriously beyond our powers of understanding that they remain heroes for us. And it is a belief in a mysterious, unknowable quality in men that substantiates man's sense of his own importance in the universe. However, if a playwright comes to believe that all human actions are in reality predictable behavioral responses, and his moral judgments of these actions can be dissolved by psychological understanding, how can he pattern a tragedy or create characters with stature? If there can be no possibility for an appraisal of personality as such, why should Hamlet's death be any more significant than that of Rosencrantz and Guildenstern?

But the problem does not end here. For once the dramatist dismisses the possibility of passing moral judgments on his characters' actions, he comes face to face with an even more frightening spectre—guilt that has no form of expiation and thus turns into anxiety. It has long been known that art must ultimately fail in its attempts to come to grips with the facts of death. Perhaps this is also true of anxiety. How can there be drama in an Age of Anxiety? What kind of play will be produced when the central conflict is between something and nothing? Many of the arts may be able to express the condition of anxiety; but the theatre, because of the objective reality and irremovable presence of the living actor, and because the drama is essentially an embodiment of the conflict between at least two opposing recognizable and nameable forces, is incapable of dealing with anxiety, or it does so to its own great peril. Beginning with the Watchman in the opening scene of the *Orestia* right on through the ghosts of Elsinore and the tormented heroes of Schiller and Kleist, the theatre has always found a way to transform anxiety into fear; that is, give it a definite object. But when we come to such plays as Ibsen's *Ghosts* and *The Master Builder* and Strindberg's *There Are Crimes and Crimes* and *The Ghost Sonata,* we discover that although this process of objectification is attempted, it is not totally successful. And when the transformation does not take place, the form and content of drama begin to change in uncontrollable ways, as some of the plays of Beckett and Ionesco, Pinter and Albee will attest. It is difficult enough to find a meaning for man in a world that views a return to nothingness as the ultimate reality, but it is next to impossible to create a dramatic "action" which can encompass the terror of being on the edge of the abyss. Kierkegaard, and more recently Paul Tillich, have declared that this threat of nothingness is the central anxiety of modern man. Many modern playwrights have sought to overcome the despair of this situation by maintaining that the only meaning of life is to be found in that death which is inevitable. But this is not an assertion that gives meaning to any of the particularities of life; in fact, it drains them of meaning. At best, it is a method of redeeming existence from meaningless anarchy by showing that the pattern of life is simple and imperturbable. But such a pattern, though it may appear to conquer chaos, is too abstract to live successfully in the theatre.

In life as we experience it, we are conscious of our physical natures, our social situation, and our unique psychic existence; and we live on all three of these levels simultaneously. For this reason it is impossible for us to act or make a choice without some element of human behavior—what we do out of physical necessity or because of social habit—playing a significant role in our decision. At the same time, because of the simultaneity of our being, it is impossible for us to understand completely the individuality of our actions. But in the theatre we see life as pure deed, that is, life in which the arbitrariness of human behavior has been eliminated and in which the mysterious transformations of individuality have been fixed. Thus, in contrast to a person in life, who is recognized by the continuity of his being and finally can only be known through intuition, a character in a play is an identity who is defined by the coherence of his acts. For this reason the deeds of a dramatic action are always public, and the characters best suited to drama are men and women who, either by fate or choice, lead a public life and whose deeds are of public concern. This explains why kings, princes, and nobility have traditionally been the most suitable subjects for drama. But as the increasing dominance of the machine in modern life has gradually destroyed the direct relation between a man's intention and his deeds, public figures have ceased to be our most appropriate heroes because, as W. H. Auden points out, "the good and evil they do depends less upon their characters and intentions than upon the quantity of impersonal force at their disposal."

Our world, it would seem, has become almost too big for the playwright. Power is too impersonal, great deeds are collective achievements, and the great man is one who is capable of withstanding some of the pressures of a mass society and manages, somehow, to maintain a face and stance more or less his own. Compare, for example, the achievement of a Lindbergh (our last "lone" hero) to that of a Colonel Glenn, who was interchangeable with five other astronauts. Or, how can the power of a Napoleon be envisioned today? In our times power is so enormous that it is barely visible and those who govern are little more than incidental and easily replaceable expressions of that power. Power is like an iceberg; the largest part is submerged—in abstraction, anonymity, and bureaucracy. Government, like modern physics, has lost its physical reality and can be expressed only in statistics and formulae. Indeed, the true men of action in our time, those who transform the world, are not the statesmen and politicians, but the scientists. Unfortunately, their most significant actions are not suitable subjects for the theatre, because their deeds are concerned with things, not people, and are, therefore, speechless.

But what are the implications of this for the theatre? Who are the true representatives of a world whose heroes are nameless? As the Swiss playwright Duerrenmatt put it: "Any small-time crook, petty government official, or policeman better represents our world than a senator or president. Today art can only embrace victims if it can reach men at all; it can no longer come close to the mighty. Creon's secretaries close Antigone's case."

That there has been a shift in attitude toward the heroic is easily seen when we examine any one of the many modern adaptations of the Greek tragedies. For example, today most people find Anouilh's *Antigone* much more a reflection of their attitudes and thus more immediately interesting than Sophocles' tragic working of the theme. The characters and the dilemma of their situation seem more human. Antigone is not a hard and almost inhuman girl, with such a monomaniacal fixity of purpose that she rejects all other feelings and desires. In the modern version she is, humanly, both weak and strong. She has a lover in Haemon, whom she rejects; but she is also a helpless little girl who runs to "Nanny" for comfort and strength; as she approaches death, she is afraid and seeks the consolations of even the most calloused of guards. Creon is not a blind and power-mad tyrant; he is a businessman king who is caught in the complex web of compromise and expediency which will not allow abstract moral principles to upset the business of government.

However, what the play gains in humanity it loses in tragic force. The sense of Antigone's aloneness and Creon's moral blindness, and of the inevitable destruction implicit in their conflict, has been softened. Anouilh's Antigone is not alone and unloved, and his Creon is not blind. We pity their situation because they are two quite attractive people caught up in a situation which neither of them likes but which they cannot control. They are victims in a disordered world which they have not created and which they have no moral obligation to correct. As the play ends, we are left with an ambiguity which allows for no reconciliation.

One of the most important functions of the hero, both in art and life, is to supply those images, values, and ethical standards which people aspire to and which they would like, if possible, to incorporate into their own lives. It would seem, however, that increasingly our modern industrialized society not only does not need heroes, but it actually suppresses or perverts our need of them. In their important book *Industrialism and Industrial Man*, Kerr, Dunlop, Harbison, and Myers convincingly demonstrate that "like ideologies, the great personality—the one great figure around whom historians so frequently weave their story—began to seem less important. Instead of ideologies and dominant personalities, we became increasingly attentive to the inherent nature of the particular industrializing system and the basic strategy and forces at work within it." Only the system, then, is important, and it fills men's remaining need for heroes by promoting celebrities, those heroes of the surface who play well their constantly shifting roles.

Furthermore, specialization—the key operative principle of an industrial society—produces not only pluralism in our economic system but also a pluralistic deviation of heroic types. However, when there are and can be so many heroic types—one cannot even begin to count all the heroes of the popular imagination—you begin to get a leveling; and with that leveling not only is the stature of heroism diminished, but the individual's sense of his own identity is actually invalidated.

Traditionally, the hero is always best described in terms of those forces that urge him to spiritual redemption. Maxwell Anderson once wrote that "from the point of view of the playwright, the essence of a tragedy, or even a serious play, is the spiritual awakening, or regeneration, of his hero." But the one thing that characterizes the hero of surfaces—and this is certainly in large measure due to industrialization and bureaucracy—is precisely the fact that he lacks the dimensions of spiritual awareness, personal morality, and social responsibility. Paul Tillich wrote in his *The Religious Situation* that "the fundamental value in ethics of a capitalistic society is economic efficiency—developed to the utmost degree of ruthless activity." Such an ethical standard is hardly conducive to the creation of great heroes in the drama.

That we live in an antiheroic age is a commonplace. Carlyle proclaimed its coming in the nineteenth century when he said: "We shall either learn to know a hero . . . when we see him, or else go on to be forever governed by the unheroic." This transformation has occurred; we have accepted it; we are even used to it. Whatever nostalgia we may still occasionally feel is more than adequately taken care of by television. In the place of the hero we have the celebrity, that triumph of the ordinary. In our time, hero worship has become horizontal; indeed, we even look down to a "man like myself."

While the advent of psychology as a systematized field of study may have been the most powerful single force to shape the modern theatre, actually the process of internalization had begun much earlier. For instance, it is clear from Hebbel's essays on the drama that the despair of old Anton's "I don't understand the world any more" in the final scene of *Maria Magdalena* is much more than an expression of the age-old frustration of the parent who does not understand the behavior of his children. It also reflects his dimly understood but tremendously painful realization that it is not longer possible for him to comprehend what the world has become or to imagine what the future will be like. Until the Industrial Revolution, patterns of life were passed on from father to son with the confidence that these patterns would satisfy the needs and desires of each new generation. Such confidence was justified, for life changed so gradually and imperceptibly that when changes did occur they were easily assimilated into the shared life of the community. But by the middle of the nineteenth century the effects of the Industrial Revolution had begun to be felt on all levels of society. Technology, with its ever-increasing capacity to transform man's way of living, not only made the future so unpredictable that it soon became impossible for him to imagine what his life would be like twenty years hence, but in its singular concern with the individual's functional qualities technology tended to isolate him from his fellows and invalidate his spiritual values and metaphysical concerns. At the same time, the discoveries of the nineteenth-century archeologists, and the ensuing interest in anthropology, tended to break down provincial and absolutist attitudes concerning human nature. Early anthropologists like Mannhardt, Robertson-Smith, Tylor and the great James Frazer made it clear that human nature was not something fixed and unchanging but only that kind of behavior exhibited in each culture. In fact, as early as 1860 scholars were demonstrating that human nature is so plastic that it can, as Frazer was later to point out in the Preface to the first edition of *The Golden Bough* (1890), "exhibit varieties of behavior which, in the animal Kingdom could only be exhibited by different species." Furthermore, by the middle of the century, democracy was finally beginning to be established both as a way of life and as a form of government. Today we tend to forget what a revolutionary idea democracy is and the shattering effects that it had upon the values of eighteenth- and nineteenth-century Europe. Tocqueville told us long ago: "Not only does democracy make every man forget his ancestors, but it hides his descendants and separates his contemporaries from him, it throws him back forever upon himself alone and threatens in the end to confine him entirely within the solitude of his own heart." In short, by the middle of the nineteenth century every established view of God, human nature, social organization, and the physical universe was beginning to be seriously challenged if not invalidated. And this revolutionary climate had a profound effect on the theatre.

Of all the arts, theatre is the only art that has always concerned itself with human destinies. Dramatic action is historical in the sense that the perpetual present of each moment on the stage is created out of past events and is directed toward a definite, if yet unknown, future. In previous ages the destiny of any dramatic action was significant because the ever-changing events in the lives of dramatic heroes could be meaningfully related to eternity, that is, to some permanent value or idea such as Fate, the Gods, or Heaven and Hell, which transcends the human condition and which is believed in by the dramatist and/or his audience.

In the plays of Buechner and Hebbel we discover the first indications in the theatre of that sense of alienation from both God and Society which underscores the fact that man's belief in eternity had been shaken. And one of the most significant aspects of Ibsen's work (at least after *Peer Gynt*, 1867) is the fact that the realm of ultimate value has either disappeared or has become so mysterious that it has ceased to have dramatic relevance. In its place we find instead a belief in some form of social ideal or societal structure; first, as the agent of some unknown Destiny, and then as Destiny itself. But when society begins to assume the role of Destiny, that is, is thought of as the determining force for good or evil in the lives of men, man cannot help but feel eventually that the meaning of his Destiny has been drastically reduced. For Society, as Robert Bolt writes in the Preface to his *A Man for All Seasons*, "can only have as much idea as we have what we are about, for it has only our brains to think with. And the individual who tries to plot his position by reference to our society finds no fixed points, but only the vaunted absence of them, 'freedom' and 'opportunity'; freedom for what, opportunity to do what, is nowhere indicated. The only positive he is given is 'get and spend' . . . and he did not need society to tell him that. In other words we are thrown back by our society upon ourselves, which of course sends us flying back to society with all the force of rebound."

Any mind capable of spiritual aspiration seeks in the actions of the dramatic hero that which affirms the vitality of the free will in any given situation. Man's free will may be defeated by the forces of Destiny—in fact, the great plays have always testified that the destroying forces of Destiny are as much a part of the hero's character as his free will; it may be paralyzed and thus incapable of action; it may be submerged by the battle in such a way as to become part of that Destiny; it may even turn out to be an illusion; but it must always be an active force if we are to believe that we are partaking in human greatness. Such a Destiny must be greater than an aggregate of human beings or an expression of social patterns.

Ironically, the revolt of Ibsen and Shaw against the conventional nineteenth-century drama was motivated by a desire to enlarge the range of Destiny in the theatre. In their attempts to present man in his total historical and social setting, they were rebelling against the narrow and private worlds that had been dominating the stage since the Restoration. But in spite of their efforts, nothing could change the fact that in the two hundred years since Shakespeare the world of the spirit had greatly diminished. The Ekdals' attic and Mrs. Warren's drawing room were not—and never could be—the same as Elsinore or Cleopatra's barge.

Nonetheless, the pioneers of the modern drama had revitalized the theatre precisely because they belived that significant social issues should be dealt with in the theatre. Thus for nearly three decades the theatre had a vitality of spirit and a forcefulness of manner which it had lacked for more than a century for the very reason that its context had been reduced. To the playwright writing at that time the human and social problems, which were the source materials of the naturalistic play, appeared capable of solution if only man and society would learn to use their common sense; which usually meant one of two things—the acceptance of a less rigid standard of social morality or the espousal of some form of socialism. But with the collapse of the established social order in the first World War, the validity of these too-easy solutions was impugned, and beginning with the plays of the early German Expressionists (written 1912–1916) the positive optimism of the Edwardian era gave way to a sense of bewilderment, exasperation, and defeatism, only occasionally tempered by the slim hope that the war had brought man to the threshold of a "New Age." The theatre reflects these changes from confidence to doubting and despair, from complacent faith in cherished values to an anxious questioning, from a rigorous but rigid morality to the mystic evangelism, the fanatical polemics, and the frivolous apathy of a disintegrating world. These changes are most apparent in the Jekyll and Hyde theatre of the German Expressionists whose nerve-shattered playwrights alternated between a militant idealism and grotesque nightmares. But one need only compare Shaw's *Heartbreak House* to *Major Barbara*, Pirandello's *Right You Are, If You Think You Are* to *Liolá*, or Hauptmann's *Winter Ballad* to *The Weavers* to realize that the effects of the collapse of the old order were widespread and were reflected in the works of established writers as well as those of the new generation. Immediately after the war the theatre on the continent was dominated by attitudes of emotionalism and cynicism, but these gradually gave way to feelings of frustration, futility, and despair, and by the middle of the 1920's the serious drama of Europe had become almost totally introspective and psychological in its orientation.[1]

---

[1] Because they were essentially isolated from the main currents of European history in the first two decades of the century, the Irish and American theatres were not immediately effected by the spreading paralysis which was transforming the rest of modern drama. But it is clear from O'Casey's *The Plow and the Stars* (1926) and *The Silver Tassie* (1927) that the Abbey Theatre could not withstand for long the theatre's introspective tendencies, and there was no serious American drama until O'Neill's plays were first produced right

Obviously, this tendency toward paralyzing introspection has by no means been accepted by everyone writing for the theatre. In fact, a large segment of the modern theatre might be best described as a reaction against the despair and de-humanizing implications of the modernist position. These "resistance movements" have sought to discover the means, both formal and substantive, whereby the possibility and validity of selfhood and human integrity, personal responsi-bility, and morally significant judgments could be reasserted in the theatre. Some playwrights—especially Eliot, Fry, Betti, and Claudel—have turned to orthodox Christian belief to provide a metaphysical structure for their drama. Others, like Lorca and Synge, have written out of the traditions and value systems of premodern hieratic societies. Probably the largest group of all is composed of those dramatists who have sought to escape the deadly strictures of modernism by turning to classical mythology.

All of these writers share one common and fundamental at-titude: each of them was in some way rebelling against the conditions of the modern world. They were not only conscious of that lack of a sense of community which inevitably occurs in an increasingly democratic society; more important, they were aware of man's growing sense of his own isolation. The modern world, with its growing collectivism, paradoxically tends to throw man back upon himself, while at the same time it increasingly tends to destroy the individual's sense of his own selfhood. This creates an impasse which the modern dramatist, for the most part, has been unable to overcome.

Joseph Warren Beach, in analyzing the problems of modern fiction, describes the reaction of many writers to this condi-tion in this way: "One of the hardest things for man to bear is spiritual isolation. The sense that he stands alone in the universe goes terribly against his gregarious instincts. He has an over-powering impulse to construct a system which will enable him to feel that he does not stand alone but is in-timately associated with some force or group infinitely more powerful and significant than himself." It is clearly evident in the work of all those playwrights who have rebelled against

---

after the war. In the twenty years between O'Neill's *Beyond the Horizon* (1920) and *The Iceman Cometh* (1941) the American theatre repeated the Continental cycle in its own terms, and by the beginning of the Second World War all of the Western theatre had reached that No Man's Land between comedy and tragedy, between pathetic aspirations and ridiculous bewilderment, between never-beginning action and never-ending talk.

modernism that they too are seeking to construct a system that will restore meaning to life and validity to art. In the end, however, they have not been completely successful, because they have all too often had to deny the realities of the modern world in the process. Furthermore, they have not accepted the wisdom of Brecht's statement that "when one sees that our world of today no longer fits into the drama, then it is merely that the drama no longer fits into the world." By insisting upon values that we may once have cherished but which no longer in actuality exist, the playwrights of the resistance have not been able to revitalize the theatre or its audiences. And most important, they have not succeeded in stretching the imaginations of men in order that they might conquer that sense of isolation and despair that pervades the modern world. And this brings us to the playwrights of the mid-twentieth century.

In an age dominated by space orbits and telestars, the fear of nuclear war, the tension of cold war diplomacy, and the insecurity of a defense economy, our greatest uncertainty is whether or not in the midst of epochal disorder man has any good chance, to borrow Faulkner's phrase, of prevailing; and if he does, what kind of man will prevail?

This uncertainty has had a profound effect on our theatre, and if there is one thing that characterizes the work of almost all of our serious playwrights of the last two decades it is that their plays express the contemporary theatre's tremendous concern to find a metaphor for universal modern man as he lives on the brink of disaster—a metaphor that expresses the inalienable part of every man, that irreducible part of each of us that exists after all the differences have been stripped away and which is beyond and beneath all that is social, political, economic, religious, and ideological. In short, they are searching for a metaphor of man left face to face with himself.

Such an idea of the theatre has tremendous implications for the drama, and we are just now becoming aware of them. First of all, it abolishes the traditional linear plot because our contemporary playwrights are not interested in presenting an action in any Aristotelian sense but are, rather, in dramatizing a condition. Whenever one asks what the central action of a Beckett, Ionesco, or Pinter play is, he come a cropper; "action" for the contemporary playwright is an artificial concept. He is concerned with showing life as it is, and in life there is no central action, there are only people, and the only thing that is basic to each individual is the ontological solitude of his being. The dramatist's only concern is to create in his plays a situation which will reveal the private drama that each man has inside himself and which is enacted every day in the random, apparently meaningless, and undramatic events of our common routine. "History," said James Joyce's Stephen Daedalus, "is a nightmare from which I must awake." The rapidity of historical change and the apparent powerlessness of the individual to affect Collective History has led in the theatre to a retreat from history. Instead of tracing the history of an individual who is born, grows old, and dies, many modern playwrights have devoted their attention to the timeless passionate moments of life, to states of being. They want to express the paradox, the contradiction, and the incompleteness of experience. They are attempting to suggest the raggedness, the confusion, the complexity of motivation, the "discontinuous continuity," and the basic ambiguity of all human behavior. They are, in short, pursuing the premises of modernism to their fullest and most logical conclusions. The writers of the contemporary theatre are facing the "facts of life." If the dramatic meaning of their plays is that drama is no longer possible, they would contend that any other meaning would be artificial, illusory, false; if the dialogue in their plays consists of meaningless clichés and stereotyped phrases, they would insist that this is the way we talk; if their characters are constantly changing their personalities, these playwrights would point out that no one today is really consistent or truly integrated. If the people in their plays seem to be helpless puppets without any will of their own, they would argue that we are all passively at the mercy of blind fate and meaningless circumstance. They call their theatre "Anti-Theatre," and this they insist is the true theatre of our times. If they are correct, so be it! Then history has again followed its own inexorable laws. The very forces that gave life and strength to the modern theatre have caused its decline and death.

But the theatre is always dying, and with equal regularity, like the phoenix, it is resurrected. No one can say with certainty what its new form will be, but that there will be a future seems certain. First, largely because of the development of college and university theatre programs in this country and the large increase in the number of professional repertory theatres here and abroad, there are more people who have experienced good theatre than ever before. And this enlarged audience wants and needs theatre, and it will not be satisfied for long with the maimed rites of psychological and moral cliché, or impassioned jeremiads from prophets of doom, or the meandering contemplations of writers who are morbidly consumed in introspection and self-analysis. Fortunately, there are audiences who want and need the theatre, and they go to the theatre in the hopeful anticipation that the stage will be capable of accommodating all of the terrible-wonderful emotions and insoluble dilemmas of our shared life together. This demand insistence by audiences on a drama that deals with the significant issues and concerns of our public life will, I believe, force our playwrights to open up new frontiers in the drama and thus extend the boundaries of the theatre. The second great hope of the theatre is that, in spite of the overriding temper of despair and the dominance of antitheatricality in current drama, our playwrights still find human action significant, still find it necessary to write plays, and, in the very act of writing, attest to the miracle of life. We live in one of the most dramatic ages in the history of mankind, and if the past is any kind of reliable guide to what the future of the theatre will be, we have good reason to believe that the theatre of tomorrow can be as dramatic as the world in which we live today.

MASTERPIECES OF THE
MODERN GERMAN THEATRE

GEORG BUECHNER

1813–1837

GEORG BUECHNER is usually referred to as the first truly modern dramatist. His career as a playwright was a case of "instantaneous ripeness"; he wrote his first play at the age of twenty and his meteoric career ended with his tragic death at the age of twenty-four. Buechner's modernity lies in the fact that he was the first to fuse the realistic social concerns—which we generally associate with Ibsen, Hauptmann, and Zola—with the anguish of isolation and social alienation that did not become a dominant theme in the theatre until the twentieth century. His profoundly moving plays, with their episodic structure, their staccato-like language, and their serious concern for the conflicts of the little man, strangely prefigure the work not only of Brecht but also the writers of the Theatre of the Absurd.

FROM BUECHNER'S LETTERS[1]

Translated by Maurice Edwards

LETTER TO HIS FIANCEE, NOVEMBER 1833.

I have been studying the history of the French Revolution.
I have felt as if crushed beneath the gruesome fatalism of
History. I find in human nature a terrifying sameness, in the
human condition an inexorable force, granted to all and to
none. The individual mere froth on the wave, greatness sheer
chance, the mastery of genius a marionette play, a ridiculous
struggle against brazen law; to recognize it, the supreme
achievement, to control it impossible. . . .

I intend to bow no more before the parade horses and
bystanders of History. I have accustomed my eyes to the sight
of blood. But I am no guillotine blade. *Must* is one of the
curses which baptized man. There is the terrifying dictum:
"For it must needs be that offenses come; but woe to that
man by whom the offense cometh!" What is it in us that lies,
murders, steals? I do not want to pursue this thought any
further. Oh, if I could but lay this cold tormented heart on
your breast!

LETTER TO GUTZKOW FROM DARMSTADT, FEBRUARY 21, 1835.

Dear Sir:

Perhaps you may have observed, or even, in less fortunate
instance, your own experience may already have told you
that there is a degree of misery which makes one forget every
consideration and benumbs every feeling. True, there are

[1] From *Buechner's Letters* by Georg Buechner, translated by Maurice Edwards, Volume 6, Number 3, March, 1962 of *The Tulane Drama Review*. Copyright by *The Tulane Drama Review* © 1961. Printed by permission of *The Tulane Drama Review*.

people who maintain that in such a case one ought rather starve himself out of this world; but I came upon the living refutation of this position in an only recently blinded captain I met on the street who declared he would shoot himself were he not forced to live in order to support his family. That is terrible. You will easily perceive that there could be similar circumstances hindering one from making an anchor of one's body to be thrown from the wreck of this world into the water; and you will therefore not wonder at my breaking open your door, bursting into your room, thrusting a manuscript[2] onto your breast, and demanding charity. I ask you to read this manuscript as quickly as possible and, in the event your conscience as a critic will allow, to recommend it to Mr. Sauerländer, and to answer forthwith.

As to the work itself, I can tell you no more than that the most unfortunate circumstances forced me to write it in at most five weeks. I say this to motivate your judgment of the author, not of the drama as such. What I should make of it, I myself do not know; I know only that I have every reason to blush as far as History is concerned; still, I console myself with the thought that, with the exception of Shakespeare, all poets stand like schoolboys before History and Nature. . . .

Should the tone of this letter perhaps cause you to wonder, consider that it is easier for me to beg in rags than to extend a supplication in dresscoat; and almost easier, with pistol in hand, to say: *"la bourse ou la vie!"* than to whisper with trembling lips: "God bless you!"

LETTER TO HIS FAMILY FROM STRASSBURG, JULY 28, 1835.

I must say a few words about my play. First let me observe that permission to make a few changes has been liberally abused: on well-nigh every page, something omitted, something added, and nearly always in a way most detrimental to the whole. Often the sense is entirely distorted or else totally gone, and almost downright nonsense takes over. Besides, the book literally abounds in the most dreadful misprints. They sent me no proofs. The title page is insipid, and it bears my name—which I had expressly forbidden; moreover, it is not on the title page of my manuscript. In addition, the editor stuck several vulgarities into my mouth which never in my life would I have uttered. I have read Gutzkow's brilliant

[2] *Danton's Death.*

critique and noted there to my joy that I have no inclination to conceit. Moreover, as to the so-called immorality of my book, my answer is as follows:

The dramatic poet is, in my eyes, nothing but a writer of History, but is superior to the latter in that he creates History for the second time. He transplants us directly into the midst of the life of an era, giving us, instead of a dry account of it, characters rather than characteristics, and figures rather than descriptions. His foremost task is to get as close as possible to history as it really happened. His book must be neither more nor less moral than history itself; but history was not created by the good Lord to provide suitable reading matter for young females, and so I must not be blamed either if my drama is so little suited to that. I can hardly make paragons of virtue out of a Danton and the bandits of the Revolution! If I wished to describe their dissoluteness, I had to make them dissolute; if I wished to show their godlessness, I had to let them speak like unbelievers. If a few indecent expressions result, one need only reflect on the well-known obscenity of the speech of that time—of which what I let my people utter is only a weak distillation. There remains but to reproach me for having chosen such a subject. But this objection was refuted long ago. Were one to let it stand, the greatest masterpieces of literature would have to be repudiated. The poet is not a teacher of morals; he invents and creates characters, he brings past epochs back to life, and people may then learn from these as they learn from the study of history and their observation of what happens around them in human life. . . . In that case (if one *so* wished), one ought not to study history at all because so very many immoral things are reported therein; one would have to go blindfold through the streets not to see the indecencies, and must needs cry out against a God who created a world in which so much debauchery takes place. If, moreover, someone were then to tell me that the poet should not represent the world as it is, but rather as it should be, I would answer that I don't wish to make it better than the Good Lord, Who surely created the world as it ought to be.

Further, as to the so-called idealist poets, I find that they have given us almost nothing but marionettes with sky-blue noses and affected pathos, certainly not people of flesh and blood who make me feel their joy and suffering, and whose comings and goings fill me with horror or admiration. In short, I think highly of Goethe or Shakespeare, but very little of Schiller. That, moreover, the most unfavorable critiques are yet to appear is understood; for governments must demonstrate through their paid penmen that their opponents are stupid asses or immoral yokels. Besides, in no way do I consider my work perfect and will gratefully accept any genuine aesthetic criticism. . . .

Three more refugees have drifted in here; Nievergelder is among them; in Giessen two students were arrested again. I am extremely careful. Here we know of no one arrested on the border. History must be a fairy tale.

Letter to his Family from Strassburg, January 1, 1836.

. . . . By the way, I definitely do not belong to the so-called Young Germany, the literary party of Gutzkow and Heine. Only a total misunderstanding of our social conditions could make people believe it possible to effect a complete reform of our religious and social ideas. Then too, though I by no means share their concept of marriage and Christianity, I am nevertheless annoyed when people a thousandfold more sinful in practice than these are in theory pull moral faces and throw stones at young, diligent talent. I go my own way and remain in the field of drama which has nothing to do with all these controversial issues. I draw my characters in accordance with Nature and History and laugh at those who would like to make me responsible for their morality or immorality. I have my own thoughts about that. . . .

Letter to his Family, September 1836.

I have not let my two plays out of my hands yet; I am still dissatisfied with much in them and do not wish it to go as it did the first time. This is work one cannot be ready with at a set time as a tailor with his clothes.

WOYZECK

by GEORG BUECHNER

1836

WOYZECK[1]

Translated by Carl Richard Mueller

CHARACTERS

WOYZECK

MARIE

CAPTAIN

DOCTOR

DRUM MAJOR

SERGEANT

ANDRES

MARGARET

PROPRIETOR OF THE BOOTH

CHARLATAN

OLD MAN WITH BARREL-
  ORGAN

JEW

INNKEEPER

APPRENTICES

KATHY

KARL THE TOWN IDIOT

GRANDMOTHER

POLICEMAN

SOLDIERS, STUDENTS,
  YOUNG MEN and GIRLS,
  CHILDREN, JUDGE,
  COURT CLERK, PEOPLE

[1] *Woyzeck* by Georg Buechner, translated by Carl Richard Mueller, printed by permission of the translator. Copyright © 1963 by Carl Richard Mueller. All rights reserved. Performance rights in all media, whether amateur or professional, must be obtained from Hill and Wang, Inc., 141 Fifth Avenue, New York, N.Y. 10010.

Scene 1

[*At the* CAPTAIN'*s. The* CAPTAIN *in a chair.* WOYZECK *shaving him.*]

CAPTAIN. Not so fast, Woyzeck, not so fast! One thing at a time! You're making me dizzy. What am I to do with the ten extra minutes that you'll finish early today? Just think, Woyzeck: you still have thirty beautiful years to live! Thirty years! That makes three hundred and sixty months! And days! Hours! Minutes! What do you think you'll do with all that horrible stretch of time? Have you ever thought about it, Woyzeck?

WOYZECK. Yes, sir, Captain.

CAPTAIN. It frightens me when I think about the world . . . when I think about eternity. Busyness, Woyzeck, busyness! There's the eternal: that's eternal, that is eternal. That you can understand. But then again it's not eternal. It's only a moment. A mere moment. Woyzeck, it makes me shudder when I think that the earth turns itself about in a single day! What a waste of time! Where will it all end? Woyzeck, I can't even look at a mill wheel any more without becoming melancholy.

WOYZECK. Yes, sir, Captain.

CAPTAIN. Woyzeck, you always seem so exasperated! A good man isn't like that. A good man with a good conscience, that is. Well, say something, Woyzeck! What's the weather like today?

WOYZECK. Bad, Captain, sir, bad: wind!

CAPTAIN. I feel it already. Sounds like a real storm out there. A wind like that has the same effect on me as a mouse. [*Cunningly.*] I think it must be something out of the north-south.

WOYZECK. Yes, sir, Captain.

CAPTAIN. Ha! Ha! Ha! North-south! Ha! Ha! Ha! Oh, he's a stupid one! Horribly stupid! [*Moved.*] Woyzeck, you're a good man, but [*with dignity*] Woyzeck, you have no morality! Morality, that's when you have morals, you understand. It's a good word. You have a child without the blessings of the Church, just like our Right Reverend Garri-

son Chaplain says: "Without the blessings of the Church."
It's not *my* phrase.

WOYZECK. Captain, sir, the good Lord's not going to look at a
poor worm just because they said Amen over it before they
went at it. The Lord said: "Suffer little children to come
unto me."

CAPTAIN. What's that you said? What kind of strange answer's
that? You're confusing me with your answers!

WOYZECK. It's us poor people that . . . You see, Captain, sir
. . . Money, money! Whoever hasn't got money . . . Well,
who's got morals when he's bringing something like me
into the world? We're flesh and blood, too. Our kind is
miserable only once: in this world and in the next. I think
if we ever got to Heaven we'd have to help with the thunder.

CAPTAIN. Woyzeck, you have no virtue! You're not a virtuous
human being! Flesh and blood? Whenever I rest at the
window, when it's finished raining, and my eyes follow the
white stockings along as they hurry across the street . . .
Damnation, Woyzeck, I know what love is, too, then! I'm
made of flesh and blood, too. But, Woyzeck: Virtue! Virtue!
How was I to get rid of the time? I always say to myself:
"You're a virtuous man [*moved*], a good man, a good man."

WOYZECK. Yes, Captain, sir: Virtue. I haven't got much of
that. You see, us common people, we haven't got virtue.
That's the way it's got to be. But if I could be a gentleman,
and if I could have a hat and a watch and a cane, and if
I could talk refined, I'd want to be virtuous, all right. There
must be something beautiful in virtue, Captain, sir. But I'm
just a poor good-for-nothing!

CAPTAIN. Good, Woyzeck. You're a good man, a good man.
But you think too much. It eats at you. You always seem
so exasperated. Our discussion has affected me deeply. You
can go now. And don't run so! Slowly! Nice and slowly
down the street!

Scene 2

[*An open field. The town in the distance.* WOYZECK *and*
ANDRES *cut twigs from the bushes.* ANDRES *whistles.*]

WOYZECK. Andres? You know this place is cursed? Look at
that light streak over there on the grass. There where the

toadstools grow up. That's where the head rolls every night. One time somebody picked it up. He thought it was a hedgehog. Three days and three nights and he was in a box. [*Low.*] Andres, it was the Freemasons, don't you see, it was the Freemasons!

ANDRES [*sings*].

> Two little rabbits sat on a lawn
> Eating, oh, eating the green green grass . . .

WOYZECK. Quiet! Can you hear it, Andres? Can you hear it? Something moving!

ANDRES [*sings*].

> Eating, oh, eating the green green grass
> Till all the grass was gone.

WOYZECK. It's moving behind me! Under me! [*Stamps on the ground.*] Listen! Hollow! It's all hollow down there! It's the Freemasons!

ANDRES. I'm afraid.

WOYZECK. Strange how still it is. You almost want to hold your breath. Andres!

ANDRES. What?

WOYZECK. Say something! [*Looks about fixedly.*] Andres! How bright it is! It's all glowing over the town! A fire's sailing around the sky and a noise coming down like trumpets. It's coming closer! Let's get out of here! Don't look back! [*Drags him into the bushes.*]

ANDRES [*after a pause*]. Woyzeck? Do you still hear it?

WOYZECK. It's quiet now. So quiet. Like the world's dead.

ANDRES. Listen! I can hear the drums inside. We've got to go!

Scene 3

[*The town.* MARIE *with her* CHILD *at the window.* MARGRET. *The Retreat passes,* THE DRUM MAJOR *at its head.*]

MARIE [*rocking* THE CHILD *in her arms*]. Ho, boy! Da-da-da-da! Can you hear? They're coming! There!

MARGRET. What a man! Built like a tree!

MARIE. He walks like a lion.

[THE DRUM MAJOR *salutes* MARIE.]

MARGARET. Oh, what a look he threw you, neighbor! We're
  not used to such things from you.
MARIE [sings].

            Soldiers, oh, you pretty lads . . .

MARGRET. Your eyes are still shining.
MARIE. And if they are? Take *your* eyes to the Jew's and let
  him clean them for you. Maybe he can shine them so you
  can sell them for a pair of buttons!
MARGRET. Look who's talking! Just look who's talking! If it
  isn't the Virgin herself! I'm a respectable person. But you!
  Everyone knows you could stare your way through seven
  layers of leather pants!
MARIE. Slut! [*Slams the window shut.*] Come, boy! What's it
  to them, anyway! Even if you are just a poor whore's baby,
  your dishonorable little face still makes your mother happy!
  [*Sings.*]

            I have my trouble and bother
            But, baby dear, where is your father?
            Why should I worry and fight
            I'll hold you and sing through the night:
            Heio popeio, my baby, my dove
            What do I want now with love?

[*A knock at the window.*]

  Who's there? Is it you, Franz? Come in!
WOYZECK. Can't. There's roll call.
MARIE. Did you cut wood for the Captain?
WOYZECK. Yes, Marie.
MARIE. What is it, Franz? You look so troubled.
WOYZECK. Marie, it happened again, only there was more.
  Isn't it written: "And there arose a smoke out of the pit,
  as the smoke of a great furnace"?
MARIE. Oh, Franz!
WOYZECK. Shh! Quiet! I've got it! The Freemasons! There was
  a terrible noise in the sky and everything was on fire! I'm
  on the trail of something, something big. It followed me all
  the way to the town. Something that I can't put my hands
  on, or understand. Something that drives us mad. What'll
  come of it all?
MARIE. Franz!

WOYZECK. Don't you see? Look around you! Everything hard and fixed, so gloomy. What's moving back there? When God goes, everything goes. I've got to get back.

MARIE. And the child?

WOYZECK. My God, the boy!—Tonight at the fair! I've saved something again. [*He leaves.*]

MARIE. That man! Seeing things like that! He'll go mad if he keeps thinking that way! He frightened me! It's so gloomy here. Why are you so quiet, boy? Are you afraid? It's growing so dark. As if we were going blind. Only that street lamp shining in from outside. [*Sings.*]

> And what if your cradle is bad
> Sleep tight, my lovey, my lad.

I can't stand it! It makes me shiver! [*She goes out.*]

Scene 4

[*Fair booths. Lights. People.* OLD MAN *with a* CHILD, WOYZECK, MARIE, CHARLATAN, WIFE, DRUM MAJOR, *and* SERGEANT.]

OLD MAN [*sings while* THE CHILD *dances to the barrel-organ*].

> There's nothing on this earth will last,
> Our lives are as the fields of grass,
> Soon all is past, is past.

WOYZECK. Ho! Hip-hop there, boy! Hip-hop! Poor man, old man! Poor child, young child! Trouble and happiness!

MARIE. My God, when fools still have their senses, then we're all fools. Oh, what a mad world! What a beautiful world!

[*They go over to* THE CHARLATAN *who stands in front of a booth, his* WIFE *in trousers, and a monkey in costume.*]

CHARLATAN. Gentlemen, gentlemen! You see here before you a creature as God created it! Yet it is nothing this way! Absolutely nothing! But now look at what Art can do. It walks upright. Wears coat and pants. And even carries a saber. This monkey here is a regular soldier. So what if he *isn't* much different! So what if he *is* still on the bottom rung of the human ladder! Hey there, take a bow! That's the way! Now you're a baron, at least. Give us a kiss!

[*The monkey trumpets.*]

This little customer's musical, too. And, gentlemen, in here you will see the astronomical horse and the little lovebirds. Favorites of all the crowned heads of Europe. They'll tell you anything: how old you are, how many children you have, what your ailments are. The performance is about to begin. And at the beginning. The beginning of the beginning!

WOYZECK. You know, I had a little dog once who kept sniffing around the rim of a big hat, and I thought I'd be good to him and make it easier for him and sat him on top of it. And all the people stood around and clapped.

GENTLEMEN. Oh, grotesque! How really grotesque!

WOYZECK. Don't you believe in God either? It's an honest fact I don't believe in God.—You call that grotesque? I like what's grotesque. See that? That grotesque enough for you? —[*To* MARIE.] You want to go in?

MARIE. Sure. That must be nice in there. Look at the tassels on him! And his wife's got pants on!

[*They go inside.*]

DRUM MAJOR. Wait a minute! Did you see her? What a piece!

SERGEANT. Hell, she could whelp a couple regiments of cavalry!

DRUM MAJOR. *And* breed drum majors!

SERGEANT. Look at the way she carries that head! You'd think all that black hair would pull her down like a weight. And those eyes!

DRUM MAJOR. Like looking down a well . . . or up a chimney. Come on, let's go after her!

Scene 5

[*Interior of the brightly lighted booth.* MARIE, WOYZECK, PROPRIETOR OF THE BOOTH, SERGEANT, *and* DRUM MAJOR.]

MARIE. All these lights!

WOYZECK. Sure, Marie. Black cats with fiery eyes.

PROPRIETOR OF THE BOOTH [*bringing forward a horse*]. Show your talent! Show your brute reason! Put human society to shame! Gentlemen, this animal you see here, with a tail on its torso, and standing on its four hoofs, is a member of all the learnèd societies—as well as a professor at our university where he teaches students how to ride and fight. But that requires simple intelligence. Now think with your double reason! What do you do when you think with your double reason? Is there a jackass in this learnèd assembly?

[*The nag shakes its head.*]

How's that for double reasoning? That's physiognomy for you. This is no dumb animal. This is a person! A human being! But still an animal. A beast.

[*The nag conducts itself indecently.*]

That's right, put society to shame. As you can see, this animal is still in a state of Nature. Not ideal Nature, of course! Take a lesson from him! But ask your doctor first, it may prove highly dangerous! What we have been told by this is: Man must be natural! You are created of dust, sand, and dung. Why must you be more than dust, sand, and dung? Look there at his reason. He can figure even if he can't count it off on his fingers. And why? Because he cannot express himself, can't explain. A metamorphosed human being. Tell the gentlemen what time it is! Which of you ladies and gentlemen has a watch? A watch?

SERGEANT. A watch? [*He pulls a watch imposingly and measuredly from his pocket.*] There you are, my good man!

MARIE. I want to see this. [*She clambers down to the first row of seats;* THE SERGEANT *helps her.*]

DRUM MAJOR. What a piece!

Scene 6

[MARIE's *room.* MARIE *with her* CHILD.]

MARIE [*sitting, her* CHILD *on her lap, a piece of mirror in her hand*]. He told Franz to get the hell out, so what could he do! [*Looks at herself in the mirror.*] Look how the stones shine! What kind are they, I wonder? What kind did he say they were? Sleep, boy! Close your eyes! Tight! Stay that way now. Don't move or he'll get you! [*Sings.*]

> Hurry, lady, close up tight
> A gypsy lad is out tonight
> And he will take you by the hand
> And lead you into gypsyland.

[*Continues to look at herself in the mirror.*] They must be gold! I wonder how they'll look on me at the dance? Our kind's got only a little corner in the world and a piece of broken mirror. But my mouth is just as red as any of the fine ladies with their mirrors from top to bottom, and their handsome gentlemen that kiss their hands for them! I'm just a poor common piece!

[THE CHILD *sits up.*]

Quiet, boy! Close your eyes! There's the sandman! Look at him run across the wall! [*She flashes with the mirror.*] Eyes tight! Or he'll look into them and make you blind!

[WOYZECK *enters behind her. She jumps up, her hands at her ears.*]

WOYZECK. What's that?
MARIE. Nothing.
WOYZECK. There's something shiny in your hands.
MARIE. An earring. I found it.
WOYZECK. I never have luck like that! Two at a time!
MARIE. Am I human or not?
WOYZECK. I'm sorry, Marie.—Look at the boy asleep. Lift his arm, the chair's hurting him. Look at the shiny drops on his forehead. Everything under the sun works! We even sweat in our sleep. Us poor people! Here's some money again, Marie. My pay and something from the Captain.
MARIE. God bless you, Franz.
WOYZECK. I've got to get back. Tonight, Marie! I'll see you tonight! [*He goes off.*]
MARIE [*alone, after a pause*]. I *am* bad, I *am!* I could run myself through with a knife! Oh, what a life, what a life! We'll all end up in hell, anyway, in the end: man, woman, and child!

Scene 7

[*At the* DOCTOR'S. THE DOCTOR *and* WOYZECK.]

DOCTOR. I don't believe it, Woyzeck! And a man of your word!
WOYZECK. What's that, Doctor, sir?

DOCTOR. I saw it all, Woyzeck. You pissed on the street! You were pissing on the wall like a dog! And here I'm giving you three groschen a day plus board! That's terrible, Woyzeck! The world's becoming a terrible place, a terrible place!

WOYZECK. But, Doctor, sir, when Nature . . .

DOCTOR. When Nature? When Nature? What has Nature to do with it? Did I or did I not prove to you that the *musculus constrictor vesicae* is controlled by your will? Nature! Woyzeck, man is free! In Mankind alone we see glorified the individual's will to freedom! And you couldn't hold your water! [*Shakes his head, places his hands behind the small of his back, and walks back and forth.*] Have you eaten your peas today, Woyzeck? Nothing but peas! *Cruciferae!* Remember that! There's going to be a revolution in science! I'm going to blow it sky-high! *Urea Oxygen.* Ammonium hydrochloratem hyperoxidic. Woyzeck, couldn't you just *try* to piss again? Go in the other room there and make another try.

WOYZECK. Doctor, sir, I can't.

DOCTOR [*disturbed*]. But you could piss on the wall. I have it here in black and white. Our contract is right here! I saw it. I saw it with these very eyes. I had just stuck my head out the window, opening it to let in the rays of the sun, so as to execute the process of sneezing. [*Going toward him.*] No, Woyzeck, I'm not going to vex myself. Vexation is unhealthy. Unscientific. I'm calm now, completely calm. My pulse is beating at its accustomed sixty, and I am speaking to you in utmost cold-bloodedness. Why should I vex myself over a man, God forbid! A man! Now if he were a Proteus, it would be worth the vexation! But, Woyzeck, you really shouldn't have pissed on the wall.

WOYZECK, You see, Doctor, sir, sometimes a person's got a certain kind of character, like when he's made a certain way. But with Nature it's not the same, you see. With Nature [*he snaps his fingers*], it's like *that!* How should I explain, it's like——

DOCTOR. Woyzeck, you're philosophizing again.

WOYZECK [*confidingly*]. Doctor, sir, did you ever see anything with double nature? Like when the sun stops at noon, and it's like the world was going up in fire? That's when I hear a terrible voice saying things to me!

DOCTOR. Woyzeck, you have an *aberratio!*

WOYZECK [*places his finger at his nose*]. It's in the toadstools, Doctor, sir, that's where it is. Did you ever see the shapes the toadstools make when they grow up out of the earth? If only somebody could read what they say!

DOCTOR. Woyzeck, you have a most beautiful *aberratio mentalis partialis* of a secondary order! And so wonderfully developed! Woyzeck, your salary is increased! *Idée fixe* of a secondary order, and with a generally rational state. You go about your business normally? Still shaving the Captain?

WOYZECK. Yes, sir.

DOCTOR, You eat your peas?

WOYZECK. Just as always, Doctor, sir. My wife gets the money for the household.

DOCTOR. Still in the army?

WOYZECK. Yes, sir, Doctor.

DOCTOR. You're an interesting case. Patient Woyzeck, you're to have an increase in salary. So behave yourself! Let's feel the pulse. Ah yes.

Scene 8

[MARIE's *room.* DRUM MAJOR *and* MARIE.]

DRUM MAJOR. Marie!

MARIE [*looking at him, with expression*]. Go on, show me how you march!—Chest broad as a bull's and a beard like a lion! There's not another man in the world like that! And there's not a prouder woman than me!

DRUM MAJOR. Wait till Sunday when I wear my helmet with the plume and my white gloves! Damn, that'll be a sight for you! The Prince always says: "My God, there goes a real man!"

MARIE [*scoffing*]. Ha! [*Goes toward him.*] A man?

DRUM MAJOR. You're not such a bad piece yourself! Hell, we'll plot a whole brood of drum majors! Right? [*He puts his arm around her.*]

MARIE [*annoyed*]. Let go!

DRUM MAJOR. Bitch!

MARIE [*fiercely*]. You just touch me!

DRUM MAJOR. There's devils in your eyes.

MARIE. Let there be, for all I care! What's the difference!

Scene 9

[*Street.* CAPTAIN *and* DOCTOR. THE CAPTAIN *comes panting along the street, stops; pants, looks about.*]

CAPTAIN. Ho, Doctor, don't run so fast! Don't paddle the air so with your stick! You're only courting death that way! A good man with a good conscience never walks as fast as that. A good man . . . [*He catches him by the coat.*] Doctor, permit me to save a human life!

DOCTOR. I'm in a hurry, Captain, I'm in a hurry!

CAPTAIN. Doctor, I'm so melancholy. I have such fantasies. I start to cry every time I see my coat hanging on the wall.

DOCTOR. Hm! Bloated, fat, thick neck: apoplectic constitution. Yes, Captain, you'll be having *apoplexia cerebria* any time now. Of course you could have it on only one side. In which case you'll be paralyzed down that one side. Or if things go really well you'll be mentally disabled so that you can vegetate away for the rest of your days. You may look forward to something approximately like that within the next four weeks! And, furthermore, I can assure you that you give promise of being a most interesting case. And if it is God's will that only one half of your tongue become paralyzed, then we will conduct the most immortal of experiments.

CAPTAIN. Doctor, you mustn't scare me that way! People are said to have died of fright. Of pure, sheer fright. I can see them now with lemons in their hands. But they'll say: "He was a good man, a good man." You devil's coffinnail maker!

DOCTOR [*extending his hat toward him*]. Do you know who this is, Captain? This is Sir Hollowhead, my most honorable Captain Drilltheirassesoff!

CAPTAIN [*makes a series of folds in his sleeve*]. And do you know who this is, Doctor? This is Sir Manifold, my dear devil's coffinnail maker! Ha! Ha! Ha! But no harm meant! I'm a good man, but I can play, too, when I want to, Doctor, when I want to . . .

[WOYZECK *comes toward them and tries to pass in a hurry.*]

Ho! Woyzeck! Where are you off to in such a hurry? Stay awhile, Woyzeck! Running through the world like an open razor, you're liable to cut someone. He runs as if he had to shave a castrated regiment and would be hung before he discovered and cut the longest hair that wasn't there. But on the subject of long beards . . . What was it I wanted to say? Woyzeck, why was I thinking about beards?

DOCTOR. The wearing of long beards on the chin, remarks Pliny, is a habit of which soldiers must be broken——

CAPTAIN [*continues*]. Ah, yes, this thing about beards! Tell me, Woyzeck, have you found any long hairs from beards in your soup bowl lately? Ho, I don't think he understands! A hair from a human face, from the beard of an engineer, a sergeant, a . . . a drum major? Well, Woyzeck? But then he's got a good woman. It's not the same as with the others.

WOYZECK. Yes, sir, Captain! What was it you wanted to say to me, Captain, sir?

CAPTAIN. What a face he's making! Well, maybe not in his soup, but if he hurries home around the corner I'll wager he might still find one on a certain pair of lips. A pair of lips, Woyzeck. I know what love is, too, Woyzeck. Look at him, he's white as chalk!

WOYZECK. Captain, sir, I'm just a poor devil. And there's nothing else I've got in the world but her. Captain, sir, if you're just making a fool of me . . .

CAPTAIN. A fool? Me? Making a fool of you, Woyzeck?

DOCTOR. Your pulse, Woyzeck, your pulse! Short, hard, skipping, irregular.

WOYZECK. Captain, sir, the earth's hot as coals in hell. But I'm cold as ice, cold as ice. Hell is cold. I'll bet you. I don't believe it! God! God! I don't believe it!

CAPTAIN. Look here, you, how would you . . . how'd you like a pair of bullets in your skull? You keep stabbing at me with those eyes of yours, and I'm only trying to help. Because you're a good man, Woyzeck, a good man.

DOCTOR. Facial muscles rigid, taut, occasional twitches. Condition strained, excitable.

WOYZECK. I'm going. Anything's possible. The bitch! Anything's possible.—— The weather's nice, Captain, sir. Look, a beautiful, hard, gray sky. You'd almost like to pound a nail in up there and hang yourself on it. And only because of that little dash between Yes and Yes again . . . and No. Captain, sir: Yes and No: did No make Yes or Yes make No? I must think about that. [*He goes off with long strides, slowly at first, then faster and faster.*]

DOCTOR [*shouting after him*]. Phenomenon! Woyzeck, you get a raise!

CAPTAIN. I get so dizzy around such people. Look at him go! Long-legged rascals like him step out like a shadow running away from its own spider. But short ones only dawdle along. The long-legged ones are the lightning, the short ones the thunder. Haha . . . Grotesque! Grotesque!

Scene 10

[MARIE'S *room*. WOYZECK *and* MARIE.]

WOYZECK [*looks fixedly at her and shakes his head*]. Hm! I don't see it! I don't see it! My God, why can't I see it, why can't I take it in my fists!

MARIE [*frightened*]. Franz, what is it?—You're raving, Franz.

WOYZECK. A sin so swollen and big—it stinks to smoke the angels out of Heaven! You have a red mouth, Marie! No blisters on it? Marie, you're beautiful as sin. How can mortal sin be so beautiful?

MARIE. Franz, it's your fever making you talk this way!

WOYZECK. Damn you! Is this where he stood? Like this? Like this?

MARIE. While the day's long and the world's old a lot of people can stand in one spot, one right after the other. —Why are you looking at me so strange, Franz! I'm afraid!

WOYZECK. It's a nice street for walking, uh? You could walk corns on your feet! It's nice walking on the street, going around in society.

MARIE. Society?

WOYZECK. A lot of people pass through this street here, don't they! And you talk to them—to whoever you want—but that's not my business!—Why wasn't it me!

MARIE. You expect me to tell people to keep off the streets— and take their mouths with them when they leave?

WOYZECK. And don't you ever leave your lips at home, they're too beautiful, it would be a sin! But then I guess the wasps like to light on them, uh?

MARIE. And what wasp stung you! You're like a cow chased by hornets!

WOYZECK. I saw him!

MARIE. You can see a lot with two eyes while the sun shines!

WOYZECK. Whore! [*He goes after her.*]

MARIE. Don't you touch me, Franz! I'd rather have a knife
in my body than your hands touch me. When I looked at
him, my father didn't dare lay a hand on me from the time
I was ten.

WOYZECK. Whore! No, it should show on you! Something!
Every man's a chasm. It makes you dizzy when you look
down in. It's got to show! And she looks like innocence
itself. So, innocence, there's a spot on you. But I can't
prove it—can't prove it! Who can prove it? [*He goes off.*]

Scene 11

[*The guardhouse.* WOYZECK *and* ANDRES.]

ANDRES [*sings*].

> Our hostess she has a pretty maid
> She sits in her garden night and day
> She sits within her garden . . .

WOYZECK. Andres!

ANDRES. Hm?

WOYZECK. Nice weather.

ANDRES. Sunday weather. —They're playing music tonight outside the town. All the whores are already there. The men
stinking and sweating. Wonderful, uh?

WOYZECK [*restlessly*]. They're dancing, Andres, they're dancing!

ANDRES. Sure. So what? [*Sings.*]

> She sits within her garden
> But when the bells have tollèd late
> Then she waits at her garden gate
> Or so the soldiers say.

WOYZECK. Andres, I can't keep quiet.

ANDRES. You're a fool!

WOYZECK. I've got to go out there. It keeps turning and turning in my head. They're dancing, dancing! Will she have
hot hands, Andres? God damn her, Andres! God damn her!

ANDRES. What do you want?

WOYZECK. I've got to go out there. I've got to see them.

ANDRES. Aren't you ever satisfied? What's all this for a whore?

WOYZECK. I've got to get out of here! I can't stand the heat!

Scene 12

[*The inn. The windows are open. Dancing. Benches in front of the inn.* APPRENTICES.]

FIRST APPRENTICE [*sings*].

> This shirt I wear, it is not mine
> And my soul stinketh of brandywine . . .

SECOND APPRENTICE. Brother, let me be a real friend and knock a hole in your nature! Forward! I'll knock a hole in his nature! Hell, I'm as good a man as he is; I'll kill every flea on his body!

FIRST APPRENTICE. My soul, my soul stinketh of brandywine! —And even money passeth into decay! Forget me not, but the world's a beautiful place! Brother, my sadness could fill a barrel with tears! I wish our noses were two bottles so we could pour them down one another's throats.

THE OTHERS [*in chorus*].

> A hunter from the Rhine
> Once rode through a forest so fine
> Hallei-hallo, he called to me
> From high on a meadow, open and free
> A hunter's life for me.

[WOYZECK *stands at the window.* MARIE *and* THE DRUM MAJOR *dance past without noticing him.*]

WOYZECK. Both of them! God damn her!

MARIE [*dancing past*]. Don't stop! Don't stop!

WOYZECK [*seats himself on the bench, trembling, as he looks from there through the window*]. Listen! Listen! Ha, roll on each other, roll and turn! Don't stop, don't stop, she says!

IDIOT. Pah! It stinks!

WOYZECK. Yes, it stinks! Her cheeks are red, red, why should she stink already? Karl, what is it you smell?

IDIOT. I smell, I smell blood.

WOYZECK. Blood? Why are all things red that I look at now? Why are they all rolling in a sea of blood, one on top of the other, tumbling, tumbling! Ha, the sea is red! —Don't stop! [*He starts up passionately, then sinks down again onto the bench.*] Don't stop! Don't stop! [*Beating his hands together.*] Turn and roll and roll and turn! God, blow

out the sun and let them roll on each other in their lechery!
Man and woman and man and beast! They'll do it in the
light of the sun! They'll do it in the palm of your hand like
flies! Whore! That whore's red as coals, red as coals! Don't
stop! Don't stop! [*Jumps up.*] Watch how the bastard takes
hold of her! Touching her body! He's holding her now,
holding her . . . the way I held her once. [*He slumps down
in a stupor.*]

FIRST APPRENTICE [*preaching from a table*]. I say unto you,
forget not the wanderer who standeth leaning against the
stream of time, and who giveth himself answer with the
wisdom of God, and saith: What is Man? What is Man?
Yea, verily I say unto you: How should the farmer, the
cooper, the shoemaker, the doctor, live, had not God created
Man for their use? How should the tailor live, had not God
implanted in Man his sense of shame? And the soldier,
had not God endowed Man with the need to slaughter
himself? And therefore doubt ye not, for all things are
lovely and sweet! Yet the world with all its things is an
evil place, and even money passeth into decay. In conclusion, my beloved brethren, let us piss once more upon the
Cross so that somewhere a Jew will die!

[*Amid the general shouting and laughing* WOYZECK *wakens.*
PEOPLE *are leaving the inn.*]

ANDRES. What are you doing there?

WOYZECK. What time is it?

ANDRES. Ten.

WOYZECK. Is that all it is? I think it should go faster—I want
to think about it before night.

ANDRES. Why?

WOYZECK. So it'll be over.

ANDRES. What?

WOYZECK. The fun.

ANDRES. Why are you sitting here by the door?

WOYZECK. Because it feels good, and because I know—a lot
of people sit by doors, but they don't know—they don't
know till they're dragged out feet first.

ANDRES. Come with me!

WOYZECK. It feels good here like this—and even better if I
laid myself down . . .

ANDRES. There's blood on your head.

WOYZECK. *In* my head, maybe. —If they all knew what time

it was they'd strip themselves naked and put on a silk shirt
and let the carpenter make their bed out of wood shavings.

ANDRES. He's drunk. [*Goes off with the others.*]

WOYZECK. The world is out of order! Why did the street-lamp
cleaner forget to wipe my eyes—everything's dark. Devil
damn you, God! I lay in my own way: jump over myself.
Where's my shadow gone? There's no safety in the kennels
any more. Shine the moon through my legs again to see
if my shadow's here. [*Sings.*]

> Eating, oh, eating the green green grass
> Eating, oh, eating the green green grass
> Till all the grass was go-o-one.

What's that lying over there? Shining like that? It's making
me look. How it sparkles. I've got to have it. [*He rushes off.*]

Scene 13

[*An open field.* WOYZECK.]

WOYZECK. Don't stop! Don't stop! Hishh! Hashh! That's how
the fiddles and pipes go. —Don't stop! Don't stop! —Stop
your playing! What's that talking down there? [*He stretches
out on the ground.*] What? What are you saying? What?
Louder! Louder! Stab? Stab the goat-bitch dead? Stab?
Stab her? The goat-bitch dead? Should I? Must I? Do I
hear it there, too? Does the wind say so, too? Won't it ever
stop, ever stop? Stab her! Stab her! Dead! Dead!

Scene 14

[*A room in the barracks. Night.* ANDRES *and* WOYZECK *in a
bed.*]

WOYZECK [*softly*]. Andres! [ANDRES *murmurs in his sleep.
Shakes* ANDRES.] Andres! Hey, Andres!

ANDRES. Mmmmm! What do you want?

WOYZECK. I can't sleep! When I close my eyes everything
turns and turns. I hear voices in the fiddles: Don't stop!
Don't stop! And then the walls start to talk. Can't you hear
it?

ANDRES. Sure. Let them dance! I'm tired. God bless us all. Amen.

WOYZECK. It's always saying: Stab! Stab! And then when I close my eyes it keeps shining there, a big, broad knife, on a table by a window in a narrow, dark street, and an old man sitting behind it. And the knife is always in front of my eyes.

ANDRES. Go to sleep, you fool!

WOYZECK. Andres! There's something outside. In the ground. They're always pointing to it. Don't you hear them now, listen, now, knocking on the walls? Somebody must have seen me out the window. Don't you hear? I hear it all day long. Don't stop. Stab! Stab the——

ANDRES. Lay down. You ought to go to the hospital. They'll give you a schnapps with a powder in it. It'll cut your fever.

WOYZECK. Don't stop! Don't stop!

ANDRES. Go to sleep! [*He goes back to sleep.*]

Scene 15

[THE DOCTOR's *courtyard*. STUDENTS *and* WOYZECK *below,* THE DOCTOR *in the attic window.*]

DOCTOR. Gentlemen, I find myself on the roof like David when he beheld Bathsheba. But all I see are the Parisian panties of the girls' boarding school drying in the garden. Gentlemen, we are concerned with the weighty question of the relationship of the subject to the object. If, for example, we were to take one of those innumerable things in which we see the highest manifestation of the self-affirmation of the Godhead, and examine its relationship to space, to the earth, and to the planetary constellations . . . Gentlemen, if we were to take this cat and toss it out the window: how would this object conduct itself in conformity with its own instincts towards its *centrum gravitationis?* Well, Woyzeck? [*Roars.*] Woyzeck!

WOYZECK [*picks up the cat*]. Doctor, sir, she's biting me!

DOCTOR. Damn, why do you handle the beast so tenderly! It's not your grandmother! [*He descends.*]

WOYZECK. Doctor, I'm shaking.

DOCTOR [*utterly delighted*]. Excellent, Woyzeck, excellent! [*Rubs his hands, takes the cat.*] What's this, gentlemen? The new species of rabbit louse! A beautiful species . . . [*He pulls out a magnifying glass; the cat runs off.*] Animals, gentlemen, simply have no scientific instincts. But in its place you may see something else. Now, observe: for three months this man has eaten nothing but peas. Notice the effect. Feel how irregularly his pulse beats! And look at his eyes!

WOYZECK. Doctor, sir, everything's going dark! [*He sits down.*]

DOCTOR. Courage, Woyzeck! A few more days and then it will all be over with. Feel, gentlemen, feel!

[*They fumble over his temples, pulse, and chest.*]

DOCTOR. Apropos, Woyzeck, wiggle your ears for the gentlemen! I've meant to show you this before. He uses only two muscles. Let's go, let's go! You stupid animal, shall I wiggle them for you? Trying to run out on us like the cat? There you are, gentlemen! Here you see an example of the transition into a donkey: frequently the result of being raised by women and of a persistent usage of the Germanic language. How much hair has your mother pulled out recently for sentimental remembrances of you? It's become so thin these last few days. It's the peas, gentlemen, the peas!

Scene 16

[*The inn.* WOYZECK. THE SERGEANT.]

WOYZECK [*sings*].

> Oh, daughter, my daughter
> And didn't you know
> That sleeping with coachmen
> Would bring you low?

What is it that our Good Lord God cannot do? What? He cannot make what is done undone. Ha! Ha! Ha!——
But that's the way it is, and that's the way it should be. But to make things better is to make things better. And a respectable man loves his life, and a man who loves his life has no courage, and a virtuous man has no courage. A man with courage is a dirty dog.

SERGEANT [*with dignity*]. You're forgetting yourself in the presence of a brave man.

WOYZECK. I wasn't talking about anybody, I wasn't talking about anything, not like the Frenchmen do when they talk, but it was good of you. ——But a man with courage is a dirty dog.

SERGEANT. Damn you! You broken mustache cup! You watch or I'll see you drink a pot of your own piss and swallow your own razor!

WOYZECK. Sir, you do yourself an injustice! Was it *you* I talked about? Did I say *you* had courage? Don't torment me, sir! My name is Science. Every week for my scientific career I get half a guilder. You mustn't cut me in two or I'll go hungry. I'm a *Spinosa pericyclia;* I have a Latin behind. I am a living skeleton. All Mankind studies me. ——What is Man? Bones! Dust, sand, dung. What is Nature? Dust, sand, dung. But poor, stupid Man, stupid Man! We must be friends. If only you had no courage, there would be no science. Only Nature, no amputation, no articulation. What is this? Woyzeck's arm: flesh, bones, veins. What is this? Dung. Why is it rooted in dung? Must I cut off my arm? No, Man is selfish, he beats, shoots, stabs his own kind. [*He sobs.*] We must be friends. I wish our noses were two bottles that we could pour down each other's throats. What a beautiful place the world is! Friend! My friend! The world! [*Moved.*] Look! The sun coming through the clouds—like God emptying His bedpan on the world. [*He cries.*]

Scene 17

[*The barracks yard.* WOYZECK. ANDRES.]

WOYZECK. What have you heard?

ANDRES. He's still inside with a friend.

WOYZECK. He said something.

ANDRES. How do you know? Why do I have to be the one to tell you? Well, he laughed and then he said she was some piece. And then something or other about her thighs—and that she was hot as a red poker.

WOYZECK [*quite coldly*]. So, he said that? What was that I dreamed about last night? About a knife? What stupid dreams we get!

ANDRES. Hey, friend! Where you off to?

WOYZECK. Get some wine for the Captain. Andres, you know something? There aren't many girls like she was.

ANDRES. Like who was?

WOYZECK. Nothing. I'll see you. [*Goes off.*]

Scene 18

[*The inn.* DRUM MAJOR, WOYZECK, *and* PEOPLE.]

DRUM MAJOR. I'm a man! [*He pounds his chest.*] A man, you hear? Anybody say different? Anybody who's not as crocked as the Lord God Himself better keep off. I'll screw his nose up his own ass! I'll . . . [*To* WOYZECK.] You there, get drunk! I wish the world was schnapps, schnapps! You better start drinking! [WOYZECK *whistles.*] Son-of-a-bitch, you want me to pull your tongue out and wrap it around your middle?

[*They wrestle;* WOYZECK *loses.*]

You want I should leave enough wind in you for a good old lady's fart? Uh!

[*Exhausted and trembling,* WOYZECK *seats himself on the bench.*]

The son-of-a-bitch can whistle himself blue in the face for all I care. [*Sings.*]

> Brandy's all my life, my life
> Brandy gives me courage!

A MAN. He sure got more than he asked for.

ANOTHER. He's bleeding.

WOYZECK. One thing after another.

Scene 19

[*Pawnbroker's shop.* WOYZECK *and* THE JEW.]

WOYZECK. The pistol costs too much.

JEW. So you want it or not? Make up your mind.

WOYZECK. How much was the knife?

JEW. It's straight and sharp. What do you want it for? To cut your throat? So what's the matter? You get it as cheap here

as anywhere else. You'll die cheap enough, but not for
nothing. What's the matter? It'll be a cheap death.

WOYZECK. This'll cut more than bread.

JEW. Two groschen.

WOYZECK. There! [*He goes out.*]

JEW. There, he says! Like it was nothing! And it's real money!
—Dog!

Scene 20

[MARIE'*s room.* THE IDIOT. THE CHILD. MARIE.]

IDIOT [*lying down, telling fairy tales on his fingers*]. This one
has the golden crown. He's the Lord King. Tomorrow I'll
bring the Lady Queen her child. Bloodsausage says: Come,
Liversausage . . .

MARIE [*paging through her Bible*]. "And no guile is found in
his mouth." Lord God, Lord God! Don't look at me!
[*Paging further.*] "And the Scribes and Pharisees brought
unto him a woman taken in adultery, and set her in the
midst . . . And Jesus said unto her: Neither do I condemn
thee; go, and sin no more." [*Striking her hands together.*]
Lord God! Lord God! I can't. Lord God, give me only so
much strength that I may pray.

[THE CHILD *presses himself close to her.*]

The child is a sword in my heart. [*To* THE IDIOT.] Karl!—
I've strutted it in the light of the sun, like the whore I am
—my sin, my sin!

[THE IDIOT *takes* THE CHILD *and grows quiet.*]

Franz hasn't come. Not yesterday. Not today. It's getting
hot in here! [*She opens the window and reads further.*]
"And stood at his feet weeping, and began to wash his
feet with tears, and did wipe them with the hairs of
her head, and anointed them with ointment." [*Striking her
breast.*] Everything dead! Saviour! Saviour! If only I might
anoint Your feet!

Scene 21

[*An open field.* WOYZECK.]

WOYZECK [*buries the knife in a hole*]. Thou shalt not kill.
Lay here! I can't stay here! [*He rushes off.*]

Scene 22

[*The barracks.* ANDRES. WOYZECK *rummages through his belongings.*]

WOYZECK. Andres, this jacket's not part of the uniform, but you can use it, Andres.

ANDRES [*replies numbly to almost everything with*] Sure.

WOYZECK. The cross is my sister's. And the ring.

ANDRES. Sure.

WOYZECK. I've got a Holy Picture, too; two hearts—they're real gold. I found it in my mother's Bible, and it said:

> O Lord with wounded head so sore
> So may my heart be evermore.

My mother only feels now when the sun shines on her hands . . . that doesn't matter.

ANDRES. Sure.

WOYZECK [*pulls out a paper*]. Friedrich Johann Franz Woyzeck. Soldier, Rifleman, Second Regiment, Second Battalion, Fourth Company. Born: the Feast of the Annunciation, twentieth of July. Today I'm thirty years old, seven months and twelve days.

ANDRES. Go to the hospital, Franz. Poor guy, you've got to drink some schnapps with a powder in it. It'll kill the fever.

WOYZECK. You know, Andres—when the carpenter puts those boards together, nobody knows who it's made for.

Scene 23

[*The street.* MARIE *with little* GIRLS *in front of the house door.* GRANDMOTHER. *Later* WOYZECK.]

GIRLS [*singing*].

> The sun shone bright on Candlemas Day
> And the corn was all in bloom
> And they marched along the meadow way
> They marched by two and two.
> The pipers marched ahead
> The fiddlers followed through
> And their socks were scarlet red . . .

FIRST CHILD. I don't like that one.

SECOND CHILD. Why do you always want to be different?

FIRST CHILD. *You* sing for us, Marie!

MARIE. I can't.

SECOND CHILD. Why?

MARIE. Because.

SECOND CHILD. But *why* because?

THIRD CHILD. Grandmother, *you* tell us a story!

GRANDMOTHER. All right, you little crab apples! Once upon a time there was a poor little girl who had no father and no mother. Everyone was dead, and there was no one left in the whole wide world. Everyone was dead. And the little girl went out and looked for someone night and day. And because there was no one left on the earth, she wanted to go to Heaven. And the moon looked down so friendly at her. And when she finally got to the moon, it was a piece of rotten wood. And so she went to the sun, and it was a faded sunflower. And when she got to the stars, they were little golden flies, stuck up there as if they were caught in a spider's web. And when she wanted to go back to earth, the earth was an upside-down pot. And she was all alone. And she sat down there and she cried. And she sits there to this day, all, all alone.

WOYZECK [*appears*]. Marie!

MARIE [*startled*]. What!

WOYZECK. Let's go. It's getting time.

MARIE. Where to?

WOYZECK. How should I know?

Scene 24

[*A pond by the edge of the woods.* MARIE *and* WOYZECK.]

MARIE. Then the town must be out that way. It's so dark.

WOYZECK. You can't go yet. Come, sit down.

MARIE. But I've got to get back.

WOYZECK. You don't want to run your feet sore.

MARIE. What's happened to you?

WOYZECK. You know how long it's been, Marie?

MARIE. Two years from Pentecost.

WOYZECK. You know how much longer it'll last?

MARIE. I've got to get back. Supper's not made yet.

WOYZECK. Are you freezing, Marie? And still you're so warm.
Your lips are hot as coals! Hot as coals, the hot breath of
a whore! And still I'd give up Heaven just to kiss them
again. Are you freezing? When you're cold through, you
won't freeze any more. The morning dew won't freeze you.
MARIE. What are you talking about?
WOYZECK. Nothing. [*Silence.*]
MARIE. Look how red the moon is! It's rising.
WOYZECK. Like a knife washed in blood.
MARIE. What are you going to do? Franz, you're so pale.

[*He raises the knife.*]

MARIE. Franz! Stop! For Heaven's sake! Help me! Help me!
WOYZECK [*stabbing madly*]. There! There! Why can't you
die? There! There! Ha, she's still shivering! Still not dead?
Still not dead? Still shivering? [*Stabbing at her again.*] Are
you dead? Dead! Dead! [*He drops the knife and runs
away.*]

[*Two* MEN *approach.*]

FIRST MAN. Wait!
SECOND MAN. You hear something? Shh! Over there!
FIRST MAN. Whhh! There! What a sound!
SECOND MAN. It's the water, it's calling. It's a long time since
anyone drowned here. Let's go! I don't like hearing such
sounds!
FIRST MAN. Whhh! There it is again! Like a person, dying!
SECOND MAN. It's uncanny! So foggy, nothing but gray mist
as far as you can see—and the hum of beetles like broken
bells. Let's get out of here!
FIRST MAN. No, it's too clear, it's too loud! Let's go up this
way! Come on! [*They hurry on.*]

Scene 25

[*The inn.* WOYZECK, KATHY, INNKEEPER, IDIOT, *and* PEOPLE.]

WOYZECK. Dance! Everybody! Don't stop! Sweat and stink!
He'll get you all in the end! [*Sings.*]

> Oh, daughter, my daughter
> And didn't you know
> That sleeping with coachmen
> Would bring you low?

[*He dances.*] Ho, Kathy! Sit down! I'm so hot, so hot! [*Takes off his coat.*] That's the way it is: the devil takes one and lets the other get away. Kathy, you're hot as coals! Why, tell me why? Kathy, you'll be cold one day, too. Be reasonable. —Can't you sing something?

KATHY [*sings*].

> That Swabian land I cannot bear
> And dresses long I will not wear
> For dresses long and pointed shoes
> Are clothes a chambermaid never should choose.

WOYZECK. No shoes, no shoes! We can get to hell without shoes.

KATHY [*sings*].

> To such and like I'll not be prone
> Take back your gold and sleep alone.

WOYZECK. Sure, sure! What do I want to get all bloody for?

KATHY. Then what's that on your hand?

WOYZECK. Me? Me?

KATHY. Red! It's blood!

[PEOPLE *gather round him.*]

WOYZECK. Blood? Blood?

INNKEEPER. Blood!

WOYZECK. I think I cut myself. Here, on my right hand.

INNKEEPER. Then why is there blood on your elbow?

WOYZECK. I wiped it off.

INNKEEPER. Your right hand and you wiped it on your right elbow? You're a smart one!

IDIOT. And then the giant said: "I smell, I smell the flesh of man." Pew, it stinks already!

WOYZECK. What do you want from me? Is it your business? Out of my way or the first one who . . . Damn you! Do I look like I murdered somebody? Do I look like a murderer? What are you looking at? Look at yourselves! Look! Out of my way! [*He runs off.*]

Scene 26

[*At the pond.* WOYZECK, *alone.*]

WOYZECK. The knife! Where's the knife? I left it here. It'll give me away! Closer! And closer! What is this place?

What's that noise? Something's moving! It's quiet now.
—It's got to be here, close to her. Marie? Ha, Marie! Quiet.
Everything's quiet! Why are you so pale, Marie? Why are
you wearing those red beads around your neck? Who was
it gave you that necklace for sinning with him? Your sins
made you black, Marie, they made you black! Did I make
you so pale? Why is your hair uncombed? Did you forget
to twist your braids today? The knife, the knife! I've got
it! There! [*He runs toward the water.*] There, into the
water! [*He throws the knife into the water.*] It dives like
a stone into the black water. No, it's not out far enough
for when they swim! [*He wades into the pond and throws
it out farther.*] There! Now! But in the summer when they
dive for mussels? Ha, it'll get rusty, who'll ever notice it!
Why didn't I break it first! Am I still bloody? I've got to
wash myself. There, there's a spot, and there's another . . .
[*He goes farther out into the water.*]

Scene 27

[*The street.* CHILDREN.]

FIRST CHILD. Let's go find Marie!
SECOND CHILD. What happened?
FIRST CHILD. Don't you know? Everybody's out there. They
    found a body!
SECOND CHILD. Where?
FIRST CHILD. By the pond, out in the woods.
SECOND CHILD. Hurry, so we can still see something. Before
    they bring it back. [*They rush off.*]

Scene 28

[*In front of* MARIE'S *house.* IDIOT, CHILD, WOYZECK.]

IDIOT [*holding* THE CHILD *on his knee, points to* WOYZECK *as
    he enters*]. Looky there, he fell in the water, he fell in the
    water, he fell in the water!
WOYZECK. Boy! Christian!
IDIOT [*looks at him fixedly*]. He fell in the water.
WOYZECK [*wanting to embrace* THE CHILD *tenderly, but it
    turns from him and screams*]. My God! My God!

IDIOT. He fell in the water.

WOYZECK. I'll buy you a horsey, Christian. There, there. [THE CHILD *pulls away. To* THE IDIOT]. Here, buy the boy a horsey!

[THE IDIOT *stares at him.*]

Hop! Hop! Hip-hop, horsey!

IDIOT [*shouting joyously*]. Hop! Hop! Hip-hop, horsey! Hip-hop, horsey!

[*He runs off with* THE CHILD. WOYZECK *is alone.*]

Scene 29

[*The morgue.* JUDGE, COURT CLERK, POLICEMAN, CAPTAIN, DOCTOR, DRUM MAJOR, SERGEANT, IDIOT, *and others.* WOYZECK.]

POLICEMAN. What a murder! A good, genuine, beautiful murder! Beautiful a murder as you could hope for! It's been a long time since we had a murder like this!

[WOYZECK *stands in their midst, dumbly looking at the body of* MARIE; *he is bound, the dogmatic atheist, tall, haggard, timid, good-natured, scientific.*]

FRIEDRICH HEBBEL

1813–1863

FRIEDRICH HEBBEL was the first successful writer of serious middle-class drama in the modern theatre. Although Hebbel's name is usually linked with those writers of the "Storm and Stress" period of nineteenth-century German romanticism, it is probably more correct to consider him as a forerunner of that revolution in the theatre usually attributed to Ibsen and Strindberg. In fact, Hebbel openly rejected both the sentimentality and the romantic neo-Shakespeareanism which dominated early nineteenth-century drama, and sought to dramatize the essential social and moral conflicts of his own time. He lived in a period of great social, economic, political, and philosophical ferment, and the sense of upheaval and change is mirrored in all his work. Furthermore, he was greatly influenced by the philosophy of Hegel, whose theories of the dialectic in history led Hebbel to believe that the most significant dramas of life were the result of the conflicts of historical process. "Great drama," he wrote, "occurs at the transition from one epoch to the next and expresses the clash of world views." In Hebbel's view, then, a time of crisis was the essential condition of drama, and in all his work he sought to represent in powerful images the issues and conflicts of an emerging middle-class morality.

A WORD ABOUT THE DRAMA[1]

by Friedrich Hebbel

1843

ART HAS to do with life, inner and outer life, and one may well say that it represents both simultaneously: purest form and highest content. The main categories of art and their laws result directly from the difference of the elements which in every instance are taken from life and worked over. Life, however, appears in twofold form, as Being and as Becoming, and art fulfills its task most completely when it maintains an even balance between the two. Only in this way can it assure itself of both present and future, which must be of equal importance; only in this way can it become what it ought to become: life in life. For that which is wholly complete stifles the creative spirit, without which it remains ineffectual, and the quivering embryo excludes form.

Drama represents the life process as such. And indeed not merely in the sense that it presents life to us in its entire breadth, an aspect also characteristic of epic poetry, but in the sense that it visualizes for us the critical relationship which the individual, released from the original nexus, bears to the whole, a part of which, despite his incomprehensible freedom, he still remains. Drama, therefore, as is fitting for the highest form of art, refers itself equally to Being as to Becoming: to Being, in that it may never tire of repeating the eternal truth: that life as individualization, which knows no moderation or bounds, does not engender guilt merely by accident,

[1] "A Word About the Drama" by Friedrich Hebbel, translated by Carl Richard Mueller. Reprinted from *The Modern Theatre*, edited by Robert W. Corrigan, © Copyright, Robert W. Corrigan, 1964. Printed by permission of The Macmillan Company and the translator.

but necessarily and essentially contains and conditions it; and to Becoming, in that with the ever new material furnished it by changing time and its deposit, history, it must prove that man, however the things about him may change, remains according to his nature and his destiny eternally the same. In this regard we may not overlook the fact that dramatic guilt does not, like the original sin of Christianity, originate in the direction of the human will, but emanates directly from the will itself, from the inflexible, arbitrary expansion of the ego, and that therefore it is a matter of complete indifference dramatically whether the hero founders while engaged in an excellent or a reprehensible endeavor.

The stuff of drama consists of plot and characters. The former we will not discuss here, for among the moderns, at least, it has been assigned a subordinate position, and anyone who doubts this may prove it to himself by examining a play of Shakespeare and asking himself what it was that fired the author to write the play, the plot or the people he lets appear in it. The treatment of characters, on the other hand, is of the utmost importance. These must never appear as finished persons, as people who can play their way through all kinds of relationships and, like actors, enjoy or suffer good fortune or misfortune respectively, but only externally, not inwardly, not in heart and spirit. This is the death of drama, death before birth. Drama only comes alive when it visualizes for us how the individual attains form and firmness of character and resolution in the struggle between his personal will and the general will of the world, which always modifies and changes his deed—the expression of freedom, through the event—the expression of necessity; and in so doing it explains to us the nature of all human action, which as soon as it tries to manifest a personal [*inneres*] motive, always simultaneously releases a resisting motive which is intended to restore equilibrium. And although the fundamental Idea, upon which the (here presumed) dignity and worth of the drama depends provides the circle within which all must move in planetary fashion, nevertheless the poet must still provide for a diversification of interest, both properly and without violating the true unity; or more properly, for the realization of the totality of life and the world; and also guard against placing all of his characters at an equal distance from the center, as so often happens in the so-called lyrical dramas. The most complete picture of life arises when the principal character is to the subordinate and opposing characters what fate, with which he wrestles, is to him; and when, in the same manner, everything, down to the lowest level, is mutually developed, conditioned and mirrored.

The question now is: What is the relationship between drama and history and to what extent must it be historical? To the same extent, I think, that it is now in and of itself, and insofar as art may be considered the highest form of historical recording; because art cannot possibly represent the most imposing and significant life processes without those decisive historical crises which history evokes and calls forth, the integration or the gradual disintegration of the religious and political forms of the world, as the principal conductor and fundament of all civilization—in a word: art and history must conjointly provide us with the atmosphere of the times. Recorded history, which even Napoleon called a fable agreed upon, this motley, checkered, monstrous chaos of dubious facts and one-sided or badly drawn character sketches, will sooner or later exceed the capacity of human comprehension, and in this way the newer drama, especially the plays of Shakespeare, which is to say all of them and not merely those specifically called historical, might quite naturally assume the same relationship to distant posterity as the Greek drama has assumed to us. Then, and very likely not before, will we cease narrow-mindedly trying to discover a common identity between art and history, and cease anxiously comparing the historical situation and character with their artistic counterparts: for then we will have learned to understand that through such means the almost nonexistent agreement between the first and the second portrayal can be brought out, not, however, that between image and truth; we will have learned to understand that the drama is symbolic, not merely in its totality, which is self-evident, but that it is symbolic in each of its elements, and that it must be regarded as symbolic; in the same way the painter, when he endows his figures with red cheeks and blue eyes, does not distill his colors from human blood, but quite naturally and as a matter of course uses cinnabar and indigo.

But the content of life is inexhaustible and the medium of art is limited. Life knows no conclusion; the thread on which it spins its phenomena merges into the infinite. Art on the other hand must come to a conclusion, it must, as best it can, tie the thread into a circle. This is the point Goethe must have had in mind when he said that in all the forms of art there is something untrue. This something untrue can, of course, be detected in life itself, for not even life can offer a single form into which all of its elements are equally merged; it cannot, for example, fashion the most perfect man without withholding from him the merits which constitute the most perfect woman; and the two buckets in the well, only one of which can always be full, are the most characteristic symbol of all creation. This fundamental lack shows itself to be far worse and more critical in art than in life, where the totality always intercedes and compensates for the individual, and this for the reason that in art a lack in one place must absolutely be compensated for in another.

I will illustrate this thought by applying it to the drama. The most superior dramas of all literatures demonstrate that only by giving one or more of the main characters a measure of consciousness of the world and of himself which far exceeds reality can the poet complete the invisible ring in which the picture of life which he has set up moves. Omitting the Greeks, whose treatment of character was something else, I will only remind the reader of Shakespeare, and, omitting the perhaps too compelling evidence of Hamlet, draw attention to the monologues in *Macbeth* and *Richard,* as well as those of the Bastard in *King John.* Some, be it remarked in passing, have at times wanted to see in this obvious defect in Shakespeare a virtue, a particular excellence (even Hegel did so in his *Aesthetics*), instead of being content with the proof that the reason lay not in the poet but in art. But what is accordingly found in the greatest dramatists as a consistent trait in whole characters is also often met with in single culminating moments when the word accompanies the deed or perhaps even precedes it. It is this, to draw a most important conclusion, which differentiates the conscious presentation in art from the unconscious presentation in life; that art, if it does not want to fail in its effect, must bring to itself sharp and complete outlines, while life, which does not first have to fight to establish itself in our belief, and which in the end may be indifferent to whether or not and how it has been understood, may content itself with a half-hearted Ah! or Oh!, with a facial expression or a gesture. Goethe's statement, with which he dared to touch on the most dangerous secret of art, is often repeated, but mostly in regard to what is superficially called form. The boy sees in the most profound Bible verse only his good friends the twenty-six letters of the alphabet which were used to express it.

The German drama seems to be in the ascendant again. What task has it now to solve? The question might be cause for surprise, for the most obvious answer in any case must be: The same which drama has had to solve in all ages. But one can ask further: Shall it come to grips with the present? Shall it turn back to the past? Or shall it be social, historical, or philosophical? Respectable talents have already entered upon these three different directions. Gutzkow has taken up the social theme. Four of his plays are available to us, and they make a better impression in their totality than taken separately, because they are obviously correlates which illumine the heights and the depths of the social condition with sharp, cutting lights.

Others have taken up historical drama. I believe, and I have explained it above, that the true historical character of the drama does not lie in its subject matter, and that a pure creation of fancy, even a love story, can be very historical if only the spirit of life moves in it and keeps it fresh for posterity, which does not want to know what our grandfathers looked like to us in our imaginations, but what we ourselves really were. I do not wish to imply in any way that our poets should fabricate their works out of thin air; on the contrary, when history or legend offers them a point of reference they ought not to scorn it in a ridiculous self-conceit of invention, but make grateful use of it. I want only to contest the widespread delusion that the poet can give anything but himself, anything but his own life process. This he cannot do, nor need he do it: for if he lives truthfully, if he does not creep pettily and obstinately into his own paltry ego, but permits himself to become permeated with those unseen elements which are in flux at all times, preparing new forms and figures, then he can confidently follow the inclination of his spirit, he can be certain that in expressing his needs he is expressing the needs of the world, that in the efforts of his imagination are the pictures of the future; it follows from this that it lies not in his province to become personally involved in any street fight which might come about. For the poet history is the vehicle for the embodiment of his views and ideas; whereas, to turn the statement around, he is not the resurrecting angel for history. Those who understand me will find that Shakespeare and Aeschylus confirm my view rather than contradict it. Philosophical dramas are also available. In these everything rests upon whether metaphysics issues from life, or whether life is to issue from metaphysics. In the first case something healthy will result, though by no means a new genre; in the other a monstrosity.

Now there is a possibility for a fourth kind of drama, one which unites the various tendencies characterized here, and which for that very reason permits no single tendency to predominate. This drama is the goal of my own endeavors, and if I have failed to make myself clear in the efforts themselves, in my *Judith* and my soon to appear *Genoveva*, then it would be foolish to try to help them with abstract explanations.

PREFACE TO *MARIA MAGDALENA*[1]

by Friedrich Hebbel

1844

THE FUNCTION OF DRAMA, as the summit of all art, is to clarify the existing state of the world and man in their relationship to the Idea, that is, to that moral center which conditions all things, and which we must accept as existing, if only for the sake of the self-preservation of those things. The drama is possible only when in this state of affairs a decisive change takes place. By drama I mean the highest, epoch-making drama, because there exist a second and third kind, a partial-nationalistic and a subjective-individual kind, which are to the first as single scenes and characters are to the complete play, but which must represent the drama until a universal genius appears, and which, if he does not, must take his place as *disjecti membra poetae*. It is therefore in every way a product of the age, but only in the sense in which such an age is the product of all preceding ages, the connect-

[1] "Preface to *Maria Magdalena*" by Friedrich Hebbel, translated by Carl Richard Mueller, printed by permission of the translator. Copyright © 1962 by Carl Richard Mueller. All rights reserved.

ing link between a series of centuries about to close, and a new series about to begin.

To the present, history has produced only two ages of crisis in which the highest drama could have been possible. Accordingly it has appeared only twice: once among the ancient Greeks when classical antiquity's concept of the world proceeded from its original simplicity to the stage of reflection, a progress at first disintegrative and finally destructive; and once among the moderns when a similar self-division proceeded from the Christian concept of the world. When paganism was on the wane, Greek drama evolved itself and devoured it. It laid bare the nerve of the idea which wound its way through all the variegated divine forms of Olympus, or, if you prefer, it gave form to Fate. Thus we have the boundless suppression of the individual by those moral forces with which he finds himself not in accidental but in necessary conflict, the very conflict which in *Oedipus* reaches such dizzying heights. Shakespearean drama developed along the lines of Protestantism and emancipated the individual. Thus we have the terrible dialectic of his characters, who, inasmuch as they are men of action, crowd out and impinge upon all living about them in their unrestrained expansion; and, inasmuch as they are men of thought, like Hamlet, are equally unrestrained in their introspection, and attempt, through the boldest and most terrifying questions, to drive God from the world as though He were a bungled piece of work.

After Shakespeare, Goethe was the first to lay again the foundation for a great drama; this he accomplished with his *Faust* and his *Wahlverwandtschaften*, a work rightly called dramatic. He did, or rather he began to do, the only thing remaining. He placed the dialectical problem directly in the Idea; he placed the contradiction, which for Shakespeare existed only in the individual, directly in the center around which the individual turns, that is, in such comprehensible aspects of the Idea as the individual can grasp. In so doing, he tried to divide that point, that Idea, into two parts, the point towards which the straight line of Greek drama and the crooked line of Shakespearean drama seemed both to lead. It need surprise no one that I pass over Calderón, to whom many assign an equal position. Calderón's dramas are indeed admirable in their logical development, and he has incorporated into the literature of the world an imperishable symbol with his play, *Life is a Dream*. This play, however,

contains only past, no future; in its rigid dependence on dogma
it assumes what it should prove. It is because of content,
then, and not of form that it must be assigned a subordinate
position.

Goethe, however, only showed the way. One can scarcely
say he took the first step, for when, in *Faust*, he rises too high
up into the cold regions where the blood begins to freeze,
he turns around; and in the *Wahlverwandtschaften* he assumes,
like Calderón, what he is to prove or demonstrate. I cannot
explain how Goethe, in every respect an artist, and a great
artist, was able, in his *Wahlverwandtschaften*, to offend so
against the inner form, or logic, of this work in that, not
unlike an absent-minded analyst who brings an automaton
into the dissecting room instead of a real body, he made the
central point of his work a marriage—that between Eduard
and Charlotte—which from the start was not only invalid but
immoral as well, and which he treated and used as though it
were its exact opposite, a marriage completely justified. The
fact that he did not go more deeply into the main problem
of the novel, and that, just as in *Faust*, when he had to choose
between an enormous perspective and a signboard painted
over with figures from the catechism, he chose the signboard,
and in so doing degraded the birth pangs of a humanity struggling for a new form, which we justly see in Part One, but
which in Part Two is reduced to mere phases of a sickness
which is cured later through an arbitrary and makeshift-
psychological act—all this emanated from his quite particularly complicated individuality which I have no need to
analyze here, since I have only to indicate how far he went.
I hope it is not necessary to note that the foregoing, quite
well-motivated objections to *Faust* and the *Wahlverwandtschaften* are by no means meant to cast aspersions on the
immeasurable worth of these two world-famous and historical
works, but to show the relationship which existed between
the poet and the ideas incorporated in the works, and to prove
where these ideas remained formless.

Goethe, therefore, to use his own expression, indeed entered
upon the great heritage of his time, but he did not consume it.
He realized well enough that human consciousness was trying
to expand, that it wanted to burst another ring, but he could
not resign himself to a childlike trust in history; and since
he was not able to resolve the dissonances which arose from
the transitory conditions, into which he as a youth was

violently drawn, he turned from them with decision, indeed
with repugnance and disgust. But these conditions were not
therefore eliminated. They have passed down to the present
day. They have, in fact, increased, and all fluctuations and
ruptures in our public as well as in our private lives are to
be traced back to them. Nor are they by any means as unnatural or even as dangerous as one would like to make them
seem. For the man of this century does not, as he is accused
of, want new and unheard of institutions: he wants merely
a better foundation for those which already exist. He wants
them to rest on nothing less than morality and necessity, which
are identical, and thus exchange for that external hook onto
which till now they have in part been attached the internal
center of gravity from which they are completely to be derived. This, I am convinced, is the world-wide historical process which is taking place in our day. Philosophy since Kant,
though actually since Spinoza, has in its demoralizing and
disintegrating way prepared for this, and dramatic art, assum-
ing it still has anything left to do, must help to end it; for
the circle which we have known till now has been described,
and duplicates are superfluous and have no place in the household of literature. Just as in a similar age of crisis Aeschylus,
Sophocles, Euripides, and Aristophanes did, dramatic art
must show through great and powerful pictures how those
elements, set free as a result of the last great historical movement, but which have not completely and absolutely been
absorbed into a living organism, but only partially formed
themselves into a seeming body—dramatic art must show how
these elements, surging about confusedly and in reciprocal
conflict, are begetting a new form of humanity in which all
things will return to place, in which woman will once again
stand face to face with man, as man stands face to face with
society, and society with the Idea. Bound up with this, of
course, is the disadvantage that dramatic art must deal with
the most delicate and dubious of problems, because a breaking up of general world-wide conditions can appear only
insofar as individual conditions are broken up, just as the
earthquake cannot appear except through the collapse of
churches and houses and the unrestrained inrushing of the
sea. Of course I only call this a disadvantage in regard to
those harmless souls for whom a tragedy and a game of cards
are unconsciously reduced to serving the same purpose, because they grow uncomfortable when a spade is no longer to

be a spade. They want new combinations within the game, but no new rules.

I say to you who call yourselves dramatic poets that if you satisfy yourselves with putting on stage anecdotes, historical or otherwise, they are all one, or, at the most, with analyzing the psychological clockwork of a character, then, no matter how often you put pressure on our tear ducts or convulse us with laughter, you are not one whit better than your famous thespian cousin who lets his puppets dance in his booth. The only basis for your art is where a problem exists. But when such a problem occurs to you, when life confronts you in its brokenness together with that aspect of the Idea (for both must coincide) in which the lost unity is found again, then seize upon it and do not worry yourself with the thought that the aesthetic-minded rabble demands that the state of health be shown in the very disease itself, because all you are doing is showing the transition to that state of health and are quite unable to heal the fever unless you concern yourself with it. Let me add expressly to this that it is not the allegorical dressing up of the Idea which need concern us here, nor any philosophical dialectic, but that dialectic which is directly a part of life itself.

I said that dramatic art must help to end that world-wide historical process of our day, that process which does not desire the overthrow of existing human institutions—political, religious, and moral—but desires to give them a firmer foundation and thereby secure them from overthrow. In this sense dramatic art must be timely, like all poetry which does not restrict itself to empty representations and arabesques; in this sense and in no other is all real poetry timely. It was also in this sense that in my preface to *Genoveva* I designated my dramas as artistic offerings of the time, for I am aware that the individual life processes which I have represented, and which I have still to represent, stand in closest relationship with the general problems which presently concern us.

Poetry, we seem to say now, is not to remain either what it was or what it is: the mirror of the century and the movement of mankind in general. It seems it is to become the mirror of the day, indeed of the very hour itself. But it is the drama that comes off worst of all, not because too much or the wrong thing is demanded of it, but because nothing at all is demanded. It is meant merely to amuse, it is meant merely to bring forward a thrilling anecdote, carried, at best, in order to be piquant, by characters of unusual psychology. But on no account must it do more.

There is one question which I cannot circumvent: Is our philosophy, thus far advanced, able, alone, to solve the great problems of our age and is the point of view of art to be regarded as outdated or capable of being outdated? If art were nothing more than what most people see in it, a dream-like spinning on of the physical world, interrupted now and then by a so-called ironic remark about itself, almost a comedy of forms [*Gestaltenkomoedie*] transferred from the external theatre to the internal one, in which the veiled Idea plays hide-and-seek with itself the same as ever—if this were true, then one must of necessity answer Yes, and lay upon art the task of atoning for the four-thousand-year-old sin of usurped existence with a voluntary death. But art is not only infinitely more, it is something completely different. It is realized philosophy, just as the world is realized Idea; and that philosophy which desires no traffic with art, and which does not want to manifest itself in appearance and thereby give highest proof of its reality—that p ilosophy had best forget the world entirely. It is a matter of indifference whether it deny the first or the last phase of the life process, from which it must presume itself to be excluded, if it believes itself able to manage without representation; for philosophy cannot relate to the world, as is possible through representation, without at the same time relating to art, for it is in art alone that the world becomes a totality. No productive and natural philosophy has ever done this, it always realized that it had not the right to suppress a proof which its nakedly reproduced Idea could not save itself from; and therefore it saw in art not merely a point of view, but its own goal and culminating point.

Now, if the drama is to solve no less a problem than the world-wide historical one itself, if it is to mediate between the Idea and the condition of the world and mankind, does it not follow that it must give itself completely to history, that it must be historical? I have said e'sewhere in regard to this important point, that the drama in and of itself and without any special tendency is historical, and that art is the highest form of historical recording. This statement will be contested by no one who is versed in the skill of looking to the past as well as to the future, for he will remember that all that remains to us of the peoples of the ancient wor'd are pictures, a skill which they developed into an art, and through which they recorded their being and their works in an unbreakable form. Herein, above all, lies factual proof which ought never to be despised. He will see, too, that the presently strengthening historical process of elimination, which separates for us the significant from the insignificant, that which for us is wholly dead, though still important in itself, from that which is still relevant in the historical organism, is in continuous advance. He will see that at some future time it will thin out the ranks of illustrious names, even to the Alexanders and the Napoleons; and that even later it will retain only the physiognomies of races, and finally perhaps even only the most general development epochs of mankind, brought about through the phases of religion and philosophy.

Since the great achievements of art are far less numerous than other great achievements, for the simple reason that they result from these other achievements, and since for that reason, they increase in number far less rapidly, it becomes evident that art will long be with us and that it will pass on to posterity the general essence of history, not the extensive and indifferent list of gardeners who planted and fertilized the tree, but the fruit with its body and core, which alone is of importance, and which furthermore can offer posterity the fragrance of the atmosphere in which it ripened.

But so much for generalities. Now a word more about the drama that I am offering to the public. It is a bourgeois tragedy. The bourgeois tragedy in Germany has fallen into discredit, and chiefly because of two abuses. Principally, it is discredited because it has not been constructed of those inner elements which are inherent in it: the harsh determination with which the individuals, incapable of dialectic, stand face to face with one another in the most confined of spheres, and the terrible constraint of life in all its one-sidedness which results from this condition. Rather dramatists have patched it together out of all kinds of externals: lack of money, for example, surplus of hunger; but above all out of the conflict between the third estate and the first and second estates in love affairs. This undoubtedly gives rise to much that is pathetic, but not tragic, for the tragic must appear from the start as something necessary, as something postulated in life itself, such as death, as something which is utterly unavoidable. As soon as one can help himself with a: If only he had (thirty dollars, which a touching sentimentality bolsters with a: If only he had come to me, I live in Nr. 32); or a: If only she had been (a lady, etc.)—when one can help himself with such and like, then the impression, which was meant to stir us deeply, becomes trivial. The effect, if it is not utterly scattered to the winds, then exists in the fact that the next day the spectator will pay his poorhouse taxes more readily than before or he will treat his daughter with more consideration: facts for which the supervisor of the poorhouse and the daughter, respectively, may be grateful, but not dramatic art.

The second reason why bourgeois tragedy has fallen into discredit is that once our poets let themselves down to the people, because it occurred to them that perhaps one need only be human to have a fate, and in certain circumstances a terrible fate, they assumed it necessary to ennoble the common people with whom they occupy themselves during such lost hours through beautiful speeches which they bestow upon them from their treasure chest. Or else these poets thought it necessary to force them down below their actual station in life by imposing on them a wooden stupidity. Their characters, therefore, appear to us partly as bewitched princes and princesses, whom the magician out of sheer malice refused to turn into dragons and lions and other respectable worthies of the animal kingdom but turned instead into base bakery maids and tailor's apprentices, but also partly as living blocks of wood, whose very ability to say Yes and No is cause for no little surprise. This, if possible, was even worse, because to the absurd and the ridiculous it added the trivial, and furthermore in a most obvious manner, for it is well known that the citizen and the farmer do not pluck their figures of speech, which they use just as well as the heroes of the salon and the promenade, from the starry firmament or fish them from the sea. Rather, the artisan gathers them in his workshop, and the farmer from behind his plow, and many of us have learned that these simple people, though they may not be adept in the art of conversation, are nevertheless capable of lively speech, and know how to combine and illustrate their ideas.

These two abuses explain the prejudice against bourgeois tragedy, but they cannot justify it, because they are the fault not of the genre but of inferior tradesmen who have bungled so badly in it. It is in and of itself a matter of indifference whether the hands of a clock are made of gold or of brass; nor does it matter whether an action which is in itself significant, that is, symbolic, takes place in a lower or in a socially higher sphere. Whereas in the heroic tragedy the seriousness of the subject matter and the reflections directly bound up in it may compensate up to a point for the deficiency in the tragic form, in the bourgeois tragedy everything depends on whether or not the circle of the tragic form is completed, that is, whether or not the point has been reached where we no longer care about the fate of a single individual, arbitrarily chosen by the playwright, but are able to see in that individual fate a fate which is universally human. The tragic outcome, too, whatever the particular form it may assume, must be recognized as wholly inevitable and incontestable.

These are the only points to be concerned about in a play: the relationship of the story to the positive and negative aspects of the moral powers moving in its background—family, honor, the choice between good and evil. Never ask for the so-called "flowery diction" of the false poets, that lamentably colorful calico in which marionettes strut about; nor for the number of pretty figures, splendid aphorisms and descriptions, and other spurious adornments, to be poor in which is the first result of richness. Those hereditary sins of the bourgeois tragedy which I have mentioned above are the very ones which I have avoided, of that I am certain. But I have undoubtedly committed others in their place. What are they?

MARIA MAGDALENA

by FRIEDRICH HEBBEL

1844

MARIA MAGDALENA[1]

Translated by Carl Richard Mueller

CHARACTERS

MASTER ANTON, *a cabinet maker*

HIS WIFE

KLARA, *his daughter*

KARL, *his son*

LEONARD

A SECRETARY

WOLFRAM, *a merchant*

ADAM, *a court bailiff*

A SECOND COURT BAILIFF

A BOY

A YOUNG GIRL

SCENE

A town of moderate size.

[1] *Maria Magdalena* by Friedrich Hebbel, translated by Carl Richard Mueller, printed by permission of the trans... Copyright © 1962 by Carl Richard Mueller. All rights reserved. Performance rights in all media, whether amateur or professional, must be obtained from Literary Discoveries, Inc., 124 Spear Street, San Francisco, California 94105.

ACT ONE

[*A room in the house of the cabinet maker,* MASTER ANTON.]

[KLARA. THE MOTHER.]

KLARA. Your wedding dress? Oh, how nice it looks on you.
It's like it was just made.

MOTHER. Well, child, a fashion can go only so far and then
it turns around again and has to come back. This dress has
been out of fashion ten times, and every time it came back
in.

KLARA. This time, mother, I don't think it quite made it. Look
here, the sleeves are too wide. But you mustn't let that
worry you.

MOTHER [*smiling*]. I'd have to be *you* to let *that* happen.

KLARA. So this is what you looked like. But you must have
worn a wreath too, didn't you?

MOTHER. I should hope! Why else would I have tended that
myrtle bush in the big flowerpot for all those years.

KLARA. I remember how often I'd beg you to put it on, but
you never would; you'd always say: "It's not my bridal
dress anymore, it's my burial dress, and not a plaything."
Finally it got to where I didn't want to see it, because when
I'd look at it hanging there, so white, it would always remind me of your death, and of the day when the old women
would pull it over your head. But why today?

MOTHER. When a person is as sick as I was, and doesn't know
if she'll ever get well again, all kinds of things come into
her mind. Death is more terrible than we think. Oh, it's a
bitter thing. It wraps the world in gloom; it blows out all
the lights, one after another, that glitter around us so gay
and happy. The friendly eyes of husband and children don't
shine anymore like they used to, and there's darkness everywhere; except that in our hearts a light is kindled that makes
everything bright, and we see so much, so very much that
we don't want to see. I know of no evil in my life. I have
always followed the ways of God. I did as much in my own
home as I was able; I raised you and your brother in the
fear of the Lord and have held together the fruits of your

father's hard labor. But I always knew how to save an
extra penny for the poor, and sometimes when I sent one
of them away because I was out of humor or because there
were too many of them, well, it wasn't such a disaster after
all, because I'd always call him back and end up by giving
him twice as much as the others. And what does it all
mean? It doesn't keep us from trembling when the hour of
our death comes round. When death threatens us, we writhe
like worms, we plead to God for life, like a servant pleading to his master to let him do again the work that he's
done so badly, so that when he's paid he won't be given
less than his due.

KLARA. Mother, you mustn't! You mustn't strain yourself this
way!

MOTHER. No, my child, it does me good. Don't you see me
standing here well and healthy again? Didn't the Lord God
call me only to tell me that my festive dress isn't quite
spotless and clean yet; and didn't He let me come back
from the very gates of death and give me time to deck
myself out for my wedding in Heaven? He wasn't as merciful as all that to those seven virgins in the Gospel that you
read me about yesterday! That's why I made up my mind
that today when I go to the Lord's Supper I would wear
this dress. I wore it on the day when I made the best and
most devout promises of my life. I want it to remind me
today of the promises that I have still to keep.

KLARA. You're talking like you did when you were sick!

KARL [entering]. Good morning, mother! Tell me something,
Klara, would you put up with me if I weren't your brother?

KLARA. A golden necklace? Where did you get it?

KARL. What do I work for? Why do I stay at work two hours
later every evening than the others? You're being impertinent!

MOTHER. Quarrelling on Sunday morning! Shame on you,
Karl!

KARL. Have you a guilder for me, mother?

MOTHER. The only money I have is for the household.

KARL. Then give me some of that. I promise I won't complain
if the pancakes aren't as rich as usual for the next two
weeks. You've done it often enough before, I know *that*
much! When you were saving up for Klara's white dress
we had nothing special on the table for months. I didn't

say anything, but I knew what to expect: a new hat or something else to show off. Let *me* have something of it, too, for a change!

MOTHER. Aren't you ashamed!

KARL. If I had time now, I'd . . . [*He starts to leave.*]

MOTHER. Where are you going?

KARL. Why do you always want me to tell you that? When I do you only get embarrassed when the old bear asks where I've gone and you have to say you don't know. Well, now you won't have to be embarrassed because you *won't* know, and you won't be lying. And besides that I don't need your guilder. It's a good thing there's water in more wells than one! [*He goes off.*]

KLARA. What did he mean by that?

MOTHER. He's such a worry to me! Yes, yes, his father was right, this is what comes of it. He was just as defiant now when he demanded that guilder as he was lovable when he was a curly-headed little boy and asked me for a piece of sugar. I wonder, would he have demanded that guilder just now if I hadn't given him those pieces of sugar? It plagues me so often. I don't think he even loves me. Did you see him cry, just once, while I was so sick?

KLARA. I saw him seldom enough; most of the time only at the table. His appetite was somewhat better than mine!

MOTHER [*quickly*]. That was only natural, his work isn't easy!

KLARA. I suppose so. Men are such strange things. They're more ashamed of their tears than of their sins. A clenched fist is something else again. But tears? Father's the same way. The time they tried to let blood from your veins but nothing would come, he sat there on his joiner's bench the whole afternoon, sobbing, till I thought I couldn't bear it any longer. And then when I went over to him and put my hand to his cheek, what do you think he said? "Get this confounded splinter out of my eye! I have so much work to do and I can't get at it!"

MOTHER. I know, I know! —I never see Leonard anymore. Why's that?

KLARA. If he wants to stay away, let him!

MOTHER. I hope you're seeing him nowhere but in this house!

KLARA. Have I ever given you reason to suspect me? Do I stay too long in the evening when I go to the well?

MOTHER. No, of course you don't. But that's why I said he

could come *here* to see you, so that he wouldn't have to watch for you like a thief in the night. My mother would never put up with that either.

KLARA. I don't see him.

MOTHER. Are you angry with one another? I like him well enough, he's a serious young man. I only wish he had some position in the world. In *my* day he couldn't have waited *too* long! The men would scramble around an able scribe like cripples for a crutch, because they were hard to come by. Even unimportant people like us could make use of him. One day he would write out a New Year's greeting from a son to his father and get paid enough for the gilt letters alone to buy a doll for a child! Then the next day the father would call in the scribe and have him read the greeting secretly where they couldn't be seen; that way they wouldn't be taken unawares and the father have to admit his ignorance. That's the way scribes got paid double. That's why they were always better off than others and made the beer more expensive. Things are different now, now old people like your father and me, who know nothing about reading and writing, have to let nine-year-old schoolboys make fun of us. The world gets smarter all the time, and maybe the time will even come when we'll have to be ashamed for not knowing how to walk a tightrope!

KLARA. The church bells are ringing.

MOTHER. Well, child, I'll pray for you. And as for Leonard, you may love him just as much as he loves God, no more, no less. That's what my old mother said to me when she gave me her blessing before she died. I think I've kept it long enough now, so now I'll give it to *you*!

KLARA [*giving her a bouquet of flowers*]. Here!

MOTHER. Is it from Karl?

KLARA [*nods, then aside*]. How I wish it were! The only real happiness she can ever know has to come from him!

MOTHER. Oh, he *is* good! He *does* love me! [*She goes off.*]

KLARA [*watching her from the window*]. There she goes. Three times I dreamt I saw her lying in a coffin, and then . . . why must these terrible dreams clothe themselves in our fears and frighten us so! I must never again pay attention to dreams, never be happy because of a good one, and so never be afraid because of the bad one that always follows. How confidently she walks. I wonder who'll be the first to meet her? I know it doesn't mean anything, but . . .

[*startled*] the grave digger! He's climbing out of a grave that he's just finished digging. She's bowing to him and smiling as she looks down into that hole. And now she throws her bouquet of flowers into it and goes into the church.

[*The sounds of a choral heard.*]

They're singing: "Now thank we all our God." [*She folds her hands.*] God, my God, if my mother had died, I would never have found peace again. [*She looks toward heaven.*] But Thou art merciful, Thou are compassionate! I wish that I believed like the Catholics do, so that I could offer something to You. I would take all the money I have and buy You a lovely golden heart and wreathe it with roses. Our pastor says that offerings mean nothing to You because all things are Yours already, and we ought not to want to give You what You already possess. But everything in this house belongs to my father, and still it makes him happy when for his birthday I buy him a handkerchief with his own money and put it on his plate to surprise him. Yes, and then he always honors my gift by wearing it only on the highest holy days, at Christmas or Pentecost. One time I saw a tiny Catholic girl carrying cherries to the altar as an offering. It made me so happy to watch her! They were the first cherries of the year that they'd given the child, and I saw how much she wanted to eat them. But still she fought against her innocent desire, and to put an end to her temptation she put down the cherries so quickly that the priest who had just raised the chalice looked at her so threateningly that he frightened the child away. And then I saw the Blessed Virgin smiling so tenderly above the altar, as if she wanted to step down out of her frame to hurry after the child and kiss her. I did it for her—Leonard's coming!

LEONARD [*outside the door*]. Are you proper?

KLARA. Why so tender all of a sudden, so thoughtful? I'm no princess!

LEONARD [*entering*]. I didn't think you were alone. When I walked past I thought I saw your neighbor's daughter Barbara at the window.

KLARA. Oh, so that's the reason!

LEONARD. Why are you always so cross! A person can be

away for two whole weeks and come back and find you
as gloomy as ever.

KLARA. It wasn't always like this.

LEONARD. I should hope not! If you'd always looked this way
we'd never have become friendly.

KLARA. Would that have been so terrible?

LEONARD. You're very open, aren't you! That suits me, too.
Then that [*with reference to something*] toothache recently
didn't mean anything!

KLARA. Oh, Leonard, that wasn't right of you!

LEONARD. Not right of me to want to possess completely my
most priceless possession? Isn't that what you are? And at
a time when I was in danger of losing you? Do you think
I was blind to the looks you and the Secretary gave one
another that evening? That was quite a happy day for me!
I took you to a dance and . . .

KLARA. When will you stop tormenting me this way! Yes, I
looked at the Secretary, why should I deny it? But it
was only because of the moustache he had grown at the
university, it made him look . . . [*She stops.*]

LEONARD. So handsome, isn't that what you wanted to say?
Women, women! They'd sit up at the grossest caricature
of a soldier's brush! I've had enough of him! Why should
I hide the way I feel? He's stood in my way long enough!
That round laughable little face of his, and that forest of
hair on his head that he combs down the middle. He looks
like a white rabbit hiding behind a bush!

KLARA. I haven't praised him yet, so you needn't insult him!

LEONARD. Yet you're not exactly indifferent to him!

KLARA. We played together as children, and afterwards . . .
you know well enough.

LEONARD. Yes, I know! And that's just what I'm talking about!

KLARA. It was only natural for me to want to look at him. I
was seeing him for the first time after so long. I was surprised to see how tall he had grown and . . . [*She interrupts
herself.*]

LEONARD. Then why were you embarrassed when he looked
back at you?

KLARA. I thought he was looking at the mole on my left cheek,
to see if it had grown larger. You know that's what I
always think when anybody stares at me very hard, and that
I always get embarrassed. It seems like the mole grows
bigger as long as they're looking at me.

LEONARD. I don't care what your reasons were! I didn't like the way you looked at each other! I said to myself that I'd make sure of you that same night. "If she wants to be my wife then she'll know it and won't try anything else," I said. "If she says no, then . . ."

KLARA. I'll never forget what you said when I pushed you from me. I wanted to run away but I felt myself held back. At first I thought it was you, but it was a rosebush that held to my dress with its thorns as though they were teeth. After that night I couldn't even trust *myself* anymore. You stood in front of me like someone demanding payment for a debt, And I . . . my God!

LEONARD. I'm not sorry for that yet. I knew that it was the only way I could keep you. I swore to myself that I would make you forget him.

KLARA. When I got back home I found my mother sick, deathly sick; suddenly struck down as if by some unseen hand. My father wanted to send for me earlier, but she wouldn't let him; she didn't want to destroy my happiness. I can't tell you how I felt when I heard. I didn't go near her, I didn't dare touch her, I trembled. She said it was only childish fear and nodded for me to come to her. As I slowly went towards her she pulled me down beside her and kissed me here on the mouth. I was ashamed, I wanted to confess to her, I wanted to cry out to her what I thought and felt: that it was *my* fault she was lying there! I *did* tell her, but my tears and sobbing choked my words. She reached for my father's hand and looked up at me so peacefully and said: "She's too good to me!"

LEONARD. And now she's well. I came to congratulate her and . . . what do you think?

KLARA. What?

LEONARD. To ask your father for your hand.

KLARA. Oh!

LEONARD. Aren't you well?

KLARA. Well? I'd be dead soon if I weren't your wife. But you don't know my father. He has no idea why it has to be soon. He mustn't know and we can't tell him. I've heard him say a hundred times that he would only give his daughter to someone who had more than love in his heart for her, but bread on the table, too. He's going to say: "Wait another year, my son, or maybe two!" And what will you say to that?

LEONARD. That problem doesn't exist anymore. I have the position. I'm Treasurer now.

KLARA. Treasurer? And the other candidate? The pastor's nephew?

LEONARD. He was drunk when he arrived at the examination. He bowed to the stove instead of to the Mayor, and when he sat down he knocked three cups from the table. You know how hot-tempered the old man is. "Sir!" he roared, still trying to control himself and biting his lip. His eyes blazed through his glasses like a pair of snakes ready for the spring, and his patience was at the breaking point. Finally we got down to computing figures and [*he chuckles*] my competitor used a multiplication table of his own finding that produced some quite novel results. "His calculations are wrong!" said the Mayor, giving me a look that told me the appointment was mine. I took his tobacco-stinking hand in mine and kissed it in all humility. And here it is, signed and sealed!

KLARA. It's all so . . .

LEONARD. Unexpected? Well, it didn't quite happen by chance, you see. Why do you think I stayed away for two whole weeks?

KLARA. I have no idea. I thought because of our quarrel that Sunday.

LEONARD. I slyly set up that little disagreement myself, so that I could stay away without it seeming too unusual.

KLARA. I don't understand.

LEONARD. I mean it. I used the time well. I used it to court that hunchbacked little niece of the Mayor's, the one he's so fond of. She's as much his *right* hand as the bailiff is his *left*. Don't misunderstand me! I didn't say anything too pleasant to her, except to compliment her on her hair which, as you know, is red. In fact I said only one thing that really pleased her . . . about *you*.

KLARA. Me?

LEONARD. Why should I keep it a secret? It was done with the best of intentions. I let her think that there had never been anything between us, that there was—but that's enough of that! It lasted only long enough for me to get my hands on *this*. That gullible man-crazy little fool will find out just how much I meant of what I said when she hears our wedding banns read in church.

KLARA. Leonard!

LEONARD. Child! Child! You be harmless as a dove, my sweet, and I'll be sly as a snake, and that way, since they say man and wife are one, we'll satisfy the Gospel all the way round. [*He laughs.*] Of course it wasn't quite an accident that our young Hermann happened to be drunk at the most important moment of his life. As you know, he doesn't go in much for drinking.

KLARA. Yes.

LEONARD. That made our plan all the easier. Three glasses and that was it! A couple of friends of mine helped. "Are congratulations in order?" —"Not yet!" —"Well, it's a pretty sure thing! After all, your uncle . . ." And then: "Have a drink with us, friends!" —On my way over here this morning I found him standing looking dejectedly over the railing of the bridge into the water. I greeted him mockingly and asked if he had lost something in the river. "Yes," he said, without looking up, "and maybe I should jump in after it."

KLARA. How could you! I never want to see you again!

LEONARD. Really? [*He pretends to leave.*]

KLARA. My God, why must I be chained to him like this!

LEONARD. Stop being a child! I want you to tell me something now in confidence. Does your father still have the thousand thalers invested in the pharmacy?

KLARA. How should I know?

LEONARD. Even about something as important as that?

KLARA. My father's coming.

LEONARD. Don't misunderstand me! The only reason I asked is that the pharmacist is about to go bankrupt.

KLARA. I have to get to the kitchen! [*She goes off.*]

LEONARD [*alone*]. Well, I guess there's not much to get *here!* Master Anton's the kind of man who if he found one letter too many on his tombstone would haunt his grave till he'd scratched it out, and only because he'd think it dishonorable to take more of the alphabet than is his due!

MASTER ANTON [*enters*]. Good morning, Mr. Treasurer! [*He takes off his hat and puts on his woolen cap.*] Will you permit an old man to cover his head?

LEONARD. Then you know . . .

MASTER ANTON. I knew yesterday evening. Yesterday at dusk I went to take the measurements for the casket of my good friend Müller who just died. I heard some of your friends complaining about you. I thought right away that you must have made it. And then in the dead man's house I heard the details from the sexton. He got there just ahead of me to console the widow, and to get drunk.

LEONARD. And Klara had to learn of it from me?

MASTER ANTON. If *you're* not interested in making her happy with the news, why should *I* be? I light no candles in my house till they belong to me. That way I can be sure that no one will come along and blow them out just when we're enjoying them most.

LEONARD. Surely you couldn't think that I . . .

MASTER ANTON. Think? About you? Or anyone else? I plane my boards smooth like they ought to be, with iron tools, but I never let my thoughts do the same with people. I cured myself of that foolishness a long time ago. When I see a tree that's green I have good cause to think that it will blossom soon. And when it's blossomed that it will soon have fruit. And I have never been deceived. That's why I have kept up the custom. But about people I have no thoughts, none whatever, neither good ones nor bad ones. That way I have no need one time to grow red with embarrassment and the next pale with disappointment, when one time they deceive my fears and the next time my hopes. I only learn from them and take examples with my two eyes, but they don't think either, they only see. I thought I had learned all there was to learn about you, and now I find you here and have to admit that I only learned the half of it.

LEONARD. I think you have it all wrong, Master Anton. A tree depends on wind and weather, but human beings have laws and standards.

MASTER ANTON. Really? Yes, I suppose we old people owe death a great debt for allowing us to chase around here for so long with all these young people, and for the chance to educate ourselves by them. It used to be the stupid world believed the father was put in it to educate the son. They had it all backwards. The son is here to put the last lick of polish on the father so that the poor simple old man needn't be ashamed when he goes to meet the worms in his grave. God be praised, I have a good teacher in my son Karl. He wages a terrible war against my prejudices, and he doesn't pamper the old child with too much indulgence. This morning he taught me two new lessons, and in the most skillful way, without opening his mouth, in fact

without even showing himself. First of all he proved to me
that we needn't keep our word, and second that it is unnecessary to go to church in order to renew in ourselves
the Commandments of the Lord. Yesterday evening he
promised me that he would, and I relied on him to come,
because I thought: He will want to render thanks to the
gracious Creator for the recovery of his mother. But he
didn't come. I found my pew, which of course is a bit
narrow for two persons, quite comfortable. I wonder how
it would please him if I took up his lesson at once and made
it my own and failed to keep my *own* word? I promised
him a new suit of clothes for his birthday, and so I have
the chance to test his delight with my teachable nature.
But . . . prejudice, prejudice! I won't do it.

LEONARD. Maybe he wasn't well . . .

MASTER ANTON. Possible! All I need to do is ask my wife and
I'll know for sure he was sick. She tells me the truth about
everything under the sun, except about the boy. And if he
wasn't sick . . . this younger generation's got the better of
us there, too; they can be moved to devotion anywhere,
they can say their prayers whether they're catching birds,
taking a walk, or even at the tavern. "Our Father, Which
art in Heaven!" —"Hello, Peter, will you be at the dance?"
—"Hallowed be Thy Name!" —"Don't worry, Catherine,
we'll find it!" —"Thy will be done!" —"Damnation, I'm
not shaved yet!" —And so on to the end. And then they
give themselves their own blessing, because they're as
human as the preacher, and the power that proceeds from
his black coat can just as well come from a blue one. I'm
not against it; I'd just as soon they'd drink down seven
glasses of beer between the seven petitions of *The Lord's
Prayer.* What's the difference? I can't prove that beer and
religion don't mix. And besides that it might come into the
liturgy as a new way of taking the Lord's Supper. Of course
an old sinner like me, I'm not strong enough to go along
with the new custom. I can't catch up my devotions like
I can a beetle in the street; the chirping of sparrows can
never take the place of the organ for me; when I'm to feel
my heart lifted up, then I must first hear the heavy iron
doors of the church close behind me and imagine them
the gates to the world; the dark high walls of the church,
with their narrow windows that let in the light only dimly
as though they filter it through, must press upon me; and

in the distance I must see the charnel house with the death's head imbedded in its wall. Well . . . it's best to be on the safe side!

LEONARD. You take the matter too seriously.

MASTER ANTON. Of course! Of course I do! And today, being an honorable man, I have to confess that I was all wrong. I lost my devotion in church because of the empty place next to me. But outside under the pear tree in my garden I found it again. Does it surprise you? You see, I went home depressed and downcast, like a man who has had his harvest ruined by hailstorms, because children are like fields, you sow good seed and weeds grow up. I stood there quietly under the pear tree that the caterpillars had eaten away. "Yes," I thought, "the boy is like this tree, empty and bare!" And then suddenly it seemed to me I was terribly thirsty and had to get to the tavern at once. I deceived myself, it wasn't a glass of beer I wanted; all I was after was to find the boy and chide him; I knew well enough I could find him at the tavern. Just as I was about to leave, the wise old tree let a juicy pear fall at my feet as if to say: "This is for your thirst, and for insulting me by comparing me with your son!" I thought for a moment, bit into the pear, and went into the house.

LEONARD. Do you know the pharmacist is about to go bankrupt?

MASTER ANTON. It's not my worry.

LEONARD. Not at all?

MASTER ANTON. Of course! I'm a Christian. The man has many children.

LEONARD. And even more creditors. Even children could be called creditors.

MASTER ANTON. How is that *my* business?

LEONARD. It was my belief that you . . .

MASTER ANTON. That was settled long ago.

LEONARD. You're a cautious man. I suppose you called in your money when you saw things weren't going too well with the pharmacy.

MASTER ANTON. No, I have no worry about losing it now; I lost it a long time ago.

LEONARD. You're joking!

MASTER ANTON. Dead serious!

KLARA [looking through the doorway]. Did you call, father?

MASTER ANTON. Are your ears burning already? We haven't even talked about you yet!

KLARA. Here's the weekly paper. [*She goes out.*]

LEONARD. You're a philosopher, too, I see.

MASTER ANTON. What is that supposed to mean?

LEONARD. You know how to compose yourself.

MASTER ANTON. I carry a millstone around my neck at times as a ruff, instead of drowning myself with it . . . it gives one a stiff bearing.

LEONARD. Let whoever can follow your example!

MASTER ANTON. Anyone who finds as brave a man to share his burden with as I seem to have found in *you*, ought to be able to *dance* under the weight. You became downright pale. That's what I call sharing.

LEONARD. I'll prove to you that you haven't misjudged me!

MASTER ANTON. Of course! [*He pounds on a chest-of-drawers.*] Isn't it strange how we can't see through wood?

LEONARD. I don't understand.

MASTER ANTON. What a fool our grandfather Adam was to take Eve so naked and unprotected, without even a fig leaf. You and I would have whipped her from Paradise for a tramp. What do you say to that?

LEONARD. You're angry because of your son. I came to talk to you about your daughter's . . .

MASTER ANTON. That's enough! Perhaps I won't say no!

LEONARD. I hope you won't. I'd also like to tell you what I think. Not even the Holy Patriarchs, you know, scorned their women's dowries. Jacob loved Rachel and strove for her hand for seven years, but at the same time he was pleased with the fat ewes and rams he earned in her father's service. I don't think it was disgraceful of him, and to outdo him would only be to embarrass him. I would have been pleased, too, if your daughter had brought along a couple hundred thalers with her, and that would have been natural enough. Things would have been easier for her: when a girl brings her own bed along into the new house then she has no need to start right in by combing wool and spinning yarn. But that's not the case here. But no matter. We'll eat on Sundays as if it were Lent, and our Sunday roasts we'll save for our Christmas feast! It'll work out!

MASTER ANTON [*extending his hand*]. Well said, and I can see the Lord God nodding His approval. And so . . . I suppose

I can forget that every evening for two weeks my daughter
set an extra cup of tea on the table to no purpose. And
now that you're to become my son-in-law I'll tell you what
has become of the thousand thalers.

LEONARD [aside]. So it *is* gone! Son-in-law or not, I needn't
smile at everything he says!

MASTER ANTON. Things were bad for me in my young days.
I wasn't born into this world a prickly hedgehog, but as
time went on I got to be one. At first all my quills were
turned inwards on me, and people amused themselves by
pressing and pinching my bare soft skin, and they were
happy when I winced because they knew the stingers were
pressing my heart and entrails. I wasn't satisfied with that
so I turned my skin inside out; that way the quills pricked
their fingers and I was left in peace.

LEONARD. With the devil himself, no doubt!

MASTER ANTON. My father worked himself to death by the
time he was thirty because he allowed himself no rest either
day or night. My poor mother helped to raise me as well
as she could by her spinning. I grew up without learning
anything, and the older I became, still unable to earn, the
happier I would have been if at least I could have given
up eating. But even if sometimes at noon I had said I was
sick and pushed the plate from me, what good would it
have done? That evening my stomach would have forced
me to say I was well again. The thing that tormented me
most was that I had no skill. I could have argued with
myself that it had been my own fault, that I was tied to
the apron strings of my mother's love and purposely left
behind in her everything that could have made me useful
and skilled. I could have been ashamed every time the sun
shone on me. Just after I was confirmed a man came to visit
us in our tiny room. Master Gebhard, the one they buried
yesterday. He wrinkled his brow and twisted up his face
like he always did when he had something good in mind;
then he said to my mother: "Did you bring this boy into
the world to eat you out of house and home?" I was just
about to cut a piece from a loaf of bread, but he shamed
me so, that I quickly put it back into the cupboard. My
mother took offence at what he meant well, and taking
a firm hold on her spinning wheel she fired back at him
that her son was honest and good. "Well, we'll have to see
about that," the Master said. "If he wants he can come

along with me to my workship just as he is. It won't cost
him a penny, he'll be fed, and I'll take care of his clothes,
too; and if he wants to get up early and go to bed late then
there'll be plenty of times for him to earn a little something
extra for his old mother." My mother started to cry, and I
started to dance, and when we finally got around to talking
about it the Master stopped his ears, started out and waved
for me to come along. There was no need for me to put on
my hat, because I didn't have one. Without even saying
goodbye to my mother I followed him out, and on the next
Sunday when I had my first time off to go back, he gave me
half of a ham to take to her. God bless that good man in
his grave! I can still hear his half-angry: "Damnation, put
it under your jacket so my wife can't see it!"

LEONARD. Does it make you cry even now?

MASTER ANTON [*drying his eyes*]. Yes, as sure as the well of
my tears is choked up inside me, I can't think about it
without it tearing at my heart. God! If I ever come down
with dropsy, at least they won't have to draw *this* water off
me! [*Suddenly wheeling about.*] Tell me: what would you
do if one Sunday afternoon you went to visit a man that you
owed everything to, and you found him confused and troubled, with a knife in his hand, the same knife that he used a
thousand times before to cut the bread with for your tea,
but you found him with the bloody knife at his throat, and
his other hand pulled a scarf up high around his neck . . .

LEONARD. He wore the scarf like that until he died.

MASTER ANTON. Because of the scar. And suppose you got
there in time to save him and help him, but not only by
taking the knife from his hand and binding his wound, but
by having to give him a miserable thousand thalers that
you'd saved, yes, you *had* to give it to him so that the sick
man would take it . . . and this happened just between
the two of you, what would you do?

LEONARD. Since I'm single and without wife or child, I'd have
sacrificed the money.

MASTER ANTON. And if you'd had ten wives like the Turks and
as many children as were promised our father Abraham,
and you had one second to think it over in, you'd have . . .
well, you're to be my son-in-law! Now you know what
happened to the money. I can tell you this now because
my old Master is in his grave. But a month ago, if I had
been on my own deathbed, I would have taken the secret

with me to my grave. I placed his promise to pay back the money under his head before they nailed his coffin closed. If I'd known how to write I'd have written across it first: *Honorably paid!* But being an ignorant man, all there was left me was to tear the paper through. He'll sleep in peace now, and I hope to do the same when the time comes for me to lay myself down by his side.

THE MOTHER [*enters quickly*]. Do you still recognize me?

MASTER ANTON [*indicating the wedding dress*]. The frame's all right but the picture's not the same. It seems the cobwebs have covered it over; but it's been so many years.

MOTHER. As you can see, I have an honest husband. But there's no need for me to praise him specially, because honesty, they say, is the virtue of husbands.

MASTER ANTON. Are you sorry your hair was more golden at twenty than it is now at fifty?

MOTHER. Of course not. If it were the other way around I'd have to be ashamed for both of us.

MASTER ANTON. Then give me a kiss. I shaved today and better than usual.

MOTHER. The only reason I'll agree is to see if you still know anything about the art. It's been a long time since you thought of it.

MASTER ANTON. You're a good wife. When I die I don't want you to be the one to close my eyes for me. It's a hard thing to do. I want to be the one to do it for *you*. I want to be able to do that last kindness for you. But you must give me time for it, you hear? I'll have to steel myself first and find the courage, and not do it all wrong. But it's too soon to think of that now.

MOTHER. I thank God that we'll be together for a while longer.

MASTER ANTON. I hope so, too. Your cheeks are even rosy again.

MOTHER. What a strange man our new grave digger is. He was digging a grave as I cut across the churchyard this morning, and I asked him who it was for. "For whoever God wants it to be for," he said, "maybe even for me. It can happen to me just like to my grandfather who dug an extra grave once, and that night on the way home from the tavern he fell into it and broke his neck."

LEONARD [*who till now has been reading the newspaper*]. Since he's not from these parts, he can lie to us all he wants.

MOTHER. I asked him: "Why don't you wait till somebody

orders a grave from you?" —"I'm invited to a wedding tonight," he said, "and I'm enough of a prophet to know what I'll feel like tomorrow. And somebody's bound to play a trick on me and die so that I'll have to get up early tomorrow and dig instead of sleep it off."

MASTER ANTON. I would have told him he was a fool, because what if the grave didn't fit?

MOTHER. That's what I said, too, but he spit out his sharp answers at me like lies out of a devil's mouth. "I went by the measurements of our weaver, Mr. Veit," he said, "he's like King Saul himself and towers a whole head above us all. Let come who will, he won't find his house too small for him, and if it's too big then I'm the one to lose, because being an honorable man I never charge for more than the length of the coffin." Then I threw my bouquet of flowers into it and said: "There now, it's been ordered."

MASTER ANTON. I think the fellow was only joking, and that's sinful enough. Digging graves beforehand is like setting a trap for death. The good-for-nothing who does such things ought to be chased from his job. [*To* LEONARD *who is reading.*] Anything new? Is some kind soul looking for an old widow who can use a few hundred thalers? Or the other way around: the old widow looking for a kind soul who can give her some?

LEONARD. The police give notice of a jewelry theft. That's amazing enough in itself. At least we can see that no matter how bad the times are there are still people around us with jewelry stuck away.

MASTER ANTON. A jewelry theft? Where was this?

LEONARD. At Wolfram's, the merchant.

MASTER ANTON. At Wol . . . That's impossible! That's where my son Karl polished a writing-desk a few days ago!

LEONARD. Yes, it disappeared from the writing-desk.

MOTHER [*to* MASTER ANTON]. May God forgive you for that!

MASTER ANTON. Yes, it was a terrible thought!

MOTHER. You have never been more than half a father to your son.

MASTER ANTON. We are not going to talk about that today!

MOTHER. Just because he's not like you, do you have to think he's evil?

MASTER ANTON. Where is he now? The noon bells rang long ago. I'll wager our food is overcooked and that Klara has secret orders not to set the table before he comes.

MOTHER. Where do you *expect* him to be? At most he's out playing at bowling; and of course he has to play in an alley as far away as possible so that you won't be able to find him. The way back for him is bound to be long. And besides, I don't know what you have against the harmless game.

MASTER ANTON. Against the game? Nothing! Fashionable gentlemen *need* something to pass their time with. Without a king of cards a real king would be bored often enough, and if bowling hadn't been invented who knows whether princes and barons wouldn't play at it with our heads. But there is nothing more deceitful or outrageous than when a craftsman stakes his hard-earned pay on gaming. A man must respect what he has gained through hard labor in the sweat of his brow, he must hold it high and value it, unless he wants to lose faith in himself, unless he wants to find all he does contemptible. When I think of what a thaler means to me and then . . .

[*The bell on the outside door rings.*]

MOTHER. There he is.

[ADAM *the bailiff, and a* SECOND BAILIFF *enter.*]

ADAM [*to* MASTER ANTON]. You may go and pay off your wagers now. People in red coats with blue lapels [*he emphasizes this strongly*] would never enter your house, eh? Well, here we are. [*To the* SECOND BAILIFF.] Why did you take your hat off? Why bother when you're with your own kind?

MASTER ANTON. What do you mean "with your own kind"?

ADAM. You're right, we're not with our own kind. Scoundrels and thieves are not our kind. [*He points to the chest.*] I want that unlocked. And then you will back up three paces. So that you don't sneak anything out of it.

MASTER ANTON. What's this! What this!

KLARA [*enters with a tablecloth*]. Shall I . . . [*She is suddenly silent.*]

ADAM [*showing a paper*]. Can you read?

MASTER ANTON. How should I be able to do what my own teacher couldn't?

ADAM. Then you'll listen. Your son stands accused of stealing jewels. We already have the thief. Now we intend to search your house.

MOTHER. Sweet Jesus! [*She collapses and dies.*]

KLARA. Mother! Mother! Look at her eyes!

LEONARD. I'll get a doctor!

MASTER ANTON. That won't be necessary. I know that look. I have seen it a hundred times before. Good night, Theresa. You died as you heard the truth. That will be written on your grave.

LEONARD. But maybe if . . . [*leaving*]. It's horrible! But it saved my neck. [*Off.*]

MASTER ANTON [*pulling out a ring of keys and tossing it from him*]. There! Unlock them! One cabinet after another! Bring an axe here! The key to that trunk is lost. Scoundrels and thieves, eh? [*He turns his pockets inside out.*] Nothing here.

SECOND BAILIFF. Master Anton, get hold of yourself. We all know you're the most honest man in the town.

MASTER ANTON. Really? Really? [*Laughs.*] In that case I must have used up all the honesty in my family! My poor son! There was nothing left for him. And she . . . [*indicating the dead* MOTHER] she was too virtuous, too. Who knows, maybe my daughter has . . . [*Suddenly to* KLARA.] What has my innocent daughter to say?

KLARA. Father!

SECOND BAILIFF [*to* ADAM]. Don't you have *any* pity?

ADAM. Pity? Do you see me digging in his pockets? Am I forcing him to take his stockings off or shake out his boots? That's what I *should* have done because of how I hate that man! Ever since the time at the tavern when he took his glass and . . . he knows the story and he couldn't help but feel insulted if he had any honor in his body. [*To* KLARA.] Where is your brother's room?

KLARA [*showing him*]. Back there.

[BOTH BAILIFFS *go off.*]

KLARA. Father, he *isn't* guilty. He *can't* be guilty.

MASTER ANTON. Not guilty, and murdered his mother? [*He laughs.*]

A GIRL [*enters with a letter, to* KLARA]. It's from Leonard, the Treasurer. [*Off.*]

MASTER ANTON. There's no need to read it. He's got himself rid of you. [*Striking his hands together.*] Bravo, the scoundrel!

KLARA [*having read the letter*]. Yes! Yes! My God!

MASTER ANTON. Let him be.

KLARA. Father, father, I can't!

MASTER ANTON. Can't? You can't? What do you mean, you can't? Are you . . .

[BOTH BAILIFFS *return*.]

ADAM [*spitefully*]. Seek and ye shall find!

SECOND BAILIFF [*to* ADAM]. What are you talking about? Were you right or not?

ADAM. Keep quiet!

[*Both go off*.]

MASTER ANTON. He's innocent, but you . . . you . . .

KLARA. Father, how can you be this way!

MASTER ANTON [*takes her tenderly by the hand*]. Dear Klara . . . my Karl is no more than a scoundrel. He murdered his own mother, what else can you call it? But the father stayed behind. Will you help him? You can't ask him to do everything alone. Give me some rest. The old trunk looks as gnarled as ever, but even it is beginning to tremble. It won't take much strength to fell it, too. You won't have to put your hands to an axe. You have a lovely face. I've never praised you before in any way, but I want to tell you this today to give you courage and confidence. Your eyes, your nose, your mouth will always . . . find approval, will always . . . you know what I'm saying. You must tell me, I can't help feeling that . . . that something has already happened.

KLARA [*almost frantic, she falls with raised arms at the feet of her* MOTHER's *body and calls to her like a child*]. Mother! Mother!

MASTER ANTON. Take her hand in yours and swear to me that you are the same as on the day that she gave you birth!

KLARA. I . . . swear . . . that . . . I . . . will . . . never . . . bring . . . shame . . . upon . . . you!

MASTER ANTON. Good! [*He puts on his hat*.] It's fine weather out. I must take a long walk in it, up one street and down another. [*Off*.]

ACT TWO

[*A room in the house of the cabinet maker.*]

[MASTER ANTON *rises from the table.* KLARA *starts to clear it.*]

MASTER ANTON. You haven't eaten anything again.

KLARA. Father, I've had enough.

MASTER ANTON. Of nothing?

KLARA. I ate in the kitchen.

MASTER ANTON. A bad appetite means a bad conscience. Well, all things come to light in the end. Or was there poison in the soup, like I dreamt yesterday? Maybe a sprig of hemlock got picked into your basket of herbs by mistake? That would have been the wise thing to do.

KLARA. My God in Heaven!

MASTER ANTON. Forgive me, I . . . Oh, the devil take you and that woeful face that you stole from the Mother of God herself! Your face should be full of life when you're young. There's only one person to show off a face like that, but do you see him doing it? A man who cries over nothing but a cut finger ought to have his face slapped. No one has that right any more . . . but then self-praise is no recommendation. What was it I did when our neighbor was about to nail shut your mother's coffin?

KLARA. You tore the hammer from his hand and nailed it shut yourself. You said: "This is my masterpiece!" The choirmaster thought you had gone mad.

MASTER ANTON. Gone mad! [*Laughs.*] Gone mad! Yes, it's a wise head that lops itself off when the time's right. Mine is put on a little too tight for that, otherwise . . . A man squats himself down in the world and thinks he's sitting in good quarters behind a warm stove, and then someone puts a light on the table and he finds himself in a den of thieves; but there's no harm done, because his heart is made of stone.

KLARA. Yes, father, that's the way it is.

MASTER ANTON. What do you know about it? Do you think just because your Treasurer's run off you have the right to curse the world along with me? There'll be another one to take you out on Sunday afternoons walking. There'll be another

one to tell you your cheeks are red and your eyes blue.
And another to take you for his wife, if you deserve it.
When you've borne up under the burden of life for thirty
long years, when without complaining you have patiently
accepted sorrow and death and every other misfortune,
and then your son comes along, who was to console you
in your old age, and instead heaps shame upon you till
you want to cry out to the earth: "Swallow me, unless I
disgust you, for I am filthier than you!" —When you've
lived through this, then you can cry out all the curses that
I hold back inside me; then you can tear your hair and beat
your breast; you're not a man, you have that advantage
over me.

KLARA. Oh, Karl!

MASTER ANTON. I wonder what I'll do when I see him here
in front of me again, when he comes into this room in the
evening before we've lighted the lamps, and his head is
shaved, because hair isn't allowed in prison, and he stutters
good-evening with the latch of the door still in his hand.
I'll do something, that's for sure, but what? [*Gnashing his
teeth.*] And if they keep him there ten years, he'll find me.
I'll live long enough for that, I know that much. And as
for death, I give him notice now that from this moment
on I am a stone in front of his sickle, and that his sickle
will break to pieces before I'll move out of his path.

KLARA [*takes his hand*]. Father, you *must* lie down for half
an hour.

MASTER ANTON. So that I can dream that you've gone into
childbed? So that I can fly up and lay hands on you and
only come to my senses afterwards and say: "Dear Klara,
I didn't know what I was doing." I thank you. My sleep
has dismissed its charlatan and taken on a prophet in its
place. He points out hideous things to me with his bloody
finger, and I don't know why but everything seems possible
to me now. I shudder as much when I think of the time to
come as when I think of the glass of water that they looked
through a microscope at! —Is that right, choirmaster?
You've spelled it out to me often enough! —I did it once
in Nürnberg at the Fair, and I wouldn't drink a glass of
water the rest of the day. Last night I saw my son Karl
with a pistol in his hand, and as I kept my eyes on him he
pulled the trigger, I heard a scream, but the powder-smoke
kept me from seeing. And then when it cleared away there

was no shattered skull to see. In between my son had become a rich man, he stood there counting gold pieces from one hand into the other, and his face . . . the devil take me, he couldn't have looked more satisfied if he had worked all day and then locked his shop up behind him! But we ought to beware of that. We ought to beware of passing judgment and then standing in front of the Highest Judge ourselves.

KLARA. Calm yourself.

MASTER ANTON. "Get well," is what you meant to say! And why am I sick? Yes, doctor, hand me the drink that will make me well! Since your brother is the worst of sons, you must become the best of daughters. I stand in view of the world like a worthless bankrupt. I owed the world a good man to take my place when I could no longer fill it, but I deceived it with a scoundrel. If you become a woman like your mother was, then they'll say: "It wasn't the parents' fault the boy went wrong, because look at the daughter, she's as honorable as any, she's the best of us all." [*With terrible coldness.*] But I'll do my part, too. I'll make it easier for you. And at the moment when I see people pointing accusing fingers at you in the street, I'll go inside and . . . [*with a movement of his hand at his throat*] shave myself. And then, and I give you my solemn assurance of this, I'll shave this old fool away. You can tell them I was scared by the sound of a horse dashing through the street outside, or because the cat jumped onto the floor and overturned a chair or a mouse ran up my leg. The people who know me will shake their heads because I'm not one to scare easy, but what's the difference. Why should I want to live in a world where people have to feel sympathy for you when they wouldn't even bother spitting at your feet!

KLARA. Merciful Heaven, what can I do!

MASTER ANTON. Nothing, nothing, my poor child . . . I'm too hard on you, I know that . . . nothing . . . just stay what you are and I'll be satisfied. I've suffered such wrong that I have to do wrong, too, when it takes hold of me, so that it doesn't crush me. The other day as I was crossing the street I met that scoundrel of a thief with the pockmarks on his face, the one I had thrown in jail a couple of years ago for stealing three times from me. Before this the scoundrel didn't have the nerve to look at me, but now he comes up to me without any shame and reaches out his hand. I wanted to give him a slap on the ear but I thought better of it and didn't even bother to spit at his feet. After all, we've been kinsmen now for eight days and it's only right for relatives to greet one another. That compassionate man our pastor paid me a visit yesterday and said that a man has no one but himself to account for and that it was unchristian pride in me that I wanted to accept responsibility for my son; that way, he said, our father Adam would have to feel the same as I do. Lord, I can well believe that the peace of our forefather Adam in Paradise can no longer be disturbed just because one of his great-grandsons begins to murder or to steal! But canst Thou tell me that he did not tear his hair in torment over his son Cain? No, no, it's too much! Sometimes I want to turn around and see if my shadow hasn't grown blacker. I can bear up under anything, anything, and I have proved it . . . except shame. Hang around my neck what you like, but don't you touch the nerve that gives me life!

KLARA. Father, Karl has confessed nothing yet, and they haven't found anything either.

MASTER ANTON. What's that supposed to prove? I went around the town from one tavern and inn to the other, asking about his debts, and they came to more than he could have earned working for me for the next three months, even if he worked three times as hard. I know now why he always worked two hours later and why in spite of that he always got out of bed two hours earlier than me. But then he saw that even all this didn't help or else that it was too much trouble and took too long, so he took the advantage when an opportunity came.

KLARA. You always think the worst of Karl. You always did. Do you still remember . . .

MASTER ANTON. You're talking like your mother would have, and I'll answer you the same way that I answered her, by keeping silent.

KLARA. And what if they let Karl free? What if they find the jewels again?

MASTER ANTON. If that happens I'll hire a lawyer, and if it costs me my last penny I'll learn whether or not the mayor has the right to send the son of an honorable man to prison. And if he has the right, then I'll bow to his will, because what others have to bear up under I must be satisfied with too, even if it costs me a thousand times as much as the others. If it happens, then it was destined to happen, and when God strikes me down I shall fold my hands and answer Him: "Lord, Thou knowest the why and the wherefore of all things!" And if he hasn't the right, if that man with the golden chain around his neck was over hasty for no other reason but that the merchant whose jewels were stolen is his brother-in-law, then we will see whether there are holes in the law! They say the King knows he must pay his subjects for their loyalty and obedience with justice, and that he would want least of all to be in debt to the humblest of his subjects; well then, we'll see whether the King will leave this hole unstopped. But why should I bother even talking about such things. The boy won't come any cleaner out of this trial than his mother will rise from her grave. I'll never find any comfort in him, and therefore you must never forget the debt you owe to me, you must keep your oath, so that I will never have to keep mine. [*He starts to leave but turns around again.*] I won't be back till late tonight. I'm going to visit the timber dealer in the hills. He's the only man who can still look me in the eyes, and only because he knows nothing about my shame. He's deaf. No one can tell him anything because they'd have to shout too loud, and even then he gets it all backwards. That's why no one ever tells him anything. [*Off.*]

KLARA [*alone*]. God! God! Have mercy! Have mercy on that old man! Please take my life instead of his. There's no other way to help him. —Look there, how golden the sunlight is on the street, the children grab for it with their hands. Everything's alive, everything wants to live. Listen to me, death, because I cry out to you now! Spare just one being whose soul still trembles at the thought of you, give him time till the world grows grey and desolate for him, and take *me* in his place. I won't shudder when you reach out your cold hand to me. I'll take it bravely in mine and follow you more happily than any child of man has ever followed you.

THE MERCHANT WOLFRAM [*enters*]. Good day, Miss Klara, is your father at home?

KLARA. He just went off.

WOLFRAM. I came to . . . my jewels have been found again.

KLARA. Oh, I wish he were here! He went off without his glasses, look! If only he'll notice it and come back. How did you find them? Where? Who had them?

WOLFRAM. It was my wife who . . . tell me something very honestly, Miss. Have you ever heard anything strange concerning my wife?

KLARA. Yes.

WOLFRAM. That she . . . [*He indicates his forehead.*]

KLARA. Yes, that she's not right in her mind.

WOLFRAM [*bursting out*]. My God! My God! It was all for nothing! Every servant I ever hired I kept with me, I paid each one twice his salary and ignored their carelessness, just to buy their silence, and for all that . . . the deceitful, ungrateful creatures! And my poor children. I wanted to hide it for their sake.

KLARA. There's no need to blame your servants. They're not the ones at fault. We've known it since the time your neighbor's house burned down. Your wife leaned out the open window and laughed and clapped her hands; she even blew into the smoke like she wanted to blow it into a flame. We had only the choice of thinking that either she was a devil or mad. Hundreds of us saw her that day.

WOLFRAM. That's true enough. In that case, I suppose it would be foolish of me to ask you to keep it silent. All right, I'll tell you. The theft that put your brother in prison was the fault of her madness.

KLARA. Your own wife . . .

WOLFRAM. There was a time when she was the noblest, most sympathetic soul in the world. But I've known for a long time now that she's become malicious and that she gloats over other people's misfortunes. She shouts with delight when she sees an accident, when the maid breaks a glass or cuts her finger. Unfortunately I didn't learn till too late, till this afternoon, that she was in the habit of secreting things, of hiding money, of destroying documents. I had just laid down across the bed and wanted to fall asleep when I noticed her coming towards me very quietly; she watched me intently to see whether I had fallen asleep yet. I closed my eyes tighter, and then she took a key from the pocket of my waistcoat lying across a chair. She opened the writing desk, grabbed for a roll of money, locked it up again and returned the key to where she had found it. I was horrified, even though I controlled myself so as not to disturb her. She left the room then and I followed her. She climbed up to the top floor and threw the roll of money into a chest that had been empty since my grandfather's time; then she looked around as if she were afraid, and hurried away without noticing me. I lighted a taper and looked through the chest. There I found some toys belonging to my youngest daughter, a pair of the maid's slippers, an account book, letters, and then, fortunately or unfortunately, I don't quite know how to say it, down at the bottom, I found the jewels.

KLARA. My poor mother! It's too shameful even to talk about.

WOLFRAM. God only knows I'd gladly give up the jewels if only I could undo what has already been done. But I'm not the one who's at fault. With due respect for your father, it was only natural that I should suspect your brother. He had just finished polishing the writing desk, and the jewels seemed to disappear with him. I noticed it almost at once because I had to take some papers from the compartment where the jewels were kept. But I had no intention of using such strong measures against him. I mentioned it only provisionally to Adam the court bailiff and asked him to investigate the matter quietly. But he'd hear of no consideration being shown; he said he had to and would report the case at once, because your brother is a drunkard and a trouble maker. Unfortunately he carries enough weight with the mayor to be able to do what he wants. I don't know why, but the man seemed enraged against your father almost to the extreme. There was little chance of calming him because he held his ears shut and hurried off. He called back to me that if I had given him the jewels as a gift he couldn't be happier.

KLARA. One time at the tavern the bailiff put his glass next to my father's on the table and nodded to him like he wanted to drink a toast. My father took his glass away and said that people in red coats with blue lapels used to have to drink out of wooden steins, and that they had to wait outside by the window, or when it rained by the door, and be modest enough to take their hats off when the innkeeper handed them a drink; and if they wanted to drink a toast with anyone they'd wait till one of their own kind came by. —My God, isn't there anything impossible in this world! And my mother had to pay for this with her death!

WOLFRAM. We ought never to provoke anyone, and bad people especially. Where is your father?

KLARA. In the hills visiting the old timber dealer.

WOLFRAM. I'll ride out there and try to find him. I've already

been to see the Mayor. Unfortunately I didn't find him at
home otherwise your brother would be here by now. But
the Secretary sent off a message at once. You'll have your
brother back before evening. [*Off.*]

KLARA [*alone*]. I should be so happy now. God! God! And
all I can think of is that now I am the only one who can
still hurt him. And yet I have the feeling that something
must come soon to make everything turn out well.

THE SECRETARY [*entering*]. Good day.

KLARA [*holding onto a chair as though about to collapse*].
He's come! Why did he have to come back . . .

SECRETARY. Isn't your father at home?

KLARA. No.

SECRETARY. I have some good news for you. Your brother
. . . No, Klara, I can't talk to you in this tone of voice.
It seems as if the table and chairs and cabinets, all
our old friends that we used to skip around in circles when
we were children—Good day! [*He nods to a cabinet.*] How
are you? You haven't changed!—it seems like they're about
to put their heads together and make fun of this fool unless
he comes up with something else pretty quickly! I *must*
call you Klara like this, like I used to; and if it displeases
you then you must think: "This grown calf of a boy is
just a dreamer, I must waken him, I must go to him and
[*with gestures*] pull myself up tall so that he can see that
the girl in front of him isn't a child anymore"—this is
how tall you were when you were eleven [*he points to a
mark on the doorpost*]—"not a child anymore but a grown
girl, who can reach the sugar even when it's set on top of
the cabinet." Do you still remember? That was the place,
the mighty fortress, where it was safe from our hands even
without being locked up. When the sugar was up there we
used to kill time by slapping at the flies because we couldn't
bear seeing them so happy flying about up there, able to
get at what we couldn't have ourselves.

KLARA. I thought people forget things like that, especially
when they have to study through hundreds and thousands
of books.

SECRETARY. Oh, they forget alright. And what don't we forget
about Justinian and Gaius, too! These young school boys
who fight so hard against learning their ABCs, they know
well enough why they do it; they have premonitions even
at that age. And then without any shame whatever we lead

those innocent souls astray; we show them just enough behind the scenes to whet their appetites; and from then on there's no stopping them, they go like a streak of lightning from A to Z and so on and on until suddenly they find themselves in the middle of a *Corpus Juris*. And it's only then that they learn with dismay into what a wilderness that blasted alphabet has lured them, those same twenty-six letters that at the start promised such wonderful things.

KLARA. And what happens then?

SECRETARY [*disinterestedly*]. That's where temperaments differ. Some of them go through with it. Generally they see the light of day again after three or four years, somewhat more lean and pale however, but we shouldn't hold that against them. I belong to this group. Others lie down in the middle of a forest with the intention of merely taking a nap, but they seldom ever get up again. I have a friend who for the last three years has been drinking his beer under the shade of the *Lex Julia*. He picked the place because it calls up such pleasant memories. And there are others who grow desperate and turn back. They're the dumbest of the lot because they're let out of one thicket only on the condition that they immediately lose themselves in another one. And then there are some who are even more terrible, who never make an end. [*To himself.*] Why can't I say what I want instead of babbling on like this!

KLARA. Everything's so bright and lively today; that's why it's so lovely.

SECRETARY. Yes, it's the kind of weather that makes owls fall out of their nests, and bats commit suicide because they think they're made by the devil. And then there's the mole who digs himself so deep into the earth that he can't find his way back and has to suffocate, poor mole, unless he can find his way through to the other side and come to light again in America. It's the kind of day when an ear of corn grows twice as long, and poppies grow twice as red, ashamed for not being red enough in the first place. Why should people be left out of it? Why should they want to cheat God of the sole tribute that His world yields Him: a happy face and clear sparkling eyes that mirror all the glory of His creation and give it back to Him transfigured? In the morning when I see some hermit or other creeping out from under his doorway, his forehead wrinkled, gaping up at the sky like a sheet of blotting paper, I can't help but think: "There's bound to be rain soon; how can God help but bring on a layer of black clouds if only in anger over that man's face." We ought to summon these scoundrels to court for spoiling country picnics and destroying our harvest weather. How else would you want to give thanks for life except by living! The only way a bird can earn its voice is by singing.

KLARA. Yes, I know how right you are, how right. It almost makes me want to cry.

SECRETARY. Please, I didn't say that against you. I realize how badly things have gone for you these past eight days. I know your father, too. But, thank God, I can make things easier for you, that's why I've come. You'll see your brother again this evening; and instead of pointing at *him*, it'll be the ones who threw him into prison that people will point at. Doesn't that deserve a kiss, maybe only a sisterlike one, if nothing else? Or shall we play blind man's buff? If I don't tag you in ten minutes I'll leave empty handed and with a slap on the face to top it off.

KLARA [*to herself*]. Suddenly I feel like a thousand years old, and time standing still above me: I can't back up and I can't go forward. Why must the sun be so bright and the world so happy?

SECRETARY. Why don't you answer me? Of course, I forgot, you're engaged. Oh, Klara, why did you have to do this to me? But then . . . what right have I to complain? You're like everything that's precious and wonderful, and everything precious and wonderful should have reminded me of you; but then for years you seemed to be out of my world entirely. And it was for that reason that you . . . If only it had been a person you could have some respect for. But this Leonard . . .

KLARA [*suddenly as she hears the name*]. I've got to go to him . . . Don't you see, my brother's not a thief any longer. God, what more do I want? Leonard *will* listen to me, he *has* to. If only he'll listen to reason, it can all be like it was before. [*To the* SECRETARY.] I'm sorry, Frederick. —Why am I so weak all of a sudden?

SECRETARY. Then you're going to . . .

KLARA. Yes, I'm going to find Leonard. What else is there for me to do? There's no other way open for me now.

SECRETARY. Then you love him?

KLARA [*impetuously*]. Love him? Either I'll have Leonard or I'll kill myself! Does it surprise you now that I'd choose *him*? I'd never do it if it were only for myself.

SECRETARY. Leonard or your death? Klara, tell me what this is about or . . .

KLARA. Please don't make it worse than it is! Don't say that word again! It's you, it's you I love! There, I've said it, I've said it, I've said it! I can call it out to you now as if I were a ghost on the other side of my grave, where there is no more shame, where we pass each other by, naked and cold, because the terrible nearness of God's presence has consumed to the very roots every thought of anyone else!

SECRETARY. *Me?* You still love *me?* Klara, I felt that, too, that night I saw you in the garden.

KLARA. Did you? Yes, he felt it, too. [*Hollow as though alone.*] And then he came to me. "It has to be one or the other of us," he said. Oh, my God, my God! And then to prove to him, but to prove it to myself, too, that it wasn't true, or if it was true, to smother it inside me, I let him do what now I . . . [*bursting into tears.*] Dear God in Heaven, have mercy on me as I would have on You if You were me!

SECRETARY. Be my wife, Klara. I came here to look at you just once more like I used to. If you hadn't understood my reason for coming, I would have left without saying a word. But I offer you everything now, everything I am and everything I have. It isn't much, but there'll be more. I would have come long before this, but your mother was sick, and then she died.

[KLARA *laughs distractedly.*]

You mustn't be frightened, Klara. You're afraid because you've given him your promise. That's a terrible enough thing in itself. How could you . . .

KLARA. Why don't you ask to hear the rest of the story! I had mockery and scorn thrown in my face everytime I turned around when you went off to the university and were never heard from again. "She's still dreaming about him!" —"She must think children's play is serious business!"— "Does she get letters?" —And then my mother: "Stay with your own kind!" she said. "Pride never helped anything. This Leonard's a good enough boy, and nobody can understand why you always look down on him" —And then my own heart would say: "If he's forgotten you, then why can't you show him that you . . ." Oh, God!

SECRETARY. I *am* at fault. I *know* it. But just because something's difficult doesn't mean it's impossible. I'll get your promise back. Perhaps . . .

KLARA. My promise! Here! [*She tosses him* LEONARD's *letter.*]

SECRETARY [*reads*]. "Since I am Treasurer now . . . your brother . . . thief . . . I'm sorry . . . I have no choice with regard to my position . . ." [*To* KLARA.] He wrote this on the same day that your mother died? He expresses his condolences over her sudden death, too, I see!

KLARA. I think he does!

SECRETARY Are you blind? Klara, there's nothing to worry about now. [*Wanting to embrace her.*] Come here. I'll never let you go. Let me kiss you . . .

KLARA [*leaning against him*]. No . . . I mustn't . . . just don't let me fall . . .

SECRETARY. But, Klara, you don't love him, he's released you from your promise . . .

KLARA [*hollowly, straightening up again*]. There's nothing else for me to do but go to him, to fall at his feet and beg him to take me if he has any pity for my father.

SECRETARY. My poor Klara . . . do I understand you . . .

KLARA. Yes.

SECRETARY. And now you want to humble yourself in front of this man instead of spitting in his face. [*Taking* KLARA *impetuously into his arms.*] My poor Klara! My poor Klara!

KLARA. Go now, please go.

SECRETARY [*moodily to himself*]. A dog like that ought to be packed from the world! If only he'd agree. If only I could force him.

KLARA. Please, Frederick.

SECRETARY [*going*]. When it's dark. [*He turns around again and takes* KLARA's *hand.*] You can count on me. I know now just how much I owe you. [*Off.*]

KLARA [*alone*]. Please, God, don't let me feel hope when I know that there can be none. —I'm going, father, I'm going. Your life is safe. —God, I'm not begging You for happiness . . . I beg You for *un*happiness, for eternal unhappiness . . . and I know that You will give me that unhappiness. —Where's the letter? [*She takes it.*] There are three wells that you must pass on your way to him. And *you must go past them!* That right is still not yours. [*Off.*]

ACT THREE

Scene 1

[*A room at* LEONARD's.]

LEONARD [*at a table covered with documents; writing*]. This will make the sixth sheet since supper. It makes a man feel good to have steady work to do. There's not a man in the world who could step through that door now, not even the King himself, but I could stand up and look him straight in the eye without embarrassment. There is one person though, the old cabinet maker Master Anton. But then there's not much that he can do to me either. Poor Klara. I do feel sorry for her, I can't think about her without feeling uneasy. If only it hadn't been for that one evening. The fact is I did it more out of jealously than out of love; and the only reason she gave herself was to disprove my blaming her, because she was as cold in my arms as death. She's in for some bad times. But then it won't be so easy for me either. Every man to his own troubles. The important thing now is to see that the affair with the little hunchback is set, to make sure she doesn't get away from me when the storm breaks. With that in hand I'm sure to have the Mayor on my side and there'll be nothing to worry about.

KLARA [*enters*]. Good evening, Leonard.

LEONARD. Klara! What are you doing here? Didn't you get my letter? But then . . . perhaps you've come on your father's business, to pay his taxes. Let's see, how much would that come to? [*Paging through a day-book.*] I should know it without bothering to look it up.

KLARA. I came to give you back your letter. Here it is. Would you read it again?

LEONARD [*reading it in great seriousness*]. It's quite a reasonable letter. How can a man to whom public monies are entrusted marry into a family to which . . . [*He slurs over his words.*] to which your brother belongs?

KLARA. Leonard!

LEONARD. But then perhaps the whole town is wrong! And your brother isn't locked up in jail! That he's never been in jail! And that you are not the sister of a . . . of your brother!

KLARA. Leonard, I am my father's daughter, and I'm standing here in front of you not as the sister of a wrongly accused brother who has been set free, and he *has* been set free, not as a girl who trembles out of undeserved shame, because [*half-voice*] I tremble more on your account, but only as the daughter of an old man who gave me life.

LEONARD. And you want what?

KLARA. I didn't think you would have to ask. Oh, if only I could leave this place. My father will cut his own throat if I . . . marry me.

LEONARD. Your father . . .

KLARA. He's sworn it . . . marry me, you can kill me afterwards! I'll be more grateful to you for the one than for the other!

LEONARD. Do you love me? Did you come here because your heart forced you to it? Am I the one human being without whom you can neither live nor die?

KLARA. Answer that yourself.

LEONARD. Can you swear to me that you love me? That you love me in the way that a girl must love the man who is to bind himself to her for all eternity?

KLARA. No, I can't swear it. But I can swear *this* to you: that whether I love you or whether I do not love you is something that you will never learn. I will serve you, I will work for you, but you must never put food on my plate because I will support myself; at night I will sew and spin for others, I will go hungry when there's no work for me to do, and I would rather bite into my own flesh than be forced to go back to my father so that he can see for himself. And if you strike me because your dog isn't at hand or because you've got rid of him, I will rather swallow my tongue than utter a cry so that the neighbors can gossip about what happens between us. I can't promise that my skin won't show the welts of your lash, because I have no power over that, but I will lie, I will say that I struck my head on a cabinet or that I fell on the pavement because it was too slippery; I'll answer them even before they ask me what the bruises are from. Marry me . . . my life can't go on for too long. And if it does and you don't want to put out the costs for separation to rid yourself of me, then buy poison from the pharmacist and place it somewhere as though it were for the rats, and without your even looking in its direction I will take it, and in dying I will say to the neighbor woman that I thought it was crushed sugar.

LEONARD. Yet you won't be too surprised if I say no?

KLARA. Then God must not look at me too terribly if I come before I'm called. If I were the only one concerned, I wouldn't complain, I'd take it upon myself patiently as deserved punishment for . . . for I don't know what. And if the world were to ridicule me instead of standing by me in my torment I would love my child all the more, even if he bore the features of this man; and I would weep so often in the presence of that poor innocent that when it grew older and more intelligent it could neither scorn nor curse its mother. But I'm *not* the only one concerned, and on the Day of Judgment I will find it far easier to answer the question: "Why didst thou lay hand upon thyself?" than: "Why didst thou drive thy father to such extreme?"

LEONARD. The way you're talking you'd think you were the only person in the world. How many thonsands of people do you think have gone through this same thing before you. and given in to it; how many thousands do you think will do it after you and find their fate the same as yours? Are they all such pigheaded fools that you think you're the only one who has to stand herself in the corner for what you've done? They had fathers, too, who invented a whole stock of new curses when they first heard and talked about murder and homicide; afterwards they were ashamed of themselves and did penance for their curses and blasphemies and they sat down and rocked the cradle or fanned flies from it.

KLARA. I can see now how you believe no one keeps his word.

A BOY [*enters*]. Some flowers for you. But I'm not supposed to tell who they're from.

LEONARD. How lovely! [*Striking his forehead.*] Damnation! How stupid! I was supposed to send some too! Now how do I get out of a thing like this? I'm afraid I'm not experienced in these matters even if the little hunchback *does* take them seriously; but then she has nothing else to think about. [*He takes the flowers.*] However, I won't take them all. [*To* KLARA.] If I remember correctly, these are for shame and remorse. Wasn't it you who told me that once?

[KLARA *nods*.]

LEONARD [*to the* BOY]. I want you to pay attention to this now, boy. *These* flowers are for me. As you see I'm placing them here inside my shirt, next to my heart. But these dark ones that burn like smouldering fire, these I want you to take back to her. Understand? And when my apples are ripe you can remind me of it.

BOY. That'll be a long time yet! [*Off.*]

LEONARD. Yes, Klara, now, you were talking about keeping one's word. It is simply because I *am* a man of my word that I have answered you as I have. I wrote you off my ledger eight days ago, and you can't deny it because there's the letter. [*He hands her the letter; she takes it mechanically.*] I had my reason: your brother. You tell me now that he's been set free, and I'm happy for you. Within the last eight days I have entered into a new "liaison"; I had the right because you failed to protest my letter within the proper amount of time. I felt as justified in my own regard as I felt justified in regard to the law. And now you make an appearance, but I have already given my word as well as accepted that of another—[*to himself*] if it were only true—the fact is that my new "interest" already finds herself in the same condition as you. I *do* feel sorry for you [*He smoothes back her hair, which she allows as though she were unaware of it.*] but I know you'll understand. There's no playing around where the Mayor's concerned.

KLARA [*absentmindedly*]. No, not where the Mayor's concerned.

LEONARD. You see, you *are* being reasonable about it. And as far as your father's concerned, you can tell him to his face that he's the one at fault. You needn't look at me like that and shake your head. It's the truth, Klara, it's the truth! You tell him that and he'll understand what I mean, he'll turn over a new leaf, I can guarantee you that. Or would you rather I talk with him myself? He can be as uncivil to me as he likes, he can throw the bootjack at my head, but colic or no colic he's going to have to swallow the truth, hard as it may be, and leave you in peace. Is he at home?

KLARA [*raising herself proudly*]. I thank you. [*Wanting to leave.*]

LEONARD. Shall I walk over with you? I'm not afraid of him.

KLARA. I thank you as I would a serpent that had wound itself about me and then suddenly let me go to prey on something else. I know that I've been bitten, I know the only reason you're leaving me is that it doesn't seem worth the effort to suck the little marrow from my bones; and still I thank you, because now my death will be peaceful. Please, you must believe me, I'm not mocking you, I *do* thank you. It seems as if through you I was able to see down to the very depths of hell itself, and whatever awful share eternity may have in store for me, at least I have nothing further to do with you, and that's a consolation. A man stung by a snake is never blamed when he horribly opens the veins in his body to let the poisoned life inside him out. Perhaps God's eternal kindness will have mercy upon me in the same way when he looks at you and at me and sees what you have made of me: because why should I be *able* to do such a thing when I haven't the *right* to do it? There's one more thing: my father knows nor suspects nothing of this; to keep him from ever learning I will take my life, tonight. If I ever thought that you . . . [*She takes a step toward him distractedly.*] But that would be foolish! You can only be grateful for the fact that they'll all stand around my grave shaking their heads to no purpose, asking why such a thing happened.

LEONARD. Accidents happen! What can *we* do? Klara!

KLARA. Let me out of here! People can talk. [*Wanting to leave.*]

LEONARD. Do you really think I take you seriously?

KLARA. No.

LEONARD. Don't forget that you can't kill yourself without killing your own child as well.

KLARA. I'd rather do both than kill my own father! I know that we can't wash one sin away with another. But what I have to do concerns no one but myself. Placing the knife in my father's hand would hurt him as much as me. There's no way out for me. This is the only thing that gives me the courage and strength to ignore my fears. You will have nothing to worry about. [*Off.*]

LEONARD [*alone*]. I have to. I have to marry her. And why do I have to? Because she wants to commit an insane action to keep her father from committing an insane action. Then why should I commit a *more* insane action simply to keep her from hers? I'll agree to nothing. At least not until I'm faced with the man who'll threaten me with the insanest

action of all. And if we both happen to think alike there'll
never be an end to it. That sounds sensible enough, but
then . . . I've got to go after her. Someone's coming. Thank
God for that. What's worse than having it out with your
own thoughts.

SECRETARY [*enters*]. Good evening.

LEONARD. Oh, it's you. And to what do I owe the honor of . . .

SECRETARY. You'll find out soon enough.

LEONARD. I see, you're very frank. But then we were school
comrades together, weren't we.

SECRETARY. And may be comrades in death. [*He lays out a
pair of pistols.*] Are you versed in the art?

LEONARD. I'm afraid I don't quite understand.

SECRETARY [*cocks one of the pistols*]. See that? That's the way
it's done. Then you take aim at me, like I'm aiming at you
now, and you pull the trigger. Like this.

LEONARD. What are you talking about?

SECRETARY. That one of us must die.

LEONARD. Die?

SECRETARY. There's no need to explain.

LEONARD. I don't understand.

SECRETARY. That's not important. It'll come to you at the last
minute.

LEONARD. I have no idea . . .

SECRETARY. Then think hard. I could shoot you down now for
a mad dog that's bitten someone dear to me, without thinking anything of it. But my conscience tells me that I must
take you for a human being, at least for the next half-hour.

LEONARD. You needn't talk so loud. Suppose someone hears
you?

SECRETARY. If there were anyone around you would have
called him my this time. Well?

LEONARD. If you're doing this for Klara's sake, yes, I can
marry her. In fact, I half-way decided it while she was still
here.

SECRETARY. She was here and left without seeing you at her
feet? Come with me. Come on.

LEONARD. All right, listen to me . . . I'll do everything you
say. I'll ask her to marry me, tonight.

SECRETARY. Either I'll be the one to do that or no one. I'll
see that you never so much as touch the hem of her dress
again even if the world depends on it. Come on. We're going
into the woods. I'm going to take you by the arm, like this,

and if you make a sound on the way there. I'll . . . [*He holds up the pistol.*] just as long as we understand each other. But just so that you won't be tempted, we'll take the back way through the garden.

LEONARD. If one of those is for me . . . then let me have it.

SECRETARY. So that you can throw it away and force me either to murder you or let you run off? You can wait. When we get to where we're going I'll give you as good a one as I'll have.

LEONARD [*goes to the table and inadvertently pushes a glass from it*]. I suppose I've had my last drink.

SECRETARY. You mustn't give up so easily, my friend. It seems God and the Devil are always fighting for the upper hand in the world. Who knows which one's on top at the moment. [*Takes him by the arm and they go off.*]

Scene 2

[*A room in the house of the* MASTER ANTON. *Evening.*]

KARL [*enters*]. Nobody here. If it hadn't been for the rathole under the door where they hide the key when they go out I'd never have got in. Not that that would have mattered. I could run around the city twenty times now and imagine there's no greater pleasure in the world than using your legs. Let's have some light here. [*He lights a lamp.*] I'll bet the matches are in the same place as ever. In this house we have *two times* Ten Commandments. My hat belongs on the third nail and not on the fourth. At half-past nine every night you have to be tired. There's no freezing before St. Martinsmas and no sweating afterwards. All this goes side by side with: "Thou shalt fear and love the Lord thy God!" I'm thirsty. [*Calls.*] Mother! Damn! I'd forgotten she's gone to where not even the inkeeper's servant boy has to come when he's called. I didn't cry when I heard the funeral bells in my dark hole in the tower, but . . . you, bailiff Adam, you wouldn't let me have my last shot in the alley even though I already had the ball in my hand. If I find you, you won't have time to draw your last breath, and that may be tonight because I know where to find you at ten o'clock. After that I'll go to sea. What's keeping Klara out so late? I'm as hungry as I am thirsty. Today's Thursday,

they had veal broth. If it was winter now there would have
been cabbage, too, white cabbage before Shrove Tuesday,
green cabbage after. That's as sure as that Thursday *has*
to come once Wednesday's been so that Thursday can't ask
Friday to take his place because his feet are tired.

[KLARA *enters.*]

KARL. It's about time! You shouldn't kiss so much! Where
four lips get together, they say, there's the devil's bridge
for sure! What's that?

KLARA. Where? What?

KARL. "Where?" "What?" That in your hand?

KLARA. Nothing!

KARL. Nothing? Something I'm not supposed to see? [*He tears*
LEONARD's *letter from her.*] Give it here! When father's
not home you listen to me.

KLARA. I held so tight to it that not even the wind could tear
it from my hand. It's so strong it's pulling tiles off roofs.
On my way past the church one of them fell so close in
front of me that I kicked it with my foot. "O God," I
thought, "send another!" And I waited there. That would
have been the best way, and they would have buried me
and said: "It was an accident." But the second tile never
came.

KARL [*who has read the letter*]. Damn him, I'll . . . I'll tear
the arm off that wrote this! Bring me a bottle of wine! Or
is the money box empty?

KLARA. There's still another bottle. I bought it secretly for
mother's birthday and set it aside. It would have been
tomorrow . . . [*She turns away.*]

KARL. Then bring it here.

[KLARA *brings the wine.*]

KARL [*drinking hurriedly*]. We could begin all over again now.
Planing, sawing, hammering, and in between eating and
drinking and sleeping so that we can keep on planing and
sawing and hammering, and with a bend of the knee thrown
in on Sundays: "I thank Thee, Lord, for permitting me to
plane and saw and hammer!" [*Drinks.*] Long live the good
dog that doesn't bite his chain! [*He drinks again.*] Here's
to him again!

KLARA. Karl, you mustn't drink so much. Father says there's
the devil in wine.

KARL. And the priest says there's God in wine! [*He drinks.*] We'll see who's right. The bailiff was here, wasn't he? How did he behave?

KLARA. Like in a den of thieves. Mother collapsed and died as soon as she heard.

KARL. Good! Then tomorrow when you hear that he's been found murdered you won't condemn the murderer.

KLARA. Karl, you couldn't . . .

KARL. Am I his only enemy? Hasn't he been attacked before this? It'd be a hard thing to try to find the right man out of all those who could have done it, unless he leaves behind his hat or his cane. [*He drinks.*] But whoever it is, I wish him luck!

KLARA. You're talking like a . . .

KARL. Don't you like the idea? Then don't think about it. You won't have to put up with me much longer.

KLARA [*shuddering*]. Karl, no!

KARL. No? Do you know already that I'm going to sea? Are my thoughts as obvious as all that that you can read my mind? Or has the old bear been raging and threatening again to lock me out of the house? Hell, that's about like the warden threatening that he can't keep me in jail any longer!

KLARA. You don't understand.

KARL [*sings*].

> The ship's stout sail blows hearty, oh,
> And brisk'y blows the wind!

Yes, and now there's nothing to keep me here at this joiner's bench. Mother's dead, there's nobody now to keep me from eating fish after every storm like I liked to do from the time I was little. I've got to get out into the world! I'll never make a go of it here, or at least not until I'm sure that there's no hope for a man who's willing to risk his life.

KLARA. And you'd leave your father alone? He's sixty years old.

KARL. Alone? Won't you be here?

KLARA. Me?

KARL. Yes, you! His pet! Why ask such silly questions? He'll be happy to see me go, he'll have nothing more to grumble about . . . so why shouldn't I do it? We don't belong to- gether. There's nothing too cramped for him. He'd like to

ball up his fist and crawl into it if he could, and I'd like
to burst out of my skin like a baby out of its clothes!
[*Sings.*]

> The heaving anchor wails,
> The rudder trims the sails,
> And leaves the shore behind!

Tell me, did he doubt for even one minute that I was guilty?
Didn't he console himself like he always does with his:
"Just what I expected!" If it had been you, he would have
committed suicide. I'd like to see him if you'd gone the
way a lot of women do. He'd go around like he was in
labor himself! And what's more, with the devil!

KLARA. I wish you wouldn't talk like that! I've got to get out
of here! I've got to!

KARL. What is it?

KLARA. I've got to get to the kitchen. [*Putting her hand to her
forehead.*] Yes, of course, that's the only reason I came
back. [*Off.*]

KARL. Why is she acting like that? [*Sings.*]

> A daring seabird greets me,
> And circles round the mast!

KLARA [*re-enters*]. The last thing's done, father's evening drink
is on the fire. When I pulled closed the kitchen door behind me and thought: "You will never again come through
that door," I shuddered to my very soul. I'll leave this room
in the same way, this house, and then my life.

KARL [*He walks back and forth, singing;* KLARA *remains in the
background.*]

> And fishes bright and merry
> Boldly encircle their guest!

KLARA. Why don't you do it? Aren't you ever going to do it?
Are you going to put it off from day to day like now you're
putting it off from minute to minute? I've got to do it. And
all I do is stand here. I feel as if two tiny hands were raising
themselves inside me here, as if two eyes . . . [*Sits on a
chair.*] What's the matter with you? Are you too weak?
Then ask yourself if you're strong enough to see your father
with his throat . . . [*She rises.*] No! No! "Our Father, Which
art in Heaven . . . hallowed be Thy Kingdom . . ." God,

my head, my head . . . I can't even pray anymore. Karl!
Karl! Help me . . .

KARL. What is it?

KLARA. *The Lord's Prayer!* [*She recollects.*] I felt like I was
in the water already and sinking and had forgotten to pray!
I . . . [*Suddenly.*] "Forgive us our trespasses, as we forgive
those who trespass against us!" That's it. Yes, yes, I forgive
him, I don't even think about him anymore. Good night,
Karl!

KARL. Why are you going to bed so early? Good night.

KLARA [*like a child repeating the Lord's Prayer*]. Forgive
us . . .

KARL. Would you bring me a glass of water? But I want it
fresh.

KLARA [*quickly*]. I'll get it from the well!

KARL. If it isn't too much trouble. It isn't far.

KLARA. Thank you. Thank you. That was the only thing that
held me back. They would never have believed it otherwise.
Now they'll say. "It was an accident. She tumbled in."

KARL. And be careful, they still haven't renailed that board
on yet.

KLARA. The moon is out . . . O God, if it were not myself it
would be my father! Forgive me, as I . . . Have mercy on
me . . . have mercy . . . [*Off.*]

KARL [*sings*].

> How gladly I'd have joined them
> For my kingdom's there below!

Let's see, what comes before that . . . [*He looks at the
clock.*] What time is it? Nine. [*Sings.*]

> My heart and head are youthful,
> I came for the ride, to be truthful,
> I care not where the winds blow!

MASTER ANTON [*enters*]. I had an apology to make to you, but
if I forgive you for making debts secretly and besides that
pay them off, then I'll consider my apology made.

KARL. The one's good and the other's not necessary. If I sell
my Sunday clothes I can pay the people myself the few
thalers I owe them. I'll take care of that tomorrow. As a
sailor I won't be needing them.

MASTER ANTON. What's all this talk about?

KARL. It's not the first time you've heard it, but say what you like today, I've made up my mind.

MASTER ANTON. You're old enough, that's for sure.

KARL. It's *because* I'm old enough that I'm not going to argue about it. Fishes and birds have no right arguing which is better: air or water. There's just one more thing: either you'll never see me again or you'll put your hand on my shoulder and tell me that what I'm doing is right!

MASTER ANTON. We'll see first what happens. At least I won't have to discharge the man I called in to do your work. What else is there?

KARL. I thank you!

MASTER ANTON. I want you to tell me, when the bailiff caught you did he take you to the Mayor by the shortest route or is it true he led you through the whole town . . .

KARL. Up one street, down another, onto the market place like the Shrove Tuesday ox, but don't worry, I'll pay him off, too, before I leave.

MASTER ANTON. I can't blame you for that, but I forbid you to do it!

KARL. Ho!

MASTER ANTON. I won't let you out of my sight, and if you lay hands on the scoundrel I'll come to his defence!

KARL. I thought *you* loved mother, *too!*

MASTER ANTON. And I will prove it!

THE SECRETARY [*enters pale and unsteadily, pressing a cloth to his chest*]. Where's Klara? [*He falls back into a chair.*] My God! I didn't think I would make it here. Where is she?

KARL. She went to the . . . What's keeping her? She said something about . . . my God! [*Off.*]

SECRETARY. He's paid for his . . . he's lying out there . . . but he struck me, too . . . why, God, why . . . now I'll never . . .

MASTER ANTON. What is it? What's happened to you?

SECRETARY. It'll all be over soon. Give me your hand and promise me that you will never disown your daughter . . . Do you understand? You must never disown your daughter if she . . .

MASTER ANTON. You're talking very strangely. Why should I . . . yes, I begin to see now. Maybe I wasn't unjust to her!

SECRETARY. Give me your hand!

MASTER ANTON. No! [*Sticks both hands in his pockets.*] But

I won't stand in her way, and she knows that, I have already promised.

SECRETARY [*horrified*]. You've promised her . . . My God, I'm beginning to understand you!

KARL [*rushing in*]. Father, father, someone's fallen into the well! It can't be . . .

MASTER ANTON. Bring the tall ladder! The hooks and the ropes, too! What are you standing there for! Hurry! I don't care if it's the bailiff!

KARL. They already have all they need. The neighbors got there before me. It can't be Klara!

MASTER ANTON. Klara? [*Holding onto a table.*]

KARL. She went to get some water, and they found her handkerchief.

SECRETARY. Now I know why I was struck. It *is* Klara.

MASTER ANTON. Go and see! [*Seats himself.*] I can't. [KARL *goes off.*] But . . . [*rises again*] if I [*to the* SECRETARY] understood you right . . . then it has all turned out for the best.

KARL [*returns*]. Klara's dead. She cracked her head horribly on the rim of the well when she . . . Father, she didn't fall in, she jumped, a girl saw her!

MASTER ANTON. She should consider more carefully before she talks! It's too dark out there for her to be so certain!

SECRETARY. Do you *doubt* what happened? Yes, you'd like to, but you can't. Think of what you said to her. You were the one who pointed out to her the way to her death, and I, I'm the one to blame for her not turning back. When you suspected her all you thought about was the tongues that would hiss, but not about the worthless snakes they belonged to. What you said to her drove her to desperation; and I, instead of taking her in my arms when she opened her heart to me, I could only think of the scoundrel who could mock at me and . . . well, I'm paying now with my life for making myself dependent on a man who was worse than me. And you, standing there like a rod of iron, someday you, too, will have cause to cry out: "Klara, I wish now that you had not spared me the scorn and disapproval of these Pharisees; it humiliates me even more not to have you here beside my deathbed to wipe the sweat of anguish from my brow!"

MASTER ANTON. She spared me *nothing!* They *saw* her!

SECRETARY. She did all she could. But you weren't worthy enough for her to succeed!

MASTER ANTON. Or *she* wasn't!

[*Noises outside.*]

KARL. They're coming with her . . . [*Wanting to leave.*]

MASTER ANTON [*stands there immovably till the end; calls after him*]. In the back room, where they put her mother!

SECRETARY. I've got to see her! [*He tries to rise but falls back.*] Oh, Karl!

[KARL *helps him up, leads him out.*]

MASTER ANTON. I don't understand the world any more! [*He continues standing there reflectively.*]

GERHART HAUPTMANN

1862–1946

GERHART HAUPTMANN once described himself as "an Aeolian Harp whose strings are stirred by every slightest breeze," and the wide variety in tone, style and theme of his more than forty plays tends to substantiate the aptness of this self-evaluation. However, as our perspective on Hauptmann and his works broadens with time, his greatest contributions to the modern theatre appear to have been his leadership in creating a strong free theatre in Germany and his naturalistic dramatization of the struggles of the working classes. Hauptmann was the first modern playwright to employ the mob as a collective hero and *The Weavers* is probably his most important achievement in this regard. In dramatizing the revolt of a group of Silesian weavers in the 1840s, Hauptmann used a loose, almost symphonic, form to express the swirling character of a great upheaval in which ideals and ambitions, humanity and inhumanity, justice and injustice, courage and cowardice are entangled. His choice of form and his concern for the individual as submerged in and identified by the group began what has become a dominant type of drama in the modern theatre, and Hauptmann has been followed by such diverse writers as Galsworthy, Odets, and Wesker.

ON THE DRAMA[1]

by Gerhart Hauptmann

THE ORIGIN of everything dramatic is in any case the split or twofold ego. The first two actors were *homo* and *ratio*, or also You and I. The earliest drama which expressed itself outwardly was the first loud soliloquy. The first stage was erected nowhere else than in the head of man. It remains the smallest and yet the largest which can be erected. It represents the world, and encompasses the world more than the greatest theatres of the world.

Human speech contains the Yes and the No. And where human speech is alive, namely in the human spirit, there the Yes and the No are the two leading antagonists. The conflict or dialogue between these two forces begins in the child, when thinking begins, and ends only in death. In this Yes and No we have the first actors in the primal drama (Urdrama), two words, which can disguise themselves indeed in the I, and the Non-I or the You. Much can be said about this primal drama, the *dramatis personae* of which will become more and more numerous as life goes on and will play their roles without interruption upon the stage of consciousness longer than even the Chinese drama, namely for an entire lifetime. Unfortunately we have not time for that. *Faust*, however, is such a primal drama in objective form, Faust himself the willful Yes, Mephisto the willful No.

Perhaps there takes place in the poet's soul agglomerations in tempestuous rotation, which in dynamic concentration

[1] "On the Drama" appears in *Speeches and Essays*, Volume 17 of *The Collected Works of Gerhart Hauptmann*. This translation by F. B. Wahr is reprinted from *The Modern Theatre*, edited by Robert W. Corrigan, © Copyright, Robert W. Corrigan, 1964. Printed by permission of The Macmillan Company, the translator, and Verlag Ullstein GMBH.

create heat, light, and finally life. There is in this something like the struggle between Ormuzd and Ahriman. Above all Ormuzd and Ahriman, god and devil, are in combat with one another, and the stage where this drama takes place is in the human breast.

Every man might then be a dramatist? I believe that to be the case. Goethe sought the *Urpflanze*. One might more justly seek the Urdrama, and indeed in the human psyche itself. It is perhaps the earliest thought process.

If I do not possess the advantages of this high calling, in the view of mankind perhaps the most objective, in any case I possess its weaknesses, and one of them is the inability to let one voice speak for itself out of the polyphony of my inner spirit, even though it be my own choice. As it is today, so it always was; there were always many voices seeking to speak out within me, and I found no other possibility of bringing about some sort of order than by giving utterance to these many voices—by writing dramas. I shall have to continue to do this; for it has been up to now the highest means of expression of my spiritual life.

The drama represents one of the many efforts of the human spirit to form a cosmos out of chaos. This effort begins in the child and continues throughout life. The stage in the human mind grows from year to year, and the company of players becomes larger and larger. Its director, the intellect, is soon no longer able to keep it all in hand, for the actors grow into a countless throng.

The earliest members of the large-small world theatre in the child's mind are mother, father, brothers and sisters, relatives and whatever other human beings enter into the circle of experience. In the child's games this drama begins, theatrelike, to project itself outward. The child imitates the mother, the father, and their relation to the children. And this imitative impulse expands farther and farther, enabling the child to establish and build up his dramatic world. This world possesses throughout universal character. In it little analogies to the greatest moments of art taken as a whole are to be found, which are at the same time always seeking to represent themselves objectively. Not only the drama performed on the stages of the world go back to them, but likewise the

"Olympian Zeus" of Phidias, the "Moses," the "Pietà," and "The Last Judgment" of Michelangelo.

If we intend to limit ourselves to the art of the theatre, our task becomes complicated at the first hasty glance. In point of time and so historically, there is the Indian, Greek, Roman, Italian, French, Spanish, English and German theatre. One might designate their summits by the following names: Kalidasa, Aeschylus, Plautus, Goldoni, Molière, Calderón, Shakespeare, Goethe and Richard Wagner. But it would be a matter here of only a few happenstances, as we say, unique instances, in which great poets ennoble the theatre and lift it up into the divine, whereby human tragedy as well as human comedy find their highest expression. On the other hand, however, the theatre born out of the populace's need for sensation is of extreme variety. As regards ancient times, I would point only to the Roman Coliseum. What a great span of time to it from the cart of Thespis! Within the modern theatre a similar lapse of time can be fixed; to Verdi and Richard Wagner, let us say, from the puppet play, from the little stage of strolling players to the joy in decorative fittings and stage equipment in the drama and pantomime of the Reinhardt theatre, and from there on to Barnum and Bailey and the universal circus world.

Recent times afford the utmost in satisfying the human need for entertainment, especially in the cinema. Its rule extends in countless theatres over all five parts of the world. Millions of human beings of all races crowd through its doors daily. Who would not get dizzy in the presence of this great and general phenomenon, when he seeks to understand its significance in the mind of the people and in that of the individual? And there still remains the satisfaction derived from the great love of potpourri on the part of the people, which the radio meets universally, in that it directs through millions and millions of channels all that is spoken, sung, fiddled and trumpeted into palaces and citizens' homes, even into the snow-covered huts of poor mountain dwellers.

At the festival plays at Heidelberg on July 21, 1928, I gave a short address much like this. Later they called it "The Tree of Gallowayshire." Upon the ruins of the wall of New Abbey in Gallowayshire there grows a kind of maple tree. Forced by lack of space and nutriment, it sent forth a strong root which found firm footing in the earth beneath and grew into a sturdy trunk. And after it had freed the roots from the height of the wall, the whole tree, released from the wall, became independent. The tree in this way left its original place. It sought the strength of mother earth and penetrated it with all its roots.

The German drama for over a century and a half has passed through a similar process. Only in recent times has it reached root-soil completely. Thus I have treated in the drama peasant conditions in my homeland in *Before Dawn*, in *Drayman Henschel*, in *Rose Bernd*, the misery of poor mountain weavers, the struggles of a washerwoman to "get ahead," the sufferings of a beggar child in *The Ascension of Hannele*, of two workhouse inmates in *Schluck und Jau*, and in *The Rats* an underworld of suffering, depravity, and crime.

Then in *Florian Geyer* I have extended my drama by presenting the sufferings of our people in the historical past. But I shall not speak of myself; I had to do so in order to honor the truth, for I am to be regarded as one of the roots of the tree of Gallowayshire.

The individual is born into the elementally dramatic nature of his people, whose natural mirror he is, more or less clearly, more or less inclusively. The genius, however, is a divinely magic mirror, and thus, as Shakespeare says, in the living drama is the mirror of the age. . . .

Struggle is the father of all things and the drama one of the many forms of representing this struggle in its tragical, comical, or tragi-comical manifestations. A drama ranks higher insofar as it keeps itself aloof from party or prejudice. . . . A challenge to combat is to be presupposed, and an evil quarrel is now and then inescapably forced upon the good as well as the bad. Some kind of victory over life should be attained at the close of the drama, tragic or comic. Advocacy of dogmas as an essential aim makes a drama second-rate. The drama is not meant to prove anything, and when it is thus abused it is destroyed as an art form.

Insofar as Germany is concerned, the theatre has been freed and ennobled by the thoughts and deeds of Lessing, Goethe, Schiller, Wagner and Nietzsche. Its task, which it fulfilled a long time ago in the music of Mozart, was formulated by these men. If nothing human is to be foreign to the theatre, then it must also preserve the dignity of man, things often difficult to unite. The theatre oftentimes makes itself effective like a natural event in such a manifold manner that its high meaning is not infrequently obscured. But religious ideas too become obscured. And there exists no bright, guiding star which is never hidden by clouds. What the stage and the actor require is an emotional existence. In addition the actor must bear as a *conditio sine qua non* the burden of talent or even of genius; both stand under special laws. If a chemist deals with dangerous materials, so much more perhaps, transferred into the spiritual realm, does the actor. No wonder if at times the god-like light is extinguished for him. And yet ever and again the heavenly fixed stars shine upon the stage, which represents the world; names like Aeschylus, Sophocles, Euripides, Calderón, Shakespeare, Molière, Goethe, Schiller, Kleist, and Grillparzer beam forth, the supernatural music of Mozart, Beethoven, Richard Wagner resounds, and even the poorest comedian feels himself exalted by their rays.

Among other things I have written dramas. . . . In these dramas all kinds of figures step forth, characters imbued with the fullest vitality by my spirit. One will not find the so-called villain in these works which are meant for the theatre. I would much rather claim to have been the seemingly incorruptible and, if possible, loving counsel for almost all of my figures. Of course I could not overlook the human, all too human, because if one wishes to present the lot of human beings, whether tragically or comically, it is an inevitable life giving and also fateful factor. Whoever desires the theatre, the drama, whoever desires the genuine, clear, purifying and clarifying mirror of life, must also most decisively say Yes to the human-all-too-human. . . . The poetic art, as I understand it, reckons with fully developed human beings, spiritually strong men and women, who have become capable of making judgments and are not oversensitive and pampered by sickly vanity. It reckons with such hearers and auditors who have the courage, seeking their own instruction and purification, to look down into the abyss of life, even where it is deepest.

Recently I was speaking in Berlin of what Henrik Ibsen once said to me after he had read my early drama *Before Dawn*, namely that it was brave and courageous. That seemed to him to contain the greatest praise. . . . He was right! Courage belongs to truth to oneself, to the love of truth! Without the high courage of youth we can accomplish nothing successfully. . . . It has been said, I have turned in my art too much to the affairs of the little man, the common man, and too little to that which lies just at the heart of the human beings of our own day. Well, not only in nature are the greatest and the smallest equally astonishing. The human is the truly great and is not changed so very much by the spirit of the time that elemental things and destinies retreat behind the variations. Thus the eternal fate of man will always be a greater theme than the cerebrally conscious fate of an epoch.

Every man, and also every gifted man, is timed. He not only goes his own way through the darkness, but carries his own lantern. Many others go forth, indeed, on better paths and light the world differently. For me it is chiefly a matter of leaving behind me a work as phraseless and as rich in human experience as possible.

Perception lies at the basis of all thinking. To think is to contend, thus dramatic. Every philosopher who presents to us his system of logical constructions has erected it by decisions which he has formulated out of the conflicting voices of his inner self. Accordingly I consider the drama to be the expression of primary thought processes upon a higher level of development and, of course, without having to make those decisions which concern the philosopher.

From this kind of perception there arise series of consequences which extend the field of the drama in all directions infinitely beyond the ruling dramaturgies, so that nothing which presents itself to the outer or inner senses can be excluded from this form of thinking, which has become an art form.

So much and no more shall I say to accompany this first collection of my dramatic works; they are to be understood as a natural expression of a personality. After all it must be left to them to achieve any vital success, such as they have at present, in the struggle between love and hatred.

THE WEAVERS

by GERHART HAUPTMANN

1892

THE WEAVERS[1]

Translated by Carl Richard Mueller

CHARACTERS

DREISSIGER, *fustian manufacturer*

FRAU DREISSIGER, *his wife*

in Dreissiger's service:

    PFEIFER, *manager*

    NEUMANN, *cashier*

    AN APPRENTICE

    JOHANN, *coachman*

    A SERVANT GIRL

WEINHOLD, *tutor to Dreissiger's sons*

PASTOR KITTELHAUS

FRAU PASTOR KITTELHAUS,
his wife

HEIDE, *Police Superintendent*

KUTSCHE, *a policeman*

WELZEL, *an innkeeper*

FRAU WELZEL, *his wife*

BAECKER

MORITZ JAEGER

OLD BAUMERT

MOTHER BAUMERT, *his wife*

BERTHA BAUMERT, *their
daughter*

EMMA BAUMERT, *another
daughter*

FRITZ, *Emma's son, four
years old*

AUGUST BAUMERT,
Baumert's son

OLD ANSORGE

FRAU HEINRICH

OLD HILSE

FRAU HILSE, *his wife*

GOTTLIEB HILSE, *their son*

LUISE HILSE, *his wife*

[1] *The Weavers* by Gerhart Hauptmann, translated by Carl Richard Mueller, printed by permission of the translator. Copyright © 1965 by Carl Richard Mueller. All rights reserved. Performance rights, whether amateur or professional, must be obtained from Literary Discoveries, Inc., 124 Spear Street, San Francisco, California 94105.

ANNA WELZEL, *their daughter*

WIEGAND, *a joiner*

A TRAVELING SALESMAN

A PEASANT

A FORESTER

SCHMIDT, *a surgeon*

HORNIG, *a ragpicker*

OLD WITTIG, *blacksmith*

MIELCHEN, *their daughter, six years old*

REIMANN

HEIBER

A BOY, *eight years old*

DYEWORKERS

A large crowd of young and old weavers and weaver women

The events described in this play take place in the 1840's in Kasbach in the Eulengebirge, as well as in Peterswaldau and Langenbielau at the foot of the Eulengebirge.

ACT ONE

[*A large whitewashed room in* DREISSIGER's *house in Peters-waldau. It is the room where the weavers must deliver their finished products. To the left there are windows without curtains; in the back wall a glass door; and to the right a similar glass door through which we see a continuous flow, in and out, of weavers, men, women, and children. The right wall, like the others, is for the most part hidden by wooden shelves for storing cotton. Along this wall stands a bench on which the in-coming weavers spread their goods. They step forward in order of their arrival and present their goods for inspection.* PFEIFER, *the manager, stands behind a large table on which the goods to be inspected are placed. This he does with the use of dividers and a · magnifying glass. The inspection finished, the weavers place the cloth on the scale where an* APPRENTICE *tests it for weight. The same* APPRENTICE *then places the accepted goods on a shelf. Each time,* PFEIFER *calls out loudly to* NEUMANN, *the cashier, sitting at a small table, the amount to be paid.*

It is a sultry day towards the end of May. The clock is at the stroke of twelve. Most of the weavers resemble persons standing in front of a bar of justice where with tortuous expectation they must wait for a life-and-death decision. There is something of the oppressed about them, something characteristic of the receiver of charity, who, having passed from one humiliation to another, is conscious of the fact that he is merely tolerated and is accustomed to making himself as inconspicuous as possible. Add to this an inflexible feature in their bearing of irresolute, harassed brooding. The men all resemble one another, half dwarflike, half schoolmasterlike. They are, for the most part, flat-chested, coughing, miserable creatures with pallid faces; creatures of the loom, whose knees are bent as a result of excessive sitting. Their women, at first glance, are less of a type; they are broken individuals, harassed, worn out—whereas the men still have about them a look of pathetic gravity. The clothes of the women are ragged, while those of the men are patched. The young girls among them are not without a

[143]

certain charm: a waxlike paleness, delicate figures and large, protruding, melancholy eyes.]

CASHIER NEUMANN [*counting out money*]. That leaves sixteen silver groschen and two pfennig.

FIRST WEAVER WOMAN [*about thirty, very emaciated. She puts away the money with trembling fingers*]. Thank you.

NEUMANN [*when the* WOMAN *fails to move on*]. Well? Something wrong again?

FIRST WEAVER WOMAN [*excitedly, begging*]. I was wondering, could I have a few pfennig in advance, I need it awful bad.

NEUMANN. And I need a couple hundred thalers. Nice if all we had to do is need it—! [*Already busy counting out money to another weaver, curtly.*] Herr Dreissiger's the one who takes care of advance payments.

FIRST WEAVER WOMAN. Then maybe I could talk with Herr Dreissiger for a minute?

MANAGER PFEIFER [*formerly a weaver himself, his type is unmistakable, except that he is well fed, well groomed, cleanly shaven, and a heavy user of snuff. He calls across brusquely*]. God knows, Herr Dreissiger'd have enough to do if he had to worry about every petty request. That's what *we're* here for. [*He measures and then inspects with the magnifying glass.*] Damn! There's a draft! [*He wraps a heavy scarf around his neck.*] Close the door when you come in.

APPRENTICE [*loudly to* PFEIFER]. Might as well talk to a stone wall.

PFEIFER. All right, that's done! Weigh it!

[*The* WEAVER *places his web on the scale.*]

Why don't you learn to do your work better? It's full of lumps again. I don't even have to look at it. A good weaver doesn't put off the winding for God knows how long.

[BAECKER *enters. He is a young and exceptionally strong weaver whose unconstrained deportment is almost impudent.* PFEIFER, NEUMANN *and the* APPRENTICE *exchange knowing glances at his entrance.*]

BAECKER. Damn! Sweating like a dog again!

FIRST WEAVER [*in a low voice*]. This heat means rain.

[OLD BAUMERT *pushes through the glass door at the right. On the other side of the door one can see the weavers waiting, crowded together, shoulder to shoulder.* OLD BAUMERT *has hobbled his way forward and laid down his pack on the bench near* BAECKER's. *He sits down beside it and wipes the perspiration from his face.*]

OLD BAUMERT. I can use a rest after that.

BAECKER. Rest's better than money anytime.

OLD BAUMERT. I could use a little money too. Good day to you, Baecker!

BAECKER. Good day to you, Father Baumert! Looks like another long wait here, uh?

FIRST WEAVER. What's the difference? A weaver can wait an hour or a day. He don't count.

PFEIFER. Quiet back there! How can I hear myself think?

BAECKER [*softly*]. One of his bad days again.

PFEIFER [*to the* WEAVER *in front of him*]. How many times do we have to tell you to clean up your webs better! What do you call a mess like this? Clots of dirt in here long as my finger, and straw and all kinds of muck.

WEAVER REIMANN. But there's always a pound waste figured in.

PFEIFER. I haven't got time. That's done with.—What have *you* got?

WEAVER HEIBER [*puts down his web. While* PFEIFER *examines it he steps up to him and talks to him in a low and eager voice*]. Beg pardon, Herr Pfeifer, sir, I wanted to ask you a favor, sir, if maybe you'd be so kind and wanted to do me a good turn, sir, and not have my advance pay come off my salary this time.

PFEIFER [*measuring and inspecting, scornfully*]. Well, now! Very well done. Looks like half of the woof was left on the spool again.

WEAVER HEIBER [*continues in his own way*]. I'll be sure to make it up this week, sir. Last week I had to work two days on the estate. And then my wife's home sick too . . .

PFEIFER [*placing the web on the scales*]. Here's another fine piece of sloppy work. [*Already beginning to inspect a new web.*] You call this a selvage? Broad here, narrow there! In one place the woof's all drawn together, God knows how much, and then here the reed's been pulled apart. And you've hardly got seventy threads to the inch. Where's the rest of it? You call this honest work? Whoever heard of such a thing?

[WEAVER HEIBER, *suppressing his tears, stands there humiliated and helpless.*]

BAECKER [*in a low voice, to* BAUMERT]. Looks like those bastards would like to make us pay for our own yarn too.

FIRST WEAVER WOMAN [*who has stepped back only a few paces from the cashier's table and has looked staringly about her from time to time, seeking help, without moving from the place. She now takes heart and turns again beseechingly toward the cashier*]. I can hardly . . . I just don't know if you don't give me any advance . . . O Jesus, Lord Jesus . . .

PFEIFER [*calls across*]. What's all this calling the Lord Jesus! Let Him in peace for a while! You never bothered much about your Lord Jesus up to now. Give a little more mind to your husband, you'd be better off, so we don't see him sitting at a tavern window all day long. We can't give any advances. We have to account here for every pfennig. Besides that, it's not our money. They'd be after *us* for it later. People who work hard and understand their business and do their work in the fear of the Lord don't need advances. So that's the end of that.

NEUMANN. And if a weaver from Bielau got paid four times as much, he'd waste just four times as much and still be in debt.

FIRST WEAVER WOMAN [*loudly as if appealing to everyone's sense of justice*]. There's nobody can say I'm lazy, but I can't go on like this anymore. Two times I had a miscarriage. And for my husband, he can do only half his part too. He even went to the shepherd at Zerlau but he couldn't help him with his trouble either . . . there's nobody can do more than he's able. We do our work here, all right, we do all we can. I've not had much sleep these past weeks, but everything'll be all right soon if only I can get some strength back into my bones. But you must have a little bit of consideration then. [*Beseeching him fawningly.*] You'll be good enough, won't you, sir, and allow me a few groschen this time.

PFEIFER [*without interrupting himself*]. Fiedler: eleven silver groschen.

FIRST WEAVER WOMAN. Just a few groschen to buy our bread. The farmer, he won't give no more credit. And then there's all our children . . .

NEUMANN [*in a low voice, with comic earnestness, to the* AP-

PRENTICE]. Every year the linen weaver has another kid, lálalala, lálalala, lá, lá, lá!

APPRENTICE [*takes it up*]. And the little brat is as blind as a lid, lálalala, lálalala, lá, lá, lá!

WEAVER REIMANN [*not touching the money which the cashier has counted out for him*]. We always used to get thirteen and a half groschen for a web.

PFEIFER [*calling over*]. If it don't suit you, Reimann, all you got to do is say so. There's enough weavers around. Especially your kind. You get full pay when your web's full weight.

WEAVER REIMANN. How could anything be wrong with the weight . . .

PFEIFER. Bring us a flawless piece of cotton sometime and your pay'll be all right, too.

WEAVER RIEMANN. I don't understand how there are any mistakes in it.

PFEIFER [*as he inspects*]. Weave well, live well.

WEAVER HEIBER [*has stayed near* PFEIFER, *looking for another favorable opportunity. He smiles together with the others over* PFEIFER's *witticism, and now he starts towards him again and addresses him as before*]. What I wanted to ask you, Herr Pfeifer, sir, is if perhaps you'd be so kind as not to take the five groschen advance off this week's pay. My wife she's been abed since Shrove Tuesday. There's nothing she can do to help me. So I have to pay the girl to tend the spools. So you see . . .

PFEIFER [*taking snuff*]. Heiber, you're not the only one I've got to take care of here. The others want their turn too.

WEAVER REIMANN. This is how I got the warp—so this is how I wound it up and took it off again. I can't bring back better yarn than I got.

PFEIFER. If you don't like it then don't bother picking up anymore. We got enough around here who'd run their soles off for it.

NEUMANN [*to* REIMANN]. Do you want the money or not?

WEAVER REIMANN. How could I feel right if I took that money?

NEUMANN [*no longer troubling himself with* REIMANN]. Heiber: ten silver groschen. Take off five for advance, that leaves five silver groschen.

WEAVER HEIBER [*steps forward, looks at the money, shakes his head as though there were something he can't believe,*

then puts the money slowly and carefully into his pocket].
My God, my God— [*Sighs.*] Well——

OLD BAUMERT [*looking* HEIBER *in the face*]. Yes, yes, Franz!
There's cause enough for sighing.

WEAVER HEIBER [*speaking with difficulty*]. Then, you see, I
got a sick girl at home too. She needs a bottle of medicine.

OLD BAUMERT. What's she got?

WEAVER HEIBER. Well, you see, she's been a sick one from
when she was born. I don't know . . . well, I can tell you
this much: she's brought it with her into the world. All
kinds of troubles break out over and over on her. It's in
the blood.

OLD BAUMERT. There's trouble all over. Wherever there's poor
people there's bad luck after bad luck. There's no end to it
and no saving us.

WEAVER HEIBER. What's that there in the bundle?

OLD BAUMERT. We had nothing at all to eat at home. And so
I had our little dog killed. There's not much on him, he was
half starved away. He was a nice little dog. I didn't want
to kill him myself. I couldn't find the heart for that.

PFEIFER [*has inspected* BAECKER'*s web, calls*]. Baecker: thirteen and a half silver groschen.

BAECKER. That's a shabby piece of charity, not pay.

PFEIFER. Whoever's been taken care of has to leave. We can't
even move around for all the crowd.

BAECKER [*to the people standing about, not lowering his
voice*]. This is a shabby tip, that's all it is. And for this we're
supposed to work our treadle from early morning to late
at night. And when you've worked eighteen days over the
loom, night after night, worn out, half dizzy with the dust
and the burning heat, then you're lucky if you made thirteen
and a half silver groschen.

PFEIFER. We don't allow back talk here.

BAECKER. You don't tell *me* what not to say!

PFEIFER [*jumps up shouting*]. We'll see about that! [*Goes to
the glass door and calls into the office.*] Herr Dreissiger,
Herr Dreissiger, if you'd be so kind, sir!

DREISSIGER [*enters. He is in his early forties, fat, asthmatic,
with a severe look*]. What is it, Pfeifer?

PFEIFER [*angrily*]. Baecker here says he won't keep his mouth
shut.

DREISSIGER [*draws himself up, throws back his head, stares at*

BAECKER *with quivering nostrils*]. Yes, of course—Baecker! [*To* PFEIFER.] Is this the one?

[*The* CLERK *nods.*]

BAECKER [*impudently*]. Right enough, Herr Dreissiger! [*Pointing to himself.*] This is *this* one—[*pointing to* DREISSIGER] and that's *that* one.

DREISSIGER [*with indignation*]. Who does he think he's talking to?

PFEIFER. He's too well off, that's what! He'll skate on thin ice just once too often.

BAECKER [*roughly*]. You shut your mouth, you stinking toad. Your mother must have rode a broomstick with Satan himself to get a devil like you!

DREISSIGER [*bellowing in sudden anger*]. Hold your tongue! Hold your tongue this minute or I'll . . . [*He trembles, comes forward a few steps.*]

BAECKER [*awaiting him with determination*]. I'm not deaf. My hearing's all right.

DREISSIGER [*controls himself and asks with apparent business-like calm*]. Isn't this one of those who . . .

PFEIFER. He's a weaver from Bielau. You find them wherever there's trouble.

DREISSIGER [*trembling*]. Just let me warn you of one thing: if ever it happens again like it did yesterday evening that a horde of half-drunken wet-nosed young louts passes my house again—and singing that vile song . . .

BAECKER. I guess it's *The Song of Bloody Justice* you mean, uh?

DREISSIGER. You know which one I mean. You just let me warn you: if I ever hear it again, I'll get hold of one of you and—I promise you this on my word of honor, I'm not joking—he will be turned over to the state's attorney. And if I ever find out who's responsible for that vile thing you call a song . . .

BAECKER. It's a beautiful song!

DREISSIGER. One more word out of you and I'll send for the police—and at once. I don't fool around. We know how to take care of young louts like you. I've taken care of people a lot different from you.

BAECKER. I take your word for it. Sure, a factory owner like you can take care of two or three hundred weavers before a man can turn around, and not even a bone left over. A man like that's got four bellies like a cow and the jaws of a wolf. For him it's nothing, nothing!

DREISSIGER [*to the* CLERK]. This one gets no more work from us.

BAECKER. What do I care whether I go hungry over a loom or at the side of a road!

DREISSIGER. Get out of here! Get out!

BAECKER [*firmly*]. First I'll take my pay.

DREISSIGER. What's he got coming, Neumann?

NEUMANN. Thirteen silver groschen, five pfennig.

DREISSIGER [*takes the money overhastily from the cashier and tosses it onto the counter so that some of the coins roll onto the floor*]. There you are! Now—get out of my sight!

BAECKER. First I'll get my pay.

DREISSIGER. There's your pay; and unless you get out of here, and quick . . . It's exactly twelve . . . My dyers are just now taking off for lunch . . .

BAECKER. I get my pay in my hand. My pay belongs here. [*He touches the palm of his left hand with the fingers of his right hand.*]

DREISSIGER [*to the* APPRENTICE]. Pick it up, Tilgner.

[*The* APPRENTICE *does so and places the money in* BAECKER's *hand.*]

BAECKER. Everything done proper. [*Without hurrying he places the money in an old purse.*]

DREISSIGER. Well? [*Impatiently, since* BAECKER *does not leave.*] Shall I *help* you out?

[*Agitation has risen among the crowd of weavers. A long, deep sigh is heard. Then someone falls. All interest is turned towards the new event.*]

DREISSIGER. What's the matter here?

VARIOUS WEAVERS AND WEAVER WOMEN. Someone fainted.— It's a sick little boy.—Is it the falling sickness, or what?

DREISSIGER. What . . . what's that? Fainted, you say? [*He goes nearer.*]

AN OLD WEAVER. He just lays there.

[*Room is made. An eight-year-old* BOY *is seen lying on the ground as if dead.*]

DREISSIGER. Does anybody know the boy?

THE OLD WEAVER. Not from our village.

OLD BAUMERT. He looks like one of the Heinrichs. [*Looks at him more closely.*] Yes, yes! It's Heinrich's boy Gustav.

DREISSIGER. Where do these people live?

OLD BAUMERT. Up around us, in Kaschbach, Herr Dreissiger. He goes around playing music, and in the daytime he works at his loom. They have nine children, the tenth on the way.

VARIOUS WEAVERS AND WEAVER WOMEN. They've got a lot of trouble, those people.—It rains through their roof.—The wife can't get two shirts for all the nine children.

OLD BAUMERT [*grabbing hold of the* BOY]. Hey there, boy, what's the matter with you? Wake up now!

DREISSIGER. Get hold of him there, we'll pick him up. Whoever heard of such foolishness, letting a child weak as him make such a long trip! Pfeifer, bring some water!

WEAVER WOMAN [*helps him sit up*]. You're not going to go and die on us now, boy, are you?

DREISSIGER. Or some cognac, Pfeifer, cognac's better.

BAECKER [*forgotten by everyone, he has stood there watching. Now, with one hand on the doorknob, he calls across loud and mockingly*]. Give him something to eat, too, and he'll come round all right. [*Off.*]

DREISSIGER. That one'll come to no good end. —Grab him under the arms, Neumann. Slowly, slowly . . . there . . . there . . . we'll take him into my office. What is it?

NEUMANN. He said something, Herr Dreissiger! He moved his lips.

DREISSIGER. What do you want, boy?

THE BOY [*whispering*]. I'm hungry!

DREISSIGER [*turning pale*]. I can't understand him.

WEAVER WOMAN. I think he wants . . .

DREISSIGER. We'll see what it is. Just don't hold us up. He can lie down on my sofa. We'll hear what the doctor has to say.

[DREISSIGER, NEUMANN *and the* WEAVER WOMAN *take the* BOY *into the office. Excited agitation arises among the weavers as though they were school children whose teacher had just left the room. They stretch their limbs, they whisper, they shift from one foot to another, and within a few seconds their conversation is loud and general.*]

OLD BAUMERT. I do believe Baecker was right.

SEVERAL WEAVERS AND WEAVER WOMEN. The boy said something that sounded like that.—It's nothing new around here, people fainting with hunger.—And what'll happen with us this winter if this cutting our wages keeps up?—And with the potatoes like they are, it'll be a bad year.—They won't do anything here until they find us all laying flat on our backs.

OLD BAUMERT. The best thing to do is what the weaver in Nentwich did, put a rope around your neck and hang yourself to your loom. Here, take yourself a pinch of snuff. He gave me a few grains to take along. What have you got in your handkerchief there that's nice?

AN OLD WEAVER. A little bit of pearl barley, that's all. The wagon from the miller in Ullbrich drove along ahead of me. One of the sacks had a little hole in it. That was a very handy thing, you can believe me.

OLD BAUMERT. Twenty-two mills there are in Peterswaldau and for us there's nothing left over.

OLD WEAVER. We mustn't ever lose our courage. There's always something to come along and help us on a little farther.

WEAVER HEIBER. When we're hungry the thing to do is pray to the Fourteen Helping Saints, and if that don't fill you up then you must put a pebble in your mouth and suck away. Right, Baumert?

[DREISSIGER, PFEIFER *and the cashier return.*]

DREISSIGER. Nothing serious. The boy's wide awake again. [*He walks about excited and puffing.*] Still and all it remains a disgrace. The child's as strong as a piece of straw in a windstorm. It's quite impossible to understand how people . . . how parents could be so unreasonable. Loading him down with two bundles of cotton and making him come all that way. I'll simply have to make it clear that goods brought by children will not be accepted. [*He walks back and forth in silence again for a while.*] In any case, I urgently hope that such a thing will never happen again. Who's to be blamed for it in the end? The factory owners, of course. We get blamed for everything. If a little fellow like this one gets stuck in the snow in wintertime and falls asleep there'd be a reporter there before we know it and the gruesome story would be in all the papers in two days. The father, the parents who send a child like that out . . . why, of course, why should *they* be blamed? The factory owner's the scapegoat. The weaver is always the one they let off easy, and the factory owner is the one who gets the lash: he's the one with no feelings, the one with a heart of stone, he's the dangerous one that every presshound can bite in the leg. He lives as splendid and happy as a prince and pays his weavers starvation wages. . . . They forget in all their high-sounding phrases that a man like that has troubles, too, and sleepless nights, and he runs tremendous risks that the worker doesn't even dream about; that there are times when he's so confused that his head swims with all the addition and multiplication and division that he has to do, with calculations and recalculations; that he has a hundred different things to think about and consider and has to fight competition tooth and nail, so to speak; that not a single day goes by without aggravation and losses; but these they never mention. Think of all the dependents the factory owner has around his neck, all the people who try to suck him dry to live off him! No, no! You ought to be in *my* shoes for a while, you'd have your fill of it soon enough. [*After a moment of reflection.*] And what about *that* fellow, *that* one, *Baecker*, how did he act! Now he'll go out and shout all over town what a hard-hearted creature I am, how I discharge my weavers over insignificant matters. It that true? Am I as hard-hearted as all that?

MANY VOICES. No, Herr Dreissiger!

DREISSIGER. Well, that's the way I see it, too. And still these young louts come around singing their vile songs about us factory owners. They talk about being hungry, yet they have so much left over to be able to drink their liquor by the quart. They ought to snoop around a little more and see what conditions are like with the linen weavers. Those are the people who can talk about being in need. But those of you here, you cotton weavers, you can still thank God quietly that you're as well off as you are. And I ask you now, you old, industrious and efficient weavers that are here: can a worker who knows what a good job is make a living working for me?

A GREAT MANY VOICES. Yes, Herr Dreissiger!

DREISSIGER. There, you see!—One like that Baecker, of course, couldn't. Let me advise you to keep fellows like him in check. If things go too far, then I'll just quit. I'll give up the whole business, and then you'll see how things really are. Then you can see about finding work for yourselves. And

I can assure you, it won't be from your honorable Herr Baecker that you'll get work.

FIRST WEAVER WOMAN [*has made her way up to* DREISSIGER *and with servility and humility brushes some dust from his coat.*] You've gone and brushed yourself up against something, Herr Dreissiger, sir.

DREISSIGER. Business is miserable right now, you know that yourselves. I'm losing money instead of making it. And if, in spite of this, I always see to it that my weavers have work, then I expect a little gratitude in return. I have piles of cloths by the thousands, and right now I don't know if I'll ever be able to get rid of them. But then I heard how many weavers around here are out of work entirely, and so . . . well, Pfeifer can give you the rest of the details. But the fact is simply that in order to show you my good intentions . . . I can't, of course, hand out charity, I'm not rich enough for that, but up to a certain point I *can* give the unemployed the opportunity to earn at least *something*. The fact that I am running a tremendous risk is, of course, *my* worry. It has always been my opinion that it is better for a man to earn a piece of cheese each day than to have to starve. Am I right?

MANY VOICES. Yes, yes, Herr Dreissiger.

DREISSIGER. And therefore I am more than happy to give work to another two hundred weavers. Pfeifer will explain to you under what conditions. [*He is about to go.*]

FIRST WEAVER WOMAN [*steps into his path, speaks hastily, imploringly and urgently*]. Herr Dreissiger, if you'd be so good, sir, what I wanted to ask you in a friendly way, if maybe you'd . . . well you see I been laid up two times already.

DREISSIGER [*hastily*]. You'll have to speak with Pfeifer, my good woman, I'm late as it is. [*He leaves her standing there.*]

WEAVER REIMANN [*also steps into his path; in an injured and accusing tone*]. Herr Dreissiger, I'm sorry, I have a complaint to make. Herr Pheifer there has . . . Well, I always used to get twelve and a half groschen a web . . .

DREISSIGER [*interrupting him*]. My manager is over there. You may go to him: he's the one to see.

WEAVER HEIBER [*stopping* DREISSIGER]. Herr Dreissiger, sir —— [*stuttering and with confused haste.*] What I wanted to ask you, sir, was if maybe you could be so kind as to

. . . that is, maybe you could be so kind as to . . . that is,
maybe if Herr Pfeifer could . . . if I could . . .

DREISSIGER. What is it you want?

WEAVER HEIBER. That advance pay I had last time, well, what
I mean is that . . .

DREISSIGER. I don't understand a word you're saying.

WEAVER HEIBER. Things were awful hard up for me, sir, because . . .

DREISSIGER. That's Pfeifer's business, that is all Pfeifer's business. There is really nothing I can . . . settle your business
with Pfeifer. [*He escapes into the office.*]

[*The suppliants look helplessly at one another. One after another they step back, sighing.*]

PFEIFER [*starts his inspecting again*]. Well there, Annie, what
have you got for us today?

OLD BAUMERT. How much do we get for a web, Herr Pfeifer?

PFEIFER. Ten silver groschen a web.

OLD BAUMERT. Now what do you think of that!

[*Excitement rises among the weavers, a whispering and murmuring.*]

constant examples of misery
=> necessity

ACT TWO

[*A room in the house of* WILHELM ANSORGE *in Kaschbach in
the Eulengebirge. It is a narrow room, not six feet high, the
floor is decayed and the rafters black with soot. In the room
are two young girls:* EMMA *and* BERTHA BAUMERT, *sitting
at their looms;* MOTHER BAUMERT, *a stiff-limbed old woman,
sitting on a stool by her bed, in front of a spooling wheel;
her son* AUGUST, *twenty years old, an idiot, with a small
body and head, and long spidery limbs, sitting on a footstool, also spooling yarn.*

*The weak, rose-colored light of evening forces its way
through two small windows, holes in the left wall which are
partially stuffed with paper and straw. It falls onto the
whitish-blond loose hair of the girls, on their bare, lean
shoulders and thin waxen necks, on the folds of their coarse
blouses which except for a short skirt of the roughest linen,
constitutes their entire clothing. The warm glow falls fully
upon the face, neck and chest of the old woman: a face
emaciated to a skeleton, with folds and wrinkles in its bloodless skin, with sunken eyes which are inflamed and watery
as a result of the lint, the smoke, and from working by
lamplight; a long goiter neck with folds and sinews; a sunken
chest which is packed in cloths and scarfs.*

*A part of the right wall, along with the stove and the
stove bench, the bedstead and several loudly tinted holy
pictures, also stands in light. On the bar of the stove rags
are hung up to dry, while behind the stove all the old,
worthless rubbish is piled. On the stove bench are several
old pots and cooking utensils; potato peelings are laid out
on a paper to dry. From the rafters there hang skeins and
reels of yarn. Baskets with spools stand beside the looms.
In the back wall there is a door without a lock. Leaning
against the wall beside the door is a bundle of willow
switches. Several damaged quarter-bushel baskets lie about
near them. The room is filled with the sounds of the looms,
the rhythmic movement of the lathe which shakes both
floor and walls, the shuffle and clicking of the rapid shuttle
moving back and forth. Mixed into this is the deep constant*

whirring of the spooling wheels which resembles the hum-
ming of bumblebees.]

MOTHER BAUMERT [*in a pitiful, exhausted voice as the girls*
leave off their weaving and lean over their looms]. Do you
have to make knots again?

EMMA [*the elder of the two girls, twenty-two years old; while*
knotting threads]. This is sure some yarn!

BERTHA [*fifteen years old*]. This warp is giving us trouble, too.

EMMA. Where is he? He left at nine o'clock.

MOTHER BAUMERT. Yes, I know, I know! Don't you know
where he could be?

BERTHA. Don't you worry, mother.

MOTHER BAUMERT. It's always a worry to me.

[EMMA *goes on with her weaving.*]

BERTHA. Wait a minute, Emma!

EMMA. What's the matter?

BERTHA. I thought I heard a noise like somebody coming.

EMMA. More likely Ansorge coming home.

[*A small barefoot, ragged little boy of four comes in crying.*]

FRITZ. Mother, I'm hungry.

EMMA. Wait a while, Fritzy, wait a while! Grandpa'll be here
soon. He'll bring some bread with him and some grain.

FRITZ. I'm still hungry, mother!

EMMA. I just told you. Don't be so stupid. He'll be here right
away. He'll bring some nice bread with him and some coffee
beans. When work's over, mother'll take the potato peelings
and she'll go to the farmer with them, and then he'll give
her a nice swallow of milk for her little boy.

FRITZ. Where'd grandpa go?

EMMA. To the factory owner's, to deliver a web, Fritzy.

FRITZ. The factory owner?

EMMA. Yes, Fritzy, yes! Down to Dreissiger's in Peterswaldau.

FRITZ. That where he gets the bread?

EMMA. Yes, yes, he gets money there, and then he can buy
the bread.

FRITZ. Will he get much money?

EMMA [*intensely*]. Oh, stop it, boy, with your talking.

[*She goes on weaving like* BERTHA. *Then they both stop again.*]

BERTHA. August, go and ask Ansorge if we could have a little
light.

[AUGUST *leaves.* FRITZ *goes with him.*]

MOTHER BAUMERT [*with increasing childlike fear, almost whining*]. Children, children, where could he be so long?

BERTHA. He probably only dropped in to see Hauffen.

MOTHER BAUMERT [*cries*]. I only hope he's not in a tavern!

EMMA. You musn't cry, mother! Our father's not that kind.

MOTHER BAUMERT [*beside herself with a multitude of fears*]. Well, well . . . well, tell me what will happen if he . . . if he comes home and . . . and if he's drunk everything up and don't bring nothing home? There's not a handful of salt in the house, not a piece of bread. We need a shovel of fuel . . .

BERTHA. Don't worry, mother! The moon's out tonight. We'll take August with us and gather some wood for the fire.

MOTHER BAUMERT. So you can be caught by the forester.

[*An old weaver with a gigantic body frame, who must bend low in order to enter the room, sticks his head and upper body through the doorway. His hair and beard are quite unkempt.*]

ANSORGE. What's the matter here?

BERTHA. You *could* give us some *light!*

ANSORGE [*in a subdued voice, as though speaking in the presence of a sick person*]. It's light enough here.

MOTHER BAUMERT. Now you even make us sit in the dark.

ANSORGE I do the best I can. [*He pulls himself out through the doorway.*]

BERTHA. You see there how stingy he is?

EMMA. So now we sit here and wait till he's ready.

[FRAU HEINRICH *enters. She is a woman of thirty and pregnant. Her tired face expresses tortuous anxieties and fearful tensions.*]

FRAU HEINRICH. Good evening, everyone.

MOTHER BAUMERT. Well, Mother Heinrich, any news?

FRAU HEINRICH [*limping*]. I stepped on a piece of glass.

BERTHA. Come here, then, sit down. I'll see if I can get it out for you.

[FRAU HEINRICH *sits down, while* BERTHA *kneels in front of her and works with the sole of the woman's foot.*]

MOTHER BAUMERT. How are you at home, Mother Heinrich?

FRAU HEINRICH [*breaks out in despair*]. It can't go on like this. [*She fights in vain against a torrent of tears. Then she cries silently.*]

MOTHER BAUMERT. It would be better for our kind, Mother Heinrich, if the Good Lord had a little understanding and took us from the world altogether.

FRAU HEINRICH [*her self-control gone, she cries out, weeping*]. My poor children are starving! [*She sobs and moans.*] I don't know what to do. You can do what you want, but all you ever do is chase around till you drop. I'm more dead than alive, and still there's no use. Nine hungry mouths I've got to feed, and how will I do it? Last evening I had a little piece of bread, it wasn't even enough for the two littlest. Which one was I to give it to? They all cried out to me: Me, mama, me, mama . . . No, no! This is what happens when I can still get about. What'll happen the day I can't get up out of bed no more? The flood's washed away the couple potatoes we had. We haven't got bread nor food to eat.

BERTHA [*has removed the piece of glass and washed the wound*]. We'll tie a rag around it now. [*To* EMMA.] See if you can find one.

MOTHER BAUMERT. It's no better here with us, Mother Heinrich.

FRAU HEINRICH. You still got your girls at least. You got a husband who can work, too. Last week my husband just broke down. He had such a fit and I was so scared to heaven I didn't know what to do with him. Whenever he has an attack like that he just has to lay in bed for a good eight days.

MOTHER BAUMERT. Mine's not so much better either anymore. He's about to give out, too. It's in his chest and his back. And there's not a pfennig in the house now. If he don't bring a couple of groschen home tonight, I don't know what'll happen.

EMMA. You can believe her, Mother Heinrich. We're so hard up, father had to take Ami along with him. He had to let them butcher him so we could have something solid in our bellies again.

FRAU HEINRICH. Don't you have a handful of flour left over, maybe?

MOTHER BAUMERT. Not even that much, Mother Heinrich; not even a grain of salt left in the house.

FRAU HEINRICH. Well, then, I don't know! [*She rises, remains standing and broods.*] Then I just don't know!—I just can't help it. [*Crying out in rage and fear.*] I'd be happy if we only had pig swill! But I can't go home with empty hands. I just can't. God forgive me. I just don't know what else there is to do. [*She limps out quickly, stepping on the heel of her left foot.*]

MOTHER BAUMERT [*calls after her, warningly*]. Mother Heinrich, Mother Heinrich, you mustn't go and do nothing foolish.

BERTHA. She won't do no harm to herself. Don't you worry.

EMMA. She's always like that. [*She sits down and weaves again for a few seconds.*]

[AUGUST *lights the way for his father,* OLD BAUMERT, *with a tallow candle, as the old man drags in a bundle of yarn.*]

MOTHER BAUMERT. Jesus, Lord Jesus, where were you all this time, father?

OLD BAUMERT. There, don't snap at me all at once. Let a man catch his breath a minute first. Why don't you go and see who's come in with me?

[MORITZ JAEGER *enters through the doorway stooping. He is a robust, average-sized, red-cheeked reservist. His Hussar's cap is worn jauntily on his head, and his clothes and shoes are in good repair; he also wears a clean shirt without a collar. Having entered, he takes a military stance and salutes; energetically.*]

JAEGER. Good evening, Aunt Baumert!

MOTHER BAUMERT. Well, well, now, you're home again, are you? And you didn't forget us. Sit down over here, then. Come over here, sit down.

EMMA [*wipes off a wooden chair with her skirt and pushes it over towards* JAEGAR]. Good evening, Moritz! Did you come home again to see how us poor people live?

JAEGER. Tell me, now, Emma, I almost didn't want to believe it. And you've got a youngster here almost old enough to be a soldier. Where'd you get him?

BERTHA [*takes the little food her father has brought, puts the meat in a pan and places it in the oven, while* AUGUST *builds a fire*]. You know the weaver named Finger?

MOTHER BAUMERT. He used to live with us here once. He wanted to marry her all right, but even then he had it awful bad in the lungs. I warned the girl enough. You think she listened? Now he's long dead and forgotten and she has to see about raising the boy. But you tell me now, Moritz, how things went with you.

OLD BAUMERT. You be quiet there, mother, can't you see how good he's fed? He'll laugh us all out, he will. He brought clothes with him like a prince. And a silver watch. And on top of all that ten thalers cash.

JAEGER [takes a boastful stance, with a swaggering, self-important smile on his face]. I can't complain. I never knew a bad time in the army.

OLD BAUMERT. He was orderly to a cavalry captain. Listen to him, he talks like a regular gentleman.

JAEGER. I got so used to all their fine talk I can't get rid of it.

MOTHER BAUMERT. No, no, now I want you to tell me! And such a good-for-nothing as you was, too, and coming into all that money. No, you weren't fit for nothing; you couldn't spool one bobbin after another without having to stop. You were always gone; setting up traps for titmice and robin snares was what you really liked. Now, ain't that the truth?

JAEGER. True enough, Aunt Baumert. It wasn't robins I caught, it was swallows.

EMMA. And all we used to tell him was: swallows are poison.

JAEGER. It was all the same to me. But how have you all got on, Aunt Baumert?

MOTHER BAUMERT. Oh, Lord Jesus, so bad, so bad these last four years. I had these pains, you see. Just you look at my fingers here. I don't know if I got rheumatism or what. I'm in such misery. I can hardly move a limb. Nobody'd believe the pains I had to suffer.

OLD BAUMERT. She's in a real bad way now. She can't hold out much longer.

BERTHA. Mornings we have to put her clothes on, nights we have to take them off for her. We've got to feed her like a child.

MOTHER BAUMERT [continues in a doleful, tearful voice]. They have to help me every which way. I'm more than sick, I'm a burden. How I have prayed to the good Lord God that He should just take me. O Jesus, my Jesus, it's too much for me. I just don't know . . . maybe people think that . . . but I been used to working since I was just a little one. I could always do my job, then all of a sudden [She tries in vain to raise herself.] it just won't go anymore. I have a good husband and good children, but if all I can do is watch . . . Just you look there at those girls! They got almost no blood in them anymore. White as a sheet. It never stops here with this treadle, even if they get nothing for it. What kind of life is that for them? They never get away from that bench the whole year. There's not a dress they own that they can show for their work so that they can cover themselves sometimes and go out among the other people or go to church sometimes and find some comfort. They look like they was cut down from the gallows, girls of fifteen and twenty.

BERTHA [*at the stove*]. It's smoking again now.

OLD BAUMERT. Just you look at that smoke. Can anything be done about it, you think? It'll fall to pieces soon, that stove. Well, we'll just have to let it fall to pieces, and as for the soot, we'll just have to swallow it. We all cough, one more than the other. If you cough, you cough, and if it gets you and you choke to death, what's it matter, nobody'll ask no questions.

JAEGER. But that's Ansorge's business, he's got to fix it.

BERTHA. He'd only look at us like we was crazy. He already grumbles too much.

MOTHER BAUMERT. We take up too much room for him as is.

OLD BAUMERT. And if *we* start to grumble, we'll be out on our ears. He's had no rent from us this half-year.

MOTHER BAUMERT. A man like him that ain't married could be a little more friendly.

OLD BAUMERT. He's got nothing either, mother, things are as bad for him, too, just be glad he didn't raise the roof on us.

MOTHER BAUMERT. Still, he's got his own house.

OLD BAUMERT. There, mother, what are you talking about! There's hardly a board in this house he can call his.

JAEGER [*sits down and removes a short pipe with a nice tassle hanging from one pocket, and from the other pocket a bottle of brandy*]. Things can't go on much longer like this. I'm amazed how things look. Why, the dogs in the city live better than you people here do.

OLD BAUMERT [*eagerly*]. That's right, isn't it, isn't it? You know that! And if any one of us makes a complaint about it they just say it's the bad times.

[ANSORGE *enters with an earthenware bowl of soup in one hand and a half-finished quarter-bushel basket in the other.*]

ANSORGE. Welcome home, Moritz! You've come back, I see.

JAEGER. Thank you, Father Ansorge.

ANSORGE [*pushing his bowl into the oven*]. Just look at him now, if he don't look almost like a count.

OLD BAUMERT. Show him the nice watch you got. He brought along a new suit and ten thalers cash.

ANSORGE [*shaking his head*]. Well, well, well!

EMMA [*puts the potato peelings into a little sack*]. I'm going over now with the peelings. Maybe it'll be enough for a little milk. [*She goes out.*]

JAEGER [*while they all watch him with attention and admiration*]. You think back and remember how many times you made things hot as hell for me. That'll teach you a thing or two, Moritz, you always used to say, when you get in the army. Well, you can see, things went pretty good for me. I had my stripe in half a year. You got to be willing to work, that's the main thing. I polished the sergeant's boots; I brushed his horse, got his beer. I was fast as a weasel. I was sharp as a tack; my stuff really shined. I was the first to the stables, the first to roll call, the first in the saddle; and then when we attacked—forward march! Holy Moses and damnation! I watched like a bloodhound! I always said to myself: you'll get no help here, it's up to you now; and then I pulled myself together, and I was all right. I did so much that one time the captain said in front of the whole squadron: This is what a Hussar ought to be.

[*Silence. He lights his pipe.*]

ANSORGE [*shaking his head*]. Then you were lucky, uh? Well, well, well! Well, well, well! [*He sits down on the floor with the willow switches beside him, and with the basket between his legs he continues mending it.*]

OLD BAUMERT. Let's hope now you brought some luck with you.—Well, maybe we'll have a drink with you now, uh?

JAEGER. Sure, Father Baumert, sure, and when that's gone, there'll be more. [*He puts a coin onto the table.*]

ANSORGE [*with stupid, grinning amazement*]. Lord in Heaven, what goings-on . . . a roast there in the oven, and here a quart of brandy—— [*He drinks from the bottle.*] Your health, Moritz! Well, well, well! Well, well, well!

[*From here on the brandy bottle is handed around.*]

OLD BAUMERT. If only on Holy Days we could have a little roast like this instead of never seeing meat for months and months. —So now we'll have to wait till another little dog comes by like this one four weeks ago: and a thing like that don't happen so often in a life.

ANSORGE. Did you have to have Ami killed?

OLD BAUMERT. He would have starved to death anyway . . .

ANSORGE. Well, well, well. Well, well, well.

MOTHER BAUMERT. And he was such a nice, friendly little dog.

JAEGER. Are you still so eager around here for roast dog?

OLD BAUMERT. O Jesus, Jesus, if we only had enough of it.

MOTHER BAUMERT. Well, a little piece of meat is a good thing.

OLD BAUMERT. Don't you have taste for things like that anymore? Well, you just stay with us, Moritz, you'll get it back soon enough.

ANSORGE [sniffing]. Well, well, well—that's something good there, good smell, too.

OLD BAUMERT [sniffing]. The real thing, you might say.

ANSORGE. Tell us what you think now, Moritz. You know the way it is out there in the world. Do you think things'll ever be different here with us weavers?

JAEGER. I really hope so.

ANSORGE. We can't live here and we can't die. It's bad for us here, you can believe that. You fight to the last, but in the end you got to give in. Poverty tears the roof off from over your head and the floor from under your feet. In the old days when you could still work at the loom you could just about half get by with all kinds of trouble and misery. Nowadays month after month can go by and I can't find a piece of work. Weaving baskets is all over with too now, all you can do is stay alive at it. I weave till late into the night, and when I fall into bed I've made a groschen and six pfennigs. You got education, you tell me: can anybody get by nowadays with these rising prices? I have to toss out three thalers for house tax, one thaler for property tax and three thalers for interest. I can count on fourteen thalers pay. That leaves seven thalers the year for myself. Out of it I have food to pay for, and heat and clothes and shoes and patches and thread for mending and then I got to have a place to live in and God knows what else. Is there any wonder when you can't pay the interest?

OLD BAUMERT. Somebody ought to go to Berlin and explain to the King how things are with us.

JAEGER. There wouldn't be much good in that, Father Baumert. There's been enough said about it in the newspapers. But these rich people, they turn and they twist the news so that . . . they can bedevil the best Christians.

OLD BAUMERT [*shaking his head*]. Not to know better than that in Berlin!

ANSORGE. Tell me, Moritz, you think that's possible? Aren't there laws for such things? If a person works the skin right off his hands and still can't pay the interest, can the farmer take my house away from me? He's a farmer who wants his money. I just don't know what'll come of it all. If I have to get out of the house . . . [*speaking through his tears*] I was born here, my father sat here at his loom for more than forty years. How many times did he tell my mother: If ever I'm not here anymore, don't let the house go, he said. I worked for this house, he said. Every nail in it I paid for with a night of work, and every beam is worth a year's bread. Wouldn't you think that . . .

JAEGER. They're able to take the last thing you've got.

ANSORGE. Well, well, well! If it ever comes to that, I'd rather they carry me out than have to walk out in my old age. What's there to dying! My father was glad enough to die. —It was only at the last he got a little scared. But then when I crawled into bed with him he quieted down a bit.— When I think about it, I was just a boy of thirteen then. I was so tired out I went to sleep right beside that sick man —I didn't know no better—and when I woke up he was already cold.

MOTHER BAUMERT [*after a pause*]. Reach into the stove, Bertha, and give Ansorge his soup.

BERTHA. Here you are, Father Ansorge!

ANSORGE [*weeping as he eats*]. Well, well, well—well, well, well!

[OLD BAUMERT *has begun to eat the meat out of the pan.*]

MOTHER BAUMERT. Now, father, father, you can wait a while. Let Bertha set the table right first.

OLD BAUMERT [*chewing*]. It was two years ago I went to the Lord's Supper last. Just after that I sold my Sunday clothes. We bought a little piece of pork with the money. Since then I've had no meat till tonight.

JAEGER. What do we need meat for? The factory owners eat it for us. They wade in fat up to here. Whoever don't believe that can go down to Bielau and Peterswaldau and see for himself. He'd have an eyeful there: one factory owner's mansion after another. With glass windows and little towers and iron fences. Believe me, they don't know what bad times are. There's enough money down there for roasts and cakes, for carriages and coaches, for governesses and who knows what else! They're so stuffed with their greed they don't know what to do with all their riches out of cockiness.

ANSORGE. It was all a different thing in the old days. Then they gave the weavers enough to live on. Today they waste it all on themselves. But I say that's because those people in high places don't believe in God no more or in the devil either. What do they know about commandments and punishments? They all but steal our last piece of bread from our mouths and make us weak and eat up the little food we got whenever they can. Those are the people our troubles come from. If the factory owners was good men, there wouldn't be no bad times for us.

JAEGER. Listen to me now. I want to read you something real nice. [*He pulls some pieces of paper from his pocket.*] Come on, August, you run down to the tavern and get another quart. What's the matter, August, why are you laughing?

MOTHER BAUMERT. I don't know what it is with the boy. He's always happy. He'll laugh himself sick no matter what happens. Well, run now, run!

[AUGUST *goes off with the empty brandy bottle.*]

Ha, you know what it is tastes good, don't you, father!

OLD BAUMERT [*chewing, stimulated by the food and drink*]. Moritz, you're our man. You can read, you can write. You know how things are with us weavers. And you have a heart for the weavers, too. You ought to step in and take up our cause for us around here.

JAEGER. If that's all. Sure, I'd like to teach those mangy factory owners a thing or two. Wouldn't bother me at all. I'm an easygoing enough person, but once I get my temper up and get mad, I could take Dreissiger in one hand and Dietrich in the other and knock their heads together till sparks fly from their eyes. If we could manage to stick together we could really make a racket for those factory owners. We wouldn't need a king for that, *or* a government, all we'd have to do is say: We want this and this and we want it done this way and not that, and they'd whistle another tune soon enough. Once they see we got some guts, they'll calm down. I know their kind. They're a bunch of cowardly bastards.

MOTHER BAUMERT. That's the truth. I'm sure not bad. I was always one to say: There have to be rich people, too. But when it comes to this . . .

JAEGER. For all of me the devil can take them, they deserve it.

BERTHA. Where did father go?

[OLD BAUMERT *has left quietly.*]

MOTHER BAUMERT. I don't know where he is.

BERTHA. Do you think maybe his stomach's not used to meat anymore?

MOTHER BAUMERT [*beside herself, crying*]. You see now, there you see! He can't even keep it down. He'll vomit up that nice little piece of food.

OLD BAUMERT [*returning, crying in rage*]. No, no! It can't go on much longer with me. It has to end soon! When you finally get something good to eat you can't even keep it down. [*He sits down crying on the stove bench.*]

JAEGER [*in a sudden frantic outburst*]. And to think there are people, judges, not far from here, with their potbellies, who've got nothing to do all year long but steal a day from the Lord God. And they're the ones who say the weavers could get along well and good if they wasn't so lazy.

ANSORGE. They're not people. Those are monsters.

JAEGER. Don't you worry, he's got what he asked for. Red Baecker and me gave him a piece of our mind, and before we left, we even sang *Bloody Justice* for him.

ANSORGE. Good Lord, is that the song?

JAEGER. Yes, yes, I've got it here.

OLD BAUMERT. They call it *Dreissiger's Song*, don't they?

JAEGER. I'll read it to you.

MOTHER BAUMERT. Who wrote the song?

JAEGER. Nobody knows. Now listen. [*He reads, spelling like a schoolboy, stressing poorly, but with unmistakably strong feeling. Despair, pain, rage, hatred, and a thirst for vengeance are felt in his reading.*]

> A bloody justice rages here,
> A law that's worse than lynching,
> Where courtroom trials are not the rule,
> They kill us without flinching.

A man is slowly tortured here,
A man is tortured long,
His sighs are counted as the proof
Of his affliction's song.

OLD BAUMERT [*gripped by the song and deeply moved, he has
several times had to control himself from interrupting
JAEGER. Now he can contain himself no longer; stammering,
amid tears and laughter, to his wife*]. "A man is tortured
long." Whoever wrote that, he knew what he knew. "His
sighs are proof . . ." How does it go? "His sighs . . . affliction's song . . ." Is that it? "Counted as the proof . . ."
JAEGER [*reads*].

His sighs are counted as the proof
Of his affliction's song.

OLD BAUMERT. You know how we sigh, mother, day after day,
in bed or on our feet.
JAEGER [*while ANSORGE, who has stopped his work, sits bro-
kenly on the floor, deeply moved, and while MOTHER BAU-
MERT and BERTHA constantly wipe their eyes, he continues
to read*].

Our hangmen are the Dreissigers,
Their servants are their henchmen,
And each one takes his pound of flesh
As though it were no sin.

You scoundrels all, you brood of hell . . .

OLD BAUMERT [*trembling with rage and stamping on the floor*].
Yes! "Brood of hell! Brood of hell!"
JAEGER [*reads*].

You demons of the fire,
You eat the poor from house and home——
May curses pay your hire.

ANSORGE. Yes, yes, that's worth a curse.
OLD BAUMERT [*clenching his fists, threateningly*]. "You eat
the poor from house and home!"——
JAEGER [*reads*].

Pleading gets you nowhere here,
Begging's all in vain;
"If you don't like it, then go starve
Elsewhere," they complain.

OLD BAUMERT. How does it go? "Begging's all in vain"? Every word . . . every word . . . it's all as true as the Bible itself. "Pleading gets you nowhere here!"

ANSORGE. Well, well, well! Nothing does any good.

JAEGER [reads].

> Let every man regard our need,
> Whom misery doth bow,
> With not a bite of bread at home——
> Where is your pity now!

> Pity! that you've never known,
> And never did ask why;
> But every man must know your aim,
> To bleed us till we die.

OLD BAUMERT [jumps up, almost in a frenzy]. "Till we die." That's what it is, "bleed us till we die." Here I stand, Robert Baumert, master weaver of Kaschbach. Who can step forward and say . . . ? I have been a good man all my days, but look at me now! What do I have to show? What do I look like? What have they done to me? "A man is slowly tortured here." [He holds out his arms.] Here, feel me, feel me . . . skin and bones. "You scoundrels all, you brood of hell!" [He collapses into a chair with anger and despair.]

ANSORGE [tosses his basket into the corner, lifts himself, his whole body trembling with rage; stammers out]. And it's got to change, I say it's got to change now! We won't stand it no more! We won't stand it no more, no matter what happens!

ACT THREE

[*The taproom of the Peterswaldau village tavern. It is a large
room with a beamed ceiling supported by a wooden center
column, aroud which runs a table. In the rear wall, to the
right of the column, is an entrance door, one jamb of which
is hidden by the column. Through the door there is a large
storeroom with barrels and brewing utensils. In the corner
of the taproom, to the right of the door, is a bar: a wooden
partition, the height of a man, with compartments for bar
utensils; behind it is a cupboard containing rows of whiskey
bottles; between the partition and the liquor cabinet is a
small area for the bartender. In front of the bar stands a
table decorated with a multicolored cloth. A pretty lamp
hangs above it, and round about it are a number of cane
chairs. Not far off, in the right wall, there is a door with
"Weinstube" written above it leading into a room for more
prominent guests. Farther downstage right stands an old
grandfather's clock. To the left of the entrance door in the
back wall there is a table with bottles and glasses, and
farther on, in the corner, is the great tiled stove. There are
three small windows in the left wall, below them runs a
bench, and in front of each window is a large wooden table
with one of its ends towards the wall. Along the sides of
these tables are benches with backs, while at the window
end of each table is a single wooden chair. The entire room
is whitewashed almost blue, covered over with advertise-
ments, pictures, and colored prints, including the portrait
of Friedrich Wilhelm IV.*

SCHOLZ WELZEL, *a good-natured colossus of more than
fifty, is drawing beer from a barrel into a glass.* FRAU WEL-
ZEL *is ironing at the stove. She is a dignified, cleanly dressed
woman not yet thirty-five.* ANNA WELZEL, *a seventeen-year-
old, pretty girl with beautiful reddish-blond hair and nicely
dressed, sits behind the table with the colored cloth and
embroiders. She looks up for a moment from her work and
listens as the sounds of a funeral hymn sung by school children are heard in the distance.* MASTER WIEGAND, *the joiner,
sits in his working clothes at the same table with a glass of*

*beer in front of him. One can see that he is a man who
knows what it takes to be a success in the world, namely
cunning, quickness, and ruthless determination.* A TRAVEL-
ING SALESMAN *sitting at the column table is vigorously chewing at a chopped steak. He is of medium height, well fed,
stout, inclined to be cheerful, lively and impudent. His
clothes are in fashion. His traveling effects—handbag, sam-
ple case, umbrella, overcoat and blanket—are on the chair
beside him.*]

WELZEL [*carrying a glass of beer to the* SALESMAN, *aside to*
WIEGAND]. Seems like the devil's loose in Peterswaldau today.

WIEGAND [*with a sharp, trumpetlike voice*]. Sure, because it's
delivery day at Dreissiger's.

FRAU WELZEL. But they don't usually make such a stir.

WIEGAND. Well, it's maybe because of the two hundred new
weavers that he wants to take on now.

FRAU WELZEL [*continues ironing*]. Yes, I suppose that would
be it. If it's two hundred he wants, at least six hundred must
have showed up. There's enough of that kind around.

WIEGAND. O Jesus, yes, there's enough of them. Their kind
don't ever die out even when times are bad. They put more
children into the world than we know what to do with.

[*For a moment the hymn is heard more clearly.*]

Then there's a funeral today too. The weaver Fabish died.

WELZEL. He's been at it long enough. Running around like a
ghost all this long time.

WIEGAND. Believe me, Welzel, never in my life did I ever glue
together such a tiny little casket. That was a corpse for you,
couldn't have weighed ninety pounds.

SALESMAN [*chewing*]. I don't understand it . . . wherever you
look, in whatever paper, all you ever read is gruesome
stories about the need of the weavers. You get the impression that people in this neighborhood are three-quarters
dead from starvation. And take this funeral. I just got to
the village. Brass band, schoolmaster, school children, the
pastor, and that procession of people behind them—my
God, it's like the Emperor of China was being buried. Well,
if these people have money to pay for something like that
. . . [*He drinks the beer. After putting down his glass, with
frivolous levity.*] Isn't that right, miss? Am I right or not?

[ANNA *smiles with embarrassment and eagerly continues her embroidering.*]

I'll bet those are a pair of slippers for your papa.

WELZEL. You won't catch *my* feet in any such thing.

SALESMAN. Let me tell you that I'd give half of what I'm worth if those slippers were for me.

FRAU WELZEL. He just don't understand things like that.

WIEGAND [*after having coughed several times, moved his chair about, and made an attempt to speak*]. The gentleman seemed surprised about the funeral. Wouldn't you say, miss, that it's a rather small funeral?

SALESMAN. Yes, but the question is . . . Why, that must cost a monstrous lot of money. Where do these people come by it?

WIEGAND. If you will excuse me, sir, but there's a kind of lack of reasonableness among these poor classes of people. With your permission, I will say that they have an exaggerated idea of the respect and duty they owe to those taken from them. And if it happens to be the parent who died, you never saw such superstitiousness. The children and nearest relatives scrape together whatever they can get their hands on. And what they can't get, they borrow from the nearest man of wealth. His Eminence the pastor finds himself borrowed from, not to mention the sexton and everyone else standing about. And then there's the food and drinks and all the other things they need. I have nothing against a child's respect for his parents, but when the mourners are put in debt for the rest of their lives, then it's too much.

SALESMAN. If I may say so, the pastor should talk them out of such foolishness.

WIEGAND. If you'll excuse me, sir, I must say something in support of this, that every little community has its own house of God and has to support the shepherd of its flock. The clergy has its advantages from large funerals. The more people at a burial, the richer flows the offertory. Whoever knows the working conditions around here, sir, can tell you with unauthoritative certainty that the pastors regard quiet funerals with little favor.

[HORNIG *enters. He is a small bowlegged old man with a draw-rope around his shoulders and chest. He is a rag-picker.*]

HORNIG. Good day to you all. Could I have a small glass of schnapps? Well now, miss, have you any rags for me? Miss Anna! I have beautiful hair ribbons, and shirt bands, and garters in my cart, nice pins, hairpins, and hooks and eyes. It's all yours for a couple of rags. [*In a changed tone of voice.*] A nice white piece of paper will be made from those rags, and then your sweetheart will write you a lovely letter on it.

ANNA. Thank you, no. I don't want a boy friend.

FRAU WELZEL [*putting a heating iron into her flatiron*]. That's the way the girl is. She won't hear a word about marrying.

SALESMAN [*jumps up, apparently pleasantly surprised, goes to the covered table and holds his hand across it towards* ANNA]. That's the way to be, miss, do like me. Agreed? Give me your hand on it! We'll both of us stay single.

ANNA [*red as a beet, gives him her hand*]. But you're already married, aren't you?

SALESMAN. God forbid! You think that because I wear this ring? I only do that to protect my irresistible personality from the sordid attacks of people. But I'm not afraid of you. [*He puts the ring in his pocket.*] But seriously, miss, wouldn't you like to get even just a little bit married?

ANNA [*shaking her head*]. You leave me alone!

FRAU WELZEL. She'll stay single unless something awful special comes along.

SALESMAN. Well, why not? I know of a rich Silesian grandee who married his mother's chambermaid, and the rich factory owner Dreissiger, he married an innkeeper's daughter, who isn't half as pretty as you are, miss, and she rides around now in a carriage and with servants in livery. So why not? [*He wanders about, stretching himself and his legs while walking.*] How about a cup of coffee here?

[ANSORGE *and* OLD BAUMERT *enter, each with a pack, and sit quietly and humbly at the table to the front and left with* HORNIG.]

WELZEL. Welcome, Father Ansorge! Good to see you again!

HORNIG. Did you really crawl out again from that smoked-up nest of yours?

ANSORGE [*awkward and obviously embarrassed*]. Yes, I went and took another web again.

OLD BAUMERT. He'll do the work for ten groschen.

ANSORGE. I would never have done it, but now there's an end
    to my basket weaving, too.

WIEGAND. It's better than nothing, I always say. And he's
    doing it so that you'll have something to work at. I know
    Dreissiger good enough. A week ago I took out his storm
    windows. We talked about it then. He's doing it out of pity.

ANSORGE. Sure, sure, sure—I believe every word you say.

WELZEL [*placing a shot of schnapps in front of the weavers*].
    There you are. Tell me now, Ansorge, how long's it been
    since you had a shave? The gentleman over there wants to
    know.

SALESMAN [*calls over to them*]. Now, Herr Welzel, I said no
    such thing. I was merely struck by our good weaver's
    venerable appearance. It's not often you get to see a giant
    like him.

ANSORGE [*scratches his head in embarrassment*]. Sure, sure,
    sure—well . . .

SALESMAN. Primeval men of nature like him are rather rare
    nowadays. We've been licked so smooth by civilization . . .
    but I can still take pleasure in nature in the rough. Bushy
    eyebrows! Wild beard . . .

HORNIG. Now you let me tell you something, sir; people like
    them can't afford a barber, and a razor is even more out
    of the question. What grows grows. They can't afford to
    worry about what they look like.

SALESMAN. I beg your pardon, sir, but I had no intention . . .
    [*quietly to the innkeeper*]. Would it be all right to offer the
    hairy one a glass of beer?

WELZEL. I wouldn't try it. He wouldn't take it anyway. He's
    got strange ideas.

SALESMAN. Well, then I won't. Will you allow me, miss? [*He
    takes a place at* ANNA'*s table.*] I can assure you, miss, I
    noticed your hair the moment I came in. It's gentle bril-
    liance, it's softness, and the fullness of it! [*At the same time
    he kisses his finger tips as though enchanted.*] And it's color
    . . . like ripe wheat. Come to Berlin with hair like that and
    you'll be the toast of the town. On my word of honor, you
    could even go to the court with such hair . . . [*Leaning
    back he looks at her hair.*] Magnificent! Absolutely mag-
    nificent!

WIEGAND. That's why they've given her the name she's got.

SALESMAN. What is it then?

ANNA [*laughing constantly to herself*]. Oh, don't listen to him!

HORNIG. They call you the chestnut filly, don't they?

WELZEL. Now, now, that's enough! Don't you be confusing the girl more than she is! She already has enough silly ideas in that head of hers. Today she wants a count and tomorrow it'll be a prince.

FRAU WELZEL. You let the girl alone now, father! It's no crime if a person wants to get ahead in the world. It's a good thing everybody doesn't think like you; if they did nobody'd ever get anywhere. They'd all still be sitting here. If Dreissiger's grandfather had thought like you, they'd all of them still be poor weavers. Now they're rich as kings. And old Tromtra was nothing but a poor weaver, too, and now he's got twelve estates and besides that they made him a nobleman.

WIEGAND. Be fair now, Welzel; this time your wife knows what she's talking about. I'll vouch for it. If I thought like you, would I be boss over seven journeymen now?

HOGNIG. You know your way around all right, no denying that. While a weaver's still running about on two legs, you're already busy with his coffin.

WIEGAND. If a man's to get ahead in the world, he has to stick by his business.

HORNIG. Yes, and you do stick by your business, don't you! You know better than a doctor when death's coming for a weaver's child.

WIEGAND [*no longer smiling, suddenly furious*]. And you know better than the police where the thieves are among the weavers, and which of them end each week with a nice spool of yarn left over. You come for rags, but you don't object if there's a little yarn among them.

HORNIG. And luck comes your way in the churchyard. The more of us that go to sleep on wooden planks, the better for you. When you look at all the children's graves, you pat yourself on the belly and say: another good year; the little brats have fallen like June bugs from the trees again. That means another extra quart for me each week.

WIEGAND. At least that don't make me a receiver of stolen goods.

HORNIG. The most you ever do is bill the rich manufacturer twice, or take a couple extra planks from Dreissiger's new building when the moon happens not to be shining.

WIEGAND [*turns his back on him*]. Babble on all you want but
   don't bother me with it. [*Then suddenly.*] Hornig the liar!
HORNIG. Deadmen's butler!
WIEGAND [*to the others*]. He can put a hex on cattle.
HORNIG. You watch yourself, or I'll put one on you.

[WIEGAND *grows pale*. FRAU WELZEL, *who had gone out, returns now and places a cup of coffee in front of the* SALES-
   MAN.]

FRAU WELZEL. Should I serve your coffee in the little room, sir?
SALESMAN. I should say not! [*With a languishing glance at*
   ANNA.] I shall sit here until I die.

[A YOUNG FORESTER *and* A PEASANT *enter. The* PEASANT *carries a whip.*]

BOTH. Good day to you! [*They remain standing at the bar.*]
PEASANT. Two gingers.
WELZEL. Welcome to both of you! [*He pours them their drink;
   they both take up their glasses, clinking them together,
   drink down, and place the glasses back on the bar.*]
SALESMAN. Well, young forester, have a good march?
FORESTER. Not bad. I come from Steinseifersdorf.

[TWO OLD WEAVERS *enter and seat themselves beside* ANSORGE,
   OLD BAUMERT *and* HORNIG.] .

SALESMAN. Excuse me, but aren't you one of Count Hoch-
   heim's foresters?
FORESTER. I work for Count Keil.
SALESMAN. Of course, of course, that's what I meant to say.
   It's a little confusing with all these counts and barons and
   other worthy gentlemen. One needs a giant's memory to
   remember so much. Why do you carry an axe?
FORESTER. I took it from some wood thieves.
OLD BAUMERT. These lords of ours take great offense over a
   piece of kindling wood.
SALESMAN. Well, if you don't mind my saying so, suppose
   everyone took what he wanted . . .
OLD BAUMERT. With your permission, sir, there's the same difference here between big and little thieves. There are some
   here with wholesale lumber businesses who get rich off their
   stolen wood. But when a poor weaver does it . . .
FIRST OLD WEAVER [*interrupts* BAUMERT]. We don't dare take
   a twig, but these lords they skin us alive. We got protection

fees to pay, spinning fees, fees in kind, we got to run here and there.

ANSORGE. That's how it is: what the factory owners leave behind for us, their lordships steal from our pockets.

SECOND OLD WEAVER [*has taken a place at the next table*]. I said so myself to his lordship. I said, you'll pardon me, my lord, I just can't manage to work so many field days this year, I just can't! And why? You'll pardon me, my lord, but the rain ruined everything for me. The flood's carried off the little field I had. I have to work day and night if I'm to live. What a terrible storm! My God, my God, all I could do was stand there and wring my hands! All that good soil came rushing down the hill and into the hut. And all my good, fine seeds! O Jesus, Jesus, I screamed out at the clouds, and for eight days I cried until I almost couldn't see the road anymore. And afterwards I had to lug eighty heavy loads of soil back up the mountain.

PEASANT [*roughly*]. You sure do know how to send up a terrible complaint here. What heaven sends us, we got to take. And then if things don't go well, whose fault is it but your own? What did you do when business was good? Gambled it all away and drank it up. If you'd saved something then, you'd have something to fall back on now, instead of stealing yarn and wood.

FIRST YOUNG WEAVER [*with some of his comrades in the hallway, talks loudly through the doorway*]. A peasant's a peasant even if he sleeps till nine!

FIRST OLD WEAVER. That's just the way it is: a peasant and a nobleman, they pull at the same rope. When the weaver needs a place to live, the peasant says to him: I'll give you a little hole to live in, and you'll pay me a nice rent and help me get in my hay and my grain; and if you don't want to, you'll see where you'll land. And then you go to another one and he says the same thing.

OLD BAUMERT [*enraged*]. A weaver's like an apple that everybody takes his bite out of.

PEASANT [*flaring up*]. Oh, you poor hungry bastards, what are you good for anyway? Can you force a plow into the soil? Can you plow a straight furrow? Or toss a bundle of oats onto the wagon? You're good for nothing but being lazy and laying with your women! You dirty bastards, what help are you? [*He has paid and now goes off. The* FORESTER, *laughing, follows him.*]

[WELZEL, *the joiner, and* FRAU WELZEL *laugh loudly;* SALES-
MAN *laughs to himself. When the laughter dies down there
is a moment of silence.*]

HORNIG. A peasant like that is as dumb as his own ox. Talking
like he didn't know there was any misery here. What don't
a person see in these villages around here? I seen four, five
people lay naked on one sack of straw.

SALESMAN [*in a mildly reproving tone of voice*]. If you'll
permit me, my good man, there is some divided opinion
about the misery in these mountains, if you can read . . .

HORNIG. Oh, I can read straight on down the page, just as good
as you. No, no, I know what I've seen. I've been around
enough with these people. When a man's had a draw-rope
around his shoulders for forty years, he knows what's going
on. What happened to Fuller? His children played around
with the neighbor's geese in dung heaps. They died, those
people, naked, on the flagstones in their house. They was
so hungry they ate that stinking weaver's glue in fear of
death. Death took them off by the hundreds.

SALESMAN. If you can read, as you say, then you must know
that the government has investigated the matter and that . . .

HORNIG. Yes, we know, we know: A man comes from the
government who knows all about it better than if he'd seen
it. He wanders about a bit in the village, down there by
the brook, where the nicest houses are. Why should he
dirty his nice polished boots? And then he thinks: well, the
rest of the place must look as good as this, and climbs back
in his carriage and rides on home. And then he writes to
Berlin that there was no poverty here. But if he'd had a
little more patience and climbed up higher in the village
where the brook comes in, or across the brook on the
narrow side, or even off the road, where the little single
shacks are, the old thatch huts on the side of the hill that
are so black, so dirty and broken down sometimes that it's
not even worth a match to set them on fire—maybe then
he'd have something to write about to Berlin. It's to me
they should have come, these government gentlemen who
wouldn't believe there was any need here. I'd have showed
them something. I'd have opened their eyes for them in
these starvation pits.

[*The weaver's song is heard from outside.*]

WELZEL. They're singing the devil's song again.

WIEGAND. They're turning the whole village upside down.

FRAU WELZEL. It's like there was something in the air.

[JAEGER and BAECKER, arm in arm, at the head of a group of YOUNG WEAVERS, enter the hallway noisily and go into the taproom.]

JAEGER. Squadron, halt! Dismount!

[The new arrivals take places at the various tables at which weavers are already seated, and engage them in conversation.]

HORNIG [calls out to BAECKER]. What does this mean, your running around in a mob like this?

BAECKER [significantly]. Who knows, maybe something might happen, Right, Moritz?

HORNIG. Wouldn't that be something! Don't get yourself into trouble.

BAECKER. There's already been some blood spilt. Want to see it? [He pulls up his sleeve and shows bloody tattoo marks on his bare upper arm. As he does so, the young weavers at the other tables do the same.] We've been to Barber Schmidt's to get tattooed.

HORNIG. I see now. No wonder there's such an uproar in the streets, with louts like you babbling all over the village.

JAEGER [swaggeringly, in a loud voice]. Two quarts here, Welzel! I'll pay, You think maybe I ain't got enough to pay? Wait and see! If we wanted to we could sit here drinking schnapps and sipping coffee till tomorrow morning, just like any traveling salesman.

[Some of the young weavers laugh.]

SALESMAN [with comic surprise]. Are you referring to me?

[The innkeeper, his wife, and her daughter, the joiner WIEGAND, and the TRAVELING SALESMAN laugh.]

JAEGER. If the cap fits, wear it.

SALESMAN. If I may say so, young man, your business seems to be going quite well.

JAEGER. No complaints. I travel around selling ready-to-wear goods. I go in halves with the manufacturers. The hungrier the weaver is, the better I eat. The more they need, the better I feed.

BAECKER. Well said, Moritz! Well said!

WELZEL [*has brought the corn schnapps; on his way back to the bar he stops and slowly turns himself, with all the power of his nature and bulk, to face the weavers again; calmly, but emphatically*]. You will let the gentleman alone, he's done nothing to you.

VOICES OF THE YOUNG WEAVERS. Who's hurting him?

[FRAU WELZEL *has exchanged some words with the* SALESMAN; *she lifts his coffee cup with the remainder of the coffee and takes it into the next room. The* SALESMAN *follows her as the weavers laugh.*]

VOICES OF THE YOUNG WEAVERS [*singing*].

> Our hangmen are the Dreissigers,
> Their servants are their henchmen . . .

WELZEL. Psst! Quiet! You can sing that song wherever you want, but not in *my* house!

FIRST OLD WEAVER. He's right, you stop singing.

BAECKER [*shouts*]. But we're going to pass by Dreissiger's once more, we want to make sure *he* hears the song again.

WIEGAND. You better not go too far so that he takes it all wrong!

[*Laughter and cries of "Ho-ho!"* OLD WITTIG, *a grey-haired old smith, enters. He has on a leather apron and wooden shoes, and is sooty as though he had just come from his workshop. He waits, standing at the bar, for a glass of brandy.*]

OLD WITTIG. Let them do what they want. Dogs that bark, don't bite.

VOICES OF THE OLD WEAVERS. Wittig! Wittig!

WITTIG. Here's Wittig. What do you want with him?

VOICES OF THE OLD WEAVERS. Wittig's here—Wittig, Wittig— Come over here, Wittig, sit down with us!—Come over here, Wittig!

WITTIG. I better be careful sitting with rascals like you.

JAEGER. Come on, have a drink with us.

WITTIG. You can keep your brandy. When I drink I pay by myself. [*He takes his schnapps glass and sits with* BAUMERT *and* ANSORGE. *Tapping* ANSORGE *on the belly.*] What do you weavers use for food, sauerkraut and louse meat?

OLD BAUMERT [*ecstatically*]. And what would you say if we're not happy with that no more?

WITTIG [*stares dumbly at the weavers, with affected surprise*]. No, no, no, don't tell me it's you, Heinerle! [*Bursts out into laughter.*] Lord in Heaven, I could die laughing! Old Baumert wants rebellion. That really does it: next it'll be the tailor's turn, and then the baa-baa sheep will want a rebellion and then the mice and the rats. My God if that ain't going to be a fine dance! [*Almost helpless with laughter.*]

OLD BAUMERT. I'm no different now than I ever was, Wittig, and I still say it'd be better if it worked out peaceable.

WITTIG. It'll work out, the dirty way, but not peaceable. What was ever worked out peaceable? Did they work it out peaceable in France? Maybe Robespierre patted the hands of the rich? What he said was: Away with them all! To the guillotine with them! That's the way it has to work, *allong sangfang*. Did you ever see a roast duck fly into your open mouth?

OLD BAUMERT. If only I could make just half a living . . .

FIRST OLD WEAVER. We're in water up to our chins already, Wittig.

SECOND OLD WEAVER. We almost don't want to go home again. Work or lay abed, you starve both ways.

FIRST OLD WEAVER. At home a man's like to go mad.

ANSORGE. It's all the same to me. It'll come one way or the other.

VOICES OF THE OLD WEAVERS [*with mounting excitement*]. No peace anywhere anymore.—No spirit left to work.—Up there by us in Steinkunzendorf there's a man who sits beside the book the whole day and washes himself, naked as the Lord God made him. It's made him lose his senses.

THIRD OLD WEAVER [*raises himself up, moved by the Spirit, and begins to talk with "tongues," raising his finger threateningly*]. A judgment is nigh. Forsake your dealings with the rich and the great. A judgment is nigh. The Lord God of Sabaoth . . .

[*A number of the weavers laugh; he is pushed back into his seat.*]

WELZEL. He can't even drink a little glass without going out of his head.

THIRD OLD WEAVER [*jumps up again*]. Alas, they believe not in God, nor in heaven nor hell. Religion is a mockery . . .

FIRST OLD WEAVER. Let that be enough!

BAECKER. You let the man pray his sermon. There might be
    somebody who could take it to heart!

MANY VOICES [*tumultuously*]. Let him speak!—Let him!

THIRD OLD WEAVER [*with his voice raised*]. And therefore hell
    opened wide its soul, and its jaws gaped without measure,
    so that all who bend the right of the poor, and use force
    upon them in misery, might descend into it—thus speaks
    the Lord.

[*A great commotion.*]

THIRD OLD WEAVER [*suddenly declaims in schoolboy fashion*].

    If one regard it well
    How strange it is to tell
    Why anyone should scorn the linen weaver's ware.

BAECKER. But we're only fustian weavers.

[*Laughter.*]

HORNIG. Linen weavers are even more miserable. They wander
    about in the hills like ghosts. You people here still have
    enough nerve to talk back.

WITTIG. You think maybe the worst is over for us here? The
    little bit of strength they still got left in their bodies the
    factory owners will beat out of them soon enough.

BAECKER. He even said it: Before I'm through with these
    weavers they'll work for a crust of bread.

[*A great commotion.*]

VARIOUS OLD AND YOUNG WEAVERS. Who said that?

BAECKER. That's what Dreissiger said about the weavers.

A YOUNG WEAVER. We ought to sling the filthy bastard up by
    his ass!

JAEGER. Listen here, Wittig, you're always the one telling us
    about the French Revolution. You always had a lot to say.
    Well, maybe a time's coming soon when a man can show
    himself for what he is: a big-mouth or an honest man.

WITTIG [*infuriated*]. You say just one more thing! Have you
    heard the whistle of bullets? Have you ever stood guard in
    an enemy country?

JAEGER. I never said you were a bad one. We're friends, aren't
    we? I didn't mean anything bad by that.

WITTIG. I don't give a damn for your friendship, you bloated oaf!

[POLICEMAN KUTSCHE *enters.*]

A NUMBER OF VOICES. Shhh! Shhh! The police!

[*There is a sound of hissing which continues for an extremely long time, until finally there is complete silence.*]

KUTSCHE [*who takes a place at the center column, while the others maintain a deep silence*]. A small brandy, please.

[*Silence again.*]

WITTIG. Well, Kutsche, you've come to see that everything's all right with us here?

KUTSCHE [*without listening to* WITTIG]. Good morning, Master Wiegand!

WIEGAND [*still in the corner in front of the bar*]. Thank you, Kutsche.

KUTSCHE. How's business?

WIEGAND. Thanks for asking.

BAECKER. The Superintendent's afraid we're ruining our stomachs with all the pay we're getting.

[*Laughter.*]

JAEGER. Isn't it right, Welzel, we've been sitting here eating roast pork, and sauce, and dumplings, and sauerkraut, and now we've settled back for some champagne.

[*Laughter.*]

WELZEL. Your world's upside down today, eh?

KUTSCHE. And even if you had champagne and roast pork I still wouldn't be satisfied. I don't have champagne either and still I have to get on.

BAECKER [*with reference to* KUTSCHE's *nose*]. He waters that beet-red pickle of his with brandy and beer, that's why it's so ripe.

[*Laughter.*]

WITTIG. It's a hard life for a policeman like him: one time he has to lock up a starving beggar boy, another time he has to lead a pretty young weaver girl astray; then he's got to get stone drunk so he can beat his wife up, so that she can go running to the neighbor's in mortal terror; and then he has to ride around on horseback, lay in bed until nine. I tell you, it's not easy!

KUTSCHE. Talk all you want! Sooner or later you'll talk a rope around your neck. We already know what kind *you* are. Even the magistrate knows that seditious tongue of yours. I know someone who'd bring his wife and child to the poorhouse with his drinking and squatting in the village tavern, and get himself into jail. He'll keep on agitating and agitating until he ends up with what he deserves.

WITTIG [*laughs bitterly*]. Who knows what's to come? You may be right about that last bit. [*Bursting out even more furiously.*] But if it ever comes to that, I know who I've got to thank for it, who blabbed to the factory owners and to the lords, who shamed me and blackened my character, so that I can't get work anywhere—who turned the peasants against me and the millers, so that all week long I don't have a single horse to shoe, or a wheel to fix. I know who it is. Once I pulled this miserable beast off his horse because he was beating a poor dumb boy with a horsewhip, for stealing a few unripe pears. But let me tell you this, and you know me, if you ever get me in jail, you'd better write up your will. And if ever I hear even a whisper of it, I'll take up anything I can get, whether it's a horseshoe or a hammer, the spoke of a wheel or a water bucket, and I'll search you out, even if I have to pull you out of bed from next to your wife, and I'll beat your skull in, just as sure as my name is Wittig. [*He has jumped up and wants to attack* KUTSCHE.]

OLD AND YOUNG WEAVERS [*holding him back*]. Be reasonable, Wittig, be reasonable!

[KUTSCHE *has risen involuntarily; his face is pale.*]

KUTSCHE [*retreating during the following. The nearer he gets to the door the braver he becomes. His last words are spoken on the threshold, so as to be able to disappear immediately thereafter*]. What do you want from me? I never had anything to do with you. I never hurt you. I've got no business with you. What I came to say was to you weavers: the Superintendent of Police forbids you to sing that song, the *Dreissiger Song*, or whatever you call it. And if it doesn't stop in the streets at once, he'll take pains to give

you ample time and leisure for it in jail. You can sing there
on water and bread as long as you like. [*He goes off.*]

WITTIG [*shouts after him*]. He can't forbid us a damned thing!
And if we shout it till the windows shake, and they hear us
in Reichenbach, and if we sing until all the factory owners'
houses tumble down on their heads, and the helmets of the
superintendents dance around on their skulls, that's nobody's business but ours.

[BAECKER *has risen in the meanwhile, given the sign to sing,
and begins himself as they all join in.*]

> A bloody justice rages here,
> A law that's worse than lynching,
> Where courtroom trials are not the rule,
> To kill us without flinching.

[*The inkeeper attempts to keep them quiet, but they pay no
attention to him.* WIEGAND *covers his ears and runs away.
The weavers rise and while the following verses of the song
are sung, follow* WITTIG *and* BAECKER *who by means of
nods, etc., have given signs to break up.*]

> A man is slowly tortured here,
> A man is tortured long,
> His sighs are counted as the proof
> Of his affliction's song.

[*The greater number of the weavers sing the following verses
on the street; only a few of the younger men are still inside
the tavern paying. At the end of the next line the room is
empty except for* WELZEL, *his wife, his daughter,* HORNIG
and OLD BAUMERT.]

> You scoundrels all, you brood of hell,
> You demons of the fire,
> You eat the poor from house and home——
> May curses be your hire.

WELZEL [*calmly gathers the glasses together*]. They've sure
gone wild today.

[OLD BAUMERT *is about to leave.*]

HORNIG. What in God's name are they up to now, Baumert?
OLD BAUMERT. They're on their way to Dreissiger's to see that
he adds something to their wages.

WELZEL. Do you go along with all this crazy goings on?

OLD BAUMERT. It's like this, Welzel, I can't help it. Sometimes a young man *can* go, but an old man *must*. [*He goes off somewhat embarrassed.*]

HORNIG [*rises*]. It'll surprise me if this don't turn out bad.

WELZEL. Even these old ones are losing their heads!

HORNIG. Well, everybody's got a dream.

ACT FOUR

[*Peterswaldau.—A private room in the house of* DREISSIGER, *the textile manufacturer. It is a room luxuriously decorated in the frosty taste of the first half of the century. The ceiling, stove and doors are white; the wallpaper is of a cold lead-grey tone, with straight rows of small flowers on it. The furniture is of mahogany and upholstered in red, carved and richly decorated; the cupboard and chairs are of the same material. To the right, between two windows with cherry-red damask curtains, stands the secretary with a drop front; on the wall directly opposite it is the sofa, not far from the iron safe; in front of the sofa are table, easy-chairs and other chairs. A gun cabinet stands at the back wall. All the walls are partially hidden by bad pictures in gold frames. Above the sofa hangs a mirror with a sturdy, gilt, rococo frame around it. A single door, left, leads into the hallway, an open double door in the rear wall leads into a salon, decorated in the same uncomfortable splendor. There are two women in the salon,* FRAU DREISSIGER *and* FRAU PASTOR KITTELHAUS, *busy looking at pictures. In addition,* PASTOR KITTELHAUS *is in conversation with* WEINHOLD, *the tutor and theology student.*]

KITTELHAUS [*a small, friendly little man, enters into the front room with the tutor, both of them smoking and talking pleasantly; he looks around and finding no one there shakes his head in surprise.*] There's nothing at all surprising about it, Herr Weinhold; the fact is you are still young. When we old folks were your age—I don't mean to say we had the same ideas, but similar ones. Yes, by all means similar. And then there's always something nice about youth—all those wonderful ideals. But, alas, they are fleeting, fleeting as the April sunshine. Wait till you get to be my age! When for thirty years a man has had his say from the pulpit fifty-two times a year, not counting saints' days, then he must of necessity become more calm. Think of me sometimes, Herr Weinhold, when you have come as far as I.

WEINHOLD [*nineteen years of age, pale, thin, tall, with simple long blond hair. His movements are very restless and nerv-*

ous]. With all due respect, Herr Pastor . . . I simply don't know . . . After all, there is a great diversity in our natures.

KITTELHAUS. My dear Herr Weinhold, however restless an individual you may be—[*in a tone of reproof*]—and you are exactly that—however violently and unrestrainedly you may attack existing conditions, you will calm down in the end. Oh, yes, I quite admit that among our brethren in office there are individuals of advanced age who still play youthful pranks. One preaches against the evils of drinking, and founds temperance societies; the other composes proclamations which make undeniably gripping reading, but what good are they? They do not lessen the distress among the weavers, wherever it may exist, whereas social freedom is undermined. No, no, in cases of this sort one would really rather say: cobbler, stick to your last! And you who are keeper of souls, do not become keeper of bellies! Preach the pure Word of God, and leave the rest to Him Who provides shelter and food for the birds and will not suffer the lily of the field to perish.—But now I should like to know what has happened to our good host. He has disappeared so suddenly.

[FRAU DREISSIGER *enters the front room now with* FRAU KITTELHAUS. *She is in her thirties, a pretty woman of a healthy, robust sort. A certain discrepancy between her manner of speaking, or the way in which she moves, and her elegant, rich way of dressing is obvious.*]

FRAU DREISSIGER. You're quite right, Herr Kittelhaus, Wilhelm does this all the time. Whenever he gets an idea he runs away and lets me sit here. I've said enough about it already, but what good does it do?

KITTELHAUS. My dear, good woman, that's why he is a business man.

WEINHOLD. Unless I'm mistaken something's happened downstairs.

DREISSIGER [*enters; hot, excited*]. Well, Rosa, have you served the coffee?

FRAU DREISSIGER [*sulking*]. Why must you always run off?

DREISSIGER [*lightly*]. Oh, you wouldn't understand!

KITTELHAUS. I beg your pardon, Herr Dreissiger, but have you had any trouble?

DREISSIGER. I have trouble every day that the Good Lord lets be, my good Herr Kittelhaus. I'm used to it. Well, Rosa! Are you taking care of it?

[FRAU DREISSIGER *walks ill-humoredly to the wide, embroidered bell-pull, and tugs violently at it several times.*]

DREISSIGER. I wish—[*after a few strides*]—Herr Weinhold, that you had been along just now. You would really have seen something. And besides . . . But come, what do you say to a game of whist?

KITTELHAUS. Why, of course, Herr Dreissiger, of course! Shake the dust and burden of the day from your shoulders, and join the company!

DREISSIGER [*has walked to a window, pulls aside one of the curtains; involuntarily*]. Hoodlums!—Come here, Rosa!

[*She goes to him.*]

Do you see that tall red-haired man over there?

KITTELHAUS. They call him Red Baecker.

DREISSIGER. Tell me, is that the same man who insulted you the day before yesterday? You remember what you told me about when Johann was helping you into the carriage?

FRAU DREISSIGER [*pouts*]. I don't remember.

DREISSIGER. Will you stop sulking! I must know. I've had enough of his impudence. If he's the one, then I will make him answer for it.

[*The weavers' song is heard.*]

Will you listen to that, will you listen!

KITTELHAUS [*extremely angry*]. When will this nonsense stop! I must confess I think it is time the police step in. If you please. [*He goes to the window.*] Do you see, Herr Weinhold! Those aren't merely young people out there, there are old, steady, weavers out there, too, who for many years I have thought to be respectable, God-fearing men. And there they are. There they are, taking part in this unheard-of nonsense. They are trampling God's law under foot. Do you still insist on defending these people?

WEINHOLD. Certainly not, Herr Kittelhaus. That is, Herr Kittelhaus, *cum grano salis*. They are nothing but hungry, ignorant people. They are expressing their dissatisfaction in the only way they know. I couldn't possibly expect that such people . . .

FRAU KITTELHAUS [*small, thin, faded, looks more like an old maid than an aging wife*]. Herr Weinhold, Herr Weinhold, how *can* you!

DREISSIGER. Herr Weinhold, I'm terribly sorry . . . I did not take you into my house so that you could lecture me on humanitarianism. I must ask that you confine yourself to educating my sons, and to leave my own affairs entirely to me! Do you understand?

WEINHOLD [*stands rigid and white as death for a moment, then bows with a forced smile; softly*]. Of course, of course, I quite understand. I saw this coming; it is my wish as well.

[*He goes off.*]

DREISSIGER [*brutally*]. Then see to it as soon as possible, we need the room.

FRAU DREISSIGER. But, Wilhelm, Wilhelm!

DREISSIGER. Have you lost your senses? Would you protect a man who would stand up in defence of such vulgar, villainous libel as this song?

FRAU DREISSIGER. But, Wilhelm, he didn't, he didn't at all, he didn't . . .

DREISSIGER. Herr Kittelhaus, did he defend it or did he not defend it?

KITTELHAUS. Herr Dreissiger, you must consider his youth.

FRAU KITTELHAUS. I just don't understand, that young man comes from such a good, respectable family. His father held public office for forty years and was never guilty of the slightest misdemeanor. His mother was overjoyed when he found such a wonderful position here. But now, now he hasn't the least idea how to make the most of it.

PFEIFER [*tears open the hall door and shouts into the room*]. Herr Dreissiger, Herr Dreissiger! They've caught him.

DREISSIGER [*hastily*]. Did someone go for the police?

PFEIFER. The Superintendent is coming up the stairs now.

DREISSIGER [*in the doorway*]. Your servant, sir! I am happy that you have come.

[KITTELHAUS *indicates to the women through gestures that it were better if they retire. He, his wife, and* FRAU DREISSIGER *go into the salon.*]

DREISSIGER [*in extreme excitement to the* POLICE SUPERINTENDENT *who in the meanwhile has entered*]. Sir, I have finally had one of the chief singers of this mob taken captive by my dye-workers. I could stand it no longer. Their impudence simply knows no bounds. It's disgraceful. I have guests in my house and these scoundrels have the nerve to . . . They insult my wife whenever she goes out; my sons' lives are not safe. I risk having my guests pummeled about. I assure you that if it is possible in a well-ordered community for unoffending people like myself and my family to be publicly put to ridicule time and again . . . well then . . . then I must regret to having different ideas about law and morality.

SUPERINTENDENT [*a man of about fifty, of medium height, fat, with high blood pressure. He wears a cavalry uniform with a long sabre and spurs*]. Certainly not . . . No certainly not, Herr Dreissiger! I am completely at your disposal. You may rest at ease, I am completely at your disposal. Everything is quite in order . . . In fact I'm delighted that you've caught one of the chief troublemakers. I'm pleased that this matter is finally coming to a head. There are a few disturbers of the peace around here on whom I've had my eye for a long time.

DREISSIGER. A few young brats, that's right, a lazy rabble of louts afraid to work, that lead disgusting lives, and hang around day after day in the taverns until they've drunk down their last pfennig. But I am determined once and for all to put an end to the trade of these professional foulmouths. It is in the public interest, not merely in my interest.

SUPERINTENDENT. No doubt about it! No doubt about it, Herr Dreissiger. No one could possibly blame you. And whatever lies in my power . . .

DREISSIGER. This pack of louts should be gone after with a bullwhip.

SUPERINTENDENT. Quite right, quite right. We must make an example of them.

[KUTSCHE *enters and stands at attention. With the door to the hallway open, the sound of heavy footsteps coming up the stairs is heard.*]

KUTSCHE. I wish to report, sir, that we've taken one of the men.

DREISSIGER. Would you care to see this man, sir?

SUPERINTENDENT. Why, certainly, certainly. First of all we

must see him at close range. Would you oblige me, Herr
Dreissiger, and not speak to him just at first. I assure you
every satisfaction, or my name is not Heide.

DREISSIGER. I cannot be satisfied with that, the man must be
turned over to the magistrate without fail.

[JAEGER *is led in by five of the dye-workers whose faces,
hands, and clothes are covered with dye, having come
directly from work. The prisoner, his cap set cockily on
his head, behaves with impudent gaiety and finds himself,
as a result of his earlier consumption of liquor, in high
spirits.*]

JAEGER. Oh, you poor sons-of-bitches! You call yourselves
workers, you call yourselves comrades? Before I ever did
a thing like that—before I ever took one of my fellow
workers prisoner, I'd think my hand would wilt on my arm
first!

[*At a sign from the* SUPERINTENDENT, KUTSCHE *signifies to
the dye-workers that they take their hands from the captive.*
JAEGER *stands there free and impudent, while around him
all doors are being guarded.*]

SUPERINTENDENT [*shouts at* JAEGER]. Off with your hat, you
lout!

[JAEGER *removes his cap, but very slowly, without relinquish-
ing his ironic smile.*]

SUPERINTENDENT. What's your name?
JAEGER. What do you think I am, your swineherd?

[*His words create a great commotion among those present.*]

DREISSIGER. Who does he think he is!
SUPERINTENDENT [*changes color, is about to blow up, but
controls his rage*]. We'll see about that! I asked you what
your name is! [*Since he receives no answer, wildly.*] Answer
me or you will get twenty-five lashes!
JAEGER [*with absolute cheerfulness, and without so much as
batting an eyelid at the fury of words, calls over the heads
of those present to a pretty servant girl who, about to serve
coffee, stands wide-eyed looking at the unexpected scene*].
Well, ironing-board Emily, what are you doing with this
crowd? You better get out of here quick; a wind might come
up and blow everything away over night.

[*The girl stares at* JAEGER, *and as soon as she is aware that it is she who is being spoken to, she grows red with embarrassment, covers her face with her hands and runs out, leaving the dishes behind her just as they are.*]

SUPERINTENDENT [*almost beside himself, to* DREISSIGER]. I have never in my life come across such unheard of impudence in . . .

[JAEGER *spits on the floor.*]

DREISSIGER. May I remind you that this is not a stable!

SUPERINTENDENT. I have reached the end of my patience. Now for the last time: what is your name?

[KITTELHAUS *has during the last scene looked through the slightly open door to the salon and listened; he comes forward now, shaking with excitement, to intervene, unable to restrain himself any longer.*]

KITTELHAUS. His name is Jaeger, Herr Superintendent. Moritz. Right? Moritz Jaeger. [*To* JAEGER.] Well, say something, Jaeger, don't you remember me?

JAEGER [*seriously*]. You are Pastor Kittelhaus.

KITTELHAUS. Yes, Jaeger, the keeper of your soul! The same one who accepted you into the Community of Saints when you were but a babe in swaddling clothes. The same one out of whose hands you first received the Lord's Supper. Do you still remember? I took every pain to bring home the Word of God to your soul. Is this the thanks I have?

JAEGER [*darkly, like a humiliated schoolboy*]. I put a thaler in the plate.

KITTELHAUS. Money, money . . . Do you perhaps believe that that filthy, miserable piece of money . . . Keep your money, I prefer it that way. What nonsense! Be good. Be a Christian! Think of what you once promised. Keep the Lord's Commandments, be good and be pious. Money, money . . .

JAEGER. I'm a Quaker, Herr Kittelhaus, I don't believe in anything anymore.

KITTELHAUS. Quaker! What are you talking about! See to it that you better yourself, and forget these words that you know nothing about! The Quakers are pious people, not heathens like you. Quaker! Quaker!

SUPERINTENDENT. With your permission, Herr Kittelhaus. [*He steps between him and* JAEGER.] Kutsche, bind his hands!

VOICES FROM OUTSIDE [*yelling wildly*]. Jaeger! Jaeger! Come out!

DREISSIGER [*slightly frightened like the others present, steps automatically to the window*]. What's the meaning of this?

SUPERINTENDENT. Oh, I understand all right. It means they want this scoundrel outside again. But I'm afraid we can't do them the favor. Do you understand, Kutsche? He goes to jail.

KUTSCHE [*the rope in his hand, hesitant*]. With all due respect, sir, we may have some trouble. That's a damned big crowd down there. A regular band of devils. There's Baecker, and there's the smith . . .

KITTELHAUS. With your permission—so as not to incense them any more, would it not be better, Herr Superintendent, if we tried to do this peaceably. Perhaps Jaeger will promise to come along quietly, or . . .

SUPERINTENDENT. Do you know what you are saying! He's my responsibility! I couldn't possibly allow such a thing. Come on, Kutsche, don't waste time!

JAEGER [*puts his hands together and holds them out, laughing*]. Tighter, tighter, tight as you can. It won't be for long.

[KUTSCHE *binds him with the help of his men.*]

SUPERINTENDENT. All right now, off with you, march! [*To* DREISSIGER.] If you're worried about him escaping, let six of your dye-workers go along. They can form a guard around him. I'll ride in front and Kutsche will follow. And if anyone gets in the way he'll be beaten down.

VOICES FROM BELOW [*shouting*]. Cockadoodledo! Bowwow-wow!

SUPERINTENDENT [*threateningly toward the window*]. Rabble! I'll cockadoodle and bowwow you! Now march! [*He strides out ahead of them with sabre drawn. The others follow with* JAEGER.]

JAEGER [*shouts as he goes off*]. Let her highness Frau Dreissiger act as proud as she wants, but she's no better than us. There's hundreds of times she served my father three pfennigs of schnapps. Squadron, left. March! [*He goes off laughing.*]

DREISSIGER [*after a pause, seemingly calm*]. Well, what do you think, Herr Kittelhaus! Shall we have a game of whist? I think there's nothing to prevent us now. [*He lights a cigar, emitting short laughs as he does so; as soon as it is lighted he laughs loudly.*] I'm beginning to see the thing as quite amusing. That scoundrel! [*In a nervous burst of laughter.*] It's incredibly ludicrous. First the row at table with Weinhold—then five minutes later he takes his leave, wherever that may be! Then *this* business. And now we'll have a game of whist.

KITTELHAUS. Yes, but . . .

[*Roaring is heard from downstairs.*]

Yes, but . . . That crowd is making a terrible noise down there.

DREISSIGER. Then let's retire to another room. We won't be disturbed there.

KITTELHAUS [*shaking his head*]. If only I knew what has got into these people. I must agree with Herr Weinhold, at least until quite recently I was of the opinion that these weavers were a humble, patient, and easily handled class. Wouldn't you say so, Herr Dreissiger?

DREISSIGER. Of course they were once patient and easily handled; of course they were once well mannered and orderly. At least as long as these humanitarians left them alone. These people have had it made clear enough to them for a long time in what terrible misery they find themselves. Just think of it: all those societies and committees for the relief of distress among the weavers. Finally the weaver believes it himself, and now they've all gone out of their minds. Now let one of them come back and set their heads straight again. Now that they're started they grumble at everything. They don't like this and they don't like that. Now they want nothing but the best.

[*Suddenly a loud, swelling cry of "Hurray!" is heard from the crowd.*]

KITTELHAUS. And so with all their humanitarianism all they've succeeded in doing is making wolves out of lambs.

DREISSIGER. I wouldn't say that, Herr Kittelhaus. If you look at the matter with calm understanding, something good might come of it even yet. Perhaps such occurrences as this will not go unnoticed in leading circles. It is possible they will be convinced that this can go on no longer, that something must happen, unless our local industry is to be completely ruined.

KITTELHAUS. Tell me then, what is the cause of this enormous depression?

DREISSIGER. Foreign markets have barricaded themselves from us through high import duty. We lose our best markets there, and here at home we have to fight all kinds of competition. We're being abandoned, completely abandoned.

PFEIFER [*totters in, pale and breathless*]. Herr Dreissiger, Herr Dreissiger!

DREISSIGER [*already in the doorway to the salon and about to leave, turns, irritated*]. Well, what is it now, Pfeifer?

PFEIFER. No, no . . . leave me alone!

DREISSIGER. What's the matter?

KITTELHAUS. You're frightening us. Say something.

PFEIFER [*not yet recovered*]. No, leave me alone! I never saw anything like it! The Superintendent . . . they really got themselves into it this time.

DREISSIGER. For God's sake, man, what is it? Has someone broken his neck?

PFEIFER [*almost crying with fear, cries out*]. They've set Moritz Jaeger free. They thrashed the Superintendent and chased him off, and then they thrashed the policeman and chased him off. Without his helmet . . . his sabre broken . . . No, no!

DREISSIGER. Pfeifer, you've gone mad!

KITTELHAUS. This could mean revolution.

PFEIFER [*sitting in a chair, his whole body trembling, whimpering*]. It's serious Herr Dreissiger, it's serious!

DREISSIGER. That whole damned police force can go and . . .

PFEIFER. It's serious, Herr Dreissiger!

DREISSIGER. Oh, shut your mouth, Pfeifer! For God's sake!

FRAU DREISSIGER [*enters from the salon with* FRAU KITTELHAUS]. This is disgraceful, Wilhelm. Our whole evening has been ruined. Frau Kittelhaus just said she thought that she'd rather go home.

KITTELHAUS. My dear Frau Dreissiger, perhaps it is the best solution for right now . . .

FRAU DREISSIGER. But, Wilhelm, why don't you do something really drastic about it?

DREISSIGER. Go on and try! Go on! Go on! [*Standing helplessly in front of the* PASTOR.] Am I a tyrant? Am I a slave driver?

JOHANN, THE COACHMAN [*enters*]. Ma'am, I've got the carriage ready. Herr Weinhold's already put Jorgel and Karlchen in the wagon. If it gets much worse, we can leave.

FRAU DREISSIGER. What's there to get worse?

JOHANN. Well, I don't know, ma'am. I just thought I'd tell you. There are more people coming all the time. They already ran off the Superintendent and the policeman.

PFEIFER. It's serious, Herr Dreissiger, it's serious!

FRAU DREISSIGER [*with mounting fear*]. What's going to happen? What do these people want? Surely they can't attack us, Johann.

JOHANN. There are some awful rough ones down there, ma'am.

PFEIFER. It's serious, it's serious.

DREISSIGER. Shut up, you fool! Are the doors barred?

KITTELHAUS. Do me one favor . . . do me this favor . . . I've come to a decision . . . just one favor . . . [*To* JOHANN.] What do the people want?

JOHANN [*embarrassed*]. They want more pay, the crazy bastards.

KITTELHAUS. Very well!—I shall go out and do my duty. I shall speak seriously with these people.

JOHANN. But, Herr Kittelhaus, Herr Kittelhaus, you mustn't! They won't listen to words.

KITTELHAUS. My dear Herr Dreissiger, one word more. I should like to ask you to station some people behind the door, and as soon as I have gone out, to close it behind me.

FRAU KITTELHAUS. Joseph, you're not really going to do it.

KITTELHAUS. I am. I am. I know what I am doing. Have no fear, the Lord will protect me.

[FRAU KITTELHAUS *presses his hand in hers, steps back and wipes tears from her eyes.*]

KITTELHAUS [*while the incessant dull rumbling of a great mob of people forces its way up from below*]. I shall pretend . . . I shall pretend that I am on my way home. I want to see whether my spiritual office . . . whether or not there is still that much respect left in these people . . . I want to see . . . [*He takes his hat and walking stick.*] I go forward in the name of God.

[*He goes off accompanied by* DREISSIGER, PFEIFER, *and* JOHANN.]

FRAU KITTELHAUS. My dear Frau Dreissiger—[*She breaks into tears and throws her arms around* FRAU DREISSIGER.]— They mustn't hurt him!

FRAU DREISSIGER [*lost in thought*]. I really don't know, Frau Kittelhaus . . . what I feel. Things like this aren't possible. If that's how it is . . . then it's just like saying it's a sin to be rich. If someone had told me all this, Frau Kittelhaus, I don't know but I would rather have remained with the little I had at first.

FRAU KITTELHAUS. My dear Frau Dreissiger, there are troubles and disappointments in every way of life.

FRAU DREISSIGER. Of course, of course, that's what I tell myself, too. And just because we have more than other people . . . Lord only knows we didn't steal it. We came by every pfennig honestly. Such things are simply not possible, that people come and attack you. Is it my husband's fault if business is bad?

[*A tumultuous roaring is heard from below. While the two women still look at one another, pale and frightened,* DREISSIGER *rushes into the room.*]

DREISSIGER. Quick, Rosa, throw something over your shoulders and get into the carriage; I'll be right there! [*He rushes toward the safe, opens it and removes various valuable articles.*]

JOHANN [*entering*]. Everything's ready! But hurry before they take the back door, too!

FRAU DREISSIGER [*in panicked fright, throws her arms around the coachman*]. Dear, dear Johann! Save us, dear, dear Johann! Save my boys, oh, oh . . .

DREISSIGER. Be reasonable! Let go of Johann!

JOHANN. Ma'am, ma'am! You mustn't worry. Our horses are in good shape. Nobody can overtake us. If anyone gets in my way I'll run over him. [*He goes off.*]

FRAU KITTELHAUS [*in helpless fear*]. But my husband? But . . . but my husband? But, Herr Dreissiger, my husband?

DREISSIGER. Frau Kittelhaus, Frau Kittelhaus, he's all right. You must calm yourself, he's all right.

FRAU KITTELHAUS. Something terrible has happened to him. You just won't tell me, you just won't tell me.

DREISSIGER. Oh, never mind, they'll regret it. I know exactly who's to blame. Such a nameless, shameless piece of impudence will not stay unavenged. The devil take the community that would manhandle its own pastor. Mad dogs, that's what they are, beasts gone mad, and they will be handled accordingly.

[*To* FRAU DREISSIGER *who stands there as though in a trance.*]

Go on now, move.

[*Pounding is heard against the front door.*]

Don't you hear? The rabble has lost its senses.

[*The clatter of broken glass panes on the ground floor is heard.*]

The rabble's gone mad. There's nothing we can do but get ourselves out of here.

INDIVIDUAL VOICES FROM OFFSTAGE. Bring Pfeifer out!—Bring Pfeifer out!

FRAU DREISSIGER. Pfeifer, Pfeifer, they want Pfeifer out there.

PFEIFER [*rushes in*]. Herr Dreissiger, there are people at the back door already. We can't hold the front door more than three minutes longer. Wittig's banging at it with a pail, like a madman.

VOICES FROM BELOW [*louder and clearer*]. Bring out Pfeifer! —Bring out Pfeifer!

FRAU DREISSIGER *runs off as though chased;* FRAU KITTELHAUS *follows her.* PFEIFER *listens, grows pale, understands the calling and is gripped with maddening fear. The following is spoken at a frantic pace, while he cries, whimpers, begs, and whines. He overwhelms* DREISSIGER *with childish affections, he carresses his cheeks and arms, kisses his hands, and finally clings to him like a drunken man, thereby re- straining and fettering* DREISSIGER *without letting him go.*]

PFEIFER. Dear, good, kind, Herr Dreissiger, don't leave me behind, I always served you faithfully; and I always han- dled the people good, too. I couldn't give them more wages than you'd set. Don't leave me here, they'll kill me. If they find me they'll beat me to death. My God, my God! My wife, my children . . .

DREISSIGER [*tries in vain to free himself from* PFEIFER]. At least let go of me, man! We'll see, we'll see about it.

[*He goes off with* PFEIFER. *The room is empty for several seconds. Window glass is shattered in the salon. A loud*

*crack reverberates through the house. From below there is
a roar of "Hurray!" and then silence. Several seconds pass,
then the sounds of quiet, cautious footsteps are heard on
the stairs leading to the second floor, as well as quiet, timid
exclamations.*]

VOICES. To the left!—Upstairs!—Psst!—Slowly! Slowly! Don't
slip!—Take it easy!—Damn, what's this!—Get on there!—
We're going to a wedding!—Go on in!—Go on!

[*Young weavers, both boys and girls, appear at the door to the
hallway; they dare not enter, and one tries to push the other
on into the room from behind. After a few seconds their
shyness is overcome and the poor, thin, often sickly figures
dressed in rags or mended clothes, spread themselves out
across* DREISSIGER's *room and across the salon. They are
curious at first and look shyly at things, then they touch
them. The girls try out the sofas; groups form and admire
their reflections in the mirror. Some climb up on the chairs
to look at the pictures and to take them down; in the meanwhile other miserable forms stream in from the hallway.*]

AN OLD WEAVER [*enters*]. No, no, I don't want no part of it!
They're already tearing things apart downstairs. It's all madness! There ain't no sense or reason in it. It will all turn
out a bad thing in the end. No man who's got a clear head
would do such a thing. I'll be careful and take no part in
such crime!

[JAEGER, BAECKER, WITTIG *with a wooden pail,* OLD BAUMERT,
*and a number of young and old weavers rush in as though
chasing after something, shouting to one another with hoarse
voices.*]

JAEGER. Where's he gone?
BAECKER. Where is the slave driver?
OLD BAUMERT. If we can eat grass he can eat sawdust.
WITTIG. When we catch him we'll string him up.
FIRST YOUNG WEAVER. We'll take him by the legs and throw
him out the window onto the stones, so that he'll never
get up again.
SECOND YOUNG WEAVER [*enters*]. He's gone.
ALL. Who's gone?
SECOND YOUNG WEAVER. Dreissiger.
BAECKER. Pfeifer too?

VOICES. Let's get Pfeifer! Let's get Pfeifer!

OLD BAUMERT. Come, Pfeifer, come, here's a weaver you can starve.

[*Laughter.*]

JAEGER. Even if we don't get that Dreissiger brute . . . we'll make a poor man of him.

OLD BAUMERT. We'll make him poor as a churchmouse. We'll make a poor man of him.

[*They all rush towards the salon door with the intention of demolishing it.*]

BAECKER [*runs ahead, turns around and halts the others*]. Halt, listen to me! When we've finished here we haven't even begun. From here we go to Bielau, to Dietrich's, where they've got mechanical looms. All our misery comes from these factories.

ANSORGE [*enters from the hallway. After he has entered a few steps he remains standing, looks around, bewildered, shakes his head, strikes his forehead and says*]. Who am I? A weaver, Anton Ansorge. Has he gone mad, this Ansorge? It's true, my head is going round like a wheel. What's he doing here? What he wants to do he'll do. Where is he, Ansorge? [*He strikes his forehead again.*] I've gone crazy! I'm not responsible, I'm not right in the head. Get out, get out! Get out, you rebels. Heads out, legs out, hands out! You take my shack and I'll take your shack, come on, let's go!

[*With a howl, he goes into the salon. Those present follow him with shouting and laughter.*]

ACT FIVE

[*Langenbielau.—The small weaving room of* OLD HILSE. *To the left is a small window, in front of it a loom; to the right there is a bed with a table pushed close to it. In the right corner, a stove with a bench. Sitting around the table on a footstool, on the bed and on a wooden stool are:* OLD HILSE, *his equally old, blind, and almost deaf wife* MOTHER HILSE, *his son* GOTTLIEB, *and his wife* LUISE. *They are at morning prayers. A spooling wheel with bobbins stands between the table and the loom. All kinds of spinning, spooling, and weaving implements are stored on top of the smoke-browned ceiling beams. Long strands of yarn hang down. All sorts of trash lie about in the room. In the backwall of this very narrow, low, and shallow room is a door leading into 'he hallway. Opposite this door, at the other end of the hallway, is another door which is open, and through which we can see into a second, similar weaving room. The hallway is paved with stone and the plaster is cracked; a flight of unsteady wooden stairs leads up into the attic living quarters. A washtub on a stool is partially visible; ragged pieces of clothes and the household implements of poverty stricken people lie about in disorderly fashion. The light falls from the left into all three rooms.* OLD HILSE *is a bearded, heavy-boned man, who now as a result of age, work, sickness and hardships is a bent and wasted man. A war veteran, he has only one arm. He has a pointed nose, his face is pale, he trembles, and he is obviously only skin, bones and sinews, and has the deep-set sore eyes so characteristic of the weavers. He, his son and daughter-in-law rise; he prays.*]

OLD HILSE. Dear God, we cannot thank you enough that you in your goodness and graciousness have had pity on us on this night, too. That on this night, too, we have suffered no grief. Lord, so far does your graciousness reach, and we are poor, evil, sinful children of men, not worthy that your foot should stamp us out, so sinful and all bad are we. But you, dear Father, you want to see and accept us for the sake of your dear son, Our Lord and Savior Jesus Christ. Jesus' blood and righteousness are my adornment and my clothes of honor. And if at times we are too much cast down by your chastisement—when the oven which is to purify us burns with too terrible heat—then do not take us too sorely to task, forgive us our sins. Give us patience, Heavenly Father, so that after this suffering we may be made partakers in your eternal bliss. Amen.

MOTHER HILSE [*who is bent forward, straining to hear, weeping*]. Oh, father, what a beautiful prayer you always say.

[LUISE *goes to the washtub,* GOTTLIEB *goes into the opposite room.*]

OLD HILSE. Where's the girl?

LUISE. She went over to Peterswaldau—to Dreissiger's. She spooled a few more bobbins last night.

OLD HILSE [*speaking very loudly*]. You want me to bring you your wheel now, mother?

MOTHER HILSE. Yes, father, bring it, bring it.

OLD HILSE [*setting it down in front of her*]. Oh, how I wish I could do it for you.

MOTHER HILSE. No . . . no . . . what would I ever do with all the time I'd have?

OLD HILSE. I'll wipe your fingers for you, so you won't get grease on the yarn, you hear? [*He wipes her hands with the rag.*]

LUISE [*from the washtub*]. From where would she get grease on her fingers?

OLD HILSE. When we got no grease, we eat our bread dry— when we got no bread, then we eat potatoes—and when we got no potatoes either, then we eat dry bran.

LUISE [*sneering*]. And when we've got no black flour, we'll do like that Wengler woman down below, we'll find where a skinner has buried a rotten horse. Then we'll dig it up and live off the carrion for a few weeks. That's what we'll do, ain't it?

GOTTLIEB [*from the back room*]. You sure do like to jabber!

OLD HILSE. You should watch yourself with that godless talk! [*He goes to the loom, calls.*] Will you help me, Gottlieb— there's still a few threads to pull through.

LUISE [*from the washtub*]. Gottlieb, you're to help your father.

[GOTTLIEB *enters. The old man and his son now begin the troublesome task of putting up the threads. The threads of the warp are pulled through the eyes of the comb, or shaft of the loom. They have scarcely begun when* HORNIG *appears in the hallway.*]

HORNIG [*in the doorway to the room*]. Good luck with your work!

OLD HILSE *and* GOTTLIEB. Thank you Hornig!

OLD HILSE. Tell me now, when do you ever sleep? In the daytime you make your rounds and at night you stand guard.

HORNIG. I can't sleep no more!

LUISE. Welcome, Hornig!

OLD HILSE. Well, what's the good news?

HORNIG. It's fine news, too, master. The weavers at Peterswaldau have risked the devil and chased Dreissiger and his whole family out of the place.

LUISE [*with signs of emotion*]. Hornig's lying again as sure as he's talking.

HORNIG. Not this time, ma'am, not this time—I've got some nice children's aprons in the wagon. No, no, I'm telling you the God's truth. They chased them right out. They got to Reichenbach last night. And believe it or not, they didn't want to let them stay—for fear of the weavers. So off he went again to Schweidnitz this time.

OLD HILSE [*carefully takes up the threads of the warp and brings them near the shaft, while from the other side his son uses a wire hook to pull them through one of the eyes*]. It's about time you stopped, Hornig!

HORNIG. May I never leave this room in one piece if it's not true. Why, every child knows as much.

OLD HILSE. Tell me, am I crazy, or are you?

HORNIG. What I told you is as true as the Word of God. I wouldn't say nothing about it if I hadn't seen it, but I seen it with my own eyes. With my own eyes, just the same as I see you here, Gottlieb. They tore up the factory owner's house from the cellar to the roof. They threw his china from the attic windows—right out over the roof—I wonder how many bolts of fustian are laying in the brook now? Water can't get through, you can believe it. It's running over its sides. It looked real sulfur blue from all the indigo they threw out the window. Those sky-blue clouds of dust just came floating down. Yes, they sure tore that house apart. And not just the house, the dyeworks, too, and the warehouse! The banister's knocked in pieces, the floor's torn up and mirrors shattered, sofa and chairs, everything torn

and slashed, cut and thrown, kicked and hacked to pieces
—damnation, believe me, it's worse than in wartime.

OLD HILSE. They were weavers from around here? [*He shakes
his head slowly and unbelievingly.*]

[*Curious tenants of the house have gathered at the door.*]

HORNIG. Who else would it be? I could name every one of
them. I led the Commissioner through the house. So I
talked to a lot of them. They was as friendly as ever. They
went about their business real slow, but they did it good.
The Commissioner talked to a lot of them. And they was
as humble as ever. But they wouldn't be stopped. They
hacked up beautiful pieces of furniture like they was getting
paid for it.

OLD HILSE. You took the Commissioner through the house?

HORNIG. Well, what would I be afraid of? Those people all
know me like I was a bad coin. I never have trouble with
them. We're all friends. As sure as my name's Hornig, I
went through the house. And you can believe it or not, but
it got all soft here around my heart—and I saw it happen
to the Commissioner, too—it touched him real close. And
why? You couldn't hear a single word, they did their work
so quietlike. It made a man feel downright solemn to see
those poor hungry bastards finally take their revenge.

LUISE [*with tears in her eyes, drying them with her apron*].
Yes, yes, that's what has to happen!

VOICES OF THE NEIGHBORS. There's enough slave drivers
around here, too.—There's one just across the street.—He's
got four horses and six carriages in his stables and lets his
weavers go hungry so that he can pay for it.

OLD HILSE [*still incredulous*]. Why did it start, over there?

HORNIG. Who knows, who knows? Once there's one thing and
another time another.

OLD HILSE. What do they say?

HORNIG. Well, they say Dreissiger said that if the weavers are
hungry they can eat grass. That's all I know.

[*There is a commotion among the neighbors who angrily pass
the word from one to the other.*]

OLD HILSE. You listen to me, Hornig. For all I care, you could
say to me: Father Hilse, tomorrow you're to have a visit
from the King of Prussia. But when you tell me that

weavers, men like me and my son, should have done things like that—no! No, I will never believe it.

[MIELCHEN, *a pretty girl of seven years with long, open flaxen hair, carrying a basket, comes running in. She holds out a silver spoon toward her mother.*]

MIELCHEN. Mummy, look here what I got. You can buy me a dress with this.

LUISE. Why do you come running in like that, girl? [*With increased excitement and tension.*] What's that you've got there, tell me? You're all out of breath. And the bobbins are still in your basket. What do you mean by this, girl?

OLD HILSE. Child, where did that spoon come from?

LUISE. Maybe she found it.

HORNIG. It's worth at least two or three thalers.

OLD HILSE [*beside himself*]. Get out, girl, get out! I said get out of here now! Will you behave or do I have to beat you! And you take that spoon back from where you got it. Get out! Do you want to make all of us thieves, eh? You little brat, I'll teach you to steal. [*He looks for something to strike her with.*]

MIELCHEN [*clinging to her mother's skirt, weeping*]. No, grandfather, no, don't hit me, we—we found it. All the . . . all the bobbin children have them.

LUISE [*between fear and anxiety, bursts out*]. There now, you see, she found it. Where did you find it?

MIELCHEN [*sobbing*]. We found it in Peterswaldau, in front of Dreissiger's house.

OLD HILSE. Don't make it worse. You get out of here now or I'll teach you what it means to move.

MOTHER HILSE. What's all this?

HORNIG. I'll tell you what, Father Hilse. You let Gottleib put on a coat and take that spoon over to the police station.

OLD HILSE. Gottlieb, put on a coat!

GOTTLIEB [*already putting it on, eagerly*]. I'll go to the station and say: You mustn't blame her too much, a child like her don't understand such things. And here I'm bringing the spoon. Stop crying, girl!

[*The crying child is taken by her mother into the back room, closing the door. LUISE comes back.*]

HORNIG. That's worth at least three thalers.

GOTTLIEB. Give me a cloth, Luise, to wrap this up in. My, my, what an expensive thing. [*There are tears in his eyes, while he wraps the spoon.*]

LUISE. If we kept it we could eat for a couple weeks.

OLD HILSE. Go on, go on, hurry up! As fast as you can! Wouldn't that be something! That's all I need. See that you get that devil's spoon out of my house!

[GOTTLIEB *goes off with the spoon.*]

HORNIG. Well, I'd better get on my way, too. [*He goes out, talks for a few seconds in the hallway, then goes off.*]

[SURGEON SCHMIDT, *a round, quicksilvery little man with a wine-red, cunning face, enters the hallway.*]

SCHMIDT. Good morning, people! What lovely stories I've heard here this morning. You take care! [*Threateningly with his finger.*] Pretty sly lot, that's what you are. [*In the doorway to the front room, without entering.*] Good morning, Father Hilse! [*To a woman in the hallway.*] Well now, mother, how's the pain? Better, eh? There, you see! Well, Father Hilse, I thought I'd come to see how you're getting on. What's the matter with mother?

LUISE. Doctor, the veins are dried up in her eyes, she can't see no more.

SCHMIDT. That's from the dust and from weaving by candle-light. Tell me, do you know what this is all about? All Peterswaldau is on its way here. I got into my carriage this morning like usual, thinking nothing at all was wrong, and then I started to hear such strange things. What the devil has taken hold of these people, Father Hilse? They're raging like a pack of wolves. It's a regular revolution, a rebellion; they're plundering and marauding . . . Mielchen! Where's Mielchen?

[MIELCHEN, *her eyes still red from crying, is pushed in by her mother.*]

Say, Mielchen, look into my coat pocket.

[MIELCHEN *does so.*]

The ginger snaps are for you. Now, now, not all at once. A song first though! "Fox, you have . . ." Well? "Fox, you have stolen our goose . . ." You just wait, I know what you did; you called the sparrows on the pastor's fence a dirty name because of what they do to it. And they went and told the choirmaster. What do you have to say to that?—Almost fifteen hundred people are on the march.

[*The pealing of bells in the distance.*]

Listen to that: they're sounding the alarm bell in Reichenbach. Fifteen hundred people. It's like the world was coming to an end. It makes a person uneasy!

OLD HILSE. Are they really on their way to Bielau?

SCHMIDT. Of course, of course, I just now drove through them, right through the middle of that whole mob. What I should have done was gotten down and given them all a powder. There they were, jogging along one behind the other, grey as death and singing so that it almost turned a man's stomach. It makes you want to be sick. My Frederick up in the driver's seat was wailing like an old woman. As soon as we were past them we had to go and buy us a good stiff drink. I wouldn't be a factory owner now even if I could have rubber rims on my wheels.

[*Singing in the distance.*]

Listen to that! Like somebody knocking with his knuckles on an old, cracked boiler. It won't be five minutes before they're here. Good-bye, my friends. Don't do anything foolish. Soldiers are right behind them. Don't lose your heads. These people from Peterswaldau have sure lost theirs.

[*Bells are rung close by.*]

By God, now they're ringing our bells. That'll drive them crazy for sure. [*He goes upstairs.*]

GOTTLIEB [*returns; from the hallway, out of breath*]. I saw them, I saw them. [*To a woman in the hallway.*] They're here, auntie, they're here! [*In the doorway.*] They're here, father, they're here! They've got beanpoles and stickers and axes. They're already up there at Dietrich's house, making a terrible racket. I think they're getting paid money. O Jesus, what's going to happen here! I won't look at it. I never seen so many people in all my life! Once they get started—my God, my God, our factory owners will be really hard put.

OLD HILSE. Why did you run so! You'll chase around till you get your sickness again, then you'll be flat on your back waving your arms around like before.

GOTTLIEB [*almost joyously excited*]. I had to run, or they

would have caught me. They were already screaming at me to join them. Godfather Baumert was there, too. He said to me: Go get your five groschen, too; you're one of those poor, starving weavers, too. He even said: Go tell your father . . . Father, I'm supposed to tell you to come and help pay the factory owners back for cutting our wages. [*Passionately.*] Times are changing, he said. Now things are going to be different for us weavers. He wants us to all come and help bring it about. We're all going to have our half-pound of meat on Sundays, and Holy Days we'll have a nice blood sausage with sauerkraut. It's all going to change, he told me.

OLD HILSE [*with suppressed indignation*]. And he calls himself your godfather! And he tells you to take part in such terrible deeds! You stay out of such things, Gottlieb. There's the devil's hand in such business. They're doing the devil's work.

LUISE [*overcome with passionate excitement, vehemently*]. Yes, Gottlieb, yes, go crawl there behind the stove, in the corner, take a spoon in your hand and a bowl of buttermilk on your knee, put on a dress and say your prayers, then you'll be what your father wants.—And he calls himself a man!

[*Laughter from the people in the hallway.*]

OLD HILSE [*trembling, with suppressed rage.*] And you call yourself a good wife, eh? Just you let me tell you something. You call yourself a mother with that evil tongue of yours, you want to teach your little girl what's right, and you stir your husband up to crime and wickedness!

LUISE [*without control*]. You and all your big talk . . . did it ever give us enough food to feed even one child? Just because of that they've laid in dirt and rags . . . all four of them. They never even had a dry diaper. Yes, I call myself a mother all right, if you want to know! And if you want to know something else, that's the reason I wish these factory owners to hell and damnation—just because I am a mother.—How was I to keep such little things alive? I have cried more than I have breathed, from the minute one of the poor things came into the world, till death had pity on it and took it. And you never gave a damn. You prayed and you sang, while I ran my feet bloody trying to find a bowl of buttermilk. How many hundreds of nights have I wracked my brain how just once I could cheat the churchyard and keep my child! What did the child ever do to deserve such a miserable end!—And over there in Dietrich's house, they get bathed in wine and washed in milk. No, no . . . if it ever starts here—there aren't ten horses could hold me back. And I tell you this: if ever they storm Dietrich's house, I'll be in front of them all, and pity the man who tries to hold me back. I've had enough, and that's a fact.

OLD HILSE. You're a lost soul; there's no help for you.

LUISE [*in a frenzy*]. You're the one there's no help for. Ragpickers, that's what you are. You're disgraces, you're not men. You're no better than the gutter scrapers they spit at in the street. You're weak-livered cowards, that get scared at the sound of a child's rattle. Fools who thank their beaters for a sound thrashing. They've bled you so white you can't even turn red in the face anymore. Somebody ought to take a whip to you and beat some life into your dead bones. [*Breathless, she goes off quickly.*]

[*An embarrassed pause.*]

MOTHER HILSE. What is it with Luise, father?

OLD HILSE. Nothing, mother dear, what should be the matter with her?

MOTHER HILSE. Tell me, father, are the bells really ringing, or am I hearing things?

OLD HILSE. They must be burying someone, mother

MOTHER HILSE. And still there's no end to my life. Why can't I die?

[*Pause.*]

OLD HILSE [*leaves his work, holds himself straight, solemnly*]. Gottlieb—you heard what your wife told us. Gottlieb, look at this! [*He opens his shirt.*] There was a bullet here once, big as a thimble. And the king knows where I lost my arm. It wasn't the mice ate it off. [*He walks back and forth.*] Your wife—before she was ever thought of, I was spilling my blood for my country. And that's why she can jabber on all she wants. It's all right with me. I don't care.— Afraid? Me, afraid? What's there to be afraid of, tell me? Of a few soldiers, maybe, who'll be coming after the rioters? O Jesus, if that was all! That'd be nothing. No, no, maybe I'm a little stiff in the back, but if it ever comes to that, I got bones as strong as ivory. I'd stand up all right against a couple of miserable bayonets.—And if it really got bad? How glad I'd be, oh, how glad I'd be to leave this world behind. No need for them to ask me twice to die. Better today than tomorrow. No, no. How glad I'd be! For what would I leave behind? Who would cry over this old torture box of aches and pains, that little heap of fear and torment that we call our life, how glad I'd be to leave that behind.— But then, Gottlieb! Then there comes something else—and when we've thrown that away, then there's nothing left.

GOTTLIEB. Who knows what's to come after you're dead? Nobody's ever seen it.

OLD HILSE. You listen, Gottlieb, don't you be throwing doubt on the one thing that we poor people got left. Why else would I have sat here—why would I have worked this treadle here for forty years until I was almost dead? And why would I have sat here and watched him over there living in pride and gluttony, making himself rich on my hunger and misery? Why? Because I had hope. In all this misery I still have something. [*Pointing out the window.*] You've got your share here in this world, I've got mine in the other. That's what I've been thinking all this time. And you can tear my body to pieces—but I know what I know. We've been promised. The day of judgment is coming; but we are not the judges: Vengeance is Mine, saith the Lord Our God.

A VOICE [*through the window*]. Weavers, come out!

OLD HILSE. Go, do what you want! [*He sits down at his loom.*] But you'll never make me leave.

GOTTLIEB [*after a brief struggle with himself*]. I'm going to work, too. Come what will. [*He goes off.*]

[*The sound of the weavers' song, sung by hundreds of voices, is heard in the immediate vicinity; it sounds like a dull monotonous wailing.*]

VOICES OF THE NEIGHBORS [*in the hallway*]. O Jesus, Lord Jesus, they're coming like ants.—Where did all them weavers come from.—Stop pushing, I want to see, too.— Look at that beanpole walking in front of them all.—My God, my God, now they're coming in swarms!

HORNIG [*steps among the people in the hallway*]. How's that for a show? You don't see something like that every day. Come on up to Dietrich's house. There's a *real* show up there. He ain't got a house, or a factory, or a winecellar, or nothing anymore. They're drinking down the bottles like they was water. They don't even bother to take out the corks anymore. One, two, three, and the necks are off even if they cut their mouths open on the glass. Some of them run around bleeding like pigs—they'll do the same now for Dietrich across the street.

[*The singing of the crowd has stopped.*]

VOICES OF THE NEIGHBORS. They don't look like such bad people.

HORNIG. Never mind! You just wait! They're taking time now to look the place over first. See there, how they're looking that palace over? Look at that little fat man—he's got a horse pail along, he's the smithy from Peterswaldau, he's a dangerous man. Believe me, he can break down the thickest doors like they was pretzels. If he ever gets one of those factory owners in his hands, there'll be no helping him!

VOICES OF THE NEIGHBORS. Bang, something happened there! —That was a stone flying in the window!—I bet old Dietrich's afraid now—Look, he's hanging a sign out.—He's hanging a sign out?—What does it say?—Can't you read? —What do you think would happen to me if I couldn't read?—Well then, read it!—"You will all get satisfaction. You will all get satisfaction."——

HORNIG. He might have spared himself that one. That won't do him much good. They got their own ideas. It's the factory they want. It's the mechanical looms they want to get rid of. The looms are what's ruining the weavers; any blind man can see that. No, no! These people won't be stopped today. No magistrate or councillor could change their minds—and least of all a sign. If you ever saw them work, you'd know what they was up to.

VOICES OF THE NEIGHBORS. My God, my God, who ever saw such a crowd!—What can they want?—[*Rapidly.*] They're coming across the bridge now! [*Fearfully.*] They're coming over here? [*In utmost surprise and fear.*] They're coming, they're coming.—They're coming to get the weavers out of their houses. [*They all run off. The hallway is left empty.*]

[*A swarm of rioters surges into the hallway, dirty, dusty, their clothes torn, rumpled as though they had been up all night, their faces flushed with strain and whisky; they cry out:*

"Weavers, come out!" *Then they disperse themselves through the house.* BAECKER *and several young weavers enter* OLD HILSE'S *room; they are armed with clubs and sticks. When they recognize* OLD HILSE, *they stop, slightly cooled off.*]

BAECKER. Father Hilse, stop your slaving away. Let whoever wants to run the treadle. You won't have to do yourself any more harm by working. That'll all be taken care of.

FIRST YOUNG WEAVER. You won't have to go to bed hungry anymore.

SECOND YOUNG WEAVER. The weaver'll have a roof over their heads and a shirt for their backs.

OLD HILSE. What the devil are you doing here with sticks and axes?

BAECKER. We'll break them on Dietrich's back.

SECOND YOUNG WEAVER. We'll get them red hot and stuff them down these factory owners' throats so that they'll know how hunger can burn.

THIRD YOUNG WEAVER. Come with us, Father Hilse! We give no quarter.

SECOND YOUNG WEAVER. Nobody took pity on us. Neither God nor man. And now we're seeing to our own rights.

[OLD BAUMERT *enters, already somewhat unsteady on his feet, a newly killed rooster under his arm. He stretches out his arms.*]

OLD BAUMERT. My brothers—we are all brothers! Come to my arms, my brothers!

[*Laughter.*]

OLD HILSE. So this is what you look like now, Wilhelm!

OLD BAUMERT. Gustav, is it really you, Gustav! Poor starving weaver, come to my arms. [*He is deeply moved.*]

OLD HILSE [*muttering*]. Leave me in peace.

OLD BAUMERT. Gustav, that's the way it is. A man must have luck. Gustav, look here at me once. How do I look? A man must have luck! Don't I look like a count? [*Striking his belly.*] What do you think I've got here in my belly? There's a king's dinner in this belly. A man must have luck, that's when he gets champagne and roast rabbit.—Let me tell you something: we've made a great mistake: we've got to help ourselves.

ALL [*together*]. We've got to help ourselves! Hurray!

OLD BAUMERT. No sooner you get the first bite of good food in your belly, that's when you start feeling you're alive again. Jesus, Jesus, you feel the power come back into you like you was a bull. And the strength flies out of your arms so that you don't see where you're hitting any more. It's a damned good feeling!

JAEGER [*at the door, armed with an old cavalry sabre*]. We made a couple of pretty good attacks.

BAECKER. We know what we're doing now. One, two, three and we're inside the house, and then it's like a fire run wild, so that everything crackles and shakes, and sparks fly like at the smithy's.

FIRST YOUNG WEAVER. What do you say we have a nice little fire? We'll march to Reichenbach and burn the roofs right off of people's houses.

JAEGER. There's nothing they'd like better. Think of all the insurance money they'd get.

[*Laughter.*]

BAECKER. From here we march to Trumtra's in Freiburg.

JAEGER. We ought to see about them government officials for once. I read that all our bad luck comes from these bureaucrats.

SECOND YOUNG WEAVER. And then we'll go to Breslau. More people are joining us all the time.

OLD BAUMERT [*to* HILSE]. Here, have a drink, Gustav!

OLD HILSE. I never drink whisky.

OLD BAUMERT. That was in the old world, Gustav, we're in a new one now!

FIRST YOUNG WEAVER. Christmas don't come every day.

[*Laughter.*]

OLD HILSE [*impatiently*]. You hounds of hell, what do you want from me!

OLD BAUMERT [*somewhat startled, in an over-friendly manner*]. Why, look here, Gustav, I meant to bring you a chicken. You have to cook mother a nice soup out of it.

OLD HILSE [*touched, in a half-friendly manner*]. Well, you tell mother herself about it.

MOTHER HILSE [*with her hand cupped at her ear has, with some strain, been listening to them; now she waves him off with her hands*]. Leave me in peace. I don't want no chicken soup.

OLD HILSE. That's right, mother, I don't want none either. Least of all, not that kind. And you, Baumert, I want to tell you something! The devil stands on his head for joy when he sees us old people jabbering away like we was little children. And just so you know! Just so all of you know: me and you, we got nothing in common. I gave you no leave to come in here!

A VOICE. Who's not with us is against us.

JAEGER [*threatening, brutally*]. You got it all wrong, old man, we're not thieves.

A VOICE. We're hungry, that's all.

FIRST YOUNG WEAVER. All we want to do is live. And so we cut the rope we was hung to.

JAEGER. And we were right! [*His fist in front of the old man's face*]. Another word out of you and you'll get this right in the face.

BAECKER. Stop it now, stop it! Let the old man alone. Father Hilse, we felt this way, too, once; better dead, we used to say, than start another life like this again.

OLD HILSE. Haven't I lived it sixty years and more?

BAECKER. It makes no difference; it's got to change.

OLD HILSE. When, on Saint Nevercomes' Day?

BAECKER. What we don't get from them peaceably we'll take by force.

OLD HILSE. By force? [*Laughs.*] Then you can start digging your graves right here. They'll teach you where force is. You just wait a while, sonny!

JAEGER. Because of the soldiers? We were soldiers, too. We can take care of a few companies.

OLD HILSE. With your tongues. I believe it. And even if you do, for every two you chase away, ten will come back at you.

VOICES [*through the window*]. The soldiers are coming. Watch out!

[*Suddenly there is a general silence. For a moment the weak sound of fife and drum is heard. Into the silence there comes a short involuntary cry*: "The hell with it! I'm taking off!" *General laughter.*]

BAECKER. Who's talking about taking off? Who said that?

JAEGER. Who's afraid here of a few miserable helmets? I'll take the command. I was in the army. I know their tricks.

OLD HILSE. What will you use for guns? You going to use clubs?

FIRST YOUNG WEAVER. Let the old fool alone, he ain't right upstairs.

SECOND YOUNG WEAVER. He's out of his head, that's what.

[*Without being noticed,* GOTTLIEB *has entered among the rioters; he takes hold of the speaker.*]

GOTTLIEB. Is that how you talk to an old man?

FIRST YOUNG WEAVER. Get your hands off me, I didn't say it.

OLD HILSE [*interrupting*]. Let them jabber, Gottlieb. Have nothing to do with them. He'll know soon enough which of us is crazy: him or me.

BAECKER. Are you coming with us, Gottlieb?

OLD HILSE. No, he ain't going with you!

LUISE [*enters the hallway, calls in*]. Don't stop for them. Don't waste your time with these prayerbook jackasses. Come out on the square! You've got to come out on the square! God-father Baumert, come out as quick as you can! The major's talking to the people from up on his horse. They're to go home. If you don't hurry it'll be all over.

JAEGER [*going off*]. That's a brave husband you've got!

LUISE. Where's my husband! I see no husband here!

VOICES [*singing in the hallway*].

> Once there was a man so small,
> Heigh, diddle diddle!
> He wanted a woman big and tall,
> Heigh, diddle, heigh diddle,
> Heigh, diddle diddle!

WITTIG [*comes down from the upper story, the horse pail still in his hand, is about to go out but remains standing for a moment in the hallway*]. Come on! Anyone who ain't a coward follow me! Hurray! [*He storms out.*]

[*A group of people, with* LUISE *and* JAEGER *among them, follow him, crying:* "Hurray!"]

BAECKER. Stay well, Father Hilse, we'll see each other again. [*About to go.*]

OLD HILSE. I don't think so. I won't last five more years. And you won't be out before then.

BAECKER [*stops suddenly, surprised*]. Out of where, Father Hilse?

OLD HILSE. Out of prison; where else?

BAECKER [*laughing wildly*]. I'd never argue with that. At least you get enough to eat there, Father Hilse! [*He goes off.*]

OLD BAUMERT [*has been sitting on a stool, in a dull, brooding mood; he now rises*]. You're right, Gustav, I am a little bit drunk. But I'm still clear enough in my head. You've got your opinion of this business and I've got mine: I say that Baecker is right, even if he ends up in chains; it's always better in prison than at home. You're taken care of there; and you won't starve either. I would have been happy not to have joined them. But you must understand, Gustav, a man has got to breathe just once in his lifetime. [*He goes slowly towards the door.*] Good-bye, Gustav. If anything happens, say a little prayer for me, you hear? [*He goes off.*]

[*The rioters have all gone now. The hallway gradually becomes full again with curious neighbors,* OLD HILSE *knots at his web.* GOTTLIEB *has taken an axe from behind the stove and tests the blade unconsciously. Both of them are silently shaken. Outside one hears the hum and roar of a great crowd of people.*]

MOTHER HILSE. Look, father, look, the floors are trembling—what's happening? What will become of us?

[*Pause.*]

OLD HILSE. Gottlieb!

GOTTLIEB. What do you want?

OLD HILSE. Put down that axe.

GOTTLIEB. Then who'll cut the kindling?

[*He leans the axe against the stove. Pause.*]

MOTHER HILSE. Gottlieb, you listen to what your father tells you.

A VOICE [*singing in front of the window*].

> Stay home, stay home, my little man,
> Heigh, diddle diddle!
> Clean the dish and clean the pan,
> Heigh, diddle, heigh, diddle,
> Heigh, diddle diddle!

[*He goes past.*]

GOTTLIEB [*jumps up, rushes to the window with his fist clenched*]. Bastard! You try me once more!

[*The crack of a volley is heard.*]

MOTHER HILSE [*drawn together with fright*]. O Jesus, Jesus, it's thundering again!

OLD HILSE [*his hand on his chest, praying*]. O Lord in Heaven, protect the poor weavers, protect my poor brothers!

[*There is a short silence.*]

OLD HILSE [*who is shaken, to himself*]. There's blood flowing now.

[*At the sound of the volley,* GOTTLIEB *has jumped up and taken the axe into his hands with firm grip; he is pale, almost beside himself with his deep inner excitement.*]

GOTTLIEB. Am I still supposed to stay here like a scared dog!

A WEAVER GIRL [*calls into the room from the hallway*]. Father Hilse, Father Hilse, get away from the window. A bullet went right through ours upstairs. [*She disappears.*]

MIELCHEN [*sticks her laughing face in through the window*]. Grandfather, grandfather, they shot with their guns. Some of them fell down. One of them's turning himself all around like a wheel. And the other one's kicking like a sparrow when you tear its head off. And you should see all the blood that's coming out! [*She disappears.*]

A WEAVER WOMAN. Some of those will never get up again.

AN OLD WEAVER [*in the hallway*]. You just wait, they're going to make a run at the soldiers.

A SECOND WEAVER [*beside himself*]. Look there at the women, look at the women, look at them! Lifting their skirts up! Spitting at the soldiers!

A WEAVER WOMAN [*calls in*]. Gottlieb, take a look at your wife out there, she's more man than you ever were, running around out there in front of the bayonets, like it was a dance.

[*Four men carry a wounded man through the hallway. Silence. Then a voice is heard saying clearly: "It's Weaver Ulbrich." After another few moments of silence, the voice is heard again: "It won't last long with him; he got a bullet right* through the ear." *Men are heard ascending the wooden stairs. Suddenly from outside:* "Hurray, hurray!"]

VOICES [*from inside the house*]. Where did you get the stones? —You better clear out! From the road they're building.— Bye-bye, soldiers.—It's raining paving stones now.

[*Screams of terror and roaring spread from the street into the house itself. The door is banged shut with a cry of terror.*]

VOICES [*in the hallway*]. They're loading up again.—They'll fire another volley soon.—Father Hilse, get away from the window.

GOTTLIEB. My God, my God, my God! Are we mad dogs! Are we to eat gun powder and bullets instead of bread! [*He hesitates for a moment with the axe in his hand. To* OLD HILSE.] Do you want my wife to be shot? I won't let them! [*He rushes out.*] Let me through! I'm coming! [*He goes off.*]

OLD HILSE. Gottlieb, Gottlieb!

MOTHER HILSE. Where has Gottlieb gone?

OLD HILSE. To the devil.

VOICES [*from the hallway*]. Get away from the window, Father Hilse!

OLD HILSE. Not me! Not even if you all go mad! [*To* MOTHER HILSE, *with mounting ecstasy.*] Here is where the Heavenly Father has placed me. Isn't that right, mother? Here we will sit and do what is our duty, though the snow itself catch fire. [*He begins to weave.*]

[*There is a loud volley. Struck,* OLD HILSE *raises himself up and falls forward across his loom. At the same moment there is a strengthened, resounding cry of* "Hurray!" *Joining the cry, the people who till now have stood in the hallway surge outside.*]

OLD MOTHER HILSE [*repeats several times*]. Father, father, what's the matter with you?

[*The uninterrupted cry of* "Hurray!" *gradually fades into the distance. Suddenly in a great hurry* MIELCHEN *runs into the room.*]

MIELCHEN. Grandfather, grandfather, they're chasing the soldiers out of town, they tore down Dietrich's house, it's just like over at Dreissiger's. Grandfather!? [*She is suddenly frightened, she grows alert, sticks her finger in her mouth and cautiously approaches the dead man.*] Grandfather!?

MOTHER HILSE. Why don't you say something, father! You're scaring me.

FRANK WEDEKIND

1864–1918

FRANK WEDEKIND was the first modern dramatist to use expressionist techniques openly in the theatre. All of the German writers at the turn of the century were beginning to turn the searchlight on bourgeois values, and it is in the drama of Wedekind that we discover the clearest indication of the cynical despair and skepticism with which contemporary values were being regarded. The world of his theatre expresses the grotesque disequilibrium of middle-class society, and it is peopled by fascinating and demonically dislocated bourgeois characters.

From the beginning, German expressionism was schizophrenic in nature. On the one hand, it was idealistic and celebrated in a mystical way the need for love and universal brotherhood in a bewildering and confusing world. On the other, it stridently encouraged the grotesque dramatization of every form of brutality, cruelty, bestiality, and sensuality. Wedekind most fully embodies the Jekyll-Hyde character of this frenzied movement. All of his work is stamped with a kind of level-headed lunacy that defies analysis, and each of his plays tends to be a strange combination of Grand Guignol and farce. In Wedekind's view, the civilized world is a menagerie of wild animals, and his plays are brutal satires in which he strips the individual down to the horrifying moral nakedness of the jungle. Morality is seen as the most lucrative of all rackets, and sexual emancipation is hailed as the only means of curing a diseased society. Variations on these two anti-bourgeois ideas appear again and again in his plays, and finally serve as the foundation for everything Wedekind ever wrote.

THE ART OF ACTING: A GLOSSARY[1]

by Frank Wedekind

1910

MAX REINHARDT

Our hope and our unhappy love. The unfathomable sorcerer Klingsor. What utter and tremendous delight would Nietzsche have found in Max Reinhardt. A man for whom the impossible became possible. A cultural phenomenon of first rank. The after effects of Bismarck in the intellectual life of the German people are gradually becoming less political and far more poetic. On the other hand, the foundation of Reinhardt's theatre, in addition to its artistic importance, is gradually also becoming politically important. The reawakening of intellectual independence in southern Germany lures him from the theatre-satiated and literature-jaded city of Berlin to Frankfort and Munich.

In Munich Georg Stollberg had, of course, favorably prepared the way for him for half a generation. If Georg Stollberg hasn't the expansion drive of Reinhardt, then he has at least proved from the first day of his activity to the present to have had an equal amount of energy, consistency, and independence as Reinhardt when it comes to the question of fighting for new dramatic works for the theatre, even when it is in contradiction to the momentarily authoritative literary current. The theatre battles which raged in the Munich *Schauspielhaus* were the direct result of the uncompromising artistic convictions of Georg Stollberg, and with every day

[1] "The Art of Acting: A Glossary" by Frank Wedekind, translated by Carl Richard Mueller. Reprinted from *The Modern Theatre*, edited by Robert W. Corrigan, © Copyright, Robert W. Corrigan, 1964. Printed by permission of The Macmillan Company and the translator.

that passes it becomes clearer that it was the Munich *Schauspielhaus* which was victorious. For that reason Munich for Max Reinhardt is not a city to be conquered, but a brother-in-cause, ready to receive him with open arms. However in Stuttgart, Darmstadt, Mannheim, Karlsruhe, Heidelberg and Konstanz, the appearance of Max Reinhardt would with a single stroke call together and unite all those in southern Germany who delight in theatre, and who have only to wait for that great event which will set them in motion towards achieving their own independence. Bismarck once spoke of the "putrid fermenting of southern German lack of discipline." This appears equally as rash to me as if a southern German were to speak of the "boastful and unwarranted pride of northern German narrow-mindedness." But surely the successful development of German culture rests not upon the conflict between southern German lack of discipline and northern German narrow-mindedness, but rather upon the co-operation between northern German proficiency and southern German richness of soul, between northern German freshness of intellect and southern German depth of feeling. If ever there was a common leader for this co-operative effort, one who stands high enough to make both elements serve his purpose, then it is Max Reinhardt.

Why then do we say "our unhappy love"?

Because in the metropolis of Berlin he is the only one who can be considered as being interested in a new art. Because he, like all others who are alone in their endeavor, very often does not have enough time. Because he is claimed by the illustrious dead—all of these facts add only to his fame and glory. His ability to make possible the impossible is something which he has proved with my tragedy of childhood, *Spring Awakening*. But his sorcery does not always work advantageously with the plainly possible. Since it is his profession to change water into wine, it happens at times, when there is no water at hand, that he changes wine into a beverage which bears little relationship to its original vine. But these are small failings which are inseparable from the great phenomena of all ages.

TRANSITION

The works of the naturalist playwrights owed their uncommonly rapid dissemination not least of all to the advantage that they were childishly simple to act. This is no objection to their literary and social qualities. The actor stuck his hands in his pocket, placed himself with his back to the audience next to the prompt-box, and waited with the greatest of ease until he heard the word called out to him. If he happened to misunderstand the word, then there was no particular harm done, because his audience for the most part consisted of stagehands playing cards behind the scenes. For years the spectator demanded nothing more of the actor than that he should not break the mood with the spoken word.

The actors who celebrated their triumphs in this form of art are no longer of any use to us. The drama of today concerns itself with far more serious problems and cultivates a far higher art form than the naturalists could ever manage. The fact that the literary production of today cannot point to a series of successes is surely no proof whatever that its stage technique exists on a lower level than those dramas of twenty years ago. More than one of today's practicing dramatists have found themselves dissatisfied, not because their stagecraft was too bad, but on the contrary, because it was too good for the abilities of today's literary theatre.

COMPENSATION

The collective thrashings which the press has seen fit to bestow upon me for my dramas I would now like to pass on undiminished and unmitigated to today's German acting profession. It has for years now proved itself unfit to present effectively the works of today's aspiring German dramatists.

IBSEN

Ibsen gave us a new conception of life [*Weltanschauung*], a new picture of man, new knowledge of the soul, but no new drama. Hebbel was a stronger dramatist than Ibsen, and Goethe and Schiller were stronger dramatists than Hebbel. How could it have been otherwise? For just as surely as the life of the German people is dramatically weaker than that of the neo-Latin people, it is certain that it is ten times more dramatic than the life of the Norwegians. German mirth is more lively than Scandinavian; a pair of German lovers is far more ardent and bold; German wit is sharper and more spicy; a fight between Germans ends more bloodily than in Sweden or in Norway. The blood of Ibsen's women of fate, Rebecca

West and Hedda Gabler, flows in the veins of our old maids. This conviction led me to believe twenty years ago that the highest ideal of art would be to unite the unsurpassed mastery of Ibsen's picture of man with the equally unsurpassed dramatic technique of Schiller's *Love and Intrigue*.

For twenty years now the modern German actor has known no higher ideal than to be able to play Ibsen. This means lamentably little to the art of acting. To be sure, Ulrik Bendel and Eylert Lövborg require a passion of spirit and liveliness. Both are episodic figures. Herbert Eulenberg is not the only dramatist writing today whose plays demand to be carried by the passion of spirit and liveliness of an Eyelert Lövberg. Should an Ibsen actor tackle such a problem, then the play will be lost, because the actor lacks the endurance. He grows short of breath, he hasn't learned enough. In the most exciting situations he tiredly drags himself from one couch to the next in order to rally new strength.

And the reviews—the divinely inspired X. X. has truly outdone himself in this role. His ingenious ability deserved a more challenging task. It is a pity that today's theatre cannot produce more works for these thespian demigods.

STRANGE HAPPENSTANCE

In face of the most grateful roles to be found in my plays, the German actor has for twenty years now been playing the *timid lover*. Unfortunately I have never written a role for precisely this department of acting.

BERLIN

The ten-year-old, almost absolute control of a single direction of taste which made it possible to exhaust the situation artistically in the widest measure is understandable only when one realizes that Berlin considers as its own cause the battle for this direction of taste. Since interest in naturalism is declining, Germany has only one great artistic event to record, an event which, save for the lively interest manifested by Berlin, would never have reached such heights of development. This event is *Max Reinhardt*.

Considering that both these German artistic events were in every respect the children of Berlin and are only to be understood in regard to the favorable conditions predominating in Berlin at the time, it would be utterly against reason to suppose that suddenly this fertile mother should fail to bring forth and nourish other children. It may be true that at the moment Berlin is somewhat tired and in need of rest. But for this reason suddenly to let fly with the damning: "Away with Berlin!" would be screaming ingratitude.

I say: No, on the contrary! Let us continually hold up Berlin as a shining example for all German towns. Let us demand that every German town try, within the limits of its powers, to rival Berlin. There must be no slavish imitations, but there must also be no envy or injustice. When our art possesses an invigorating power, then it will harm neither Berlin nor any other town. And we could not possibly render German culture a greater service.

ON THE MISERY AND DEATH OF THE GERMAN ART OF ACTING
(REPLY TO THE ATTACK: "ON THE MISERY AND DEATH OF THE GERMAN DRAMA.")

Those actors whose art exceeds that of any critic, whose ability decides absolutely and without argument the fate of today's dramatic productions, storm out of a performance of *The Bride of Messina*, in which they have acted the lead roles, and cry: "Schiller! The inept idiot! Just ask the public what an abominable impression this miserable play made on it! The scribbler! Just think, if it weren't for us!"

Not one of them has the least idea about the world-historical charade which Schiller builds up through powerful verses, compared with which Ibsen's *Master Builder* is a broken-winded eccentricity which they idolize as revelation only because for twenty years they learned nothing more demanding.

And so Schiller becomes our companion in misery, parodying himself in so doing: it is not that the hero is destroyed while the idea conquers; no one is at all concerned about the idea; rather, the play fails while the direction succeeds.

How is that possible?

The actor who today is praised as exemplary lacks the ability and endurance to carry a play. He is unsurpassed in changes and episodes and for that reason the darling of directors. The fact that he can sing-song conversation pieces is certainly not to his discredit; it misleads him, however, into passing over the author's passion of spirit and liveliness in the tone of voice of the conversation piece. Then the critics scream that the author is utilizing a wooden German. Unfortunately the actor hasn't the ability to portray greatness as something self-evident, to remain exultantly naïve, to show human warmth and depth of feeling convincingly bound up with strength and liveliness. If he speaks naïvely, obviously, then what he says is not understood, because he has neglected his speech techniques for twenty years. Should he want to appear powerful, heroic, vivacious, then every word will appear deliberately stressed, overworked, conscious, intellectualized, so that there will be no trace of naturalness or of the obvious. The actor of today makes of every God-created human being who is not by nature intellectually lazy, a bloodless, overdrawn, desk-created whim.

An art of acting which grows into an unbridgeable yawning gap between author and audience.

ALBERT STEINRÜCK

In the character of my Lulu in *Earth Spirit* I tried to draw a fine example of a woman, and explain how a creature highly gifted by nature, even though she may have sprung from the dregs of society, achieves complete development in the company of men to whom she is far superior in matters of common sense.

Under the command of the bourgeois narrow-mindedness of German naturalism, the splendid creature I intended became a paragon of malevolent unnaturalness, and through the years I was decried as a fanatical, pitiless inquisitor of woman, an exorcising misogynist.

This fact can in no way do damage to the acting genius of a Gertrud Eysoldt. On the contrary, I was convinced from the beginning that had my *Earth Spirit* been played ten years ago as I had envisioned it, and without the interpretation of Gertrud Eysoldt, it would have aroused only displeasure and moral indignation. Frau Eysoldt played precisely that type of woman and beauty which was in current literary and artistic vogue in Berlin. Moreover, Albert Steinrück's Dr. Schön was from the beginning the most fascinating embodiment of a brutal beast of prey that I could have imagined. Albert Steinrück, a deeply moving Gabriel Borkmann, a demonic Master Builder Solness, is spoken of far more in regard to his presentations of active, determined characters than passive, brooding ones, by virtue of his inherent acting energy. Today's drama is not so inclined to give extravagant praise to the paralytic condition as was the drama of the 1890s. But it is all the more inclined to extol the unflinching intellect, passion, and high-spiritedness. And for that it no longer needs a theatrical interpreter of dreams, but theatrical energy. When Albert Steinrück has his hands free he is one of our greatest hopes.

DILETIANTISM

In view of the literary minds of all nations—and I believe that today my voice may also be heard abroad—I herewith appeal to the professional honor of the German actor:

For five years now actors everywhere in Germany where I have appeared in one of my own plays have acknowledged and eulogized me for the work I have done, but these same actors seem unable to concern themselves in the least about the fact. Of every role I have played during the last five years, the critics have written that any actor could have played it immeasurably better, and that in these roles I show myself to be a miserable, incapable, obtrusive dilettante. To date it has never occurred to any actor to oppose this observation whether by word or deed. I have no desire to contradict the critics; I could wish nothing better for myself than for them to be right. But then, my most honored actors, when will you finally set about to prove in those places where I have appeared that you are qualified to praise my taste? Just for once play an unmutilated *The Tenor*, especially since the mutilated ones are more than a hundred years in the past. Play a Karl Hetmann, a King Nicolo, a Marquis of Keith, a Marquis Casti-Piani. Do you consider it an honor for the German art of acting that a playwright is compelled to act the leading roles in his own plays unless he wants the critics to make nothing more of him than a bungling author of unstageable literary dramas? Answer that for me. If I hadn't acted, then, of course, you would have had as easy a time with me as with my companions in misfortune: Arthur Vollmöller, Herbert Eulenberg, Josef Ruederer, Wilhelm von Scholz and others, whose stage techniques even today are a Book of Seven Seals to you, and who must let themselves be dismissed by the critics with a sympathetic shrug of the shoulders. And so, of course, you found just recently that I too am a justification for your convenience. You maintain that my plays are so lacking in content and are so superficial that no spectator could possibly find any interest in them, unless for the same money there were thrown into the bargain the added sensation of seeing the author on stage as an utterly incompetent dilettante. Besides that, you spread the rumor that unless I am personally able to star in my own plays I will withhold them from production. But all this will no longer be of any avail to you. Since for five years now you have, with cheerful openness, relished the work I have done, I challenge you today, on the honor of your profession, to show at last how the roles of Gerardo, Karl Hetmann, King Nicolo and the Marquis of Keith can be acted more artfully and with greater effect than they have been by me. It is only after you have proved this to me that you will be justified in disparaging me to your own high honor.

Should you ignore this summons, then I believe we will know what to expect of you.

EXECUTIONS

Today's theatre seems to have more to do with executions than with productions. My own experience is meager by comparison with that of my professional comrades. My play *Such Is Life* was executed in Munich, Berlin, and Frankfort-on-the-Main. My *Marquis of Keith* was twice broken on the wheel in Berlin during a ten-year period. My *Earth Spirit* was executed in Hamburg and Breslau prior to its Berlin production. My harmless farce *The Love Potion* was pilloried in Leipzig, Nürnberg, and Breslau. . . . I should think that for premières actors would prefer to change the word "production" to "supreme penal court," something more in keeping with the effect they produce. . . . The office of executioner has its professional honor, too, as soon as it stops bothering itself with worthless subjects.

FIORENZA

In a country in which not a day goes by but one reads in the papers of a new and immortal feat performed by some immeasurably gifted genius of a director, it must seem somewhat odd that a work such as the *Fiorenza* of Thomas Mann, a work so richly poetic in the plasticity of its characters, in the dramatic soundness of its dialogue, in the stageworthiness of its technique, should become four years old and in these years have known only two stage productions.

It deserves by virtue of its poetic greatness and beauty to have been made a repertory piece of every German theatre long ago—those same theatres which claim to be the guardians of art. And every director and stage designer worth his salt will already have in his mind a particular conception of how *Fiorenza* must be staged. Such a thing is as self-evident as that the same directors and designers must have preconceived, personal ideas about staging Goethe's *Faust* and Schiller's *The Robbers*.

But what happens instead?

German theatres and the art of German acting have successfully hushed up this distinguished play for four whole years, despite the fact that in its final scene between Savanarola and the dying Lorenzo di Medici, there exists the most exalted, ingenious, and dramatically effective writing which has ever been done for the German stage. Or is there something missing in dramatic effectiveness in the remaining four acts of *Fiorenza*? The first act offers as its high point the relation of what happened in the cathedral. The second act shows the splendid band of artists, the dialogue between the two brothers, and then the love dialogue between Fiore and Piero.

Despite this the play has lain fallow for four years while our directors permit their art to be praised to the skies and at the same time publically proclaim the misery and death of the German drama.

FOR THE PUBLIC

When I recently appeared at Düsseldorf, I elicited a general headshaking and shrugging of shoulders, because I rolled my *R*s, because I failed to turn my back to the audience, and because I did not veil my plays in muslin. In short, because I proceeded on the barbaric assumption that the spectator wanted to hear and see something for his money. I am firmly of the conviction that for the past twenty years our literary theatre has, first, had far too little theatre in it, and second, has been far too literary. I am convinced that for the past twenty years our literary theatre has offered far too little pleasure and amusement. I am for that reason an abomination to the snobs and philistines of art.

Moreover, I know of two actors who share my opinion in this regard, Josef Kainz and Josef Jarno.

By chance I heard both of them express the conviction that even the gloomy Ibsen is made excessively gloomy by his contemporary high priests. Engstrand and Pastor Manders, whose comic elements go back to the Hofmarschall von Kalb, must willy-nilly hold fast to a gloomy human destiny for their characterizations. I retorted dryly: It's good box office. It will be done even in despite of Ibsen, even if it makes Ibsen turn over in his grave.

In the entire range of my plays there is not a single leading male role which I did not write for either one or the other of those two incomparably great actors: Kainz and Jarno. Jarno has thanked me by his unexcelled characterization of my Marquis of Keith, and Kainz by his warm-hearted, honest interest in my Karl Hetmann. Both actors have one thing in common: the exceedingly rare gift of being able to play a role almost immediately as though they were riding a hurdle race. The acting routine of the actor enchants the public by the way it lightly pushes aside with a red pencil every hurdle it encounters and plays only the remaining platitudes. That is how they have managed to ruin my *The Tenor* through the years. The great, celebrated actor, on the other hand, persists at each single hindrance as though it were a labor of Hercules, while during the intermissions he celebrates wild orgies which seem never to end. When and how he arrives at his mark does not bother him in the least. Nevertheless, naturalism has drummed into the public a hardy endurance, one which is scarcely to be outdone.

DICTATORIAL DIRECTION

The expression 'dictatorial direction' stems from Wilhelm von Scholz, to whom I herewith express my thanks for it.

The dictatorial director is a man who will not be shoved into the shadows by any theatre piece, regardless of its strength and virtues.

In one of my plays, the dictatorial director was afraid of being shoved into the shadows by one of my most effective scenes. What was he to do? He came to his own rescue in that, without any cause whatever, he brought onto stage a real, live donkey. The experiment was a splendid success. My play failed, but the donkey found himself extolled to the high heavens by all the critics.

CONCLUSION

. . . I am not fighting against a station, but against a state of things. I am not fighting to repress, but to awaken new life. I am firmly convinced that this quarrel will be dispatched remarkably soon. Afterwards the former friendship will continue on an even firmer basis, and perhaps we will be able to be more mutually thankful to one another than has been the situation till now.

THE MARQUIS OF KEITH

by FRANK WEDEKIND

1900

THE MARQUIS OF KEITH[1]

Translated by Carl Richard Mueller

CHARACTERS

CONSUL CASIMIR, *a merchant*

HERMANN CASIMIR, *his son, fifteen years old*

THE MARQUIS OF KEITH

ERNST SCHOLZ

MOLLY GRIESINGER

ANNA, COUNTESS WERDENFELS, *a widow*

SARANIEFF, *a painter*

ZAMRIAKI, *a composer*

SOMMERSBERG, *a writer*

RASPE, *a police inspector*

OSTERMEIER, *proprietor of a brewery*

KRENZL, *a master builder*

GRANDAUER, *a restaurateur*

FRAU OSTERMEIER

FRAU KRENZL

BARONESS VON ROSENKRON, *divorcée*

BARONESS VON TOTLEBEN, *divorcée*

SASCHA

SIMBA

A BUTCHER'S HELPER

A BAKERY WOMAN

A PORTER

PATRONS OF THE HOFBRÄUHAUS

The place of the action is Munich, late summer, 1899.

[1] *The Marquis of Keith* by Frank Wedekind, translated by Carl Richard Mueller. Reprinted from *The Modern Theatre*, edited by Robert W. Corrigan, © Copyright, Robert W. Corrigan, 1964. Printed by permission of The Macmillan Company and the translator. All rights reserved. Performance rights, in all media, whether amateur or professional, must be obtained by applying to the translator c/o The Macmillan Company, 866 East Third Avenue, New York, N.Y., 10022.

ACT ONE

[*A workroom, the walls of which are covered with pictures. In the rear wall to the right there is a door leading into the hallway, and to the left, a door leading into a waiting room. A door in the right wall leads into the living room. Downstage left is a writing table on which unrolled plans are lying; on the wall beside the writing table is a telephone. There is a divan downstage right, with a smaller table in front of it; somewhat upstage center is a larger table. Bookcases with books; musical instruments, bundles of notes and documents.*

The MARQUIS OF KEITH *is seated at the writing table, engrossed in one of the plans. He is a man of about twenty-seven: medium height, slender and bony; he would have an exemplary figure were it not for the limp in his left leg. His features are vigorous, though at the same time nervous and somewhat hard. He has piercing grey eyes, a small, blond mustache. His unmanageable short, straw-blond hair is carefully parted in the middle. He is dressed in a suit well chosen for its social elegance, but by no means foppishly. He has the rough red hands of a clown.*

MOLLY GRIESINGER *enters from the living room and places a covered tray on the small table in front of the divan. She is a plain sort of creature, brunette, somewhat shy and harassed, wearing a plain house dress, but at the same time she possesses large, black, soulful eyes.*]

MOLLY. There you are, my dear, tea, caviar and cold cuts. Do you realize you were up by nine this morning?

KEITH [*without moving*]. Thank you, my dear child.

MOLLY. You must be terribly hungry. Have you had word yet whether the Fairyland Palace will be built?

KEITH. Can't you see I'm busy?

MOLLY. Yes, you're always busy when I come in. That means that all I ever learn about you and your enterprises has to come from your lady friends.

KEITH [*without turning in his chair*]. I once knew a woman who stopped up both her ears whenever I talked about plans. She would say: "Come and tell me when you've *done* something!"

MOLLY. Well, I suppose it's my misfortune that you've already known every kind of woman.

[*A bell rings.*]

Merciful heaven, now who could *that* be! [*She goes into the hall to open the door.*]

KEITH [*to himself*]. That poor miserable creature!

MOLLY [*returns with a card*]. A young gentleman would like to see you. I told him you were very busy.

KEITH [*after reading the card*]. Just who I wanted to see!

[MOLLY *brings in* HERMANN CASIMIR, *a fifteen-year-old student in a very elegant cycling costume. She then goes off into the living room.*]

HERMANN. Good morning, Herr Baron.

KEITH. To what do I owe the honor?

HERMANN. I suppose it were best if I come right out with it. I was at the Café Luitpold last night with Saranieff and Zamriaki. I told them that I absolutely had to have a hundred marks. And so Saranieff thought I might come to you for it.

KEITH. All Munich must think I'm an American railroad baron!

HERMANN. Zamriaki said you always have money on hand.

KEITH. I've patronized Zamriaki because he's the greatest musical genius since Richard Wagner. But these highway robbers certainly aren't proper kind of company for you!

HERMANN. I find these highway robbers interesting. I met the gentlemen at an anarchist meeting.

KEITH. Your father must be delightfully surprised to find you spend your time at revolutionary meetings.

HERMANN. Why doesn't my father let me leave Munich!

KEITH. Because you're still too young for the great world.

HERMANN. But I find that a person my age can learn infinitely more by direct experience than by scooting about on a schoolbench till he's come of age.

KEITH. Actual experience merely causes you to lose the abilities you brought with you into the world along with your flesh and blood. And this is especially true of you, the son and sole heir of our greatest German financial genius. What has your father to say about me?

HERMANN. My father never speaks to me.

KEITH. But he does speak to others.

HERMANN. That's possible. I spend as little time at home as I can.

KEITH. I'm afraid you're at fault there. I have followed your father's financial operations ever since I was in America. Your father completely rejects the possibility that there is another soul alive who can be as clever as he. That's why, up till now, he's so obstinately refused to join my enterprise.

HERMANN. However I may try, I can't imagine ever finding pleasure in leading the kind of life my father does.

KEITH. It's simply that your father lacks the ability to interest you in his profession.

HERMANN. The important thing in this world is not merely to live; the important thing is to learn to know both life *and* the world.

KEITH. Your desire to learn to know the world will only end you in a ditch at the side of the road. Just remember that the most important thing is to learn to put the greatest value on the circumstances into which you were born. That will guard you against degrading yourself quite so cheerfully.

HERMANN. Do you mean by pumping you for money? And yet I'm certain there must be things of a higher value than wealth!

KEITH. Theoretically perhaps. These things are called "higher" because they are the *products* of material possessions and are only made possible *through* material possessions. You, of course, are free to devote yourself to either an artistic or a scientific profession because your father has already made a fortune. If in doing so, however, you disregard the primary guiding principle of the world, then you are merely dropping your inheritance into the hands of swindlers.

HERMANN. If Jesus Christ had chosen to act according to this guiding principle of the world . . .

KEITH. You will kindly remember that Christianity liberated two-thirds of mankind from slavery. There's not a single idea—social, scientific or artistic—that deals with anything other than goods and property. That's why anarchists are the sworn enemies of ideas. And don't think that the world will ever change itself in this regard. Man either adjusts or he is eliminated. [*He has seated himself at the writing table.*] I'll give you the hundred marks. But do come around sometime when you aren't in need of money. How long is it since your mother died?

HERMANN. It will be three years this spring.

KEITH [*giving him a sealed note*]. You will take this note to the Countess Werdenfels, Brienner Strasse number twenty-three. Give her my best regards. I seem not to have any cash today.

HERMANN. Thank you, Herr Baron.

KEITH [*leading him out; as he closes the door behind him*]. Thank you, it was my pleasure. [*With this he returns to the writing table, rummages in the plans.*] You would think his old man were a dog catcher the way he treats me. Let's see, I must arrange a concert as soon as possible. That way public opinion will force him into joining my enterprise. If worst comes to worst I will simply have to do without him.

[*A knock at the door.*]

Come in!

[ANNA, *the widowed* COUNTESS WERDENFELS, *enters. She is a voluptuous beauty of thirty. White skin, turned-up nose, sparkling eyes, luxuriant chestnut-brown hair.*]

KEITH [*going to meet her*]. Well, here you are, my queen! I've just sent young Casimir to you with a small request.

ANNA. Oh, so that was the young Herr Casimir, was it?

KEITH [*after kissing her hastily on the mouth which she has offered him*]. He'll be back if he finds you not at home.

ANNA. He doesn't look in the least like his father.

KEITH. Let's forget about his father. I've just approached a number of people whose social ambitions assure me their burning enthusiasm for my enterprise.

ANNA. But everyone knows that old Casimir loves to patronize young actresses and singers.

KEITH [*devouring* ANNA *with his eyes*]. Anna, as soon as you appear in front of me I become another person; it's as though you were the living pledge of my good fortune. But won't you have some breakfast? There's tea here, and caviar and cold cuts.

ANNA [*seats herself on the divan and eats*]. I have a lesson at eleven. I dropped in for only a moment. Madame Bianchi tells me that in a year's time I could be the leading Wagnerian soprano of Germany.

KEITH [*lighting a cigarette*]. Perhaps in a year you'll have improved so much that the best Wagnerian sopranos will be seeking *your* patronage.

ANNA. That's all right with me. With my limited woman's intelligence I really can't see how I could possibly reach the top so soon.

KEITH. I'm afraid *I* can't tell you that beforehand either. I simply let myself be driven along without resistance until I arrive at a place where I feel comfortable enough and say to myself: "This is the place to build!"

ANNA. And in that, my dear, I shall be your most faithful accomplice. For some time now my delirious love of life has brought me round to thoughts of suicide.

KEITH. One man steals what he wants, the other receives it as a gift. When I came out into the world my boldest aspiration was to die a village schoolmaster somewhere in Upper Silesia.

ANNA. You would have had a hard time dreaming then that someday Munich would be lying at your feet.

KEITH. My only knowledge of Munich was from a class in geography. If my career till now hasn't been exactly spotless, then one oughtn't to forget the depths out of which I rose.

ANNA. I pray fervently to God every night that He may transfer some of your remarkable energy to *me*.

KEITH. Nonsense, I haven't the slightest bit of energy.

ANNA. Yet it's a necessity of your existence to keep running your head through stone walls.

KEITH. My talent is restricted by the unfortunate fact that I'm unable to breathe in a bourgeois atmosphere. If for that very reason I also achieve what I want, then I certainly will never assume the least bit of credit for it. There are other people, of course, who find themselves planted on a certain level of society on which they can vegetate their whole lives away without ever coming into conflict with the world.

ANNA. You on the other hand fell from the heavens an utterly individualized personality.

KEITH. I'm a bastard. Intellectually my father was a very prominent man, especially in matters concerning mathematics and other such exact sciences, and my mother was a gypsy.

ANNA. If only I had your skill in reading the secrets in men's faces! Then I could grind their noses into the dirt with the tip of my toe.

KEITH. These are accomplishments which cause more distrust in people than they are likely to give benefit to you. That's why bourgeois society has harbored a secret aversion of me ever since I came into this world. This bourgeois society by means of its cautiousness, and against its own will, has made my fortune for me. The higher I climb the more I'm trusted. In fact I'm waiting for the time when the crossing of the philosopher with the horse thief will be appreciated at its full value.

ANNA. There's no other topic of conversation in the city besides your Fairyland Palace.

KEITH. This Fairyland Palace is nothing more than a rallying point for my powers. I know myself too well to suppose that I could ever start auditing account books at this time in my life.

ANNA. Then what's to become of *me*? Do you suppose I thrill to the prospect of taking singing lessons for the rest of my life? You said only yesterday that the Fairyland Palace was being built especially for me.

KEITH. But not for you to dance around on your hind legs the rest of your life and be crucified by those nitwits of the press. What you need are more high points in your past.

ANNA. Well it's certain I can't produce a family tree like Mesdames von Rosenkron and von Totleben.

KEITH. And you needn't envy either of them because of it.

ANNA. I should hope not! What feminine attributes *should* I be jealous of them for?

KEITH. I inherited these two ladies as legacies from my predecessor when I took over the concert agency. As soon as I've established my position they can peddle radishes or write novels for a living if they like.

ANNA. I'm more concerned about my boots than about your love for me. And do you know why? Because you are the most inconsiderate being in the world, and because you care about nothing else in this world than your sensual gratifications! That's why if you were to leave me all I could feel for you would be pity. But just you take care that you aren't the one who gets left!

KEITH [*carressing* ANNA]. I have a life of sudden reversals behind me, but now I am seriously considering building a house; a house with the highest ceilings possible, a park and a broad flight of stairs leading to the entrance. And there must be beggars, too, to decorate the driveway. I'm through with the past and I have no desire to turn back. There were too many times when I had to fight for my existence. I would never advise a friend to take my life as an example.

ANNA. Of course. You're indestructible.

KEITH. I can attribute everything I've achieved up to now to that fact. You know, Anna, I believe that even had we been born in two separate worlds we would have had to find one another after all.

ANNA. I'm indestructible too.

KEITH. Even if Providence hadn't destined us for one another because of our fabulous similarity of taste, there's still one other thing that we have in common . . .

ANNA. Robust healthiness.

KEITH [*seats himself beside her and caresses her*]. As far as women are concerned, cleverness, good health, sensitivity and beauty are inseparable; any one of them leads inevitably to the other three. If this inheritance is increased in our children . . .

[SASCHA, *a thirteen-year-old errand boy in livery jacket and knee breeches, enters from the hallway and places an armful of newspapers on the center table.*]

KEITH. What does Councillor Ostermeier have to say?

SASCHA. The Herr Councillor gave me a letter. It's there with the newspapers. [*He goes off into the waiting room.*]

KEITH [*having opened the letter*]. I can thank your being with me for this! [*Reads.*] ". . . I have been told several times now about your plans and find myself extremely interested. I shall be at the Café Maximilian at noon today . . ." The world just now has been placed in the palm of my hand! Now I can turn my backside on old Casimir if he decides to come along. With these "worthy" gentlemen on my side my absolute power remains undisputed.

ANNA [*has risen*]. Could you give me a thousand marks?

KEITH. Do you mean to tell me you're broke again?

ANNA. The rent is due.

KEITH. That can wait till tomorrow. Just don't worry about it.

ANNA. Whatever you think best. Count Werdenfels prophesied on his deathbed that one day I would learn about the less agreeable side of life.

KEITH. If he had known you for your true worth he might even still be alive today.

ANNA. Up till now his prophecy has remained unfulfilled.

KEITH. I'll send you the money tomorrow noon.

ANNA [*while* KEITH *accompanies her out*]. No, please don't; I'll come for it myself.

[*The stage remains empty for a moment. Then* MOLLY GREIS-INGER *enters from the living room and clears away the tea things.* KEITH *returns from the hallway.*]

KEITH [*calling*]. Sascha! [*Removes one of the pictures from the wall.*] This will have to help me through the next two weeks.

MOLLY. Do you mean to say you hope we can continue living this way?

SASCHA [*enters from the waiting room*]. Herr Baron?

KEITH [*gives him the picture*]. Go over to Tannhäuser's. He's to place this Saranieff in his window. I'll let it go for three thousand marks.

SASCHA. Very well, Herr Baron.

KEITH. I'll be along in five minutes. Wait! [*He takes a card from his writing-table on which "3000 M" is written and fastens it to the frame of the picture.*] Three thousand Marks! [*Goes to the writing-table.*] First I'll have to dash off a newspaper article about it.

[SASCHA *goes off with the picture.*]

MOLLY. I'd like just once to see a single trace of success from all this talking so big!

KEITH [*writing*]. "The Aesthetical Ideal in Modern Landscape Painting."

MOLLY. If this Saranieff knew how to paint you wouldn't have to write newspaper articles about him.

KEITH [*turning around*]. I beg your pardon?

MOLLY. I know, you're busy.

KEITH. What was it you wanted to say?

MOLLY. I received a letter from Bückeberg.

KEITH. From your mama?

MOLLY [*finds the letter in her pocket and reads*]. "You are both welcome at any time. You could move into the two front rooms on the third floor. That way you could wait quietly till your transactions in Munich are completed."

KEITH. Can't you understand, my dear child, that you're undermining my credit with these little letters of yours?

MOLLY. We haven't even any bread for tomorrow.

KEITH. Then we'll eat at the Hotel Continental.

MOLLY. I wouldn't be able to swallow a mouthful in fear that meanwhile the bailiff would lay hold of our beds.

KEITH. He's still deliberating that prospect. Why is it the only things you can think about in that little head of yours are food and drink? You could make your existence so endlessly more enjoyable if only you appreciated its lighter side more. You cherish the most unyielding affection for misfortune.

MOLLY. I think it's *you* who cherish this affection for misfortune! Other people seem to have an awfully easy time of it; they never have to give a second thought to their professions. That's why they exist for one another in comfortable homes where nothing ever threatens their happiness. And you, with all your talents, run about endangering your health like a madman, and for all that there's never so much as a penny in the house for days on end.

KEITH. Still, you've always had enough to eat! If you never spend anything for clothes, that's scarcely *my* fault. As soon as I've finished writing this newspaper article I'll have three thousand marks in the palm of my hand. Then you can take a cab and buy up everything you can think of at the moment.

MOLLY. He'll pay three thousand marks for that picture like I'll put on silk stockings for your sake.

KEITH [*rises unwillingly*]. You're a real jewel!

MOLLY [*throws her arms around his neck*]. Have I hurt you, darling? Please, forgive me! But what I just told you, I'm solemnly convinced of it.

KEITH. Even if the money only lasts till tomorrow evening I still won't regret the sacrifice.

MOLLY [*wailing*]. I know it was hateful of me. Why don't you beat me!

KEITH. The Fairyland Palace is as good as built.

MOLLY. Then at least let me kiss your hand! Please let me kiss your hand!

KEITH. If only I can maintain my composure for the next couple of days.

MOLLY. Why won't you let me? How can you be so inhuman?

KEITH [*pulls his hand out of his pocket*]. It's high time, I think, you took council with yourself; otherwise the enlightenment may suddenly come of its own accord.

MOLLY [*covering his hand with kisses*]. Why won't you beat me? I know I deserve it!

KEITH. You're cheating yourself of happiness with all the means a woman has at her disposal.

MOLLY [*jumps up indignantly*]. Don't ever suppose that I'll let myself be frightened by these flirtations of yours! We're bound too closely together. Once that band breaks I won't hold you anymore; but as long as you're in misery you belong to me.

KEITH. It will be your undoing, Molly, this fearing my good fortune more than death. If tomorrow my hands are free you won't stay here another moment.

MOLLY. As long as you know that, then everything's fine.

KEITH. But I am not in misery!

MOLLY. Just let me keep on working here for you until your hands *are* free.

KEITH [*seats himself again at the writing-table*]. All right, do what you have to do. But you know there's nothing I like less about a woman than seeing her have to work.

MOLLY. I won't make a monkey or a parrot out of myself for your sake. I can't very well ruin you by standing over a washtub, instead of running around half naked with you to fancy-dress balls.

KEITH. This doggedness of yours is something superhuman.

MOLLY. I can well believe that it's above your capacity for understanding.

KEITH. Even if I *did* understand you, it still wouldn't help you.

MOLLY [*triumphantly*]. I don't have to put one over on you, but I can give it to you in black and white if you like! I wouldn't be one bit happier if I constrained myself and made me think myself better than God had made me— *because you love me!*

KEITH. That goes without saying.

MOLLY [*triumphantly*]. Because you can't live without my love! Keep your hands as free as you want! My staying here only depends on whether I let you have some love left over for other women! Let your women dress themselves up as vulgarly as they can and idolize you as much as they please; it saves me going to comedies. You and your ideals! I know all about that! If it ever came to your doing anything about your ideals—and a lot of chance there is of that—I'd happily let myself be buried alive.

KEITH. If only you'd be happy with what fortune offers you!

MOLLY [*tenderly*]. But what *does* it offer me, my sweet? We knew these same endless fears in America too. And in the end everything always went to pieces. In Santiago you weren't elected president and you were nearly shot because you didn't have brandy on the table on the decisive evening. Do you still remember how you cried out: "A dollar, a dollar, a republic for a dollar!"

KEITH [*jumps up enraged and goes to the divan*]. I was born into this world a cripple. I do not feel myself condemned to be a slave because of it, any more than I feel I should hinder myself from regarding the most luxurious pleasures of life as my rightful inheritance, just because I was born a beggar.

MOLLY. You'll never do anything *but* regard those pleasures as long as you live.

KEITH. Only death can change what I've just said. And death would never have the nerve to come near to me for fear of making a fool of himself. If I die without having lived, then I'll come back as a ghost.

MOLLY. Your only trouble is a swelled head.

KEITH. But I *am justified!* When you were just an irresponsible fifteen-year-old child you left school and ran off with me to America. If we were to part now and you were left to your own resources, you'd come to the worst end possible.

MOLLY [*throws her arms around his neck*]. Then come to Bückeberg with me. My parents haven't seen their Molly for three whole years. They'll be so happy they'll give you half their wealth. And the two of us could live there together.

KEITH. In Bückeberg?

MOLLY. There would be no more troubles for you!

KEITH [*freeing himself*]. I'd rather have to pick up cigar butts in cafés.

SASCHA [*returns with the picture*]. Herr Tannhäuser says he can't put the picture in his window. Herr Tannhäuser says he already has a dozen pictures by Herr Saranieff.

MOLLY. I knew that from the start!

KEITH. That's why I keep you here! [*Goes to the writing-table and tears up the writing paper.*]. At least I needn't write a newspaper article about it anymore!

[SASCHA *goes into the waiting room after putting the picture on the table.*]

MOLLY. These Saranieffs and Zamriakis are people of an entirely different sort from us. They know how to turn people's pockets inside out. The two of us are just too simple for the great world!

KEITH. Your kingdom hasn't come yet. Leave me alone. Bückeberg will just have to wait.

MOLLY [*as the bell rings in the corridor, claps her hands maliciously*]. The bailiff! [*She hurries to open the door.*]

KEITH [*looks at his watch*]. What else can we sacrifice to fortune?

MOLLY [*accompanies* ERNST SCHOLZ *into the room*]. The gentleman refuses to give me his name.

[ERNST SCHOLZ *is a slender, extremely aristocratic figure of about twenty-seven years of age; black wavy hair, a Van-dyke beard, and under his strong elongated eyebrows large water-blue eyes with an expression of helplessness.*]

KEITH. Gaston! Where have you come from?

SCHOLZ. Your welcome is a good sign. I've changed so, that I presumed you would never recognize me.

[MOLLY, *after looking at* SCHOLZ, *decides against removing the breakfast dishes for fear of disturbing the two men. She goes into the living room without the dishes.*]

KEITH. You seem worn out; but then life never was a game!

SCHOLZ. At least not for me. That's precisely why I've come. It's only because of you that I've come to Munich.

KEITH. I thank you; whatever I have left over from my business is yours.

SCHOLZ. I know how bitter a struggle life is for you. But now I want to get to know you personally. I would like to place myself under your moral guidance for a time, but only on the condition that you allow me to help you as much as you need with my financial resources.

KEITH. But why? I'm just now at the point of becoming direc-tor of a gigantic company. And I rather assume you're doing well too? If I'm not mistaken, we saw each other last four years ago.

SCHOLZ. At the legal convention in Brussels.

KEITH. You had passed your State examination just a while before.

SCHOLZ. And you were already writing for every conceivable newspaper. You may recall how I reproached you for your cynicism that time at the ball in the Palace of Justice.

KEITH. You had fallen in love with the daughter of the Danish ambassador, and you broke out in a rage when I maintained that women are by nature for more materialistic than men, even after we've experienced the finest of luxuries.

SCHOLZ. I find you no different now than I did during the whole of our youth, a monster of unscrupulousness; however, you were perfectly right.

KEITH. I've never had a more flattering compliment in all my life.

SCHOLZ. I'm a broken man. Although I detest your entire conception of life from the depths of my soul, I entrust to you as of now the unsolvable riddle of my existence.

KEITH. God be praised you're finally escaping your gloom and turning around to the sun!

SCHOLZ. Don't think this a cowardly capitulation on my part. I've tried every means at my disposal to solve this riddle, and failed every time.

KEITH. All the better for you to have that behind you. During the Cuban revolution I was to have been shot along with twelve conspirators. I naturally fell down with the first shot and stayed "dead" until they came to bury me. It was from that day that I actually felt myself the master of my fate. [*Jumping up.*] We assume no obligations at birth, and we have nothing to throw away except our life. Anyone who lives on after death is outside the rules. That time in Brussels you intended to go into the civil service, didn't you?

SCHOLZ. I decided on our ministry of railroads.

KEITH. I never understood why, with your great wealth, you never chose to live like a great lord, according to your tastes.

SCHOLZ. I intended first to become a useful member of human society. Had I been born the son of a day laborer than it would have happened as a matter of course.

KEITH. One can help his fellow man best in this world by working to his own advantage in as far-reaching a manner as possible. The further my interests extend, the greater the number of people I can provide with a means of livelihood. Whoever imagines that by standing by his post and feeding his children he's accomplishing something useful is only pulling the wool over his own eyes. The children would thank their creator if they had never been brought into the world, and a hundred poor devils are struggling for the same post!

SCHOLZ. The fact is I could see no compelling reason why I should saunter around the world like a worthless idler just

because I was a rich man. I have no artistic talent, and I
didn't think myself insignificant enough to believe my only
vocation in life was to marry and nurture children.

KEITH. Then you've given up the civil service?

SCHOLZ [*hangs his head*]. Because I was the cause of a terrible disaster while I still held office.

KEITH. When I came back from America someone who had
met you the year before in Constantinople told me that
you had travelled for two years but that now you were
at home and on the verge of being married.

SCHOLZ. I broke my engagement just three days ago. Up till
now I'd been only half a man. Since that day on which I
became my own master I allowed myself to be guided by the
single conviction that I could not enjoy my existence until
I had justified it through honest work. This one-sided point
of view has led me today to where I seek nothing but
material satisfaction, and this out of a sheer sense of duty,
nothing else, as though I were doing penance. But no
sooner do I want to open my arms to life than I'm paralyzed
by remembering those unfortunate people who lost their
lives in the most horrible way as a result of my exaggerated
conscientiousness.

KEITH. What's all this about?

SCHOLZ. I had changed one of the regulations of the railroad.
There was a constant danger that this regulation could not
be carried out to the letter. Naturally my fears were exaggerated, but with every day that passed I saw this disaster
draw nearer. I lack that intellectual equilibrium which those
people have who come from a home worthy of human
beings. The first day after my new regulation was introduced
there was a collision of two express trains; it cost the lives
of nine men, three women and two children. I even had to
inspect the scene of the disaster. It isn't my fault that I'm
still alive after seeing the sight.

KEITH. And then you began to travel?

SCHOLZ. I went to England, to Italy, but I still felt myself
completely cut off from all human activity. In gay, happy
surroundings, amid deafening music, I suddenly hear a
shrieking cry, because I am unexpectedly reminded of the
disaster. Even in the Orient I lived like a frightened owl.
To be quite honest, ever since the day of the disaster I
have been convinced that I can only buy back my joy in

living through self-sacrifice. But in order to do that I must have access to life. I had hoped to find that access to life a year ago when I became engaged to a lovely girl of humble origins.

KEITH. And you wanted to turn the creature into the Countess Trautenau?

SCHOLZ. I am no longer the Count Trautenau. That's something you can't understand. The press placed my name and rank in effective contrast with the disaster I had caused. I felt myself bound by duty to my family to assume another name. For two years now my name has been Ernst Scholz. That way, too, my engagement could surprise no one; but some disaster would have emerged from that too. In her heart, not a spark of love; in mine, only the need to sacrifice myself; our association, an endless chain of trivial misunderstandings. I've given the girl an ample enough dowry to make her a desirable choice for anyone of her station in life. She was so happy with her newly won freedom that she could scarcely express herself. And now, finally, I must learn the difficult art of forgetting myself. We can look death in the eye with clear consciousness; but no one can really live until he can forget himself.

KEITH [*throws himself into a chair*]. My father would turn over in his grave if he knew that you . . . were asking me for my advice.

SCHOLZ. In that way life contradicts theoretical wisdom. Your father contributed his share towards my one-sided development too.

KEITH. My father was as selfless and conscientious as the mentor and tutor of a Count Trautenau had to be. You were his model student, and I his whipping boy.

SCHOLZ. Don't you remember how, when you were at our castle, the chambermaids used to kiss you with such tenderness, and then with even greater preference when *I* happened to be around! [*Rising.*] I shall spend the next two to three years singly and solely [*with tears in his voice*] teaching myself to be an epicurean.

KEITH [*jumping up*]. What do you say we go to the dance this evening at the Nymphenburg! That's as unworthy of our sort of people as you can possibly imagine. But with all the rain and sleet pouring itself down over my head I feel enticed to bathe myself in the mire again.

SCHOLZ. I don't particularly want to hear market cries.

KEITH. You won't hear a single loud word spoken, just a hollow roar as though the ocean had been uprooted from its depths. Munich is Arcadia and Babylon at the same time. The silent Saturnalian frenzy here that seizes upon the soul at every opportunity has a fascination for even the most jaded beings.

SCHOLZ. How could I possibly be jaded! To this day I have quite literally never enjoyed a moment of my life.

KEITH. We'll have to guard ourselves against the people on the dance floor! In such places my appearance attracts them like flies to carrion. But I'll lay you a wager that you'll forget yourself for all that. In three months from now you'll even be able to forget yourself when you think back to this evening.

SCHOLZ. I have also asked myself in all seriousness whether it is not my tremendous wealth, perhaps, which is the single source of my misfortune.

KEITH [indignant]. That's blasphemy!

SCHOLZ. In fact I have already debated whether I should not also renounce my wealth as I have my title. As long as I am alive this renunciation could only be for the benefit of my family. In any case, I can decide upon an advantageous disposition of my property on my deathbed, that is to say, after it has ruined my life. If from my youth on I had had to struggle for my livelihood, then, with my moral earnestness and industry, I'd be in the midst of a brilliant career instead of being an outcast.

KEITH. Or else you'd be revelling with your lower-class girl in the most common sort of trashy lovemaking and then clean the dirty boots of your "fellow men."

SCHOLZ. I'd gladly exchange that for my lot anytime.

KEITH. Just don't ever make yourself believe that this railroad disaster is what's standing between you and your life. The only reason you find satisfaction in these hideous memories is that you're too dull to provide yourself with a more delicate nourishment.

SCHOLZ. You may be right. That's precisely why I should like to submit myself to your spiritual guidance.

KEITH. We'll find something to sink our teeth into tonight. I'm afraid I can't invite you to have breakfast with me. I have a business meeting at twelve with a local bigwig. But

I'll give you a few lines to take to my friend Raspe. Spend the afternoon with him; we'll meet at six tonight at the Hofgarten Café. [*He has gone to the writing-table and writes a note.*]

SCHOLZ. What sort of business are you in?

KEITH. I'm an art dealer, I write for the newspapers, I have a concert agency—none of it worth talking about. You've come just at the right time to see the founding of a large-scale concert hall which is being built exclusively for my artists.

SCHOLZ. [*takes the pictures from the table and looks at it*]. You have a nice picture gallery.

KEITH [*jumping up*]. I wouldn't give ten thousand marks for that. A Saranieff. [*Turns the picture around in his hands.*] This is the way you have to hold it.

SCHOLZ. I know nothing about art. While travelling I didn't set foot inside a single museum.

KEITH [*gives him the note*]. The gentleman is an international authority on crime; so you mustn't be too open with him at first. Really a charming man. People never know whether they ought to keep an eye on me, or whether I'm here to keep an eye on them.

SCHOLZ. Thank you for your kind reception. Well then, at six tonight, at the Hofgarten Café.

KEITH. Then we'll drive out to the Nymphenburg. And I thank you that you have finally come around to having faith in me.

[KEITH *accompanies* SCHOLZ *out. The stage is empty for a moment. Then* MOLLY GRIESINGER *enters from the living room and clears the tea service from the table.* KEITH *returns immediately.*]

KEITH [*calling*]. Sascha! [*Goes to the telephone and rings.*] Seventeen thirty-five. Inspector Raspe!

SASCHA [*enters from the living room*]. Herr Baron!

KEITH. My hat! My overcoat!

[SASCHA *hurries into the hall.*]

MOLLY. I beg of you, don't have anything to do with this patron! He wouldn't have come unless he wanted to exploit us.

KEITH [*speaking into the telephone*]. Thank God you're there!

Just wait ten minutes. You'll see for yourself. [*To* MOLLY *while* SASCHA *helps him into his overcoat.*] I must hurry to the newspaper offices.

MOLLY. What should I answer mama?

KEITH [*To* SASCHA]. A carriage!

SASCHA. Yes, Herr Baron! [*Goes off.*]

KEITH. Give her my deepest regards. [*Goes to the writing-table.*] The plans—the letter from Ostermeier—tomorrow morning all Munich must know that the Fairyland Palace will be built!

MOLLY. Then you're not coming to Bückeburg?

KEITH [*the plans rolled up together under his arm, takes his hat from the table, center, and crams it onto his head*]. I can't help but wonder how he's going to turn himself into an epicurean! [*Goes off hurriedly.*]

ACT TWO

[*In the study of the* MARQUIS OF KEITH *the center table is laid for breakfast: champagne and a large dish of oysters. The* MARQUIS OF KEITH *is seated on the writing-table with his left foot on a stool, while* SASCHA, *kneeling in front of him, buttons his shoes with a buttonhook.* ERNST SCHOLZ *stands behind the divan as he tries out a guitar which he has taken from the wall.*]

KEITH. What time did you get back to your hotel this morning?

SCHOLZ [*with a radiant smile*]. At ten.

KEITH. Wasn't I right to leave you alone with that charming creature?

SCHOLZ [*smiling blissfully*]. After last night's discussions about art and modern literature I'm beginning to ask myself whether I shouldn't start taking lessons from this girl. I was even more surprised that she asked you whether she could wait on your guests at the garden party that you plan to astonish all Munich with?

KEITH. She quite simply considers it an honor. Besides, there's time enough to talk about the garden party later. I'm leaving for Paris tomorrow for a couple of days.

SCHOLZ. This comes at a most inopportune time for me.

KEITH. Come along then. I want one of my artists to sing for Madame Marquesi before she makes her debut here.

SCHOLZ. Must I bring back those mental torments that I once lived through in Paris?

KEITH. Won't last night's experience help you to jump that hurdle? Well then, spend your time during my absence with Saranieff the painter. He's bound to run into us sometime today.

SCHOLZ. The girl told me that this Saranieff's studio is a regular chamber of horrors full of the most terrifying abominations ever perpetrated on man. And then she ran on in the most delightfully charming way about her childhood, how when she was a girl in the Tyrol she spent all summer long sitting in the cherry trees and how on winter evenings till dark came on she would go sleighing with the village children. How can a girl like this possibly consider it an honor to serve at your party!

KEITH. The girl considers it an honor because it accords her an opportunity to fight against the unbounded contempt with which our bourgeois society treats her.

SCHOLZ. But how do they justify this contempt? How many hundreds of women in the best social circles have their lives ruined because the stream of life has dried up inside them, in the same way that in this girl it overflows its banks. This girl in all her exuberant joy can never be guilty of a sin like the soul-killing discord which my parents endured together for twenty years!

KEITH. What is sin!

SCHOLZ. Yesterday I was certain that I knew. But today I can confess without despair what thousands upon thousands of other well established persons like myself have experienced: that the man who has failed in life looks with bitter envy at the creature who has wandered from the path of virtuous living!

KEITH. The happiness of these creatures would never be so despised were it not the most unprofitable of all businesses imaginable. Sin is a mythological name for bad business. Good business always works its way into the existing social order! No one knows that better than I. I, the Marquis of Keith, despite that I am the talk of all Munich, and despite my reputation in Europe, I am just as much outside the boundaries of society as that girl. That's the only reason that I'm giving the garden party. I'm unspeakably sorry that I can't receive the poor thing as one of my guests. It will be in far better taste if she appears among my hired help.

SASCHA [has risen]. Would the Herr Baron like me to call a carriage?

KEITH. Yes.

[SASCHA goes off.]

KEITH [stamping his feet into his boots]. You've read, I suppose, that the Fairyland Palace Company was established yesterday?

SCHOLZ. How could I have seen a newspaper since yesterday?

[They both take their places at the breakfast table.]

KEITH. The entire enterprise rests on a beer brewer, a master builder, and a restaurant owner. They are the caryatids that support the pediment of the temple.

SCHOLZ. Incidentally, your friend Raspe, the police inspector, is a charming person.

KEITH. He's a scoundrel; yet I like him for another reason.

SCHOLZ. He told me he was originally a theology student, but lost his faith through too much studying and then tried to regain it the same way as the prodigal son.

KEITH. He sank deeper and deeper till finally the arm of the law caught him up and made good his lost faith again by detaining him for two years under lock and key.

SCHOLZ. The girl absolutely couldn't understand why I had never learned to ride a bicycle. She thought it very reasonable of me not to have ridden a bicycle in Asia and Africa because of the wild animals. But she thought I ought certainly to have begun in Italy!

absurd

KEITH. I'll warn you again, my friend, don't be too open with people! The truth is our most priceless possession and we can never be too sparing with it.

SCHOLZ. Is that why you laid on to the title "Marquis of Keith?"

KEITH. I have as much right to be called the Marquis of Keith as you have to be called Ernst Scholz. I am the adopted son of Lord Keith, who in the year 1863 . . .

SASCHA [*enters from the hall, announcing*]. Herr Professor Saranieff!

[SARANIEFF *enters. He wears a black walking coat with sleeves which are somewhat too long, light trousers which are somewhat too short, thick shoes and glaring red gloves; his rather long, straight, black hair is cut straight all the way around; on a black ribbon in front of his promising eyes he wears a pince-nez à la Murillo; his profile is expressive; he wears a small Spanish mustache. After greeting them he hands his top hat to* SASCHA.]

SARANIEFF. I wish you good fortune from the bottom of my heart, my good friend. At last the cables are cut and the balloon may rise!

KEITH. The Command of my enterprise is awaiting me; I'm afraid there isn't time to invite you to breakfast.

SARANIEFF [*sitting down at the table*]. Then I shall release you from the obligation to invite me.

KEITH. Sascha, set another place!

[SASCHA *has hung up the hat in the hall and goes off into the living room.*]

SARANIEFF. I am amazed that the name of the great Casimir isn't listed among the members of the Fairyland Palace Company.

KEITH. That's simply because I don't wish to waive credit for being the creator of my own work. [*Introducing them.*] Saranieff, the painter—Count Trautenau.

SARANIEFF [*taking a glass and plate and helping himself; to* SCHOLZ]. Count, I already know you inside and out. [*To* KEITH.] Simba was just with me; she is presently sitting for a Böcklin.

KEITH [*to* SCHOLZ]. Böcklin was a great artist himself. [*To* SARANIEFF.] You really needn't boast about such tricks!

SARANIEFF. Make me famous, and I'll no longer have need for such tricks! I'll pay you thirty percent for life. Zamriaki's mind is already tottering like a rotting fencepost because he utterly insists on becoming immortal through honorable means.

KEITH. My only concern is his music. For a genuine composer the mind is always a hindrance.

SCHOLZ. To want to be immortal one must first have an extraordinary love for life.

SARANIEFF [*to* SCHOLZ]. Incidentally, our Simba described you to me as a highly interesting person.

SCHOLZ. Yes, I can well imagine she doesn't meet old grump-usses like me every day.

SARANIEFF. She categorized you with the Symbolists. [*To* KEITH.] And then she raved about an imminent party for the Fairyland Palace, with an extraordinary fireworks display.

KEITH. You can't very well dazzle a dog with fireworks. But the rational man always feels insulted if you fail to give him any. In any case, I'll be going to Paris for a few days beforehand.

SARANIEFF. Undoubtedly they want your opinion on a joint German-French mutual aid treaty?

KEITH. But don't say anything about it!

SCHOLZ. I had no idea you were active in politics too!

SARANIEFF. Can you think of a single thing in which the Marquis of Keith isn't active?

KEITH. I don't want people to say that I don't take an interest in my own times!

SCHOLZ. Doesn't one find enough to occupy his time if he takes life seriously?

SARANIEFF. In any case, you take it too damned seriously! Did a washer woman in Gizeh, at the foot of the pyramids, exchange one of your collars by mistake?

SCHOLZ. You seem to have been quite thoroughly informed about me. Would you permit me to visit you someday in your studio?

SARANIEFF. If you have no objection we can have our coffee there right now. You'll even find your Simba still there.

SCHOLZ. Simba?—Simba? You always seem to be talking about Simba. The girl told me her name was Kathi!

SARANIEFF. Her real name is Kathi; but the Marquis of Keith dubbed her Simba.

SCHOLZ. Undoubtedly because of her wonderfully red hair.

KEITH. Good will or no good will, I have no information on the subject.

SARANIEFF. She has made herself comfortable on my Persian divan and at the moment is sleeping off her hangover from yesterday.

[MOLLY GRIESINGER *enters from the living room and lays a place for* SARANIEFF.]

SARANIEFF. My heartiest thanks, dear madam; but as you can see, I have already finished. You will pardon me, I hope, if I haven't yet taken the opportunity of kissing your hand.

MOLLY. Save your compliments for more worthy opportunities!

[*The bell rings in the corridor;* MOLLY *goes to answer it.*]

KEITH [*looks at his watch and rises*]. You will have to excuse me, gentlemen. [*Calls.*] Sascha!

SARANIEFF [*wiping his mouth*]. We shall go with you, of course. [*He and* SCHOLZ *rise.*]

[SASCHA *enters from the waiting room with the coats and helps* KEITH *and* SCHOLZ *put theirs on.*]

SCHOLZ [*to* KEITH]. Why didn't you tell me you were married?

KEITH. Here, let me straighten your tie. [*He does so.*] You must give more attention to your outward appearance.

[MOLLY *returns from the hall with* HERMANN CASIMIR.]

MOLLY. The young Herr Casimir wishes to see you.

KEITH [*to* HERMANN]. Did you deliver my kind regards yesterday?

HERMANN. The Countess herself was waiting for money from you!

KEITH. Would you wait here just a moment? I shall be right back. [*To* SCHOLZ *and* SARANIEFF.] Ready, gentlemen?

SARANIEFF [*takes his hat from* SASCHA]. With you through thick and thin!

SASCHA. The carriage is waiting, Herr Baron.

KEITH. Sit with the driver!

[SCHOLZ, SARANIEFF, KEITH *and* SASCHA *go off.*]

MOLLY [*gathering the breakfast dishes together*]. I wish I knew what you wanted in this madhouse! You would be much more sensible to stay at home with your mama!

HERMANN [*wanting to leave the room at once*]. My mother is no longer alive, my dear madam; but I wouldn't want to bother you.

MOLLY. Oh, for Heaven's sake, don't go! You're not bothering anyone. I just can't understand these inhuman parents who don't keep their children from associating with such highway thieves! I had a happy home like you and was neither older nor wiser than you are when without thinking I jumped into the bottomless abyss.

HERMANN [*very agitated*]. My God, I *must* find a way! I'll be ruined if I stay in Munich any longer! But the Marquis is bound to refuse me his help if he even suspects what I have in mind. I beg you, madam, don't betray me!

MOLLY. If only you knew how I feel you wouldn't have any fear of my being concerned with your stories! I hope things don't turn out worse for you than for me! If my mother had let me work like I'm working now, instead of sending me ice-skating every free afternoon, I'd still have a life of happiness ahead of me!

HERMANN. But—if you're so terribly unhappy and you know —that you could still be happy, why—why don't you get a divorce?

MOLLY. Oh, for Heaven's sake, don't talk about things you don't understand! You have to be married first if you want to get a divorce.

HERMANN. I'm sorry. I—I thought you *were* married.

MOLLY. God only knows, I don't want to complain about any-one! But in order to get married anywhere in the world you first need papers. And to have papers is something beneath his dignity! [*A bell rings in the corridor.*] This place is like a post office from morning till night! [*Goes off into the hall.*]

HERMANN [*pulling himself together*]. Why do I go shooting my mouth off like that!

[MOLLY *leads in the* COUNTESS WERDENFELS.]

MOLLY. You may wait here for my husband if you like. He should be back very soon. May I introduce you?

ANNA. Thank you. We've met.

MOLLY. Of course! Then I won't be needed. [*Goes into the living room.*]

ANNA [*sits down on the bench of the writing-table beside* HERMANN *and places her hand on his*]. Now, I want you to tell me honestly and openly, my dear young friend, what you do at school with so much money?

HERMANN. I won't tell you.

ANNA. But I'd like very much to know!

HERMANN. I can believe it!

ANNA. Aren't you stubborn!

HERMANN [*pulls his hands from hers*]. I will not be bargained with!

ANNA. And who's bargaining with you? Don't flatter yourself! You see, I divide human beings into two large classes. The young and interesting and the old maids.

HERMANN. In your opinion, of course, I'm an old maid.

ANNA. Yes, unless you can tell me why you need all that money.

HERMANN. But I couldn't possibly because I'm an old maid!

ANNA. Oh, but I could tell from the first time I laid eyes on you that you were young and interesting!

HERMANN. And I am, too; otherwise I'd be content to stay here in Munich.

ANNA. But you want to go out into the world!

HERMANN. And you would like very much to know where. To Paris—to London.

ANNA. Nowadays Paris isn't at all fashionable.

HERMANN. I don't really care about going to Paris.

ANNA. Now why wouldn't you rather stay here in Munich? You have a father with more money than . . .

HERMANN. Because there's nothing here to experience! I'll die if I stay here in Munich, and especially if I have to spend anymore time at school. An old school friend writes me from Africa that when you're unhappy in Africa you're ten times happier than when you're happy in Munich.

ANNA. Let me tell you something: your friend is an old maid. Don't go to Africa. Stay here in Munich with us and really experience something.

HERMANN. But there's no chance of that here!

[MOLLY *shows in* POLICE INSPECTOR RASPE. RASPE, *in his early twenties, is dressed in a light-colored summer suit and straw hat and has the innocent childlike features of an angel by Guido Reni. Short blond hair, the start of a mustache. When he feels himself being watched he clamps his blue pince-nez onto his nose.*]

MOLLY. My husband will be back very soon, if you would care to wait. May I introduce you . . .

RASPE. I really don't know, my good madam, whether it would be of any real service to the Baron if you introduce me.

MOLLY. Well, all right then!—For Heaven's sake! [*She goes into the living room.*]

ANNA. May I say your precautions are quite superfluous. We have met.

RASPE [*seating himself on the divan*]. Hmm—I'm afraid I shall have to recollect . . .

ANNA. When you have sufficiently recollected yourself, then I should like to ask you not to introduce me either.

RASPE. How is it that I've never heard you spoken of here?

ANNA. Only a change of name. I was told that you had spent two years in absolute solitude.

RASPE. Whereupon you naturally concealed the fact that you had known me during my days of glory.

ANNA. Whom haven't we known in his day of glory!

RASPE. You're quite right. Pity is blasphemy. What could I do? I was the sacrifice of the insane confidence which everyone offered me.

ANNA. But now you're young and interesting again?

RASPE. Now I make use of that same insane confidence which everyone offered me for the well being of my fellow human beings. By the way, can you tell me something more specific about this epicurean?

ANNA. I'm very sorry; no one has put him through his paces for me yet.

RASPE. I'm extremely surprised. A Herr Scholz wants to train himself here in Munich to be an epicurean.

ANNA. And for that reason the Marquis of Keith introduces him to a Police Inspector?

RASPE. He's quite harmless. I scarcely knew what to do with him. For his education's sake I took him to the Hofbräuhaus. It's right next door here.

[MOLLY *opens the entrance door and shows in* CONSUL CASIMIR. *He is a man in his middle forties, rather heavy set, dressed in opulent elegance; a full face with a luxuriant black beard, powerful mustache, bushy eyebrows, and hair parted carefully down the center.*]

MOLLY. My husband is not at home. [*Off.*]

CASIMIR [*without greeting anyone, goes straight toward* HERMANN]. There is the door! To think that I had to hunt you down in a robbers' den like this!

HERMANN. You'd never have looked for me here if you weren't afraid for your business!

CASIMIR [*threatening him*]. Will you be quiet! I'll show you what it means to move!

HERMANN [*pulls out a pocket revolver*]. Don't touch me, papa! Don't touch me! I'll shoot myself if you touch me!

CASIMIR. I'll make you pay for this when I get you home!

RASPE. Why should he let himself be treated like an animal?

CASIMIR. Must I be insulted as well here?

ANNA [*approaches him*]. If you please, sir, this is bound to cause an accident. You must calm yourself first. [*To* HERMANN.] Be reasonable; go with your father.

HERMANN. I have nothing to go home for. He doesn't even notice when I drink myself senseless because I don't know why I'm alive!

ANNA. Then tell him quietly what you have in mind; but don't threaten your father with that revolver. Give me that thing.

HERMANN. Is that what you thought I wanted?

ANNA. You won't regret it. I'll give it back to you when you've quieted down. Do you take me for a liar?

[HERMANN *hesitantly gives her the revolver.*]

ANNA. Now you ask your father to forgive you. If you have a spark of honor in your body you couldn't possibly expect your father to make the first move.

HERMANN. But I will not be ruined!

ANNA. You will first ask for forgiveness. You can be quite certain then that your father can be reasoned with.

HERMANN. I—I beg you to . . . [*He sinks to his knees and sobs.*]

ANNA [*tries to stand him up*]. Aren't you ashamed of yourself! Look your father in the eye!

CASIMIR. He has his mother's nerves!

ANNA. Prove to your father that he can have confidence in you. Now you will go home and when you've quieted down you will tell your father all about your plans and your wishes. [*She leads him out.*]

CASIMIR [*to* RASPE]. Who is this woman?

RASPE. Today is the first time I've seen her in two years. At the time she was a saleswoman in a shop on Perus Strasse and her name was Huber if I'm not mistaken. However if you want to know anything further . . .

CASIMIR. I thank you. Your faithful servant! [*Goes off.*]

[MOLLY *enters from the living room to remove the breakfast dishes.*]

RASPE. Pardon me, my good woman; did the Baron really intend to be back before dinner?

MOLLY. Oh, for God's sake, don't ask me such ridiculous things!

ANNA [*re-enters from the hall; to* MOLLY]. May I help you carry something off?

MOLLY. You're asking me if you can help me . . . [*She puts the serving tray back down on the table.*] Whoever wants to can clear the table; I didn't eat off it! [*Goes off into the living room.*]

RASPE. That bit with the boy was extremely well done.

ANNA [*sits down at the writing-table*]. I envy him the carriage his father is taking him home in.

RASPE. Tell me, whatever happened to the Count Werdenfels who used to give one champagne party after another two years ago?

ANNA. That happens to be my own name now.

RASPE. I should have guessed! Would you be so good as to

convey to the Count my sincerest congratulations on his choice.

ANNA. I'm afraid that is no longer possible.

RASPE. Obviously then you've separated.

ANNA. Yes, obviously.

[*Voices are heard in the hallway.*]

I'll explain it to you some other time.

[KEITH *enters with* HERR OSTERMEIER, HERR KRENZL, *and* HERR GRANDAUER, *all of them more or less large-bellied, bleary-eyed Munich Philistines.* SASCHA *follows them.*]

KEITH. What a remarkable stroke of luck! I can introduce you at once to one of our leading artists. Sascha, remove this stuff!

[SASCHA *goes into the living room with the breakfast dishes.*]

KEITH [*introducing them*]. Herr Ostermeier, the brewery proprietor; Herr Krenzl, the master builder; Herr Grandauer, the restaurateur: the caryatids of the Fairyland Palace—the Countess Werdenfels. But your time is limited, gentlemen, and you did come to see the plans. [*Takes the plans from the writing-table and unrolls them on the center table.*]

OSTERMEIER. Take your time, my honored friend. Five minutes one way or the other won't matter.

KEITH [*to* GRANDAUER]. Would you hold this, please.—What you see here is the large concert hall with its sliding ceiling and skylight, so that in the summer it can serve as an exhibition palace. Next to it here there is a smaller theatre which I intended to make popular by means of the most modern of artistic decorations, something, you know, which is a cross between a dance hall and a death chamber. The most modern of styles is always the cheapest and the most effective advertising.

OSTERMEIER. Hm—didn't you forget the toilets?

KEITH. Here you can see a completely detailed sketch of the cloak room and the toilet facilities.—And here, Herr Master Builder, is the façade: the driveway, pediment and caryatids!

KRENZL. I sure wouldn't want being one of them caryatids!

KEITH. Just a little joke of mine, my good sir!

KRENZL. What'd my old lady have to say if I let myself be

chiselled into one of them caryatids way up there, and even more on a Fairyland Palace!

GRANDAUER. Let me tell you, the main thing I want to have as the owner of the restaurant is room.

KEITH. My dear Herr Grandauer, we have proposed to devote the entire ground floor to the restaurant.

GRANDAUER. You can't go crowding folks into a place for eats and drinks like you can for listening to that there music.

KEITH. And for afternoon coffee, my dear Herr Grandauer, here you have a terrace on the mezzanine with a magnificent view overlooking the grounds of the Isar.

OSTERMEIER. And now, my good friend, I'd like to ask you to let us have a look at your preliminary expense sheet.

KEITH [*producing a sheet of writing*]. Four thousand shares at five thousand makes approximately twenty million marks. —I'm operating on the assumption, gentlemen, that each of us subscribes to forty preferred shares, and that we pay for them at once. You see, the estimated profit is extraordinarily low.

KRENZL. The only question now is if the local authorities say all right to what we want.

KEITH. That's why, in addition to the shares, we are going to issue a number of interest-drawing bonds and place a portion of them at the city's disposal for worthy purposes.—It is proposed that members of the governing board receive ten percent of the net profit before deductions for depreciation reserves.

OSTERMEIER. All as it should be. Can't ask for more than that.

KEITH. As far as the stock exchange is concerned, we'll need to work some on that. I'm going to Paris tomorrow for that very purpose. In two weeks from today we shall have our founders' party at my villa on Brienner Strasse.

[ANNA *starts.*]

OSTERMEIER. Sure would be nice to get Consul Casimir to come along with us by the time of the party!

KRENZL. That'd be the smartest thing, all right. Get Consul Casimir with us and the authorities would say yes to anything.

KEITH. I hope, gentlemen, that we shall be able to call a general meeting of the board before the party. You will see then how I shall take into consideration your suggestions regarding Consul Casimir.

OSTERMEIER [*shakes his hand*]. Have a nice trip to Paris, then, my good friend. Let's have a word out of you from Paris. [*Bowing to* ANNA.] May I take the liberty of bidding you farewell; my compliments.

GRANDAUER. Farewell; may I take the liberty of wishing you a good afternoon.

KRENZL. My best regards. Good day!

[KEITH *leads the gentlemen out*.]

ANNA [*after he has returned*]. What can you possibly be thinking of, announcing your founders' party at my house?!

KEITH. I shall have a dress made for you in Paris that will make it wholly unnecessary for you to be able to sing. [*To* RASPE.] And you, Herr Police Inspector, I shall expect you at our founders' party to utilize all the charm of your personality in bewitching the wives of our three caryatids.

RASPE. The ladies will find nothing to complain of.

KEITH [*giving him some money*]. Here are three hundred marks. I'm bringing fireworks back from Paris, the likes of which the city of Munich has never seen.

RASPE [*pocketing the money*]. He got this from the epicurean.

KEITH [*to* ANNA]. I use every mortal according to his talents, and I must recommend a certain degree of caution in regard to my close friend, Police Inspector Raspe.

RASPE. When a man looks as though he had been cut down from the gallows, like yourself, getting through life honestly is no art. I'd like to see where you'd be today if you had my angelic face!

KEITH. With your face I'd have married a princess.

ANNA [*to* RASPE]. If I'm not mistaken, you were first introduced to me under a French name.

RASPE. I no longer use French names since I've become a useful member of human society.—Permit me to pay you my respects. [*Goes off*.]

ANNA. With my serving staff I am not equipped to give big suppers!

KEITH [*calls*]. Sascha!

SASCHA [*enters from the waiting room*]. Herr Baron?

KEITH. Would you like to help serve at a garden party for my friends?

SASCHA. That would be a real pleasure, Herr Baron. [*Goes off*.]

KEITH. May I introduce you today to my oldest boyhood friend, the Count Trautenau?

ANNA. I've never had much luck with counts.

KEITH. That's all right. All I ask is that you don't discuss my domestic relations with him. The fact is he is a moralist, both by nature and by conviction. He's already questioned me closely today about my family life.

ANNA. Good Heavens, this man doesn't really want to become an epicurean, does he?

KEITH. That makes it all the more contradictory! Ever since I've known him he's lived a life of sacrifice, without realizing that there are really two souls in his breast.

ANNA. That too! I find that just one is too many. But isn't his name Scholz?

KEITH. One of his souls is named Ernst Scholz, the other Count Trautenau.

ANNA. Thank you anyway, but I want nothing to do with people who can't make up their minds!

KEITH. Why, he's a paragon of decision. The world has no more pleasures to offer him unless he starts from the bottom up.

ANNA. But man is always supposed to climb higher!

KEITH. Why are you so upset?

ANNA. Because you are trying to pair me off with this frightful monster!

KEITH. He's gentle as a lamb.

ANNA. I thank you very much, but no personification of disaster will even enter my boudoir!

KEITH. But you don't understand me. At the moment I cannot do without his confidence, and for that reason I don't want to expose myself to his disapproval. If he fails to get to know you, all the better for me, because I won't have his reproaches to look forward to.

ANNA. Who can ever tell where your calculations are going to lead!

KEITH. What did you have in mind?

ANNA. I thought you wanted to use me as a whore for your friend.

KEITH. Do you really think me capable of such a thing?

ANNA. You said just a moment ago that you use every mortal according to his talents. And who could ever doubt that I possess the talent of a whore?

KEITH [taking ANNA in his arms]. Anna—I am going to Paris tomorrow, not to work out the stock exchange or to buy fireworks, but because I must breathe some fresh air, because I must stretch out my arms unless I want to see the façade topple that I have so carefully erected here in Munich. Anna, would I be taking you with me to Paris if you weren't everything to me?—Do you know something, Anna? Not a night goes by but I see you in my dreams with a diadem in your hair. If you were ever to ask me to get a star for you from the firmament, I wouldn't be afraid, I'd find the ways and means to do it.

ANNA. Use me as a whore!—You'll see whether or not I yield a profit!

KEITH. All I can think of at this moment is the concert dress that I will have made for you at St. Hilaire's . . .

SASCHA [*enters from the hall*]. A Herr Sommersberg would like to see you.

KEITH. Show him in. [*To* ANNA, *describing the dress.*] A silvery torrent of mauve silk and paillettes from shoulder to knee, so tightly laced and cut so deep in front and back that the dress will appear a glittering jewel on your slender body!

[SOMMERSBERG *has entered. In his late thirties, deeply lined face, hair and beard streaked with grey and unkempt. A heavy winter overcoat covers his shabby clothes, torn kid gloves.*]

SOMMERSBERG. I am the author of *Songs of a Happy Man*. I don't look it.

KEITH. I looked like that once myself.

SOMMERSBERG. I would never have found the courage to come to you if it weren't for the fact that I have had almost nothing to eat for almost two days.

KEITH. That's happened to me a hundred times. How can I help you?

SOMMERSBERG. Just a little something—for my lunch . . .

KEITH. Is that all the use you think I can be to you?

SOMMERSBERG. I'm an invalid.

KEITH. But you still have half a lifetime ahead of you!

SOMMERSBERG. I have wasted my life living up to the expectations people had set for me.

KEITH. Perhaps you may still find a current which will take you out to the open sea. Or are you afraid for your life?

SOMMERSBERG. I can't swim; and here in Munich resignation isn't so hard to bear.

KEITH. Why don't you come to our founders' party in two weeks from today? Brienner Strasse. You'll be able to make some necessary contacts there. [*Gives him some money.*] Here are a hundred marks. Keep enough of this money in reserve so that you can rent a dress suit for the evening.

SOMMERSBERG [*hesitantly taking the money*]. I feel as if I were deceiving you . . .

KEITH. Just don't deceive yourself! And in doing so you will be doing a good turn for the next poor devil who comes to me.

SOMMERSBERG. Thank you, Herr Baron. [*Goes off.*]

KEITH. Don't mention it. [*He closes the door and puts his arms around* ANNA.] And now, my queen, we're off to Paris!

ACT THREE

[*A room overlooking a garden is lighted with electric lamps; a wide glass door in the right side wall leads into the garden. The middle door in the back wall leads into the dining room where dinner is being served. When the door is opened one sees the upper end of the table. In the left wall is a curtained door into the game room. Near the door is an upright piano. Downstage right, a lady's writing-table; downstage left, a settee, chairs and table, etc. In the upstage right corner there is a door which leads into the hallway. A toast is being drunk in the dining room. As the glasses clink,* SOMMERSBERG, *in shabbily elegant evening dress, and* KEITH, *in a full-dress suit, enter the salon through the center door.*]

KEITH [*closing the door behind him*]. You've composed the telegram?

SOMMERSBERG [*a paper in hand, reading*]. "The founders of the Munich Fairyland Palace Company brought together yesterday evening the notable citizens of the gay city on the Isar for a highly spirited garden party at the villa of the Marquis of Keith on Brienner Strasse. Until after midnight a magnificent fireworks display delighted the residents of the neighboring streets. We wish to extend to this enterprise begun under such favorable auspices . . ."

KEITH. Excellent!—Whom can I send to the telegraph office . . .?

SOMMERSBERG. Let me take care of that. After all the champagne I've had, a little fresh air will do me good.

[SOMMERSBERG *goes off into the hallway; at the same time* ERNST SCHOLZ *enters; he is in a full-dress suit and an overcoat.*]

KEITH. You've certainly kept us waiting long enough.

SCHOLZ. And I've merely come to tell you I can't stay.

KEITH. They're making a laughing stock of me! Old Casimir has already left me in the lurch; but at least he sent a congratulatory telegram.

SCHOLZ. I don't belong with people! You complain about being outside society; I'm outside humanity!

KEITH. Haven't you every pleasure now that a man can dream of?

SCHOLZ. Pleasure? What pleasure? This frenzied whirl of pleasurable sensations I'm reveling in now leaves no line of distinction between myself and a barbarian. To be sure, I have learned to go into raptures over Rubens and Richard Wagner. The disaster which earlier aroused pity in me has become almost insupportable in its ugliness. And so I've become an all the more devout enthusiast of the artistic achievements of dancers and acrobats.—If only, after all this, I had made just one step of progress! It's for my money's sake that I'm treated like a human being. But as soon as I actually want to be one I find myself ramming against invisible walls!

KEITH. If you can envy those lucky dogs who take root whereever they find room and then are blown away as soon as the wind changes, then don't look to me for pity! This world is a damned sly beast, and it's no easy thing to conquer. But succeed once and you're proof against any misfortune.

SCHOLZ. If such phrases give you any sort of satisfaction then I'm afraid there's nothing I can hope for from you. [*He is about to leave.*]

KEITH [*holds him back*]. They are not phrases! There's no misfortune today that can touch me. We're too well acquainted with one another, misfortune and I. Misfortune for me is as favorable an opportunity as anything else. Any stupid ass can suffer misfortune; the trick of the matter is to know how to exploit it to one's own advantage!

SCHOLZ. You hang around the world's neck like a whore to a pimp. You can't understand that a man can become as loathesome to himself as carrion if he exists only for himself.

KEITH. Then in the name of all the devils in hell will you be satisfied with your godly way of life! Once you have this purgatory of earthly vice and joy behind you you'll look down on this poor miserable sinner as if I were a Father of the Church!

SCHOLZ. If only I were in possession of my human birthright! Better to crawl into the wilderness like a wild animal than to have to beg to be excused for my existence every step of the way!—I can't stay here!—I met the Countess Werdenfels yesterday.—How I could have offended her is something I cannot understand. I suppose I unintentionally assumed the tone I've grown accustomed to using with our Simba.

KEITH. I've received more slaps on the ear from women than I have hairs on my head! But no one has ever laughed at me behind my back because of it!

SCHOLZ. I'm a man without breeding!—And with a woman for whom I have the highest regard!

KEITH. A man like you, whose every step from his youth on has given rise to a spiritual conflict, can be the master of his times and rule the world long after the rest of us have become food for worms!

SCHOLZ. And then there's our little Simba who's playing the waitress here tonight!—The most experienced diplomat never had to deal with as ticklish a situation as this!

KEITH. Simba doesn't know you!

SCHOLZ. I'm not afraid that Simba will be too friendly with me; I'm afraid Simba will be insulted if I ignore her here without the slightest provocation.

KEITH. How could you insult her by doing that! She understands class distinctions a hundred times better than you!

SCHOLZ. Believe me, I've learned all there is to know about class distinctions! God knows, they're the fetters that show man his utter weakness in its most extreme form!

KEITH. I suppose you think *I* have no weakness to combat! It makes no difference whatever whether my conduct is as correct as the course of the planets, or whether my dress is as elegant and well chosen as possible, these things are no more capable of changing these plebeian hands of mine than you can make an intellect out of an imbecile! With my intellectual endowments I should long ago have enjoyed a better position in society were it not for these hands.— Come, you'd do best to put your overcoat in the next room!

SCHOLZ. Leave me alone! I couldn't talk calmly with the Countess today if I wanted to.

KEITH. Then talk with the two divorcées; they're both experiencing conflicts similar to yours.

SCHOLZ. Both at the same time?!

KEITH. Neither one of them is over twenty-five, absolute beauties, ancient Nordic aristocracy, and so ultramodern in their principles that they make me feel like an old flint-lock beside them.

SCHOLZ I rather feel that I'm not far from being a modern myself.

[SCHOLZ *goes off into the game room;* KEITH *is about to follow him but at that moment* SARANIEFF *enters from the hallway.*]

SARANIEFF. Tell me, is there anything left to eat?

KEITH. Please leave your coat outside! I haven't eaten all day long.

SARANIEFF. One needn't worry so about it in here. But first I must ask you something very important.

[SARANIEFF *hangs his hat and coat in the hallway; meanwhile* SASCHA *in frock coat and satin breeches enters from the gameroom with a filled champagne cooler on his way into the dining room.*]

KEITH. When you set off the fireworks later, Sascha, be sure you're careful with the big mortar! There's all hellfire in that one!

SASCHA. Oh, I'm not scared, Herr Baron! [*He goes off into the diningroom, closing the door behind him.*]

SARANIEFF [*re-enters from the hallway*]. Have you any money?

KEITH. But you've just sold a picture! Why do you think I sent my friend to see you?

SARANIEFF. What do you expect me to get from a squeezed lemon like him? Why, you've already stripped him to his shirt. He has to wait three days before he can pay me a pfennig.

KEITH [*gives him a note*]. Here are a thousand marks.

[SIMBA, *a typical Munich girl, ruddy complexion, with nimble movements, luxuriant red hair, in a tasteful black dress with white pinafore, enters from the dining room with a serving tray of half-empty wine glasses.*]

SIMBA. The Herr Councillor wants to drink another toast to the Herr Baron.

[KEITH *takes one of the glasses from the tray and goes to the table through the open door.* SIMBA *goes off into the game room.*]

KEITH. Ladies and gentlemen! This evening's celebration signifies the beginning of an era for Munich which will eclipse everything that has gone before. We are creating here in this city a center for the arts in which all the arts of the world will find a welcome home. If our project has been the cause of general astonishment, then you must be mindful of the fact it is always only the truly astounding which wins the crown of greatest success. I empty my glass in honor of the principle which has ordained Munich a city of the arts, in honor of Munich's citizens and its lovely women.

[*While the glasses are still clinking,* SASCHA *enters from the dining room, closes the door behind him and goes into the game room.* SIMBA *enters from the game room with a platter of cheese under a glass cover on her way into the dining room.*]

SARANIEFF. Simba! Have you been struck blind?! Can't you see, Simba, that this epicurean of yours is about to escape from your snare and be gathered up again by this Countess from Perusa Strasse?!

SIMBA. What are you doing out here? Go on, sit at the table!

SARANIEFF. Me sit with the caryatids!—Simba! Do you want all that lovely money that your epicurean has in his pockets to be devoured by the insane Marquis of Keith?!

SIMBA. Go on, now, let me alone! I have to serve!

SARANIEFF. The caryatids don't need any more cheese! It's time they wiped their mouths and put an end to it! [*He places the cheese platter on the table and takes* SIMBA *on his knee.*] Simba! Don't you feel anything for me anymore! Am I to have to beg for twenty mark pieces from the Marquis of Keith amid wailing and the gnashing of teeth, while you can fetch thousand mark notes fresh from their source?

SIMBA. Thanks! Nobody in the world ever plagued me like this epicurean with his compassion, that stupid compassion of his! He's trying to tell me I'm a martyr of civilization! Ever hear anything like that? Me a martyr of civilization! I said to him, I said: "Tell your society ladies that! They'll like it when you call them martyrs of civilization, because otherwise they're nothing!" A martyr of civilization he calls me, when I can drink champagne and have all the fun I want!

SARANIEFF. Simba! If I were a woman of your qualities this epicurean would have to pay for every muggy glance with an ancestral castle!

SIMBA. That's the way he talks all right! He asks me why he's a man. Like there aren't enough ghosts in the world! Ever hear me ask why I'm a girl?

SARANIEFF. Nor do you ask us to throw away fifty million marks on some confounded idea of yours!

SIMBA. Oh, those sad millions! You know, there's only once I've seen this epicurean laugh since I met him. I told him, this epicurean, that he had to learn to ride a bicycle. And so he learned. We took a ride to Schleissheim and while we were in the woods looking around a thunderstorm broke out like I thought the world would come to an end. It was then, for the first time since I met him, that he started to laugh. Oh, and how he laughed! "There," I said, "now you're a real epicurean!" He laughed at every stroke of lightning! The more it lightninged and thundered the crazier he laughed!—"Don't stand there under the trees," I said, "that's where the lightning'll hit!"—"No lightning's going to hit me," he said, and laughed and laughed!

SARANIEFF. Simba! Simba! At that very moment you could have become an imperial countess!

SIMBA. Thanks! What I could have become is a Social Democrat. World betterment, humanitarianism, those are his specialties. No thanks, I wasn't made for the Social Democrats. They're too moralistic for me! Let them get into power once and goodbye champagne suppers.—Have you seen my lovey?

SARANIEFF. Have I seen your lovey? I thought I was your lovey!

SIMBA. That could be almost anybody!—You see, I have to keep close watch on him, otherwise the Marquis of Keith won't engage him for his new Fairyland Palace.

[SOMMERSBERG *enters from the hallway.*]

SIMBA. Here he is! Where in heaven's name have you been all this time?

SOMMERSBERG. I was sending off a telegram to the newspapers.

SARANIEFF. My God, the graves have begun to open! Sommersberg! Aren't you ashamed to come back from the dead to be secretary of this Fairyland Palace?!

SOMMERSBERG [*indicating* SIMBA]. This angel has restored me to the world.

SIMBA. Oh, go on, lovey!—He comes and asks me where he can get some money.—"Go to the Marquis of Keith," I said. "If he's all out, you won't find another pfennig in the city of Munich."

[RASPE, *dressed in the most elegant evening clothes, a small chain with an Order on his chest, enters from the game room.*]

RASPE. Simba, this is simply scandalous, making the Fairyland Palace Company wait for its cheese!

SIMBA [*catches up the cheese platter*]. Holy Mother of God!— I'll be there!

SARANIEFF. Why don't you just stay with the old crones you are hired to take care of!

SIMBA [*taking* RASPE's *arm*]. You let this boy alone, you hear?—You'd both be happy enough if you were as handsome as he is!

SARANIEFF. Simba—you are a born whore!

SIMBA. I'm what?

SARANIEFF. You are a born whore!

SIMBA. Say that again?

SARANIEFF. You are a born whore!

SIMBA. I'm not a born whore. I'm a born cheese spit. [*Goes off into the dining room with* RASPE.]

SOMMERSBERG. I even dictate her love letters for her.

SARANIEFF. Then it's you I have to thank for destroying my castles in the air!

[SASCHA *enters from the game room with a lighted lantern.*]

SARANIEFF. My God, what are you all got up for! You want to marry a countess too?

SASCHA. I'm going to set off the fireworks in the garden now. Wait'll I set off the big mortar, that'll open their eyes! The Herr Marquis said there's all hellfire in that one! [*Goes off into the garden.*]

SARANIEFF. His master's afraid if he sets off the fireworks himself he might go up with them!—There's no wonder fortune never lets him up in the saddle! He's no sooner mounted than he rides the poor beast to its shame till there's not a shred of flesh on its ribs!

[*The center door opens and the guests leave the dining room.*]

Come, Sommersberg! Now our Simba can dish us up a real Lucullan feast!

[*The guests stream into the salon; at their head,* RASPE *between* FRAU COUNCILLOR OSTERMEIER *and* FRAU KRENZL; *then* KEITH *with* OSTERMEIER, KRENZL, *and* GRANDAUER; *then* ZAMRIAKI *with* BARONESS VON ROSENKRON *and* BARONESS VON TOTLEBEN, *and finally* SCHOLZ *and* ANNA—SARANIEFF *and* SOMMERSBERG *sit down at the table in the dining room.*]

RASPE. Will your royal highnesses join me in a cup of exquisite coffee?

FRAU OSTERMEIER. My, I don't think there could possibly be another cavalier as gracious as you in all southern Germany!

FRAU KRENZL. The noblemen of our Royal House could certainly take you as an example!

RASPE. I give you my absolute word of honor that this is the most blessed moment of my life. [*Goes off with both ladies into the game room.*]

OSTERMEIER [*to* KEITH]. All the same it was nice of old Casimir, you know, to send us a congratulatory telegram. But then, you see, my dear friend, old Casimir is a very cautious man!

KEITH. Never mind! Never mind! We'll have old Casimir with us by the time of our first general meeting.—Won't you gentlemen have some coffee?

[OSTERMEIER, KRENZL *and* GRANDAUER *go off into the game room.*]

BARONESS VON ROSENKRON [*to* KEITH, *who is about to follow the gentlemen*]. Promise me now, Marquis, that you will let me study to be a dancer at the Fairyland Palace.

BARONESS VON TOTLEBEN. And that you'll let me learn to be a trick rider!

KEITH. I swear to you, my lovely goddesses, that we will not open the Fairyland Palace without you!—What's the matter with you, Zamriaki? You're as pale as a corpse . . .

ZAMRIAKI [*a slender, short conservatory musician, with long, black, wavy hair parted down the middle; speaks with a Polish accent*]. On my symphony I am working day and night. [*Takes* KEITH *to one side.*] If you permit me, Herr Marquis, I like to ask for advance of twenty Marks on salary of conductor for Fairyland Palace Orchestra.

KEITH. With the greatest pleasure. [*Gives him the money.*] Could you perhaps give us a sampling soon of your new symphony in one of my Fairyland Palace concerts?

ZAMRIAKI. I play the Scherzo. Scherzo will be great success.

BARONESS VON ROSENKRON [*at the glass door into the garden*]. My, just look at this sea of light! Look, Martha, look!— Come, Zamriaki, take us into the garden!

ZAMRIAKI. I come, ladies! I come! [*He goes into the garden with* BARONESS VON ROSENKRON *and* BARONESS VON TOTLE-BEN.]

KEITH [*following them*]. Damnation, people, stay away from the big mortar! It's loaded with my most splendid rockets! [*Goes off into the garden.*]

[SIMBA *closes the center door from inside the dining room.* ANNA *and* SCHOLZ *stay behind alone in the salon.*]

ANNA. I can't imagine what in the world I could have taken amiss. Have you ever experienced this tactlessness you speak of in your relations with any other women?

SCHOLZ. Quite impossible. But you see, I'm as happy now as a person who has been locked inside a prison since his earliest childhood, and now for the first time in his life breathes the free air. That's why I'm still so distrustful of myself with every step I take; I'm that afraid of losing my newfound happiness.

ANNA. I can imagine it must be fascinating to live one's life in the dark without ever opening one's eyes!

SCHOLZ. You see, Countess, if I could exchange my existence for one which strives for the common good, I could never render my Creator sufficient thanks.

ANNA. I thought you came to Munich to learn to be an epi-curean?

SCHOLZ. This learning to be an epicurean is only a means to an end for me. I give you my most sacred assurance of that! But you mustn't think me a hypocrite because of it!—Oh, there's still so much good still to fight for in this world! I'll find my rightful place. The more blows Fortune rains down upon my head, the more precious this bag of bones will be to me, that seemed so unspeakably burdensome till now. And I am absolutely certain of this one fact: if I am ever successful at putting myself at the service of my fellow men I shall never, never once assume any credit for it! Whether my path lead me upwards or whether it lead me downwards I belong solely to that terrible and pitiless race whose interest resides in self-preservation!

ANNA. Maybe the only reason famous people become famous

is that they couldn't endure traffic with us common run-of-the-mill people!

SCHOLZ. You still do not understand me, Countess.—As soon as I have found my proper sphere of activity I shall be the most modest and grateful member of society. I've even begun riding a bicycle here in Munich. It made me feel as though I hadn't seen the world since the days of my childhood. Every tree, every body of water, the mountains, the heavens, they were all one great revelation which I seemed to have had a presentiment of in a former life.— May I invite you to a cycling party sometime?

ANNA. What would you say to tomorrow morning at seven? Or aren't you one for getting up early?

SCHOLZ. Tomorrow morning at seven! I see my life spread out before me like an endless spring landscape!

ANNA. Just don't keep me waiting!

[ZAMRIAKI, BARONESS VON ROSENKRON and BARONESS VON TOTLEBEN return from the garden. SIMBA enters from the game room.]

BARONESS VON ROSENKRON. Oh, but it's cold!—Martha, we'll have to take our shawls the next time we go out. Play us a cancan, Zamriaki! [To SCHOLZ.] Do you dance the can-can?

SCHOLZ. I regret that I do not, madam.

BARONESS VON ROSENKRON [to BARONESS VON TOTLEBEN]. Then let us dance together!

[ZAMRIAKI has seated himself at the piano and begun a waltz.]

BARONESS VON ROSENKRON. Do you call that a waltz, Maestro?

ANNA [to SIMBA]. But you can do the waltz, can't you?

SIMBA. If madam wishes . . .

ANNA. Come on!

[BARONESS VON ROSENKRON, BARONESS VON TOTLEBEN, ANNA and SIMBA dance the waltz.]

BARONESS VON ROSENKRON. More tempo, please!

[KEITH returns from the garden and turns off all the electric lights but one, so that the salon is only dimly lighted.]

ZAMRIAKI [breaks off playing with annoyance]. I come with each beat closer to my symphony.

BARONESS VON TOTLEBEN. But why is it so dark all of a sudden?

KEITH. So that my rockets make more of an impression! [*He opens the door to the dining room.*] If you please, ladies and gentlemen . . .

[RASPE, HERR *and* FRAU OSTERMEIER *and* HERR *and* FRAU KRENZL *enter the salon.* SIMBA *goes off.*]

KEITH. It pleases me to be able to announce to you that in the course of the next few weeks the first of our great Fairyland Palace concerts will take place. These concerts shall serve as publicity for our enterprise. Countess Werdenfels will introduce us to some songs of very recent composition, while our conductor Herr Zamriaki will personally direct excerpts from his symphonic poem *The Wisdom of the Brahmans.*

[*General applause. In the garden a rocket rises hissingly into the air, casting a reddish shimmer into the salon.* KEITH *turns off all the electric lights and opens the glass door.*]

KEITH. Into the garden, ladies and gentlemen! Into the garden if you care to see something!

[*A second rocket rises into the air as the guests leave the salon.* KEITH, *who is about to follow them, is held back by* ANNA. *The stage remains dark.*]

ANNA. Just what do you mean announcing I'm to take part in your Fairyland Palace concert?

KEITH. If you want to wait until your teacher declares you ready for the public, you might grow old and grey without ever having sung a note. [*Throws himself into a chair.*] At last, at last this perilous rope dancing bit is coming to an end! For ten years I had to dissipate my powers so as not to lose my equilibrium. From this day on my way is upwards!

ANNA. And just where am I supposed to get the cheek to step in front of the Munich public with my so-called singing?!

KEITH. I thought you were going to be the best Wagnerian singer in Germany inside of two years.

ANNA. I said that only in jest.

KEITH. How was I to know that!

ANNA. Other concerts are prepared for months in advance!

KEITH. I haven't denied myself thousands of times in my life-time only to pattern myself after other people. If your so-called singing doesn't please them, then they'll be intoxicated by the brilliance of your Parisian concert dress.

ANNA. If only the others saw me with vour eyes!

KEITH. I'll see they use the right glasses!

ANNA. I no sooner come within your sight than you hear and see the most fantastic sort of daydreams. You overrate my appearance as much as you overrate my art.

KEITH [*jumping up*]. I have never been suspected of overrating women, but I knew all there was to know about you from the first moment I laid eyes on you! Is it any wonder I looked for you for ten years on two separate continents! You might have made my acquaintance several times, but at the time vou were either in the clutches of a bandit like myself or else I was reduced to such a level that there would have been little point in my entering your luminous circle of society.

ANNA. Just because you're losing vour mind out of love for me, is that any reason why I should heap the scorn of all Munich on my own back?

KEITH. Other women have heaped quite different things on themselves for my sake!

ANNA. I haven't become infatuated with vou yet!

KEITH. That's what thev all say! You might as well surrender to vour inevitable good fortune. I shall inspire you with the necessary degree of ingenuousness for your first appearance—even if I have to drive you out there with a loaded revolver!

ANNA. You just keep pushing me around like an animal and you'll see how soon it will be over between us!

KEITH. You can be confident in the fact that I'm a man who takes life damned seriously! Perhaps I may like to bathe in champagne, but for all that I can deny myself every one of life's pleasures, like few other people can. Not a single moment of my existence is bearable to me unless I've made at least one step of progress towards my goal!

ANNA. And it's about time you reached that goal!

KEITH. Do you really think, Anna, that I would arrange this Fairyland Palace concert if I were not absolutely certain of the fact that it will yield a brilliant triumph for you?— Let me tell you something: I am a man of *faith* . . .

[*In the garden a rocket rises hissingly into the air.*]

. . . I believe in nothing so firmly as in the fact that our efforts and sacrifices are rewarded in this world!

ANNA. You'd *have* to believe like that to overwork yourself like you do!

KEITH. And if we are not rewarded then our children will be.

ANNA. But you haven't any children!

KEITH. Then you will give them to me, Anna—children with my intelligence, with robust, healthy bodies and aristocratic hands. And for that I shall build you a home fit for a queen, such as a woman of your stamp deserves! And I shall place a spouse at your side with the power of fulfilling every desire mirrored in your great, black eyes. [*He kisses her passionately. In the garden some fireworks are set off which for a moment bathe the couple in a dark red glow.*]—Go into the garden. The caryatids are dying for the privilege of kneeling before our Divinity!

ANNA. Aren't you coming too?

KEITH [*turns on two of the electric lights so that the salon is dimly lighted*]. I want to dash off a newspaper article about our concert. The notice must appear in tomorrow morning's paper. In it I shall congratulate you in advance for your eminent triumph.

[ANNA *goes into the garden.* KEITH *sits at the table and notes down a few words.* MOLLY GRIESINGER, *a colored shawl over her head, enters excitedly and provoked from the hallway.*]

MOLLY. I have to speak to you for a moment.

KEITH. As long as you want, my child; you aren't disturbing me at all. I told you though that you wouldn't be able to hold out at home alone.

MOLLY. I pray to Heaven for some dreadful disaster to overtake us! That's the only thing left that can still save us!

KEITH. But why won't you come with me, if I ask you to?

MOLLY [*shuddering*]. To your friends?

KEITH. The people in these rooms are the business on which we both live! But you find it unbearable that I should be here with my thoughts and not with you!

MOLLY. Can that surprise you?—You know, when you're with these people you're an entirely different person; you're someone I've never known, whom I've never loved, whom I would never in my life have followed so much as a single step, to say nothing of sacrificing home, family, happiness, everything.—You're so good, so wonderful, so dear!—But with these people—to me you're worse than—than dead!

KEITH. Go home and dress yourself up a little; Sascha will go with you. You *mustn't* be alone tonight.

MOLLY. Yes, I'm just in the mood to get dressed up. The way you're carrying on frightens me so that I feel as if the world's going under tomorrow. I have the feeling that I must do something, whatever it may be, to keep these horrors from us.

KEITH. As of yesterday I am drawing a yearly salary of one hundred thousand marks. You needn't fear any longer that we'll die of hunger.

MOLLY. Don't joke like that! You're sinning against *me!* I can scarcely express any more what it is that frightens me!

KEITH. Then tell me what I can do to calm you. I'll do it at once.

MOLLY. Come with me! Come with me out of this murderers' den where all they want to do is destroy you. It's true that I've complained to people about you; but I did it because I couldn't look at your childish delusions any longer. You're so stupid! Really you are! You let yourself be taken in by the lowest, commonest swindlers, and you patiently let them cut your throat!

KEITH. It's better, my child, to suffer evil than to do evil.

MOLLY. Yes, if you only knew!—But they make certain your eyes stay closed. These people flatter you by saying you're a marvel of cleverness and diplomacy! And only because your vanity strives towards nothing higher than to be just that! At the same time they are quietly and cold-bloodedly placing the rope around your neck!

KEITH. What is this terrible thing you're so afraid of?

MOLLY [*whimpering*]. I can't tell you! I can't make myself say it!

KEITH. Please, you *must* say it; you'll be able to laugh about it then.

MOLLY. I'm afraid that . . . I'm afraid that . . .

[*A muffled report sounds from the garden;* MOLLY *screams and falls to her knees.*]

KEITH [*helping her up*]. That was the large mortar.—You must calm yourself!—Come, have a couple glasses of champagne; then we'll go out and look at the fireworks together . . .

MOLLY. Those fireworks have been burning inside me for four-teen days now!—You were in Paris!—Who was with you in Paris!—I swear to you by everything that's holy that I never trembled for you, that I never suffered anything, if only you will come with me now!

KEITH [*kisses her*]. Poor creature!

MOLLY [*throws her arms passionately around his neck and covers him with kisses*]. You're dear!—You're wonderful! —You're good!—[*She lets loose of him, smiling.*] All I wanted was to see you today, just once, with your friends. You know there are times when I'm a little . . . [*She turns her fist in front of her forehead.*]

KEITH [*wants to keep her back*]. You're staying here, girl . . .!

[MOLLY *rushes out through the hall door.* SCHOLZ *enters from the garden through the glass door, limping and holding his knee.*]

SCHOLZ [*very pleased*]. Please don't be alarmed!—Put out the light so the people outside can't see me. No one noticed anything. [*He drags himself to the chair into which he lets himself down.*]

KEITH. What's the matter with you?

SCHOLZ. Turn the lights out first.—It's nothing. The big mortar exploded! A piece of it struck me in the knee!

[KEITH *has put the light out; the stage is dark.*]

KEITH. That could only happen to you!

SCHOLZ [*in a blissful voice*]. The pains are already beginning to subside.—Believe me, I'm the most fortunate creature under the sun! In any case I won't be able to go cycling tomorrow with the Countess Werdenfels. But what does that matter? [*Jubilantly.*] I have overcome the evil spirits; happi-ness lies before me; I belong to life! From this day forward I am another man . . .

[*A rocket rises from the garden and bathes* SCHOLZ'S *features in a dark red glow.*]

KEITH. Damnation!—I almost didn't recognize you then!

SCHOLZ [*jumps up from the chair and hops about the room triumphantly on one foot, while holding onto his injured knee with his hands.*] For ten long years I took myself to be an outcast! Outlawed by society! Now I realize that it was all just my imagination! All just my imagination! Nothing but imagination!

ACT FOUR

[*In the garden room of the* COUNTESS WERDENFELS *a number
of rather large laurel wreaths are lying about on the arm
chairs; a splendid bouquet of flowers is placed in a vase
on the table.* ANNA, COUNTESS WERDENFELS, *dressed in an
attractive morning costume, is found in conversation with*
POLICE INSPECTOR RASPE *and* HERMANN CASIMIR. *It is fore-
noon.*]

ANNA [*a piece of colored paper in her hand, to* HERMANN].
Let me thank you, my young friend, for the lovely verses
you composed for me after our first Fairyland Palace concert yesterday evening.—[*To* RASPE.] But I find it highly
unusual that you, sir, should come to me, especially on this
particular morning, with such serious rumors concerning
your friend and benefactor.

RASPE. The Marquis of Keith is neither my friend nor my
benefactor. Two years ago I asked him to give evidence
at my trial as a psychiatric expert. He might have saved
me a year and a half in prison. But instead, he absconded
to America with a fifteen-year-old girl!

[SIMBA, *in a tasteful maid's uniform, enters from the hallway
and hands* ANNA *a card.*]

SIMBA. The gentleman would like to see you.
ANNA [*to* HERMANN]. Good Lord, your father!
HERMANN [*frightened, looking at* RASPE]. How could my
father suspect I came here!
RASPE. He didn't hear it from me.
ANNA [*lifts the curtain to the game room*]. Go in there. I'll
send him on his way.

[HERMANN *goes into the game room.*]

RASPE. It's best, then, if I pay my respects and be on my way
too.
ANNA. Yes, I should like that.
RASPE [*bowing*]. Madam! [*Off.*]
ANNA [*to* SIMBA]. You may show the gentleman in.

[SIMBA *shows* CONSUL CASIMIR *in; he is followed by a lackey from whom he has taken a bouquet of flowers;* SIMBA *goes off*.]

CONSUL CASIMIR [*handing her the flowers*]. You will permit me, madam, to extend to you my sincere congratulations on your triumph of yesterday evening. Your debut has taken all Munich by storm; you could not, however, have made a more lasting impression on any of your listeners than you did on me.

ANNA. Even if that were the case, I must still be overwhelmed with your coming personally to tell me so.

CASIMIR. Do you have a moment?—It has to do with a purely practical matter.

ANNA [*invites him to be seated*]. I'm certain you'll find yourself on the wrong track.

CASIMIR [*after both have been seated*]. We shall see presently. —I wanted to ask you if you would be my wife.

ANNA. How am I to understand you?

CASIMIR. That is why I am here, so that we can come to an understanding over it. Permit me to make it clear to you from the start that you will naturally be required to give up the enticing artistic career which you embarked on yesterday evening.

ANNA. Surely you can't have considered this step thoroughly enough yet.

CASIMIR. A man of my age, madam, takes no step that is ill considered. Later, yes—or earlier. Would you care to tell me what other scruples may come to mind?

ANNA. Surely you must know that I cannot give an answer to such a proposal.

CASIMIR. I'm quite aware of that. I am speaking, however, for that time in the not too distant future, when you shall be utterly free to make your own decisions concerning yourself and your future.

ANNA. At this moment I really can't imagine any such possibility.

CASIMIR. Today, as you see, I am the most respected man in Munich, but tomorrow I might be under lock and key. I should not find fault with my best friend if by chance he should ask himself whether to stand by me in such a reversal of fortune.

ANNA. Would you also not find fault with your wife if *she* should consider the same question?

CASIMIR. My wife, certainly; my mistress, never. I want no answer from you just yet. I am speaking only for the time when you may find yourself with nowhere to turn or when the situation alters and frees you from all obligations; in short then, for the time when you need someone to turn to.

ANNA. And then you will make me your wife?

CASIMIR. At all events that must appear almost insane to you; yet that is all to the honor of your modesty. But in such a case one is only accountable to oneself. As you may perhaps know, I have two small children at home, girls of three and six. Then, as you might well imagine, there are other considerations . . . As for you, I shall take all responsibility upon myself that you do not dissapoint my expectations—even in spite of yourself.

ANNA. I must admire your self-confidence.

CASIMIR. You may have absolute confidence in me.

ANNA. But after a success like yesterday evening!—It seemed as though an entirely different spirit came over the Munich public.

CASIMIR. Believe me, I sincerely envy the founder of the Fairyland Palace for this subtle shrewdness of his. Incidentally, I must express to you my particular compliments on your choice of a concert dress for yesterday. You displayed so aristocratic an assurance in it, and it showed your figure to such extraordinary effect, that I must confess I found it quite impossible to devote proper attention to your recital.

ANNA. Please don't think that I in any way overrate the applause in regard to my artistic accomplishments.

CASIMIR. I certainly would not blame you for it in any case; but your teacher has told me that a success like yours last night has brought misfortune to many people. And then there is one thing that you must not forget; where would the most celebrated singer today be if rich men did not consider it their moral duty to listen to her without hope of return. No matter how splendid the salary may be in individual cases, the fact remains that these people almost always live on charity.

ANNA. I was amazed at the reception the public gave every one of the numbers.

CASIMIR [*rising*]. Until the unfortunate symphony of this Herr Zamriaki. Furthermore, I have no doubt whatever that with time we shall come around to praising the noise occasioned by this Herr Zamriaki as a divine artistic revelation. Let us allow the world its ways, hope for the best, and be prepared for the worst. You will permit me, madam, to bid you good day. [*Off.*]

[ANNA *seizes both her temples, goes to the game room, lifts the curtain and steps back.*]

ANNA. You didn't even close the door!

[HERMANN CASIMIR *enters from the game room.*]

HERMANN. How could I ever have dreamed I could live through an experience like this!

ANNA. Go on now, so that your father will find you at home.

HERMANN [*notices the second bouquet*]. The flowers are from him?—I seem to have inherited *that* from him too.—Except that to him the expense means nothing.

ANNA. Where do you get the money for such insane expenses?

HERMANN [*significantly*]. From the Marquis of Keith.

ANNA. Please, you must go now! You look tired. I hope your round of drinking didn't last too long last night!

HERMANN. I helped save the composer Zamdiaki's life.

ANNA. Do you consider that one of your worthy accomplishments?

HERMANN. What better have I to do?

ANNA. It is nice of you, of course, to have a heart for unfortunate people; but you mustn't sit at the same table with them. Misfortune is contagious.

HERMANN [*significantly*]. The Marquis of Keith told me the same thing.

ANNA. Go now! Please!

[SIMBA *enters from the hallway and hands* ANNA *a card.*]

SIMBA. The gentleman would like to see you.

ANNA [*reading the card*]. "Representative of the South German Concert Agency."—Tell him to come back in two weeks.

[SIMBA *goes off.*]

HERMANN. What answer will you give my father?

ANNA. I think it's time you left! You're becoming impertinent!

HERMANN. I'm going to London—even if I have to steal the

money. Then my father won't have any reason to complain about me.

ANNA. That will be more to your benefit than to his.

HERMANN [*uneasily*]. I owe that much to my two little sisters. [*Off.*]

ANNA [*reflects a moment, then calls*]. Kathi!

[SIMBA *enters from the dining room.*]

SIMBA. Yes, madam?

ANNA. I want to get dressed.

[*A bell rings in the corridor.*]

SIMBA. At once, madam. [*Goes to open the door.*]

[ANNA *goes off into the dining room. Immediately following,* SIMBA *shows in* ERNST SCHOLZ; *he walks supported by an elegant crutch, limping on his stiff knee, and carrying a large bouquet of flowers.*]

ERNST SCHOLZ. I've had no opportunity, my dear child, to thank you for your tactful, sensitive conduct recently at the garden party.

SIMBA [*formally*]. Does the Herr Baron wish to be announced to my mistress?

[KEITH *enters from the hallway in a light-colored overcoat, with a bundle of newspapers in his hand.*]

KEITH [*removing his overcoat*]. It's an act of Providence that I should find you here! [*To* SIMBA.] What are you still doing here?

SIMBA. Madam has taken me on as a housemaid.

KEITH. You see, I brought you luck.—You may announce us!

SIMBA. Very well, Herr Baron. [*Goes off into the game room.*]

KEITH. The morning papers are already coming out with the most enthusiastic reviews of our concert yesterday! [*He sits down at the table downstage left and pages through the newspapers.*]

SCHOLZ. Have you had any word yet where your wife is staying?

KEITH. She's with her parents in Bückeberg. Where did you suddenly disappear to yesterday during the banquet?

SCHOLZ. I had the most vital need to be alone. How *is* your *wife?*

KEITH. Thank you: her father is about to go bankrupt.

SCHOLZ. Surely you'll have enough left over to protect her family from such an extremity!

KEITH. Have you any idea what the concert yesterday cost me?

SCHOLZ. I find you take things too lightly!

KEITH. Do you really want me to help you hatch the eggs of eternity?

SCHOLZ. I would consider myself fortunate if I could cede some of my excess sense of duty to you.

KEITH. God protect me from that! I need all the elasticity possible to make the most of this success.

SCHOLZ [self-confidently]. I have to thank you that today I can stand up to life calmly and confidently. Therefore I consider it my duty to speak as frankly to you as you spoke to me two weeks ago.

KEITH. The only difference is that I didn't ask you for your advice.

SCHOLZ. To my mind that's merely another reason for complete and open frankness. Through my exaggerated zeal for duty I was guilty of the death of twenty people; but *you* behave as though one had absolutely *no* duty to his fellow men. You take great pleasure in playing with the lives of others!

KEITH. No one ever got away from me with more than a black eye.

SCHOLZ [with growing self-confidence]. That is your personal good fortune! But you are not conscious of the fact that others have precisely the same claims to the pleasures of life as you. And as far as morality is concerned, that sphere in which we see man's highest achievement, why, you haven't the slightest understanding of it.

KEITH. You do remain true to yourself, don't you!—You come to Munich with the express purpose of training yourself to be an epicurean and through some oversight train yourself to be a moralist.

SCHOLZ. By means of the variegated life here in Munich I have arrived at a modest yet all the more reliable evaluation of myself. During these last two weeks I have passed through such tremendous inner transformations that if you wanted to listen to me I actually *could* speak as a moralist.

KEITH [irritated]. The fact is that you can't endure my good fortune!

SCHOLZ. I don't believe in your good fortune! I'm so unspeakably happy that I could embrace the entire world, and quite honestly and frankly I wish you the same. But you will never have it as long as you jeer in your puerile way at the highest values of life. Before I came to Munich I was able only to appreciate the *spiritual* significance of the relationship between men and women, because at the time sensual gratification seemed vulgar to me. I've learned that it's the other way around. But you, in your entire life, have never valued a woman for anything higher than her sensual gratification. As long as you refuse to make those concessions to the moral order, as I have had to do, you will find that just that long will your good fortune stand on feet of clay!

KEITH [*to the point*]. Things are really quite different. I can thank these last two weeks for my *material* freedom, and as a result I am finally able to enjoy my life. And you can thank these last two weeks for your *spiritual* freedom, and as a result *you* are finally able to enjoy *your* life.

SCHOLZ. With the difference that all *my* pleasures are concerned with becoming a useful member of human society.

KEITH [*jumping up*]. Why should anyone even *want* to become a useful member of human society?!

SCHOLZ. Because otherwise one has no justification for his existence!

KEITH. I need no justification for my existence! I asked no one for my existence and I deduce from that my justification for existing according to my own dictates.

SCHOLZ. And so with extraordinary calm of spirit you give over your wife to misery, she who shared every danger and hardship with you these last three years!

KEITH. What am I to do! My expenses are so horrendous that I never have so much as a pfennig left over for my own use. I paid up my share of the founding capital with the first installment of my salary. For a moment I considered laying hold of the money that had been placed at my disposal to defray the costs of the preliminary work. But I can't do that.—Or would you advise me to?

SCHOLZ. I can let you have ten or twenty thousand marks if you find it necessary, if you can't help yourself in any other way. Just by chance I received a draft today from my steward for more than ten thousand marks. [*Takes the draft from his portfolio and hands it to* KEITH.]

KEITH [*tears the paper from his hand*]. Just don't come to me tomorrow and say you want the money back!

SCHOLZ. I don't need it just now. The other ten thousand marks I'll have to have sent through my banker in Breslau.

[ANNA *enters from the game room, dressed in elegant street clothes.*]

ANNA. Pardon me for keeping you waiting, gentlemen.

SCHOLZ [*hands her the flowers*]. I could not deny myself the pleasure, madam, of wishing you luck with all my heart on the first morning of your very promising career.

ANNA [*places the flowers in a vase*]. Thank you. In last night's excitement I completely forgot to ask how your injuries are coming along.

SCHOLZ. Heaven knows, they're not worth talking about. My doctor says that if I wanted to I could be climbing mountains inside of a week. What pained me yesterday was the resounding and scornful laughter that Herr Zamriaki's symphony occasioned.

KEITH [*has seated himself at the writing-table*]. I can do nothing more than give people the opportunity of showing what they can do. Whoever can't play his part will be left behind. I can find any number of conductors in Munich.

SCHOLZ. Wasn't it you who said of him that he's the greatest musical genius since Richard Wagner?

KEITH. Just because I *own* a nag, do you think I'd *call* it that? I must be prepared at every moment to answer for the accuracy of my accounts. [*Rising.*] I've just been to the municipal council about the caryatids. They're questioning whether the Fairyland Palace is something which Munich really needs. The answer was unanimously in the affirmative. A city like Munich could not even begin to dream of all it needs!

SCHOLZ [*to* ANNA]. I presume madam has world-embracing plans to discuss with her fortunate impressario.

ANNA. Thank you, no; we have nothing to discuss with one another. Are you planning on leaving us already?

SCHOLZ. May I have the honor of calling on you again in the next few days?

ANNA. I should be pleased; you are always welcome.

[SCHOLZ *has shaken* KEITH's *hand; goes off.*]

KEITH. The morning papers have come out with enthusiastic critiques of your performance yesterday.

ANNA. Have you had any news about Molly?

KEITH. She's with her parents in Bückeberg. She's revelling in an ocean of petit bourgeois sentimentality.

ANNA. The next time we won't let ourselves be so frightened for her! And besides that, she really needed to prove to you how completely unnecessary she is to you!

KEITH. God be praised that passion for you is a book with seven seals. If a woman isn't capable of making a man happy then the least she wants to do is set the roof afire over his head!

ANNA. Nevertheless you ought to inspire somewhat more confidence in your business enterprises! It isn't particularly pleasant sitting on top of a volcano day and night!

KEITH. Why must everything I hear today be a moral lecture!

ANNA. Because you act as though you were in constant need of a sedative! You don't know what rest is. I've found that as soon as one is in doubt about doing one thing in preference to another, the best thing to do is *nothing at all*. It's only by doing things that one makes himself susceptible to all kinds of unpeasantries. I do as little as I possibly can and I've always been happy because of it. You can't blame anyone for not trusting you when all you do is chase after your own good fortune day and night like a starving wolf.

KEITH. I can't help it if I'm insatiable.

ANNA. But sometimes there are people sitting in sleighs with loaded rifles, and then they go bang-bang.

KEITH. I'm bulletproof. I still have two Spanish bullets from Cuba here in my limbs. And besides that I possess the most inviolable guarantee of my good fortune.

ANNA. This is the absolute limit!

KEITH. The limit, at least, of the human herd mentality!—It must be twenty years now since that young Trautenau and I stood in short pants at the altar of the village church. My father was playing the organ. The village priest handed each of us a picture with a Bible verse on it. Since that time I have scarcely seen the inside of a church, but my confirmation verse has fulfilled itself in such ways that I've often been amazed beyond belief. And even today when some calamity or other arises I always smile scornfully in recollection of that saying: "We know that all things work together for good to them that love God."

ANNA. "Them that love God"?—And you want to be capable of this love?

KEITH. Concerning the question *whether I love God*, I have

tested all existing religions and in no religion have I found that there is any difference between love of God and love of one's own well-being. Love of God is everywhere only a summary and symbolic way of expressing love of oneself.

[SIMBA *enters from the hallway.*]

SIMBA. Would the Marquis care to come out for a moment. Sascha is here.

KEITH. Why doesn't the boy come in?

[SASCHA *enters with a telegram.*]

SASCHA. I didn't know if I should or if I shouldn't, because the Herr Baron said not to deliver telegrams in company.

KEITH [*breaks the seal on the telegram, wads it into a ball in his hand and throws it away.*] Damnation!—My overcoat!

ANNA. From Molly?

KEITH. No!—I only hope to God nobody finds out about it!

ANNA. Then she isn't with her parents in Bückeberg?

KEITH [*while* SASCHA *helps him into his coat*]. No!

ANNA. But you just said . . .

KEITH. Is it *my* fault she's not in Bückeberg? You no sooner have a bit of luck in the world than you find a noose around your neck!

[KEITH *and* SASCHA *go off.*]

SIMBA [*picks up the telegram and hands it to* ANNA]. The Marquis forgot his telegram.

ANNA. Do you know where Sascha came from?

SIMBA. Sascha's from the country. His mother's a house-keeper.

ANNA. Surely then his name can't be Sascha?

SIMBA. At first his name was Seppi, but the Herr Marquis christened him Sascha.

ANNA. Bring me my hat.

[*The bell rings in the corridor.*]

SIMBA. Right away, madam. [*Goes to open the door.*]

ANNA [*reads the telegram*]. ". . . Molly is not here. Please answer by return wire if you have any sign of Molly. In anxious fear . . ."

[SIMBA *returns.*]

SIMBA. The Herr Baron forgot his gloves.

ANNA. Which baron?

SIMBA. The epicurean.

ANNA [*searches hastily*]. Merciful Heaven, where could his gloves be . . . !

[ERNST SCHOLZ *enters.*]

SCHOLZ. Will you permit me two more words, madam?

ANNA. I was just about to go out. [*To* SIMBA.] My hat, quickly!

[SIMBA *goes off.*]

SCHOLZ. My friend's presence prevented me from expressing myself as openly as I . . .

ANNA. Perhaps you might care to wait for a more suitable opportunity.

SCHOLZ. I hoped to be able to wait a few days for your decision. But my feelings, Countess, have overcome me! And so that there can be no doubt in your mind that my offer seeks only to gain you happiness, permit me to say, to confess to you that I—that I am quite unspeakably—in love with you.

ANNA. Well? And what were your offers?

SCHOLZ. Before you, as an artist, are able to reap the fruits of uncontested recognition you will find many obstacles in your path . . .

ANNA. I know that; however, I don't expect to sing anymore!

SCHOLZ. You don't want to sing anymore? How many unfortunate artists would give up half their lives to be able to buy your talent!

ANNA. Is that all you have to say to me?

SCHOLZ. I'm afraid I have offended you again without even realizing it. Naturally you expected me to offer you my hand . . .

ANNA. You mean to say that isn't what you intended?

SCHOLZ. I wanted to ask you if you would be my *mistress.*— I could not honor you as my wife any more highly than I could honor the mistress in you. [*From here on he speaks with the ruthless, aggressive deportment of a madman.*] Whether as wife or mistress, I offer you my life, I offer you everything that I possess. You know that it was only after the most absolute self-conquest that I was able to accept the moral attitudes that are the standard here in Munich. If my happiness should be dashed to pieces on that conquest which I won over myself in order to be able to share in the happiness of my fellow man, that would be the most *revolting of farces!*

ANNA. I thought you were doing it only to become a useful member of human society!

SCHOLZ. I dreamed of bettering the world like a prisoner behind iron bars dreams of snow-covered mountains! Now I can hope for only one thing more, to make this woman happy whom I love so unspeakably, so that she will never regret her choice.

ANNA. I'm sorry to have to tell you that I find myself indifferent towards you.

SCHOLZ. Indifferent towards me? I have never had more proof of dedication from *any* woman than I have from you!

ANNA. That's not my fault. Your friend described you to me as a philosopher who couldn't be bothered with reality.

SCHOLZ. It was reality that wrested me from my philosophy! I'm not one of those who rail against earthly vanity all their lives, and who, when they are deaf and lame, have to be kicked along by death before they will accept him!

ANNA. The Marquis of Keith is helped out of his misfortunes by his confirmation verse! He considers it an infallible magic formula before which police and bailiff take to their heels!

SCHOLZ. I do not lower myself to the level of believing in omens! If this fortune hunter is right, then I received just as infallible a magic formula against misfortune at my confirmation as he did. The priest gave me the verse: "Many are called, but few are chosen."—But that doesn't bother me! Even if I had the most certain proofs that I do *not* belong to the chosen, it could only strengthen me in my fearless battle against my destiny!

ANNA. Please spare me this fearless battle of yours!

SCHOLZ. I swear to you that I would rather renounce my reason than let myself be convinced through this reason that there are certain people who through no fault of their own are from the very beginning shut off from all happiness!

ANNA. Complain about that to the Marquis of Keith.

SCHOLZ. But I'm not complaining! The longer the hard school of misfortune endures the more hardened my intellectual resistance will become. It is an enviable transformation which people like myself enter into. *My soul is indestructible!*

ANNA. I congratulate you!

SCHOLZ. Therein lies my irresistible power! The less you feel for me the greater and more powerful becomes my love for you, and the sooner do I see the moment when you will say: "I fought against you with all at my command, and still I love you!"

ANNA. Heaven protect me from it!

SCHOLZ. Heaven will *not* protect you from it! When a man of my strength of will, which has remained unbroken through all adversity, concentrates all his thought and endeavor on *one* design, then there are only two possibilities: either he achieves his goal or he loses his mind.

ANNA. Yes, I'm inclined to agree.

SCHOLZ. I will take the chance! It all depends on which is more resistant, your lack of feeling or my mind. I'm counting on the worst outcome and I will not look back till I have reached my goal; because if I cannot fashion a happy life out of the bliss which fills me at this moment, then there's no hope for me. The opportunity will never offer itself again!

ANNA. I thank you from the bottom of my heart for reminding me of that! [*She sits down at the writing-table.*]

SCHOLZ. This is the last time that the world will be spread out before me in all its glory!

ANNA [*writing a note*]. That applies to me too! [*Calls.*] Kathi—[*To herself.*] The opportunity will never offer itself to me again either.

SCHOLZ [*suddenly coming to himself*]. Why are you so suspicious, madam? Why are you so suspicious? You are mistaken, Countess!—You are harboring a terrible suspicion . . .

ANNA. Are you still unaware of the fact that you are detaining me? [*Calls.*] Kathi!

SCHOLZ. I couldn't possibly leave you like this! Give me your assurance that you do not doubt my sanity!

[SIMBA *enters with* ANNA's *hat.*]

ANNA. Where were you so long?

SIMBA. I was afraid to come in.

SCHOLZ. Simba, you know better than anyone else that I'm in possession of my five senses . . .

SIMBA [*pushing him back*]. Go on, don't talk so dumb!

ANNA. You will leave my maid alone. [*To* SIMBA.] Do you know the address of Consul Casimir?

SCHOLZ [*suddenly petrified*]. I bear the mark of Cain on my brow . . .

ACT FIVE

[*All the doors in the* MARQUIS OF KEITH's *workroom are wide open. While* HERMANN CASIMIR *seats himself at the center table* KEITH *calls into the living room.*]

KEITH. Sascha! [*Receiving no answer he goes to the waiting room; to* HERMANN.] Excuse me. [*Calls into the waiting room*] Sascha! [*Comes downstage; to* HERMAN.] So, you're going to London with your father's consent. I can give you the best of recommendations to take with you to London. [*Throws himself onto the divan.*] In the first place I recommend you leave your German sentimentality at home. Social Democracy and Anarchism won't even bring on a raised eyebrow in London anymore. But let me tell you one thing more: the only proper way to make use of one's fellow man is to play up to the good in him. Therein lies the art of being liked, the art of getting what one wants. The more abundantly you take advantage of your fellow man, the more careful you have to be that you have the right on your side. Never seek your own gain to the detriment of a virtuous man, but only to the detriment of scoundrels and blockheads. And now let me endow you with the philosophers' stone: the most splendid business in the world is morality. I'm not at the point yet of having made it my business, but I wouldn't be the Marquis of Keith if I let the opportunity slip from me.

[*The bell rings in the corridor.*]

KEITH [*calls*]. Sascha! [*Rising.*] I'll slap that rascal's ears! [*He goes into the hallway and returns with* COUNCILLOR OSTERMEIER.]

KEITH. You couldn't have come at a more opportune moment, my dear Herr Ostermeier . . .

OSTERMEIER. My colleagues on the Board of Directors, my dear friend, have commissioned me to . . .

KEITH. I have a plan to discuss with you which will increase our intake a hundredfold.

OSTERMEIER. Do you want me to say at the general meeting that I failed again today to inspect your account books?

KEITH. You're raving, my dear Herr Ostermeier! Why don't you explain to me calmly and impartially what this is all about?

OSTERMEIER. It is about your account books, dear friend.

KEITH [*irritably*]. I slave away for these bleary-eyed numbskulls . . .

OSTERMEIER. So he's right then! [*Turning to leave.*] Your servant!

KEITH [*tears open the drawer of the writing-table*]. Here, you may revel in the account books if you like! [*Turning to face* OSTERMEIER.] And who is it who's right?

OSTERMEIER. A certain Herr Raspe, a police inspector, who bet five bottles of Pommery last night in the American Bar that you don't keep account books.

KEITH [*giving himself airs*]. Well, yes, I don't keep account books.

OSTERMEIER. Then show me your notebook.

KEITH. Where would I have found time since establishing the company to set up an office!

OSTERMEIER. Then show me your notebook.

KEITH [*giving himself airs*]. I have no notebook.

OSTERMEIER. Then show me the deposit receipts the bank gave you.

KEITH. Do you think I took your money to let it out on interest?!

OSTERMEIER. Don't excite yourself, my dear friend. If you don't have any books then surely you must make notations of your expenditures somewhere. An errand boy does that much.

KEITH [*tosses his memorandum book onto the table*]. There you have my memorandum book.

OSTERMEIER [*opens it and reads*]. "A silvery torrent of mauve silk and paillettes from shoulder to knee—" That's all!

KEITH. If, after I've scored up one success after another, you care to place obstacles in my path, then you may rest assured of one thing, that you will never again see so much as one pfennig of your money whether in this world or in the next!

OSTERMEIER. Our shares in the Fairyland Palace, my dear friend, aren't so bad off. We'll see our money again. Your servant! [*About to leave.*]

KEITH [*holding him back*]. Your snooping about is undermining our enterprise! You must pardon me, sir; but I am excited because I feel towards the Fairyland Palace like a father towards his child.

OSTERMEIER. Then you needn't worry for your child's sake anymore. The Fairyland Palace is secured and will be built.

KEITH. Without *me?*

OSTERMEIER. If necessary, then without you, my dear friend!

KEITH. But you can't do that!

OSTERMEIER. At all events you are the last one who would hinder us!

KEITH. That would be a low and infamous trick!

OSTERMEIER. That would be better yet! Because we won't let ourselves be cheated by you any longer. And you call *us* the cheats!

KEITH. If you believe yourself cheated then you ought to bring an action against me for payment of your money!

OSTERMEIER. Excellent idea, my friend, if only we didn't belong to the Board of Directors!

KEITH. What are you talking about! You sit on the Board of Directors in order to support me in my work.

OSTERMEIER. That's why I've come; but you don't seem to have anything to work at.

KEITH. My dear Herr Ostermeier, you cannot expect me as a man of honor to submit myself patiently to so base an act as this. You take over the business side of the enterprise, why don't you, and let me manage the artistic side. I admit to certain faults in my managing of the business, but I was able to forgive myself for them because I knew they would never happen again, and that as soon as my position had been consolidated I would never be found at fault in even the slightest matter.

OSTERMEIER. We could have talked of this yesterday when I and the other gentlemen were here; but you were more determined to talk our ears off. I might even say to you today: let's try again—if you had only shown yourself to be an honorable person. But when all we hear are lies, well . . .

KEITH [*giving himself airs*]. Then you may tell the gentlemen that I shall build the Fairyland Palace just as surely as the idea was mine in the first place. If, however, *you* build it— and you may tell the gentlemen this too!—then I shall blow the Fairyland Palace, together with its Board of Directors and its stockholders—sky high!

OSTERMEIER. I shall give them an exact account, good neighbor! You know, I really don't like to insult people to their faces, not to mention throwing them out on their . . . Your servant! [*Goes off.*]

KEITH [*starting after him*]. . . . on their asses! I thought as much. [*To* HERMANN.] Don't leave me alone now or I'm afraid I'll go to pieces till there's nothing left of me.—How can this be possible? [*With tears in his eyes.*] After all those fireworks!—Am I to be driven like an outcast again from country to country?—No! No!—I mustn't let myself be pushed against a wall!—This is the last time in this life that the world will be spread out before me with all its glory! [*Pulling himself up straight.*] No!—I'm not only not tottering yet, but I'll take a leap that will set all Munich gaping. And while it's still shaking with astonishment, I'll fall on its prostrate body to the accompaniment of trumpets and drums, and tear it to pieces. We'll see then who'll be the first to get on his feet!

[*The* COUNTESS WERDENFELS *enters.*]

KEITH [*rushing towards her*]. My queen . . .

ANNA [*to* HERMANN]. Would you excuse us for a moment?

[KEITH *shows* HERMANN *into the living room.*]

KEITH [*closing the door behind him*]. You look terribly self-confident today.

ANNA. That's quite possible. Every day now since our Fairy-land Palace concert I've received a good half-dozen proposals of marriage.

KEITH. That means damned little to me!

ANNA. But not to me.

KEITH [*scornfully*]. Have you fallen in love with him?

ANNA. Whom do you mean?

KEITH. The epicurean!

ANNA. Are you making fun of me?

KEITH. Then whom *do* you mean?

ANNA [*indicating the living room*]. His father.

KEITH. And you want to talk with me about this?

ANNA. No, I wanted only to ask whether you had had any sign of Molly.

KEITH. No, but what's this about Casimir?

ANNA. What's this about Molly—Are you keeping her disappearance a secret?

KEITH [*uneasily*]. To be quite honest, I'm less afraid *she* has met with some misfortune than that her disappearance might pull the ground out from under *my* feet. If that seems somewhat inhuman, then I've paid for it by sitting out the last three nights in the telegraph office.—My only crime against her is that since we have known one another she has never once heard an angry word from me. She lets herself be eaten up with longing for her petit bourgeois world where, brow to brow, they drudge and humiliate themselves, and love one another! No free view, no free breath! Nothing but love! As much as possible and of the commonest sort!

ANNA. Suppose they don't find Molly, what then?

KEITH. I can be comforted with the prospect that once my house has collapsed about me she will come back penitent and smiling and say: "I'll never do it again!"—She's reached her goal; I can start packing.

ANNA. And what's to become of *me?*

KEITH. Up till now you've gained the most from our enterprise, and I hope you'll continue to gain by it. You can't lose anything because you haven't invested anything.

ANNA. Are you so sure?

KEITH. —I see . . . !

ANNA. I'm glad!

KEITH. —What did you answer him?

ANNA. I wrote him that I couldn't give him an answer just yet.

KEITH. That's what you wrote him?

ANNA. I wanted to talk with you about it first.

KEITH [*takes her by the wrist and thrusts her from him*]. If all you had in mind was to talk with me about it—then marry him!

ANNA. A person as contemptuous of feelings as you surely ought to be able to discuss a purely practical matter calmly!

KEITH. My feelings have nothing to do with this! What infuriates me is that you have so little family pride as to sell your birthright for a mess of pottage!

ANNA. Whatever you have no part in is a mess of pottage!

KEITH. I know my weaknesses; but these men are domestic animals! The one of them is weak in the head and the other weak in the spine! Do you want to bring creatures into the world who can't see before the eighth day?—If it's all over with me, I will gladly give you whatever glow of spirit I've embued you with for use in your career. But if you take refuge from your artist's fate behind a sack of money, then you are worth no more today than the grass that one day will grow on your grave!

ANNA.—If only you had the faintest idea where Molly could be!

KEITH. You needn't revile me on top of it all! [*Calls.*] Sascha!

ANNA. If you absolutely insist that we should part . . .

KEITH. Of course I insist on it.

ANNA. Then give me back my letters!

KEITH [*scornfully*]. Do you plan to write your memoirs?

ANNA. No, but they *could* find their way into the wrong hands.

KEITH [*jumping up*]. Sascha!

ANNA. What is it you want Sascha for?—I sent him on an errand.

KEITH. How did you come to do that?!

ANNA. Because he came to me. I've done so a number of times. When worst comes to worst the boy always knows where he can earn something.

KEITH [*sinks into the chair by the writing-table*]. My Sascha! [*Wipes a tear from his eye.*] You didn't forget him either! —If you leave the room now, Anna, I shall break down like an ox in a slaughterhouse.—Give me a reprieve!

ANNA. I have no time to lose.

KEITH. Only until I've accustomed myself to doing without you, Anna!—I need mental clarity now more than ever . . .

ANNA. Are you going to give me back my letters?

KEITH. You're dreadful!—But of course you're doing it out of pity! I should at least be able to curse you now that you are no longer my mistress.

ANNA. As long as you live you'll never learn to judge a woman properly!

KEITH [*straightening himself up proudly*]. I will not renounce my belief even on the rack! You're on the road to good fortune; that's human enough. You will always remain to me what you once were.

ANNA. Then give me back my letters.

KEITH. No, my child! Your letters I shall keep for myself. Otherwise I shall doubt one day on my deathbed whether perhaps you were not a phantom after all. [*Kissing her hand.*] Good luck!

ANNA. Even without you! [*Goes off.*]

KEITH [*alone, wrenched by spasms of the heart*]. —Ah!—Ah! This is my death!—[*He plunges for the writing-table, re-*

moves a handful of letters from the drawer and hurries after her.] Anna! Anna!

[*In the open doorway he is met by* ERNST SCHOLZ. SCHOLZ *walks without even a trace of his injury.*]

KEITH [*starting back*]. . . . I was just going to drive to your hotel.

SCHOLZ. There's no sense in that. I'm leaving.

KEITH. Then at least give me the twenty thousand marks you promised me yesterday!

SCHOLZ. You'll get no more money from me.

KEITH. The caryatids will crush me! They want to take my directorship away from me!

SCHOLZ. That only confirms me in my resolution.

KEITH. It's a matter of overcoming a momentary crisis!

SCHOLZ. My wealth is far more important than you! My wealth will secure for the members of my family a free and lofty position of power for all time! Whereas you will never arrive at any point where you will be able to be of use to anyone!

KEITH. You parasite, where do you have the gall to accuse me of being useless?

SCHOLZ. Let's not argue!—I am finally fulfilling the greatest renunciation which many a man must agree to in this life.

KEITH. What's that?

SCHOLZ. I've torn myself from my illusions.

KEITH [*scornfully*]. I suppose you're revelling again in the love of a girl from the lower classes?

SCHOLZ. I've torn myself from everything.—I am entering a private sanatorium.

KEITH [*crying out*]. There is nothing more shameful than the betrayal of your own person!

SCHOLZ. I can well understand your anger.—During these last three days I have fought through the most terrible battle that can be allotted a mortal man.

KEITH. So that you could crawl away a coward?—So that as the victor you could renounce your worth as a human being?

SCHOLZ [*flaring up*]. I am not renouncing my worth as a human being! You have no cause to insult or to jeer at me! —If a man is forced against his will into accepting the restraints in which I find myself now, then he may very well lose his worth as a human being. And because of that he remains relatively happy; he protects his illusions.—A man who settles his account with reality dispassionately, like myself, has to forfeit neither the respect nor the sympathy of his fellow men.

KEITH [*shrugs his shoulders*]. If I were you I'd take a little more time to think it over.

SCHOLZ. I've thought it through thoroughly. It is the last duty which my fate has left to fulfill.

KEITH. Once you're in it's not so easy to get out.

SCHOLZ. If I had even the slightest hope of getting out again, I'd never go in. The renunciation which I have burdened myself with, the self-conquest and joyful hope which I have been able to wrest from my soul, I undertook in order to change my fate. God be damned that there is no longer any doubt that I am different from other men.

KEITH [*very proudly*]. God be praised that I have never *doubted* that I was different from other men!

SCHOLZ [*very calmly*]. God be damned or God be praised— up till now I have always thought of you as the most cunning of scoundrels!—I have given up even this illusion. A scoundrel can count on good fortune just as surely as an honorable man can count on his good conscience staying with him through an irrevocable misfortune. Your good fortune exists no more than mine, except that you don't realize it. Therein lies the horrible danger that hangs over you!

KEITH. The only danger hanging over me is that tomorrow I will have no money!

SCHOLZ. However long you live you'll never have money tomorrow!—I wish I knew that you were safe from your hopeless delusion. That's why I've come to see you this last time. I am profoundly convinced that the best thing for you is to come with me.

KEITH [*with impatient suspicion*]. Where?

SCHOLZ. To the sanatorium.

KEITH. Give me the thirty thousand marks and I'll come with you!

SCHOLZ. If you come with me you won't need money anymore. You'll find a more comfortable home than perhaps you may ever have known. We'll have a carriage and horses, we'll play billiards . . .

KEITH [*embracing him*]. Give me the thirty thousand marks!

Do you want me to fall prostrate at your feet? I could be
arrested on the spot!

SCHOLZ. Has it really gone that far? [*Pushing him back.*] I
don't give sums like that to madmen!

KEITH [*shouts*]. You're the madman!

SCHOLZ [*calmly*]. I'm the one who has come to his senses.

KEITH [*scornfully*]. If you want to go to a lunatic asylum just
because you've come to your senses, then—go ahead!

SCHOLZ. You're one of those they bring there by force!

KEITH. I suppose you'll resume your title again once you've got
into the lunatic asylum?

SCHOLZ. Haven't you gone bankrupt on two continents in every
conceivable way that bourgeois life permits?!

KEITH [*venomously*]. If you consider it your moral duty to
free the world of your superfluous existence then I'm certain
you can find more radical means than going for drives or
playing billiards!

SCHOLZ. I tried that long ago.

KEITH [*shouts at him*]. Then what are you still doing here?!

SCHOLZ [*gloomily*]. I failed at that like I have at everything
else.

KEITH. I suppose you shot someone else by mistake!

SCHOLZ. They cut the bullets from between my shoulders,
quite near the spinal column.—This is the last time in your
life that someone will extend you a helping hand. You already know the kind of experiences that are in store for you.

KEITH [*throws himself on his knees in front of* SCHOLZ *and
clasps* SCHOLZ's *hands*]. Give me the forty thousand marks
and I'm saved!

SCHOLZ. That won't save you from the penitentiary!

KEITH [*starts up in terror*]. Shut up!

SCHOLZ [*pleading*]. Come with me, then you'll be out of
danger. We grew up together; I see no reason why we
shouldn't wait for the end together too. Bourgeois society
judges you a criminal and subjugates you to all kinds of
inhuman medieval tortures . . .

KEITH [*moaning*]. If you won't help me, then go, I beg you!

SCHOLZ [*tears in his eyes*]. Don't turn your back on your only
refuge! I know you didn't choose your pitiable fate anymore than I chose mine.

KEITH. Go away! Go away!

SCHOLZ. Come with me. Come.—You have a companion in

me as gentle as a lamb. It would be a dim ray of light in the night of my life if I knew how to rescue my boyhood friend from his terrible fate.

KEITH. Go away! I beg you!

SCHOLZ.—From this moment on you must entrust yourself to my guidance, as I once wanted to entrust myself to you . . .

KEITH [*cries out in despair*]. Sascha! Sascha!

SCHOLZ.—You must never forget that you have a friend who will welcome you at any time. [*Goes off.*]

KEITH [*crawls about, searching*]. Molly!—Molly!—This is the first time in my life that I have whimpered on my knees in front of a woman! [*He suddenly hears a sound from the direction of the living room.*] There . . . ! There . . . ! [*After opening the door to the living room.*] Oh, it's you?

[HERMANN CASIMIR *enters from the living room.*]

KEITH. I can't ask you to stay here any longer. I'm—I'm not quite well. I must first—sleep on it—for a night, to be master of the situation again.—Have a good . . . a good . . .

[*Heavy footsteps and many voices are heard from the stairs.*]

KEITH. Listen . . . The noise! The uproar!—That's bad . . .

HERMANN. Lock the door then, why don't you?

KEITH. I can't!—I can't!—It's her!

[*A number of patrons from the neighboring Hofbräuhaus drag in* MOLLY's *lifeless body. Water drips from her body, her clothes hang from her in shreds. Her undone hair covers her face.*]

A BUTCHER'S HELPER. Here's the bastard we want!—[*To the others behind him.*] Right?—All right! [*To* KEITH.] Look here what we fished up! Look here what we're bringin' you! Look here—if you got the guts!

A PORTER. We pulled her out of the sewer! From under the iron bars! She must have been in the water a whole week!

A BAKERY WOMAN. And all the while the filthy little scoundrel runs around with his shameless crew! He hasn't paid for his bread in six weeks! He let his poor wife go begging at all the shops to see what she could get to eat! It would have made a stone cry to see the way she looked at the end!

KEITH [*retreats to his writing-table, while the crowd presses around him with the body*]. I beg of you, just calm yourselves!

THE BUTCHER'S HELPER. Shut your mouth, you swindler! Or I'll clout you one in the face that'll knock you off your feet!—Look here!—Is it her or not?—Look at her, I said!

KEITH [*has taken hold of* HERMANN's *revolver which the* COUNTESS WERDENFELS *had left there earlier*]. Keep your hands off me unless you want to make me use this weapon!

THE BUTCHER'S HELPER. What's the coward say?—What's he say?—You goin' to give me the revolver?—haven't you done enough to *her*, you dog? Give it here, I said . . . !

[THE BUTCHER'S HELPER *grapples with* KEITH *who has succeeded in getting close to the doorway through which at that moment* CONSUL CASIMIR *enters.* HERMANN CASIMIR *in the meanwhile has gone to the body; he and the* BAKERY WOMAN *carry the body to the divan.*]

KEITH [*defending himself like a desperate man, calls*]. Police!—Police! [*Notices* CASIMIR *and clings to him.*] Save me, for God's sake! They're going to hang me!

CONSUL CASIMIR [*to the people*]. You listen to me now, because if this goes any further you'll learn to know another side of me!—Leave the woman there on the divan!—Now get out!—Or must I show you what a door's made for?—[*He pulls forward his son who wants to leave with the crowd.*] Just a minute there, little friend! You're going to take a nice lesson with you on your trip to London!

[*The Hofbräuhaus people have left now.*]

CASIMIR [*to* KEITH]. I was going to invite you to leave Munich within twenty-four hours; now, however, I think it best for you if you leave on the next train.

KEITH [*still holding the revolver in his left hand*]. I—I am not responsible for this—this disaster . . .

CASIMIR. You can settle that with yourself! But you *are* responsible for the forgery of my signature on a congratulatory telegram delivered to your founders' party on Brienner Strasse.

KEITH. I can't leave . . .

CASIMIR [*hands him a paper*]. You will sign this receipt. In it you are certifying that a sum of ten thousand marks owed to you by the Countess Werdenfels has been received from me.

[KEITH *goes to the writing-table and signs.*]

CASIMIR [*counting the money from his wallet*]. As your successor in the directorship of the Fairyland Palace Company I will request of you that in the interests of our enterprise's successful development you do not show yourself again in Munich for some time!

[KEITH, *standing at the writing-table, hands the paper to* CASIMIR *and mechanically receives the money.*]

CASIMIR [*pocketing the paper*]. Pleasant journey! [*To* HERMANN.] And you come with me!

[HERMANN *slips out shyly.* CASIMIR *follows him.*]

KEITH [*the revolver in his left hand, the money in his right, takes a few steps toward the divan, but recoils in horror. Then he looks irresolutely from the revolver to the money in turn. As he lays down the revolver behind him on the center table, with a grin on his face*]. Life is one switchback after another . . .

BERTOLT BRECHT

1898–1956

BERTOLT BRECHT was a Marxist and the prophet for the drama of the collective. But he never wore his prophet's mantle with ease, nor was he ever comfortable with his Marxist position. He was, however, the first playwright of the modern theatre to comprehend fully the effects of industrialization and collectivism upon our social structures, and he realized that these forces were creating new kinds of conflicts which were not being dealt with in the theatre. As early as 1925, he wrote: "When one sees that our world of today no longer fits into the drama, then it is merely that the drama no longer fits into the world." Brecht's epic theatre is an attempt to express the drama of a world that was gradually being transformed from a traditional community into a highly organized collective state. In using the term "epic theatre," Brecht was thinking of the drama as episodic and narrative and, therefore, more like the structure of an epic poem than the well-made play. He rejected the traditional Aristotelian idea that a play should have a beginning, middle and end, because he believed that the dramatic processes of history do not end, but only move on to the next episode. He wanted to translate this episodic nature of history into the theatre. Brecht's epic form, then, is his way of expressing the complexity, multiplicity, variety, and even the contradiction of a collective world while still maintaining that unity of form which is essential for art. Furthermore, it is a form that seeks to achieve the capacity of the novel in dealing with the central issues of the modern world, without sacrificing the immediacy and force of the actor on a stage.

The second important point that must be made about Brecht is that he was a poet. A large number of the serious dramatists of the twentieth century have been involved in the revolt against the tyranny of words in the modern theatre. They believe that the language of drama has become stereotyped and wooden because it has lost that gestural quality which is essential to all language in theatre. They realize, as George Steiner has pointed out, "that drama is language under such high pressure of feeling that the words carry a necessary and immediate connotation of gesture." In their attempts to revitalize the language of the theatre, they hope to force audiences into a new awareness of the world in which they live. But most of these dramatists, in order to achieve these ends, have tended to dislocate the very mechanism of language itself; they have practically destroyed the syntax of rational discourse. This Brecht did not do. As a poet he believed in the power of verse to deal with the contradictions of reality. He believed poetry could advance discordant persuasions simultaneously and still retain that gestural quality which is essential to the theatre.

Now, a decade after his death, Brecht's work is just being evaluated with thoroughness and objectivity, and it seems clear that he has made more important contributions to the modern theatre than any other playwright writing in the first half of the twentieth century.

THEATRE FOR PLEASURE OR THEATRE
FOR INSTRUCTION[1]

by Bertolt Brecht

A FEW YEARS back, anybody talking about the modern theatre meant the theatre in Moscow, New York and Berlin. He might have thrown in a mention of one of Jouvet's productions in Paris or Cochran's in London, or *The Dybbuk* as given by the Habima (which is to all intents and purposes part of the Russian theatre, since Vakhtangov was its director). But broadly speaking there were only three capitals so far as modern theatre was concerned.

Russian, American and German theatres differed widely from one another, but were alike in being modern, that is to say in introducing technical and artistic innovations. In a sense they even achieved a certain stylistic resemblance, probably because technology is international (not just that part which is directly applied to the stage but also that which influences it, the film for instance), and because large progressive cities in large industrial countries are involved. Among the older capitalist countries it is the Berlin theatre that seemed of late to be in the lead. For a period all that is common to the modern theatre received its strongest and (so far) maturest expression there.

The Berlin theatre's last phase was the so-called epic theatre, and it showed the modern theatre's trend of development in its purest form. Whatever was labelled "*Zeitstück*" or "*Piscator-bühne*" or "*Lehrstück*" belongs to the epic theatre.

THE EPIC THEATRE

Many people imagine that the term "epic theatre" is self-contradictory, as the epic and dramatic ways of narrating a

[1] "Theatre for Pleasure or Theatre for Instruction" from *Brecht on Theatre* translated by John Willett. Copyright © 1957, 1963, and 1964 by Suhrkamp Verlag, Frankfurt am Main. Translation and notes © 1964 by John Willett. Reprinted by permission of Hill and Wang, Inc.

story are held, following Aristotle, to be basically distinct. The difference between the two forms was never thought simply to lie in the fact that the one is performed by living beings while the other operates via the written word; epic works such as those of Homer and the medieval singers were at the same time theatrical performances, while dramas like Goethe's *Faust* and Byron's *Manfred* are agreed to have been more effective as books. Thus even by Aristotle's definition the difference between the dramatic and epic forms was attributed to their different methods of construction, whose laws were dealt with by two different branches of aesthetics. The method of construction depended on the different way of presenting the work to the public, sometimes via the stage, sometimes through a book; and independently of that there was the "dramatic element" in epic works and the "epic element" in dramatic. The bourgeois novel in the last century developed much that was "dramatic," by which was meant the strong centralization of the story, a momentum that drew the separate parts into a common relationship. A particular passion of utterance, a certain emphasis on the clash of forces are hallmarks of the "dramatic." The epic writer Döblin provided an excellent criterion when he said that with an epic work, as opposed to a dramatic, one can as it were take a pair of scissors and cut it into individual pieces, which remain fully capable of life.

This is no place to explain how the opposition of epic and dramatic lost its rigidity after having long been held to be irreconcilable. Let us just point out that the technical advances alone were enough to permit the stage to incorporate an element of narrative in its dramatic productions. The possibility of projections, the greater adaptability of the stage due to mechanization, the film, all completed the theatre's equipment, and did so at a point where the most important transactions between people could no longer be shown simply by personifying the motive forces or subjecting the characters to invisible metaphysical powers.

To make these transactions intelligible the environment in which the people lived had to be brought to bear in a big and 'significant' way.

This environment had of course been shown in the existing drama, but only as seen from the central figure's point of view, and not as an independent element. It was defined by the hero's reactions to it. It was seen as a storm can be seen when one sees the ships on a sheet of water unfolding their sails, and the sails filling out. In the epic theatre it was to appear standing on its own.

The stage began to tell a story. The narrator was no longer missing, along with the fourth wall. Not only did the background adopt an attitude to the events on the stage—by big screens recalling other simultaneous events elsewhere, by projecting documents which confirmed or contradicted what the characters said, by concrete and intelligible figures to accompany abstract conversations, by figures and sentences to support mimed transactions whose sense was unclear—but the actors too refrained from going over wholly into their role, remaining detached from the character they were playing and clearly inviting criticism of him.

The spectator was no longer in any way allowed to submit to an experience uncritically (and without practical consequences) by means of simple empathy with the characters in a play. The production took the subject matter and the incidents shown and put them through a process of alienation: the alienation that is necessary to all understanding. When something seems "the most obvious thing in the world" it means that any attempt to understand the world has been given up.

What is "natural" must have the force of what is startling. This is the only way to expose the laws of cause and effect. People's activity must simultaneously be so and be capable of being different.

It was all a great change.

The dramatic theatre's spectator says: Yes, I have felt like that too—Just like me—It's only natural—It'll never change—The sufferings of this man appall me, because they are inescapable—That's great art; it all seems the most obvious thing in the world—I weep when they weep, I laugh when they laugh.

The epic theatre's spectator says: I'd never have thought it—That's not the way—That's extraordinary, hardly believable—It's got to stop—The sufferings of this man appall me, because they are unnecessary—That's great art: nothing obvious in it—I laugh when they weep, I weep when they laugh.

THE INSTRUCTIVE THEATRE

The stage began to be instructive.

Oil, inflation, war, social struggles, the family, religion, wheat, the meat market, all became subjects for theatrical representation. Choruses enlightened the spectator about facts unknown to him. Films showed a montage of events from all over the world. Projections added statistical material. And as the "background" came to the front of the stage, so people's activity was subjected to criticism. Right and wrong courses of action were shown. People were shown who knew what they were doing, and others who did not. The theatre became an affair for philosophers, but only for such philosophers as wished not just to explain the world but also to change it. So we had philosophy, and we had instruction. And where was the amusement in all that? Were they sending us back to school, teaching us to read and write? Were we supposed to pass exams, work for diplomas?

Generally there is felt to be a very sharp distinction between learning and amusing oneself. The first may be useful, but only the second is pleasant. So we have to defend the epic theatre against the suspicion that it is a highly disagreeable, humorless, indeed strenuous affair.

Well: all that can be said is that the contrast between learning and amusing oneself is not laid down by divine rule; it is not one that has always been and must continue to be.

Undoubtedly there is much that is tedious about the kind of learning familiar to us from school, from our professional training, etc. But it must be remembered under what conditions and to what end that takes place.

It is really a commercial transaction. Knowledge is just a commodity. It is acquired in order to be resold. All those who have grown out of going to school have to do their learning virtually in secret, for anyone who admits that he still has something to learn devalues himself as a man whose knowledge is inadequate. Moreover the usefulness of learning is very much limited by factors outside the learner's control. There is unemployment, for instance, against which no knowledge can protect one. There is the division of labor, which makes generalized knowledge unnecessary and impossible. Learning is often among the concerns of those whom no amount of concern will get any further forward. There is not much knowledge that leads to power, but plenty of knowledge to which only power can lead.

Learning has a very different function for different social strata. There are strata who cannot imagine any improvement in conditions: they find the conditions good enough for them.

Whatever happens to oil they will benefit from it. And they feel the years beginning to tell. There can't be all that many years more. What is the point of learning a lot now? They have said their final word: a grunt. But there are also strata "waiting their turn" who are discontented with conditions, have a vast interest in the practical side of learning, want at all costs to find out where they stand, and know that they are lost without learning; these are the best and keenest learners. Similar differences apply to countries and peoples. Thus the pleasure of learning depends on all sorts of things; but none the less there is such a thing as pleasurable learning, cheerful and militant learning.

If there were not such amusement to be had from learning, the theatre's whole structure would unfit it for teaching.

Theatre remains theatre even when it is instructive theatre, and insofar as it is good theatre it will amuse.

THEATRE AND KNOWLEDGE

But what has knowledge got to do with art? We know that knowledge can be amusing, but not everything that is amusing belongs in the theatre.

I have often been told, when pointing out the invaluable services that modern knowledge and science, if properly applied, can perform for art and specially for the theatre, that art and knowledge are two estimable but wholly distinct fields of human activity. This is a fearful truism, of course, and it is as well to agree quickly that, like most truisms, it is perfectly true. Art and science work in quite different ways: agreed. But, bad as it may sound, I have to admit that I cannot get along as an artist without the use of one of two sciences. This may well arouse serious doubts as to my artistic capacities. People are used to seeing poets as unique and slightly unnatural beings who reveal with a truly godlike assurance things that other people can only recognize after much sweat and toil. It is naturally distasteful to have to admit that one does not belong to this select band. All the same, it must be admitted. It must at the same time be made clear that the scientific occupations just confessed to are not pardonable side interests, pursued on days off after a good week's work. We all know how Goethe was interested in natural history, Schiller in history: as a kind of hobby, it is charitable to assume. I have no wish promptly to accuse these

two of having needed these sciences for their poetic activity;
I am not trying to shelter behind them; but I must say that
I do need the sciences. I have to admit, however, that I look
askance at all sorts of people who I know do not operate
on the level of scientific understanding: that is to say, who
sing as the birds sing, or as people imagine the birds to sing.
I don't mean by that that I would reject a charming poem
about the taste of fried fish or the delights of a boating party
just because the writer had not studied gastronomy or navi-
gation. But in my view the great and complicated things that
go on in the world cannot be adequately recognized by people
who do not use every possible aid to understanding.

Let us suppose that great passions or great events have to
be shown which influence the fate of nations. The lust for
power is nowadays held to be such a passion. Given that a
poet "feels" this lust and wants to have someone strive for
power, how is he to show the exceedingly complicated ma-
chinery within which the struggle for power nowadays takes
place? If his hero is a politician, how do politics work? If he
is a businessman, how does business work? And yet there are
writers who find business and politics nothing like so passionately interesting as the individual's lust for power. How
are they to acquire the necessary knowledge? They are scarcely
likely to learn enough by going round and keeping their eyes
open, though even then it is more than they would get by just
rolling their eyes in an exalted frenzy. The foundation of a
paper like the *Völkischer Beobachter* or a business like Standard Oil is a pretty complicated affair, and such things cannot
be conveyed just like that. One important field for the playwright is psychology. It is taken for granted that a poet, if not
an ordinary man, must be able without further instruction to
discover the motives that lead a man to commit murder; he
must be able to give a picture of a murderer's mental state
'from within himself.' It is taken for granted that one only
has to look inside oneself in such a case; and then there's
always one's imagination. . . . There are various reasons why
I can no longer surrender to this agreeable hope of getting
a result quite so simply. I can no longer find in myself all
those motives which the press or scientific reports show to
have been observed in people. Like the average judge when
pronouncing sentence, I cannot without further ado conjure up
an adequate picture of a murderer's mental state. Modern psychology, from psychoanalysis to behaviorism, acquaints me

with facts that lead me to judge the case quite differently, especially if I bear in mind the findings of sociology and do not overlook economics and history. You will say: but that's getting complicated. I have to answer that it *is* complicated. Even if you let yourself be convinced, and agree with me that a large slice of literature is exceedingly primitive, you may still ask with profound concern: won't an evening in such a theatre be a most alarming affair? The answer to that is: no.

Whatever knowledge is embodied in a piece of poetic writing has to be wholly transmuted into poetry. Its utilization fulfills the very pleasure that the poetic element provokes. If it does not at the same time fulfill that which is fulfilled by the scientific element, none the less in an age of great discoveries and inventions one must have a certain inclination to penetrate deeper into things—a desire to make the world controllable—if one is to be sure of enjoying its poetry.

IS THE EPIC THEATRE SOME KIND OF "MORAL INSTITUTION"?

According to Friedrich Schiller the theatre is supposed to be a moral institution. In making this demand it hardly occurred to Schiller that by moralizing from the stage he might drive the audience out of the theatre. Audiences had no objection to moralizing in his day. It was only later that Friedrich Nietzsche attacked him for blowing a moral trumpet. To Nietzsche any concern with morality was a depressing affair; to Schiller it seemed thoroughly enjoyable. He knew of nothing that could give greater amusement and satisfaction than the propagation of ideas. The bourgeoisie was setting about forming the ideas of the nation.

Putting one's house in order, patting oneself on the back, submitting one's account, is something highly agreeable. But describing the collapse of one's house, having pains in the back, paying one's account, is indeed a depressing affair, and that was how Friedrich Niezsche saw things a century later. He was poorly disposed towards morality, and thus towards the previous Friedrich, too.

The epic theatre was likewise often objected to as moralizing too much. Yet in the epic theatre moral arguments only took second place. Its aim was less to moralize than to observe. That is to say it observed, and then the thick end of the wedge followed: the story's moral. Of course we cannot pretend that we started our observations out of a pure passion for observing and without any more practical motive, only to be completely staggered by their results. Undoubtedly there were some painful discrepancies in our environment, circumstances that were barely tolerable, and this not merely on account of moral considerations. It is not only moral considerations that make hunger, cold and oppression hard to bear. Similarly the object of our inquiries was not just to arouse moral objections to such circumstances (even though they could easily be felt—though not by all the audience alike; such objections were seldom for instance felt by those who profited by the circumstances in question), but to discover means for their elimination. We were not in fact speaking in the name of morality but in that of the victims. These truly are two distinct matters, for the victims are often told that they ought to be contented with their lot, for moral reasons. Moralists of this sort see man as existing for morality, not morality for man. At least it should be possible to gather from the above to what degree and in what sense the epic theatre is a moral institution.

Can Epic Theatre Be Played Anywhere?

Stylistically speaking, there is nothing all that new about the epic theatre. Its expository character and its emphasis on virtuosity bring it close to the old Asiatic theatre. Didactic tendencies are to be found in the medieval mystery plays and the classical Spanish theatre, and also in the theatre of the Jesuits.

These theatrical forms corresponded to particular trends of their time, and vanished with them. Similarly the modern epic theatre is linked with certain trends. It cannot by any means be practiced universally. Most of the great nations today are not disposed to use the theatre for ventilating their problems. London, Paris, Tokyo and Rome maintain their theatres for quite different purposes. Up to now favorable circumstances for an epic and didactic theatre have only been found in a few places and for a short period of time. In Berlin Fascism put a very definite stop to the development of such a theatre.

It demands not only a certain technological level but a powerful movement in society which is interested to see vital questions freely aired with a view to their solution, and can defend this interest against every contrary trend.

The epic theatre is the broadest and most far-reaching attempt at large-scale modern theatre, and it has all those immense difficulties to overcome that always confront the vital forces in the sphere of politics, philosophy, science and art.

THE CAUCASIAN CHALK CIRCLE

by BERTOLT BRECHT

1945

THE CAUCASIAN CHALK CIRCLE

English Version by Eric Bentley *and* Maja Apelman[1]

CHARACTERS

OLD MAN ON THE RIGHT

PEASANT WOMAN ON THE RIGHT

YOUNG PEASANT

A VERY YOUNG WORKER

OLD MAN ON THE LEFT

PEASANT WOMAN ON THE LEFT

AGRICULTURIST KATO

GIRL TRACTORIST

WOUNDED SOLDIER

THE DELEGATE FROM THE CAPITAL

THE STORYTELLER

GEORGI ABASHWILI, *the Governor*

NATELLA, *the Governor's wife*

LAVRENTI VASHNADZE, *Grusha's brother*

ANIKO, *his wife*

PEASANT WOMAN, *for a while Grusha's mother-in-law*

JUSSUP, *her son*

MONK

AZDAK, *village scrivener*

SHAUWA, *a policeman*

GRAND DUKE

DOCTOR

INVALID

LIMPING MAN

BLACKMAILER

LUDOVICA

INNKEEPER, *her father-in-law*

MICHAEL, *their son*
SHALVA, *an adjutant*
ARSEN KAZBEKI, *a fat prince*
MESSENGER FROM THE
   CAPITAL
NIKO MIKADZE *and* MIKA
   LOLADZE, *doctors*
SIMON SHASHAVA, *a soldier*
GRUSHA VASHNADZE, *a
   kitchen maid*
OLD PEASANT WITH THE
   MILK
CORPORAL *and* PRIVATE
PEASANT *and* HIS WIFE

STABLEBOY
POOR OLD PEASANT WOMAN
IRAKLI, *her brother-in-law,
   a bandit*
THREE WEALTHY FARMERS
ILLO SHUBOLADZE *and*
   SANDRO OBOLADZE,
   lawyers
OLD MARRIED COUPLE
SOLDIERS, SERVANTS,
   PEASANTS, BEGGARS,
   MUSICIANS, MERCHANTS,
   NOBLES, *and* ARCHITECTS

THE JUDGE: Officer, fetch a piece of chalk. You will trace below the bench a circle, in the center of which you will place the young child. Then you will order the two women to wait, each of them at opposite sides of the circle. When the real mother takes hold of him, it will be easy for the child to come outside the circle. But the pretended mother cannot lead him out.

[*The officer traces a circle with the chalk and motions the child to stand in the center of it.* MRS. MA *takes the child's hand and leads him out of the circle.* HAI-TANG *fails to contend with her.*]

THE JUDGE: It is evident that Hai-Tang is not the mother of the child, since she did not come forward to draw him out of the circle.

HAI-TANG: I supplicate you, Honored Sir, to calm your wrath. If I cannot obtain my son without dislocating his arm or bruising his baby flesh, I would rather perish under the blows than make the least effort to take him out of the circle.

THE JUDGE: A sage of old once said: What man can hide what he really is? Behold the power of the Chalk Circle! In order to seize an inheritance, Mrs. Ma has raised a young child that is not her own. But the Chalk Circle augustly brought out the truth and the falsehood. Mrs. Ma has an engaging exterior but her heart is corrupt. The true mother —Hai-Tang—is at last recognized.

From *The Chalk Circle*, an anonymous Chinese play of about 1300 A.D.

PROLOGUE

(Summer, 1945)

[*Among the ruins of a shattered Caucasian village the members of two Kolkhoz villages, mostly women and older men, are sitting in a circle, smoking and drinking wine. With them is a delegate of the State Reconstruction Commission from the capital.*]

PEASANT WOMAN ON THE LEFT [*pointing*]. In those hills over there we stopped three Nazi tanks, but the apple orchard was already destroyed.

OLD MAN ON THE RIGHT. Our beautiful dairy farm; a ruin.

GIRL TRACTORIST. I laid the fire, Comrade.

[*Pause.*]

DELEGATE. Now listen to the report. Delegates from the goat-breeding Kolkhoz "Rosa Luxemburg" have been to Nuka. When Hitler's armies approached, the Kolkhoz had moved its goat herds further east on orders from the authorities. They are now thinking of returning. Their delegates have looked at the village and the land and found a lot of it destroyed.

[DELEGATES *on right nod.*]

The neighboring fruit-culture Kolkhoz [*To the left.*] "Galinsk" is proposing to use the former grazing land of Kolkhoz "Rosa Luxemburg," a valley with scanty growth of grass, for orchards and vineyards. As a delegate of the Reconstruction Commission, I request that the two Kolkhoz villages decide between themselves whether Kolkhoz "Rosa Luxemburg" shall return here or not.

OLD MAN ON THE RIGHT. First of all, I want to protest against the restriction of time for discussion. We of Kolkhoz "Rosa Luxemburg" have spent three days and three nights getting here. And now discussion is limited to half a day.

WOUNDED SOLDIER ON THE LEFT. Comrade, we haven't as many villages as we used to have. We haven't as many hands. We haven't as much time.

GIRL TRACTORIST. All pleasures have to be rationed. Tobacco is rationed, and wine. Discussion should be rationed.

OLD MAN ON THE RIGHT [*sighing*]. Death to the fascists! But I will come to the point and explain why we want our valley back. There are a great many reasons, but I'll begin with one of the simplest. Makinä Abakidze, unpack the goat cheese.

[*A peasant woman from the right takes from a basket an enormous cheese wrapped in a cloth. Applause and laughter.*]

Help yourselves, Comrades, start in!

OLD MAN ON THE LEFT [*suspiciously*]. Is this a way of influencing us?

OLD MAN ON THE RIGHT [*amid laughter*]. How could it be a way of influencing you, Surab, you valley thief? Everyone knows you'll take the cheese and the valley, too.

[*Laughter.*]

All I expect from you is an honest answer. Do you like the cheese?

OLD MAN ON THE LEFT. The answer is: yes.

OLD MAN ON THE RIGHT. Really. [*Bitterly.*] I ought to have known you know nothing about cheese.

OLD MAN ON THE LEFT. Why not? When I tell you I like it?

OLD MAN ON THE RIGHT. Because you can't like it. Because it's not what it was in the old days. And why not? Because our goats don't like the new grass as they did the old. Cheese is not cheese because grass is not grass, that's the thing. Please put that in your report.

OLD MAN ON THE LEFT. But your cheese is excellent.

OLD MAN ON THE RIGHT. It isn't excellent. It's just passable. The new grazing land is no good, whatever the young people may say. One can't live there. It doesn't even smell of morning in the morning.

[*Several people laugh.*]

DELEGATE. Don't mind their laughing: they understand you. Comrades, why does one love one's country? Because the bread tastes better there, the air smells better, voices sound stronger, the sky is higher, the ground is easier to walk on. Isn't that so?

OLD MAN ON THE RIGHT. The valley has belonged to us from all eternity.

SOLDIER ON THE LEFT. What does *that* mean—from all eternity? Nothing belongs to anyone from all eternity. When you were young you didn't even belong to yourself. You belonged to the Kazbeki princes.

OLD MAN ON THE RIGHT. Doesn't it make a difference, though, what kind of trees stand next to the house you are born in? Or what kind of neighbors you have? Doesn't that make a difference? We want to come back just to have you as our neighbors, valley thieves! Now you can all laugh again.

OLD MAN ON THE LEFT [*laughing*]. Then why don't you listen to what your neighbor, Kato Wachtang, our agriculturist, has to say about the valley?

PEASANT WOMAN ON THE RIGHT. We've not said all *we* have to say about our valley. By no means. Not all the houses are destroyed. As for the dairy farm, at least the foundation wall is still standing.

DELEGATE. You can claim state support—here and there—you know that. I have suggestions here in my pocket.

PEASANT WOMAN ON THE RIGHT. Comrade Specialist, we haven't come here to bargain. I can't take your cap and hand you another, and say "This one's better." The other one might *be* better, but you *like* yours better.

GIRL TRACTORIST. A piece of land is not a cap—not in our country, Comrade.

DELEGATE. Don't get angry. It's true we have to consider a piece of land as a tool to produce something useful, but it's also true that we must recognize love for a particular piece of land. As far as I'm concerned, I'd like to find out more exactly what you [*to those on the left*] want to do with the valley.

OTHERS. Yes, let Kato speak.

DELEGATE. Comrade Agriculturist!

KATO [*rising; she's in military uniform*]. Comrades, last winter, while we were fighting in these hills here as partisans, we discussed how, after the expulsion of the Germans, we could build up our fruit culture to ten times its original size. I've prepared a plan for an irrigation project. By means of a cofferdam on our mountain lake, three hundred hectares of unfertile land can be irrigated. Our Kolkhoz could not only cultivate more fruit, but also have vineyards. The project, however, would pay only if the disputed valley of Kolkhoz "Rosa Luxemburg" were also included. Here are the calculations. [*She hands* DELEGATE *a briefcase.*]

OLD MAN ON THE RIGHT. Write into the report that our Kolkhoz plans to start a new stud farm.

GIRL TRACTORIST. Comrades, the project was conceived during days and nights when we had to take cover in the mountains. We were often without ammunition for our half-dozen rifles. Even getting a pencil was difficult.

[*Applause from both sides.*]

OLD MAN ON THE RIGHT. Our thanks to the Comrades of Kolkhoz "Galinsk" and all who have defended our country!

[*They shake hands and embrace.*]

PEASANT WOMAN ON THE LEFT. In doing this our thought was that our soldiers—both your men and our men—should return to a still more productive homeland.

GIRL TRACTORIST. As the poet Mayakovsky said: "The home of the Soviet people shall also be the home of Reason!"

[*The delegates excluding* OLD MAN *have got up, and with the* DELEGATE *specified proceed to study the Agriculturist's drawings. Exclamations such as:*
"Why is the altitude of all 22 meters?"—"This rock must be blown up"—"Actually, all they need is cement and dynamite"—"They force the water to come down here, that's clever!"

A VERY YOUNG WORKER ON THE RIGHT [*to* OLD MAN ON THE RIGHT]. They're going to irrigate all the fields between the hills, look at that, Aleko!

OLD MAN ON THE RIGHT. I'm not going to look. I knew the project would be good. I won't have a revolver aimed at my chest.

DELEGATE. But they only want to aim a pencil at your chest.

[*Laughter.*]

OLD MAN ON THE RIGHT [*gets up gloomily, and walks over to look at the drawings*]. These valley thieves know only too well that we can't resist machines and projects in this country.

PEASANT WOMAN ON THE RIGHT. Aleko Bereshwili, you have a weakness for new projects, That's well known.

DELEGATE. What about my report? May I write that you will all support the cession of your old valley in the interests of this project when you get back to your Kolkhoz?

PEASANT WOMAN ON THE RIGHT. I will. What about you, Aleko?

OLD MAN ON THE RIGHT [*bent over drawings*]. I suggest that you give us copies of the drawings to take along.

PEASANT WOMAN ON THE RIGHT. Then we can sit down and eat. Once he has the drawings and he's ready to discuss them, the matter is settled. I know him. And it will be the same with the rest of us.

[*Delegates laughingly embrace again.*]

OLD MAN ON THE LEFT. Long live the Kolkhoz "Rosa Luxemburg" and much luck to your horse-breeding project!

PEASANT WOMAN ON THE LEFT. In honor of the visit of the delegates from Kolkhoz "Rosa Luxemburg" and the specialist, the plan is that we all hear a presentation of the storyteller Arkadi Tscheidse.

[*Applause.* GIRL TRACTORIST *has gone off to bring the* STORYTELLER.]

PEASANT WOMAN ON THE RIGHT. Comrades, your entertainment had better be good. We're going to pay for is with a valley.

PEASANT WOMAN ON THE LEFT. Arkadi Tscheidse knows about our discussion. He's promised to perform something that has a bearing on the problem.

KATO. We wired Tiflis three times. The whole thing nearly fell through at the last minute because his driver had a cold.

PEASANT WOMAN ON THE LEFT. Arkadi Tscheidse knows 21,000 lines of verse.

OLD MAN ON THE LEFT. It's very difficult to get him. You and the Planning Commission should see to it that you get him to come north more often, Comrade.

DELEGATE. We are more interested in economics, I'm afraid.

OLD MAN ON THE LEFT [*smiling*]. You arrange the redistribution of vines and tractors, why not songs?

[*Enter the* STORYTELLER *Arkadi Tscheidse, led by* GIRL TRACTORIST. *He is a well-built man of simple manners, accompanied by four musicians with their instruments. The artists are greeted with applause.*]

GIRL TRACTORIST. This is the Comrade Specialist, Arkadi.

[*The* STORYTELLER *greets them all.*]

DELEGATE. Honored to make your acquaintance. I heard about your songs when I was a boy at school. Will it be one of the old legends?

THE STORYTELLER. A very old one. It's called "The Chalk Circle" and comes from the Chinese. But we'll do it, of course, in a changed version. Comrades, it's an honor for me to entertain you after a difficult debate. We hope you will find that the voice of the old poet also sounds well in the shadow of Soviet tractors. It may be a mistake to mix different wines, but old and new wisdom mix admirably. Now I hope we'll get something to eat before the performance begins—it would certainly help.

VOICES. Surely. Everyone into the Club House!

[*While everyone begins to move,* DELEGATE *turns to* GIRL TRACTORIST.]

DELEGATE. I hope it won't take long. I've got to get back tonight.

GIRL TRACTORIST. How long will it last, Arkadi? The Comrade Specialist must get back to Tiflis tonight.

THE STORYTELLER [*casually*]. It's actually two stories. An hour or two.

GIRL TRACTORIST [*confidentially*]. Couldn't you make it shorter?

THE STORYTELLER. No.

VOICE. Arkadi Tscheidse's performance will take place here in the square after the meal.

[*And they all go happily to eat.*]

PART ONE

1

The Noble Child

[*As the lights go up,* THE STORYTELLER *is seen sitting on the floor, a black sheepskin cloak round his shoulders, and a little, well-thumbed notebook in his hand. A small group of listeners—the chorus—sits with him. The manner of his recitation makes it clear that he has told this story over and over again. He mechanically fingers the pages, seldom looking at them. With appropriate gestures, he gives the signal for each scene to begin.*]

THE STORYTELLER.

In olden times, in a bloody time,
There ruled in a Caucasian city—
Men called it City of the Damned—
A Governor.
His name was Georgi Abashwili.
He was rich as Croesus
He had a beautiful wife
He had a healthy baby.
No other governor in Grusinia
Had so many horses in his stable
So many beggars on his doorstep
So many soldiers in his service
So many petitioners in his courtyard.
Georgi Abashwili—how shall I describe him to you?
He enjoyed his life.
On the morning of Easter Sunday
The Governor and his family went to church.

[*At the left a large doorway, at the right an even larger gateway.* BEGGARS *and* PETITIONERS *pour from the gateway, holding up thin* CHILDREN, *crutches, and petitions. They are followed by* IRONSHIRTS, *and then, expensively dressed, the* GOVERNOR'S FAMILY, *his* SERVANTS *and the* ADJUTANT.]

BEGGARS AND PETITIONERS. Mercy! Mercy, Your Grace! The taxes are too high.

—I lost my leg in the Persian War, where can I get . . .

—My brother is innocent. Your Grace, a misunderstanding . . .

—The child is starving in my arms!

—Our petition is for our son's discharge from the army, our last remaining son!

—Please, Your Grace, the water inspector takes bribes.

[ONE SERVANT *collects the petitions.* ANOTHER *distributes coins from a purse.* SOLDIERS *push the crowd back, lashing at them with thick leather whips.*]

THE SOLDIERS. Get back! Clear the church door!

[*Behind the* GOVERNOR, *his* WIFE *and the* ADJUTANT, *the* GOVERNOR'S CHILD *is brought through the gateway in an ornate carriage.*]

THE CROWD. The baby!

—I can't see it, don't shove so hard!

—God bless the child, Your Grace!

THE STORYTELLER [*while the crowd is driven back with whips*].

For the first time on that Easter Sunday, the people saw the Governor's heir.

Two doctors never moved from the noble child, apple of the Governor's eye.

Even the mighty Prince Kazbeki bows before him at the church door.

[*A* FAT PRINCE *steps forward and greets the* FAMILY.]

THE FAT PRINCE. Happy Easter, Natella Abashwili! What a day! When it was raining in the night, I thought to myself, gloomy holidays! But this morning the sky was gay. I love a gay sky, a simple heart, Natella Abashwili. And little Michael is a governor from head to foot! Tititi! [*He tickles the* CHILD.]

THE GOVERNOR'S WIFE. What do you think, Arsen, at last Georgi has decided to start building the wing on the east side. All those wretched slums are to be torn down to make room for the garden.

THE FAT PRINCE. Good news after so much bad! What's the latest on the war, Brother Georgi?

[*The* GOVERNOR *indicates a lack of interest.*]

Strategical retreat, I hear. Well, minor reverses are to be expected. Sometimes things go well, sometimes not. Such is war. Doesn't mean a thing, does it?

THE GOVERNOR'S WIFE. He's coughing. Georgi, did you hear? [*She speaks sharply to the* DOCTORS, *two dignified men standing close to the little carriage.*] He's coughing!

THE FIRST DOCTOR [*to the* SECOND]. May I remind you, Niko Mikadze, that I was against the lukewarm bath? [*To the* GOVERNOR'S WIFE.] There's been a little error over warming the bath water, Your Grace.

THE SECOND DOCTOR [*equally polite*]. Mika Loladze, I'm afraid I can't agree with you. The temperature of the bath water was exactly what our great, beloved Mishiko Oboladze prescribed. More likely a slight draft during the night, Your Grace.

THE GOVERNOR'S WIFE. But do pay more attention to him. He looks feverish, Georgi.

THE FIRST DOCTOR [*bending over the* CHILD]. No cause for alarm, Your Grace. The bath water will be warmer. It won't occur again.

THE SECOND DOCTOR [*with a venomous glance at the* FIRST]. I won't forget that, my dear Mika Loladze. No cause for concern, Your Grace.

THE FAT PRINCE. Well, well, well! I always say: "A pain in my liver? Then the doctor gets fifty strokes on the soles of his feet." We live in a decadent age. In the old days one said: "Off with his head!"

THE GOVERNOR'S WIFE. Let's go into church. Very likely it's the draft here.

[*The procession of* FAMILY *and* SERVANTS *turns into the doorway. The* FAT PRINCE *follows, but the* GOVERNOR *is kept back by the* ADJUTANT, *a handsome young man. When the crowd of* PETITIONERS *has been driven off, a young dust-stained* MESSENGER, *his arm in a sling, remains behind.*]

THE ADJUTANT [*pointing at the* MESSENGER, *who steps forward*]. Won't you hear the messenger from the capital, Your Excellency? He arrived this morning. With confidential papers.

THE GOVERNOR. Not before Service, Shalva. But did you hear

Brother Kazbeki wish me a happy Easter? Which is all very well, but I don't believe it did rain last night.

THE ADJUTANT [*nodding*]. We must investigate.

THE GOVERNOR. Yes, at once. Tomorrow.

[*They pass through the doorway. The* MESSENGER, *who has waited in vain for an audience, turns sharply round and, muttering a curse, goes off. Only one of the palace guards —*SIMON SHASHAVA—*remains at the door.*]

THE STORYTELLER.

> The city is still.
> Pigeons strut in the church square.
> A soldier of the Palace Guard
> Is joking with a kitchen maid
> As she comes up from the river with a bundle.

[*A girl—*GRUSHA VASHADZE—*comes through the gateway with a bundle made of large green leaves under her arm.*]

SIMON. What, the young lady is not in church? Shirking?

GRUSHA. I was dressed to go. But they needed another goose for the banquet. And they asked me to get it. I know about geese.

SIMON. A goose? [*He feigns suspicion.*] I'd like to see that goose.

[GRUSHA *does not understand.*]

One must be on one's guard with women. "I only went for a fish," they tell you, but it turns out to be something else.

GRUSHA [*walking resolutely toward him and showing him the goose*]. There! If it isn't a fifteen-pound goose stuffed full of corn, I'll eat the feathers.

SIMON. A queen of a goose! The Governor himself will eat it. So the young lady has been down to the river again?

GRUSHA. Yes, at the poultry farm.

SIMON. Really? At the poultry farm, down by the river . . . not higher up maybe? Near those willows?

GRUSHA. I only go to the willows to wash the linen.

SIMON [*insinuatingly*]. Exactly.

GRUSHA. Exactly what?

SIMON [*winking*]. Exactly that.

GRUSHA. Why shouldn't I wash the linen by the willows?

SIMON [*with exaggerated laughter*]. "Why shouldn't I wash the linen by the willows!" That's good, really good!

GRUSHA. I don't understand the soldier. What's so good about it?

SIMON [*slyly*]. "If something I know someone learns, she'll grow hot and cold by turns!"

GRUSHA. I don't know what I could learn about those willows.

SIMON. Not even if there was a bush opposite? That one could see everything from? Everything that goes on there when a certain person is—"washing linen"?

GRUSHA. What does go on? Won't the soldier say what he means and have done?

SIMON. Something goes on. Something can be seen.

GRUSHA. Could the soldier mean I dip my toes in the water when it's hot? There's nothing else.

SIMON. There's more. Your toes. And more.

GRUSHA. More what? At most my foot?

SIMON. Your foot. And a little more. [*He laughs heartily.*]

GRUSHA [*angrily*]. Simon Shashava, you ought to be ashamed of yourself! To sit in a bush on a hot day and wait till someone comes and dips her legs in the river! And I bet you bring a friend along too! [*She runs off.*]

SIMON [*shouting after her*]. I didn't bring any friend along!

[*As the* STORYTELLER *resumes his tale, the* SOLDIER *steps into the doorway as though to listen to the service.*]

THE STORYTELLER.

> The city lies still
> But why are there armed men?
> The Governor's palace is at peace
> But why is it a fortress?
> And the Governor returned to his palace
> And the fortress was a trap
> And the goose was plucked and roasted
> But the goose was not eaten this time
> And noon was no longer the hour to eat:
> Noon was the hour to die.

[*From the doorway at the left the* FAT PRINCE *quickly appears, stands still, looks around. Before the gateway at the right* TWO IRONSHIRTS *are squatting and playing dice. The* FAT PRINCE *sees them, walks slowly past, making a sign to them. They rise: one goes through the gateway, the other goes off at the right. Muffled voices are heard from various directions in the rear:* "To your posts!" *The palace is sur-*

rounded. The FAT PRINCE *quickly goes off. Church bells
in the distance. Enter, through the doorway, the* GOVERNOR'S
FAMILY *and procession, returning from church.*]

THE GOVERNOR'S WIFE [*passing the* ADJUTANT]. It's impossible
to live in such a slum. But Georgi, of course, will only
build for his little Michael. Never for me! Michael is all!
All for Michael!

[*The procession turns into the gateway. Again the* ADJUTANT
lingers behind. He waits. Enters the wounded MESSENGER
from the doorway. TWO IRONSHIRTS *of the Palace Guard
have taken up positions by the gateway.*]

THE ADJUTANT [*to the* MESSENGER]. The Governor does not
wish to receive military reports before dinner—especially
if they're depressing, as I assume. In the afternoon His
Excellency will confer with prominent architects. They're
coming to dinner too. And here they are!

[*Enter* THREE GENTLEMEN *through the doorway.*]

Go in the kitchen and get yourself something to eat, my
friend. [*As the* MESSENGER *goes, the* ADJUTANT *greets the*
ARCHITECTS.] Gentlemen, His Excellency expects you at
dinner. He will devote all his time to you and your great
new plans. Come!

ONE OF THE ARCHITECTS. We marvel that His Excellency in-
tends to build. There are disquieting rumors that the war
in Persia has taken a turn for the worse.

THE ADJUTANT. All the more reason to build! There's nothing
to those rumors anyway. Persia is a long way off, and the
garrison here would let itself be hacked to bits for its
Governor.

[*Noise from the palace. The shrill scream of a woman. Someone is shouting orders. Dumfounded, the* ADJUTANT *moves
toward the gateway. An* IRONSHIRT *steps out, points his
lance at him.*]

What's this? Put down that lance, you dog.

ONE OF THE ARCHITECTS. It's the Princes! Don't you know the
Princes met last night in the capital? And they're against
the Grand Duke and his Governors? Gentlemen, we'd better
make ourselves scarce.

[*They rush off. The* ADJUTANT *remains helplessly behind.*]

THE ADJUTANT [*furiously to the Palace Guard*]. Down with
 those lances! Don't you see the Governor's life is threatened?

[*The* IRONSHIRTS *of the Palace Guard refuse to obey. They
 stare coldly and indifferently at the* ADJUTANT *and follow
 the next events without interest.*]

THE STORYTELLER.

O blindness of the great!
They go their way like gods,
Great over bent backs,
Sure of hired fists,
Trusting in the power
Which has lasted so long.
But long is not forever.
O change from age to age!
Thou hope of the people!

[*Enter the* GOVERNOR, *through the gateway, between* TWO SOL-
 DIERS *fully armed. He is in chains. His face is gray.*]

Up, great sir, deign to walk upright!
From your palace the eyes of many foes follow you!
And now you don't need an architect, a carpenter will do.
You won't be moving into a new palace
But into a little hole in the ground.
Look about you once more, blind man!

[*The arrested man looks round.*]

Does all you had please you?
Between the Easter Mass and the Easter meal
You are walking to a place whence no one returns.

[*The* GOVERNOR *is led off. A horn sounds an alarm. Noise
 behind the gateway.*]

When the house of a great one collapses
Many little ones are slain.
Those who had no share in the *good* fortunes of the mighty
Often have a share in their *mis*fortunes.
The plunging wagon
Drags the sweating oxen down with it
Into the abyss.

[*The* SERVANTS *come rushing through the gateway in panic.*]

THE SERVANTS [*among themselves*]. The baskets!

—Take them all into the third courtyard! Food for five days!

—The mistress has fainted! Someone must carry her down.

—She must get away.

—What about us? We'll be slaughtered like chickens, as always.

—Goodness, what'll happen? There's bloodshed already in the city, they say.

—Nonsense, the Governor has just been asked to appear at a Princes' meeting. All very correct. Everything'll be ironed out. I heard this on the best authority . . .

[*The* TWO DOCTORS *rush into the courtyard.*]

THE FIRST DOCTOR [*trying to restrain the other*]. Niko Mikadze, it is your duty as a doctor to attend Natella Abashwili.

THE SECOND DOCTOR. My duty! It's yours!

THE FIRST DOCTOR. Whose turn is it to look after the child today, Niko Mikadze, yours or mine?

THE SECOND DOCTOR. Do you really think, Mika Loladze, I'm going to stay a minute longer in this accursed house on that little brat's account? [*They start fighting. All one hears is:* "You neglect your duty!" *and* "Duty, my foot!" *Then the* SECOND DOCTOR *knocks the* FIRST *down.*] Oh go to hell! [*Exit.*]

[*Enter the soldier,* SIMON SHASHAVA. *He searches in the crowd for* GRUSHA.]

SIMON. Grusha! There you are at last! What are you going to do?

GRUSHA. Nothing. If worst comes to worst, I've a brother in the mountains. How about you?

SIMON. Forget about me. [*Formally again.*] Grusha Vashnadze, your wish to know my plans fills me with satisfaction. I've been ordered to accompany Madam Natella Abashwili as her guard.

GRUSHA. But hasn't the Palace Guard mutinied?

SIMON [*seriously*]. That's a fact.

GRUSHA. Isn't it dangerous to go with her?

SIMON. In Tiflis, they say: Isn't the stabbing dangerous for the knife?

GRUSHA. You're not a knife, you're a man, Simon Shashava, what has that woman to do with you?

SIMON. That woman has nothing to do with me. I have my orders, and I go.

GRUSHA. The soldier is pigheaded: he is running into danger for nothing—nothing at all. I must get into the third courtyard, I'm in a hurry.

SIMON. Since we're both in a hurry we shouldn't quarrel. You need time for a good quarrel. May I ask if the young lady still has parents?

GRUSHA. No, just a brother.

SIMON. As time is short—my second question is this: Is the young lady as healthy as a fish in water?

GRUSHA. I may have a pain in the right shoulder once in a while. Otherwise I'm strong enough for my job. No one has complained. So far.

SIMON. That's well known. When it's Easter Sunday, and the question arises who'll run for the goose all the same, she'll be the one. My third question is this: Is the young lady impatient? Does she want apples in winter?

GRUSHA. Impatient? No. But if a man goes to war without any reason and then no message comes—that's bad.

SIMON. A message will come. And now my final question . . .

GRUSHA. Simon Shashava, I must get to the third courtyard at once. My answer is yes.

SIMON [very embarrassed]. Haste, they say, is the wind that blows down the scaffolding. But they also say: The rich don't know what haste is. I'm from . . .

GRUSHA. Kutsk . . .

SIMON. So the young lady has been inquiring about me? I'm healthy, I have no dependents, I make ten piasters a month, as paymaster twenty piasters, and I'm asking—very sincerely—for your hand.

GRUSHA. Simon Shashava, it suits me well.

SIMON [taking from his neck a thin chain with a little cross on it]. My mother gave me this cross, Grusha Vashnadze. The chain is silver. Please wear it.

GRUSHA. Many thanks, Simon.

SIMON [hangs it round her neck]. It would be better for the young lady to go to the third courtyard now. Or there'll be difficulties. Anyway, I must harness the horses. The young lady will understand?

GRUSHA. Yes, Simon.

[*They stand undecided.*]

SIMON. I'll just take the mistress to the troops that have stayed loyal. When the war's over, I'll be back. In two weeks. Or three. I hope my intended won't get tired, awaiting my return.

GRUSHA.

> Simon Shashava, I shall wait for you.
> Go calmly into battle, soldier,
> The bloody battle, the bitter battle
> From which not everyone returns:
> When you return I shall be there.
> I shall be waiting for you under the green elm
> I shall be waiting for you under the bare elm
> I shall wait until the last soldier has returned
> And longer.
> When you come back from the battle
> No boots will stand at my door
> The pillow beside mine will be empty
> And my mouth will be unkissed.
> When you return, when you return
> You will be able to say: It is just as it was.

SIMON. I thank you, Grusha Vashnadze. And good-bye!

[*He bows low before her. She does the same before him. Then she runs quickly off without looking round. Enter the* ADJUTANT *from the gateway.*]

THE ADJUTANT [*harshly*]. Harness the horses to the carriage! Don't stand there doing nothing, louse!

[SIMON SHASHAVA *stands to attention and goes off.* TWO SERVANTS *crowd from the gateway, bent low under huge trunks. Behind them, supported by her* WOMEN, *stumbles* NATELLA ABASHWILI. *She is followed by a* WOMAN *carrying the* CHILD.]

THE GOVERNOR'S WIFE. I hardly know if my head's still on. Where's Michael? Don't hold him so clumsily. Pile the trunks onto the carriage. Shalva, is there no news from the city?

THE ADJUTANT. None. All's quiet so far, but there's not a minute to lose. No room for all these trunks in the carriage. Pick out what you need. [*Exit quickly.*]

THE GOVERNOR'S WIFE. Only essentials! Quick, open the trunks!

I'll tell you what I need. [*The trunks are lowered and opened. She points at some brocade dresses.*] The green one! And, of course, the one with the fur trimming. Where are Niko Mikadze and Mika Loladze? I've suddenly got the most terrible migraine again. It always starts in the temples.

[*Enter* GRUSHA.]

Taking your time, eh? Go at once and get the hot water bottles!

[GRUSHA *runs off, returns later with hot water bottles; the* GOVERNOR'S WIFE *orders her about by signs.*]

Don't tear the sleeves.

A YOUNG WOMAN. Pardon, madam, no harm has come to the dress.

THE GOVERNOR'S WIFE. Because I stopped you. I've been watching you for a long time. Nothing in your head but making eyes at Shalva Tzereteli. I'll kill you, you bitch! [*She beats the* YOUNG WOMAN.]

THE ADJUTANT [*appearing in the gateway*]. Please make haste, Natella Abashwili. Firing has broken out in the city. [*Exit.*]

THE GOVERNOR'S WIFE [*letting go of the* YOUNG WOMAN]. Oh dear, do you think they'll lay hands on us? Why should they? Why? [*She herself begins to rummage in the trunks.*] How's Michael? Asleep?

THE WOMAN WITH THE CHILD. Yes, madam.

THE GOVERNOR'S WIFE. Then put him down a moment and get my little saffron-colored boots from the bedroom. I need them for the green dress.

[*The* WOMAN *puts down the* CHILD *and goes off.*]

Just look how these things have been packed! No love! No understanding! If you don't give them every order yourself . . . At such moments you realize what kind of servants you have! They gorge themselves at your expense, and never a word of gratitude! I'll remember this.

THE ADJUTANT [*entering, very excited*]. Natella, you must leave at once!

THE GOVERNOR'S WIFE. Why? I've got to take this silver dress —it cost a thousand piasters. And that one there, and where's the wine-colored one?

THE ADJUTANT [*trying to pull her away*]. Riots have broken out! We must leave at once. Where's the baby?

THE GOVERNOR'S WIFE [*calling to the* YOUNG WOMAN *who was holding the baby*]. Maro, get the baby ready! Where on earth are you?

THE ADJUTANT [*leaving*]. We'll probably have to leave the carriage behind and go ahead on horseback.

[*The* GOVERNOR'S WIFE *rummages again among her dresses, throws some onto the heap of chosen clothes, then takes them off again. Noises, drums are heard. The* YOUNG WOMAN *who was beaten creeps away. The sky begins to grow red.*]

THE GOVERNOR'S WIFE [*rummaging desperately*]. I simply cannot find the wine-colored dress. Take the whole pile to the carriage. Where's Asja? And why hasn't Maro come back? Have you all gone crazy?

THE ADJUTANT [*returning*]. Quick! Quick!

THE GOVERNOR'S WIFE [*to the* FIRST WOMAN]. Run! Just throw them into the carriage!

THE ADJUTANT. We're not taking the carriage. And if you don't come now, I'll ride off on my own.

THE GOVERNOR'S WIFE [*as the* FIRST WOMAN *can't carry everything*]. Where's that bitch Asja?

[*The* ADJUTANT *pulls her away.*]

Maro, bring the baby! [*To the* FIRST WOMAN.] Go and look for Masha. No, first take the dresses to the carriage. Such nonsense! I wouldn't dream of going on horseback!

[*Turning round, she sees the red sky, and starts back rigid. The fire burns. She is pulled out by the* ADJUTANT. *Shaking, the* FIRST WOMAN *follows with the dresses.*]

MARO [*from the doorway with the boots*]. Madam! [*She sees the trunks and dresses and runs toward the* BABY, *picks it up, and holds it a moment.*] They left it behind, the beasts. [*She hands it to* GRUSHA.] Hold it a moment. [*She runs off, following the* GOVERNOR'S WIFE.]

[*Enter* SERVANTS *from the gateway.*]

THE COOK. Well, so they've actually gone. Without the food wagons, and not a minute too early. It's time for us to get out.

A GROOM. This'll be an unhealthy neighborhood for quite a while. [*To one of the* WOMEN.] Suliko, take a few blankets and wait for me in the foal stables.

GRUSHA. What have they done with the Governor?

THE GROOM [*gesturing throat cutting*]. Ffffft.

A FAT WOMAN [*seeing the gesture and becoming hysterical*]. Oh dear, oh dear, oh dear, oh dear! Our master Georgi Abashwili! A picture of health he was, at the morning Mass—and now! Oh, take me away, we're all lost, we must die in sin like our master, Georgi Abashwili!

THE OTHER WOMAN [*soothing her*]. Calm down, Nina! You'll be taken to safety. You've never hurt a fly.

THE FAT WOMAN [*being led out*]. Oh dear, oh dear, oh dear! Quick! Let's all get out before they come, before they come!

A YOUNG WOMAN. Nina takes it more to heart than the mistress, that's a fact. They even have to have their weeping done for them.

THE COOK. We'd better get out, all of us.

ANOTHER WOMAN [*glancing back*]. That must be the East Gate burning.

THE YOUNG WOMAN [*seeing the* CHILD *in* GRUSHA'S *arms*]. The baby! What are you doing with it?

GRUSHA. It got left behind.

THE YOUNG WOMAN. She simply left it there. Michael, who was kept out of all the drafts!

[*The* SERVANTS *gather round the* CHILD.]

GRUSHA. He's waking up.

THE GROOM. Better put him down, I tell you. I'd rather not think what'd happen to anybody who was found with that baby.

THE COOK. That's right. Once they get started, they'll kill each other off, whole families at a time. Let's go.

[*Exeunt all but* GRUSHA, *with the* CHILD *on her arm, and* TWO WOMEN.]

THE TWO WOMEN. Didn't you hear? Better put him down.

GRUSHA. The nurse asked me to hold him a moment.

THE OLDER WOMAN. She's not coming back, you simpleton.

THE YOUNGER WOMAN. Keep your hands off it.

THE OLDER WOMAN [*amiably*]. Grusha, you're a good soul, but you're not very bright, and you know it. I tell you, if he had the plague he couldn't be more dangerous.

GRUSHA [*stubbornly*]. He hasn't got the plague. He looks at me! He's human!

THE OLDER WOMAN. Don't look at *him*. You are a fool—the kind that always gets put upon. A person need only say, "Run for the salad, you have the longest legs," and you run. My husband has an ox cart—you can come with us if you hurry! Lord, by now the whole neighborhood must be in flames.

[BOTH WOMEN *leave, sighing. After some hesitation,* GRUSHA *puts the sleeping* CHILD *down, looks at it for a moment, then takes a brocade blanket from the heap of clothes and covers it. Then* BOTH WOMEN *return, dragging bundles.* GRUSHA *starts guiltily away from the* CHILD *and walks a few steps to one side.*]

THE YOUNGER WOMAN. Haven't you packed anything yet? There isn't much time, you know. The Ironshirts will be here from the barracks.

GRUSHA. Coming!

[*She runs through the doorway.* BOTH WOMEN *go to the gateway and wait. The sound of horses is heard. They flee, screaming. Enter the* FAT PRINCE *with drunken* IRONSHIRTS. *One of them carries the Governor's head on a lance.*]

THE FAT PRINCE. Here! In the middle!

[ONE SOLDIER *climbs onto the* OTHER'S *back, takes the head, holds it tentatively over the door.*]

That's not the middle. Farther to the right. That's it. What I do, my friends, I do well. [*While, with hammer and nail, the* SOLDIER *fastens the head to the wall by its hair.*] This morning at the church door I said to Georgi Abashwili: "I love a clear sky." Actually, I prefer the lightning that comes out of a clear sky. Yes, indeed. It's a pity they took the brat along, though, I need him, urgently. [*Exit with* IRONSHIRTS *through the gateway.*]

[*Trampling of horses again. Enter* GRUSHA *through the doorway looking cautiously about her. Clearly she has waited for the* IRONSHIRTS *to go. Carrying a bundle, she walks toward the gateway. At the last moment, she turns to see if the* CHILD *is still there. Catching sight of the head over the doorway, she screams. Horrified, she picks up her bundle again, and is about to leave when the* STORYTELLER *starts to speak. She stands rooted to the spot.*]

THE STORYTELLER.

As she was standing between courtyard and gate,
She heard or she thought she heard a low voice calling.
The child called to her,
Not whining, but calling quite sensibly,
Or so it seemed to her.
"Woman," it said, "help me."
And it went on, not whining, but saying quite sensibly:
"Know, woman, he who hears not a cry for help
But passes by with troubled ears will never hear
The gentle call of a lover nor the blackbird at dawn
Nor the happy sigh of the tired grape picker as the Angelus
        rings."

[GRUSHA *walks a few steps toward the* CHILD *and bends over it.*]

Hearing this she went back for one more look at the child:
Only to sit with him for a moment or two,
Only till someone should come,
His mother, or anyone.

[*Leaning on a trunk, she sits facing the* CHILD.]

Only till she would have to leave, for the danger was too
        great,
The city was full of flame and crying.

[*The light grows dimmer, as though evening and night were
coming on.*]

Fearful is the seductive power of goodness!

[GRUSHA *now settles down to watch over the* CHILD *through
the night. Once, she lights a small lamp to look at it. Once,
she tucks it in with a coat. From time to time she listens
and looks to see whether someone is coming.*]

And she sat with the child a long time,
Till evening came, till night came, till dawn came.
She sat too long, too long she saw
The soft breathing, the small clenched fists,
Till toward morning the seduction was complete
And she rose, and bent down and, sighing, took the child
And carried it away.

[*She does what the* STORYTELLER *says as he describes it.*]

As if it was stolen goods she picked it up.
As if she was a thief she crept away.

2

The Flight Into The Northern Mountains

THE STORYTELLER.

When Grusha Vashnadze left the city
On the Grusinian highway
On the way to the Northern Mountains
She sang a song, she bought some milk.

THE CHORUS.

How will this human child escape
The bloodhounds, the trap setters?
Into the deserted mountains she journeyed
Along the Grusinian highway she journeyed
She sang a song, she bought some milk.

[GRUSHA VASHNADZE *walks on. On her back she carries the*
CHILD *in a sack, in one hand is a large stick, in the other
a bundle. She sings.*]

THE SONG OF THE FOUR GENERALS

Four generals
Set out for Iran.
With the first one, war did not agree.
The second never won a victory.
For the third the weather was never right.
For the fourth the men would never fight.
Four generals
And not a single man!

Sosso Robakidse
Went marching to Iran.
With him the war did so agree
He soon had won a victory.
For him the weather was always right.
For him the men would always fight.

Sosso Robakidse,
He is our man!

[*A peasant's cottage appears.*]

GRUSHA [*to the* CHILD]. Noontime is meal time. Now we'll sit
hopefully in the grass, while the good Grusha goes and buys
a little pitcher of milk. [*She lays the* CHILD *down and knocks
at the cottage door. An* OLD MAN *opens it.*] Grandfather,
could I have a little pitcher of milk? And a corn cake,
maybe?

THE OLD MAN. Milk? We have no milk. The soldiers from the
city have our goats. Go to the soldiers if you want milk.

GRUSHA. But grandfather, you must have a little pitcher of
milk for a baby?

THE OLD MAN. And for a God-bless-you, eh?

GRUSHA. Who said anything about a God-bless-you? [*She
shows her purse.*] We'll pay like princes. "Head in the
clouds, backside in the water."

[*The* OLD MAN *goes off, grumbling, for milk.*]

How much for the milk?

THE OLD MAN. Three piasters. Milk has gone up.

GRUSHA. Three piasters for this little drop?

[*Without a word the* OLD MAN *shuts the door in her face.*]

Michael, did you hear that? Three piasters! We can't afford
it! [*She goes back, sits down again, and gives the* CHILD
her breast.] Suck. Think of three piasters. There's nothing
there, but you *think* you're drinking and that's something.
[*Shaking her head, she sees that the* CHILD *isn't sucking
any more. She gets up, walks back to the door, and knocks
again.*] Open grandfather, we'll pay. [*Softly.*] May lightning strike you! [*When the* OLD MAN *appears.*] I thought it
would be half a piaster. But the baby must be fed. How
about one piaster for that little drop?

THE OLD MAN. Two.

GRUSHA. Don't shut the door again. [*She fishes a long time in
her bag.*] Here are two piasters. The milk better be good.
I still have two days' journey ahead of me. It's a murderous
business you have here—and sinful, too!

THE OLD MAN. Kill the soldiers if you want milk.

GRUSHA [*giving the* CHILD *some milk*]. This is an expensive joke. Take a sip. Michael, it's a week's pay. Around here they think we earned our money just sitting on our behinds. Oh, Michael, Michael, you're a nice little load for a girl to take on!

[*Uneasy, she gets up, puts the* CHILD *on her back, and walks on. The* OLD MAN, *grumbling, picks up the pitcher and looks after her unmoved.*]

THE STORYTELLER.

> As Grusha Vashnadze went northward
> The Princes' Ironshirts went after her.

THE CHORUS.

> How will the barefoot girl escape the Ironshirts,
> The bloodhounds, the trap setters?
> They hunt even by night.
> Pursuers never get tired.
> Butchers sleep little.

[TWO IRONSHIRTS *are trudging along the highway.*]

THE CORPORAL. You'll never amount to anything, blockhead, your heart's not in it. Your senior officer sees this in little things. Yesterday, when I made the fat gal, yes, you grabbed her husband as I commanded, and you did kick him in the belly, at my request, but did you *enjoy* it, like a loyal private, or were you just doing your duty? I've kept an eye on you blockhead, you're a hollow reed and a tinkling cymbal, you won't get promoted. [*They walk a while in silence.*] Don't think I've forgotten how insubordinate you are, either. Stop limping! I forbid you to limp! You limp because I sold the horses, and I sold the horses because I'd never have got that price again. You limp to show me you don't like marching. I know you. It won't help. You wait. Sing!

THE TWO IRONSHIRTS [*singing*].

> Sadly to war I went my way
> Leaving my loved one at her door.
> My friends will keep her honor safe
> Till from the war I'm back once more.

THE CORPORAL. Louder!

THE TWO IRONSHIRTS [*singing*].

> When 'neath a headstone I shall be
> My love a little earth will bring:
> "Here rest the feet that oft would run to me
> And here the arms that oft to me would cling."

[*They begin to walk again in silence.*]

THE CORPORAL. A good soldier has his heart and soul in it. When he receives an order, he gets a hard on, and when he drives his lance into the enemy's guts, he comes. [*He shouts for joy.*] He lets himself be torn to pieces for his superior officer, and as he lies dying he takes note that his corporal is nodding approval, and that is reward enough, it's his dearest wish. *You* won't get any nod of approval, but you'll croak all right. Christ, how'm I to get my hands on the Governor's bastard with the help of a fool like you! [*They stay on stage behind.*]

THE STORYTELLER.

> When Grusha Vashnadze came to the River Sirra
> Flight grew too much for her, the helpless child too heavy.
> In the cornfields the rosy dawn
> Is cold to the sleepless one, only cold.
> The gay clatter of the milk cans in the farmyard where the
>   smoke rises
> Is only a threat to the fugitive.
> She who carries the child feels its weight and little more.

[GRUSHA *stops in front of a farm. A fat* PEASANT WOMAN *is carrying a milk can through the door.* GRUSHA *waits until she has gone in, then approaches the house cautiously.*]

GRUSHA [*to the* CHILD]. Now you've wet yourself again, and you know I've no linen. Michael, this is where we part company. It's far enough from the city. They wouldn't want you *so* much that they'd follow you all *this* way, little good-for-nothing. The peasant woman is kind, and can't you just smell the milk? [*She bends down to lay the* CHILD *on the threshold.*] So farewell, Michael, I'll forget how you kicked me in the back all night to make me walk faster. And you can forget the meager fare—it was meant well. I'd like to have kept you—your nose is so tiny—but it can't be. I'd have shown you your first rabbit, I'd have trained you to keep dry, but now I must turn around. My sweetheart the soldier might be back soon, and suppose he didn't find me? You can't ask that, can you?

[*She creeps up to the door and lays the* CHILD *on the threshold. Then, hiding behind a tree, she waits until the* PEASANT WOMAN *opens the door and sees the bundle.*]

THE PEASANT WOMAN. Good heavens, what's this? Husband!

THE PEASANT. What is it? Let me finish my soup.

THE PEASANT WOMAN [*to the* CHILD]. Where's your mother then? Haven't you got one? It's a boy. Fine linen. He's from a good family, you can see that. And they just leave him on our doorstep. Oh, these are times!

THE PEASANT. If they think we're going to feed it, they're wrong. You can take it to the priest in the village. That's the best we can do.

THE PEASANT WOMAN. What'll the priest do with him? He needs a mother. There, he's waking up. Don't you think we could keep him, though?

THE PEASANT [*shouting*]. No!

THE PEASANT WOMAN. I could lay him in the corner by the armchair. All I need is a crib. I can take him into the fields with me. See him laughing? Husband, we have a roof over our heads. We can do it. Not another word out of you!

[*She carries the* CHILD *into the house. The* PEASANT *follows protesting.* GRUSHA *steps out from behind the tree, laughs, and hurries off in the opposite direction.*]

THE STORYTELLER.

Why so cheerful, making for home?

THE CHORUS.

Because the child has won new parents with a laugh,
Because I'm rid of the little one, I'm cheerful.

THE STORYTELLER.

And why so sad?

THE CHORUS.

Because I'm single and free, I'm sad
Like someone who's been robbed
Someone who's newly poor.

[*She walks for a short while, then meets the* TWO IRONSHIRTS *who point their lances at her.*]

THE CORPORAL. Lady, you are running straight into the arms of the Armed Forces. Where are you coming from? And when? Are you having illicit relations with the enemy? Where is he hiding? What movements is he making in your rear? How about the hills? How about the valleys? How are your stockings fastened?

[GRUSHA *stands there frightened.*]

Don't be scared, we always withdraw, if necessary . . . what, blockhead? I always withdraw. In that respect at least, I can be relied on. Why are you staring like that at my lance? In the field no soldier drops his lance, that's a rule. Learn it by heart, blockhead. Now, lady, where are you headed?

GRUSHA. To meet my intended, one Simon Shashava, of the Palace Guard in Nuka.

THE CORPORAL. Simon Shashava? Sure, I know him. He gave me the key so I could look you up once in a while. Blockhead, we are getting to be unpopular. We must make her realize we have honorable intentions. Lady, behind apparent frivolity I conceal a serious nature, so let me tell you officially: I want a child from you.

[GRUSHA *utters a little scream.*]

Blockhead, she understood me. Uh-huh, isn't it a sweet shock? "Then first I must take the noodles out of the oven Officer. Then first I must change my torn shirt, Colonel." But away with jokes, away with my lance! We are looking for a baby. A baby from a good family. Have you heard of such a baby, from the city, dressed in fine linen, and suddenly turning up here?

GRUSHA. No, I haven't heard a thing. [*Suddenly she turns round and runs back, panic-stricken. The* IRONSHIRTS *glance at each other, then follow her, cursing.*]

THE STORYTELLER.

> Run, kind girl! The killers are coming!
> Help the helpless babe, helpless girl!
> And so she runs!

THE CHORUS.

> In the bloodiest times
> There are kind people.

[*As* GRUSHA *rushes into the cottage, the* PEASANT WOMAN *is bending over the* CHILD's *crib.*]

GRUSHA. Hide him. Quick! The Ironshirts are coming! I laid him on your doorstep. But he isn't mine. He's from a good family.

THE PEASANT WOMAN. Who's coming? What Ironshirts?

GRUSHA. Don't ask questions. The Ironshirts that are looking for it.

THE PEASANT WOMAN. They've no business in my house. But I must have a little talk with you, it seems.

GRUSHA. Take off the fine linen. It'll give us away.

THE PEASANT WOMAN. Linen, my foot! In this house I make the decisions! "*You* can't vomit in *my* room!" Why did you abandon it? It's a sin.

GRUSHA [*looking out of the window*]. Look, they're coming out from behind those trees! I shouldn't have run away, it make them angry. Oh, what shall I do?

THE PEASANT WOMAN [*looking out of the window and suddenly starting with fear*]. Gracious! Ironshirts!

GRUSHA. They're after the baby.

THE PEASANT WOMAN. Suppose they come in!

GRUSHA. You mustn't give him to them. Say he's yours.

THE PEASANT WOMAN. Yes.

GRUSHA. They'll run him through if you hand him over.

THE PEASANT WOMAN. But suppose they ask for it? The silver for the harvest is in the house.

GRUSHA. If you let them have him, they'll run him through, right here in this room! You've got to say he's yours!

THE PEASANT WOMAN. Yes. But what if they don't believe me?

GRUSHA. You must be firm.

THE PEASANT WOMAN. They'll burn the roof over our heads.

GRUSHA. That's why you must say he's yours. His name's Michael. But I shouldn't have told you.

[*The* PEASANT WOMAN *nods.*]

Don't nod like that. And don't tremble—they'll notice.

THE PEASANT WOMAN. Yes.

GRUSHA. And stop saying yes, I can't stand it. [*She shakes the* WOMAN.] Don't you have any children?

THE PEASANT WOMAN [*muttering*]. He's in the war.

GRUSHA. Then maybe *he's* an Ironshirt? Do you want *him* to run children through with a lance? You'd bawl him out. "No fooling with lances in my house!" you'd shout, "Is that what I've reared you for? Wash your neck before you speak to your mother!"

THE PEASANT WOMAN. That's true, he couldn't get away with anything around here!

GRUSHA. So you'll say he's yours?

THE PEASANT WOMAN. Yes.

GRUSHA. Look! They're coming!

[*There is a knocking at the door. The* WOMEN *don't answer. Enter* IRONSHIRTS. *The* PEASANT WOMAN *bows low.*]

THE CORPORAL. Well, here she is. What did I tell you? What a nose I have! I *smelt* her. Lady, I have a question for you. Why did you run away? What did you think I would do to you? I'll bet it was something dirty. Confess!

GRUSHA [*while the* PEASANT WOMAN *bows again and again*]. I'd left some milk on the stove, and I suddenly remembered it.

THE CORPORAL. Or maybe you imagined I looked at you in a dirty way? Like there could be something between us? A lewd sort of look, know what I mean?

GRUSHA. I didn't see it.

THE CORPORAL. But it's possible, huh? You admit that much. After all, I might be a pig. I'll be frank with you: I could think of all sorts of things if we were alone. [*To the* PEASANT WOMAN.] Shouldn't you be busy in the yard? Feeding the hens?

THE PEASANT WOMAN [*falling suddenly to her knees*]. Soldier, I didn't know a thing about it. Please don't burn the roof over our heads.

THE CORPORAL. What are you talking about?

THE PEASANT WOMAN. I had nothing to do with it. She left it on my doorstep, I swear it!

THE CORPORAL [*suddenly seeing the* CHILD *and whistling*]. Ah, so there's a little something in the crib! Blockhead, I smell a thousand piasters. Take the old girl outside and hold on to her. It looks like I have a little cross-examining to do.

[*The* PEASANT WOMAN *lets herself be led out by the* PRIVATE, *without a word.*]

So, you've *got* the child I wanted from you! [*He walks toward the crib.*]

GRUSHA. Officer, he's mine. He's not the one you're after.
THE CORPORAL. I'll just take a look.

[*He bends over the crib.* GRUSHA *looks round in despair.*]

GRUSHA. He's mine! He's mine!
THE CORPORAL. Fine linen!

[GRUSHA *dashes at him to pull him away. He throws her off and again bends over the crib. Again looking round in despair, she sees a log of wood, seizes it, and hits the* CORPORAL *over the head from behind. The* CORPORAL *collapses. She quickly picks up the* CHILD *and rushes off.*]

THE STORYTELLER.

> And in her flight from the Ironshirts
> After twenty-two days of journeying
> At the foot of the Janga-Tu Glacier
> Grusha Vashnadze decided to adopt the child.

THE CHORUS.

> The helpless girl adopted the helpless child.

[GRUSHA *squats over a half-frozen stream to get the* CHILD *water in the hollow of her hand.*]
GRUSHA.

> Since no one else will take you, son,
> I must take you.
> Since no one else will take you, son,
> You must take me.
> O black day in a lean, lean year,
> The trip was long, the milk was dear,
> My legs are tired, my feet are sore:
> But I wouldn't be without you any more.
> I'll throw your silken shirt away
> And wrap you in rags and tatters.
> I'll wash you, son, and christen you in glacier water.
> We'll see it through together.

[*She has taken off the* CHILD'S *fine linen and wrapped it in a rag.*]

THE STORYTELLER.

> When Grusha Vashnadze
> Pursued by the Ironshirts
> Came to the bridge on the glacier
> Leading to the villages of the Eastern Slope
> She sang the Song of the Rotten Bridge
> And risked two lives.

[*A wind has risen. The bridge on the glacier is visible in the dark. One rope is broken and half the bridge is hanging down the abyss.* MERCHANTS, *two men and a woman, stand undecided before the bridge as* GRUSHA *and the* CHILD *arrive. One man is trying to catch the hanging rope with a stick.*]

THE FIRST MAN. Take your time, young woman. You won't get across here anyway.

GRUSHA. But I *have* to get the baby to the east side. To my brother's place.

THE MERCHANT WOMAN. Have to? How d'you mean, "have to"? I have to get there, too—because I have to buy carpets in Atum—carpets a woman had to sell because her husband had to die. But can *I* do what I have to? Can she? Andrei's been fishing for that rope for hours. And I ask you, how are we going to fasten it, even if he gets it up?

THE FIRST MAN [*listening*]. Hush, I think I hear something.

GRUSHA. The bridge isn't quite rotted through. I think I'll try it.

THE MERCHANT WOMAN. *I* wouldn't—if the devil himself were after me. It's suicide.

THE FIRST MAN [*shouting*]. Hi!

GRUSHA. Don't shout! [*To the* MERCHANT WOMAN.] Tell him not to shout.

THE FIRST MAN. But there's someone down there calling. Maybe they've lost their way.

THE MERCHANT WOMAN. Why shouldn't he shout? Is there something funny about you? Are they after you?

GRUSHA. All right, I'll tell. The Ironshirts are after me. I knocked one down.

THE SECOND MAN. Hide our merchandise!

[*The* WOMAN *hides a sack behind a rock.*]

THE FIRST MAN. Why didn't you say so right away? [*To the others.*] If they catch her they'll make mincemeat out of her!

GRUSHA. Get out of my way. I've got to cross that bridge.

THE SECOND MAN. You can't. The precipice is two thousand feet deep.

THE FIRST MAN. Even with the rope it'd be no use. We could hold it up with our hands. But then we'd have to do the same for the Ironshirts.

GRUSHA. Go away.

[*There are calls from the distance:* "Hi, up there!"]

THE MERCHANT WOMAN. They're getting near. But you can't take the child on that bridge. It's sure to break. And look!

[GRUSHA *looks down into the abyss. The* IRONSHIRTS *are heard calling again from below.*]

THE SECOND MAN. Two thousand feet!

GRUSHA. But those men are worse.

THE FIRST MAN. You can't do it. Think of the baby. Risk your life but not a child's.

THE SECOND MAN. With the child she's that much heavier!

THE MERCHANT WOMAN. Maybe she's *really* got to get across. Give *me* the baby. I'll hide it. Cross the bridge alone!

GRUSHA. I won't. We belong together. [*To the* CHILD.] "Live together, die together." [*She sings.*]

THE SONG OF THE ROTTEN BRIDGE

Deep is the abyss, son,
I see the weak bridge sway
But it's not for us, son,
To choose the way.

The way I know
Is the one you must tread,
And all you will eat
Is my bit of bread.

Of every four pieces
You shall have three.
Would that I knew
How big they will be!

Get out of my way, I'll try it without the rope.

THE MERCHANT WOMAN. You are tempting God!

[*There are shouts from below.*]

GRUSHA. Please, throw that stick away, or they'll get the rope and follow me.

[*Pressing the CHILD to her, she steps onto the swaying bridge. The MERCHANT WOMAN screams when it looks as though the bridge is about to collapse. But GRUSHA walks on and reaches the far side.*]

THE FIRST MAN. She made it!

THE MERCHANT WOMAN [*who has fallen on her knees and begun to pray, angrily*]. I still think it was a sin.

[*The IRONSHIRTS appear; the CORPORAL'S head is bandaged.*]

THE CORPORAL. Seen a woman with a child?

THE FIRST MAN [*while the SECOND MAN throws the stick into the abyss*]. Yes, there! But the bridge won't carry you!

THE CORPORAL. You'll pay for this, blockhead!

[*GRUSHA, from the far bank, laughs and shows the CHILD to the IRONSHIRTS. She walks on. The wind blows.*]

GRUSHA [*turning to the CHILD*]. You mustn't be afraid of the wind. He's a poor thing too. He has to push the clouds along and he gets quite cold doing it.

[*Snow starts falling.*]

And the snow isn't so bad, either, Michael. It covers the little fir trees so they won't die in winter. Let me sing you a little song. [*She sings.*]

THE SONG OF THE CHILD

> Your father is a bandit
> A harlot the mother who bore you.
> Yet honorable men
> Shall kneel down before you.
>
> Food to the baby horses
> The tiger's son will take.
> The mothers will get milk
> From the son of the snake.

3

In The Northern Mountains

THE STORYTELLER.

> Seven days the sister, Grusha Vashnadze,
> Journeyed across the glacier
> And down the slopes she journeyed.
> "When I enter my brother's house," she thought,
> "He will rise and embrace me."
> "Is that you, sister?" he will say,
> "I have long expected you.
> This is my dear wife,
> And this is my farm, come to me by marriage,
> With eleven horses and thirty-one cows. Sit down.
> Sit down with your child at our table and eat."
> The brother's house was in a lovely valley.
> When the sister came to the brother,
> She was ill from walking.
> The brother rose from the table.

[*A* FAT PEASANT COUPLE *rise from the table.* LAVRENTI VASH-NADZE *still has a napkin round his neck, as* GRUSHA, *pale and supported by a* SERVANT, *enters with the* CHILD.]

LAVRENTI. Where've *you* come from, Grusha?

GRUSHA [*feebly*]. Across the Janga-Tu Pass, Lavrenti.

THE SERVANT. I found her in front of the hay barn. She has a baby with her.

THE SISTER-IN-LAW. Go and groom the mare.

[*Exit the* SERVANT.]

LAVRENTI. This is my wife Aniko.

THE SISTER-IN-LAW. I thought you were in service in Nuka.

GRUSHA [*barely able to stand*]. Yes, I was.

THE SISTER-IN-LAW. Wasn't it a good job? We were told it was.

GRUSHA. The Governor got killed.

LAVRENTI. Yes, we heard there were riots. Your aunt told us. Remember, Aniko?

THE SISTER-IN-LAW. Here with us, it's very quiet. City people always want something going on. [*She walks toward the door, calling.*] Sosso, Sosso, don't take the cake out of the oven yet, d'you hear? Where on earth are you? [*Exit, calling.*]

LAVRENTI [*quietly, quickly*]. Is there a father? [*As she shakes her head.*] I thought not. We must think up something. She's religious.

THE SISTER-IN-LAW [*returning*]. Those servants! [*To* GRUSHA.] You have a child.

GRUSHA. It's mine. [*She collapses.* LAVRENTI *rushes to her assistance.*]

THE SISTER-IN-LAW. Heavens, she's ill—what are we going to do?

LAVRENTI [*escorting her to a bench near the stove*]. Sit down, sit. I think it's just weakness, Aniko.

THE SISTER-IN-LAW. As long as it's not scarlet fever!

LAVRENTI. She'd have spots if it was. It's only weakness. Don't worry, Aniko. [*To* GRUSHA.] Better, sitting down?

THE SISTER-IN-LAW. Is the child hers?

GRUSHA. Yes, mine.

LAVRENTI. She's on her way to her husband.

THE SISTER-IN-LAW. I see. Your meat's getting cold.

[LAVRENTI *sits down and begins to eat.*]

Cold food's not good for you, the fat mustn't get cold, you know your stomach's your weak spot. [*To* GRUSHA.] If your husband's not in the city, where is he?

LAVRENTI. She got married on the other side of the mountain, she says.

THE SISTER-IN-LAW. On the other side of the mountain. I see. [*She also sits down to eat.*]

GRUSHA. I think I should lie down somewhere, Lavrenti.

THE SISTER-IN-LAW. If it's consumption we'll all get it. [*She goes on cross-examining her.*] Has your husband got a farm?

GRUSHA. He's a soldier.

LAVRENTI. But he's coming into a farm—a small one—from his father.

THE SISTER-IN-LAW. Isn't he in the war? Why not?

GRUSHA [*with effort*]. Yes, he's in the war.

THE SISTER-IN-LAW. Then why d'you want to go to the farm?

LAVRENTI. When he comes back from the war, he'll return to his farm.

THE SISTER-IN-LAW. But you're going there now?

LAVRENTI. Yes, to wait for him.

THE SISTER-IN-LAW [*calling shrilly*]. Sosso, the cake!

GRUSHA [*murmuring feverishly*]. A farm—a soldier—waiting
—sit down, eat.

THE SISTER-IN-LAW. It's scarlet fever.

GRUSHA [*starting up*]. Yes, he's got a farm!

LAVRENTI. I think it's just weakness, Aniko. Would you look
after the cake yourself, dear?

THE SISTER-IN-LAW. But when will he come back if war's
broken out again as people say? [*She waddles off, shouting.*] Sosso! Where on earth are you? Sosso!

LAVRENTI [*getting up quickly and going to* GRUSHA]. You'll
get a bed in a minute. She has a good heart. But wait till
after supper.

GRUSHA [*holding out the* CHILD *to him*]. Take him.

LAVRENTI [*taking it and looking around*]. But you can't stay
here long with the child. She's religious, you see.

[GRUSHA *collapses.* LAVRENTI *catches her.*]

THE STORYTELLER.

> The sister was so ill,
> The cowardly brother had to give her shelter.
> Summer departed, winter came.
> The winter was long, the winter was short.
> People mustn't know anything,
> Rats mustn't bite,
> Spring mustn't come.

[GRUSHA *sits over the weaving loom in a workroom. She and
the* CHILD, *who is squatting on the floor, are wrapped in
blankets.*]

GRUSHA [*sings*].

THE SONG OF THE CENTER

> And the lover started to leave
> And his betrothed ran pleading after him
> Pleading and weeping, weeping and teaching:
> "Dearest mine, dearest mine
> When you go to war as now you do
> When you fight the foe as soon as you will
> Don't lead with the front line
> And don't push with the rear line
> At the front is red fire

In the rear is red smoke
Stay in the war's center
Stay near the standard bearer
The first always die
The last are also hit
Those in the center come home."

GRUSHA [*speaks*].

Michael, we must be clever. If we make ourselves as small as cockroaches, the sister-in-law will forget we're in the house, and then we can stay till the snow melts.

[*Enter* LAVRENTI. *He sits down beside his sister.*]

LAVRENTI. Why are you sitting there muffled up like coachmen, you two? Is it too cold in the room?

GRUSHA [*hastily removing one shawl*]. It's not too cold, Lavrenti.

LAVRENTI. If it's too cold, you shouldn't be sitting here with the child. Aniko would never forgive herself! [*Pause.*] I hope our priest didn't question you about the child?

GRUSHA. He did, but I didn't tell him anything.

LAVRENTI. That's good. I wanted to speak to you about Aniko. She has a good heart but she's very, very sensitive. People have only to mention our farm and she's worried. She takes everything hard, you see. One time our milkmaid went to church with a hole in her stocking. Ever since, Aniko has worn two pairs of stockings in church. It's the old family in her. [*He listens.*] Are you sure there are no rats around? If there are rats, you couldn't live here.

[*There are sounds as of dripping from the roof.*]

What's that, dripping?

GRUSHA. It must be a barrel leaking.

LAVRENTI. Yes, it must be a barrel. You've been here six months, haven't you? Was I talking about Aniko?

[*They listen again to the snow melting.*]

You can't imagine how worried she gets about your soldier husband. "Suppose he comes back and can't find her!" she says and lies awake. "He can't come before the spring," I tell her. The dear woman!

[*The drops begin to fall faster.*]

When d'you think he'll come? What do *you* think?

[GRUSHA *is silent.*]

Not before the spring, you agree?

[GRUSHA *is silent.*]

You don't believe he'll come at all?

[GRUSHA *is silent.*]

But when spring comes and the snow melts here and on the passes, you can't stay on. They may come and look for you. There's already talk of an illegitimate child.

[*The "glockenspiel" of the falling drops has grown faster and steadier.*]

Grusha, the snow is melting on the roof. Spring is here.

GRUSHA. Yes.

LAVRENTI [*eagerly*]. I'll tell you what we'll do. You need a place to go, and, because of the child [*He sighs*], you have to have a husband, so people won't talk. Now I've made cautious inquiries to see if we can find you a husband. Grusha, I *have* one. I talked to a peasant woman who has a son. Just the other side of the mountain. A small farm. And she's willing.

GRUSHA. But I *can't* marry! I must wait for Simon Shashava.

LAVRENTI. Of course. That's all been taken care of. You don't need a man in bed—you need a man on paper. And I've found you one. The son of this peasant woman is going to die. Isn't that wonderful? He's at his last gasp. And all in line with our story—a husband from the other side of the mountain! And when you met him he was at the last gasp. So you're a widow. What do you say?

GRUSHA. It's true I could use a document with stamps on it for Michael.

LAVRENTI. Stamps make all the difference. Without something in writing the Shah couldn't prove he's a Shah. And you'll have a place to live.

GRUSHA. How much does the peasant woman want?

LAVRENTI. Four hundred piasters.

GRUSHA. Where will you find it?

LAVRENTI [*guiltily*]. Aniko's milk money.

GRUSHA. No one would know us there. I'll do it.

LAVRENTI [*getting up*]. I'll let the peasant woman know. [*Quick exit.*]

GRUSHA. Michael, you cause a lot of fuss. I came to you as the pear tree comes to the sparrows. And because a Christian bends down and picks up a crust of bread so nothing will go to waste. Michael, it would have been better had I walked quickly away on that Easter Sunday in Nuka in the second courtyard. Now I *am* a fool.

THE STORYTELLER.

The bridegroom was on his deathbed when the bride arrived.
The bridegroom's mother was waiting at the door, telling her
    to hurry.
The bride brought a child along.
The witness hid it during the wedding.

[*On one side the bed. Under the mosquito net lies a very sick* MAN. GRUSHA *is pulled in at a run by her future* MOTHER-IN-LAW. *They are followed by* LAVRENTI *and the* CHILD.]

THE MOTHER-IN-LAW. Quick! Quick! Or he'll die on us before the wedding. [*To* LAVRENTI.] I was never told she had a child already.

LAVRENTI. What difference does it make? [*Pointing toward the dying* MAN.] It can't matter to him—in his condition.

THE MOTHER-IN-LAW. To him? But I'll never survive the shame! We are honest people. [*She begins to weep.*] My Jussup doesn't have to marry a girl with a child!

LAVRENTI. All right, make it another two hundred piasters. You'll have it in writing that the farm will go to you: but she'll have the right to live here for two years.

THE MOTHER-IN-LAW [*drying her tears*]. It'll hardly cover the funeral expenses. I hope she'll really lend me a hand with the work. And what's happened to the monk? He must have slipped out through the kitchen window. We'll have the whole village round our necks when they hear Jussup's end is come! Oh dear! I'll run and get the monk. But he mustn't see the child!

LAVRENTI. I'll take care he doesn't. But why only a monk? Why not a priest?

THE MOTHER-IN-LAW. Oh, he's just as good. I only made one mistake: I paid half his fee in advance. Enough to send him to the tavern. I only hope . . . [*She runs off.*]

LAVRENTI. She saved on the priest, the wretch! Hired a cheap monk.

GRUSHA. You *will* send Simon Shashava over to see me if he turns up after all?

LAVRENTI. Yes. [*Pointing at the sick* MAN.] Won't you take a look at him?

[GRUSHA, *taking* MICHAEL *to her, shakes her head.*]

He's not moving an eyelid. I hope we aren't too late.

[*They listen. On the opposite side enter* NEIGHBORS *who look around and take up positions against the walls, thus forming another wall near the bed, yet leaving an opening so that the bed can be seen. They start murmuring prayers. Enter the* MOTHER-IN-LAW *with a* MONK. *Showing some annoyance and surprise, she bows to the* GUESTS.]

THE MOTHER-IN-LAW. I hope you don't mind waiting a few moments? My son's bride has just arrived from the city. An emergency wedding is about to take place. [*To the* MONK *in the bedroom.*] I might have known you couldn't keep your trap shut. [*To* GRUSHA.] The wedding can take place at once. Here's the license. I myself and the bride's brother.

[LAVRENTI *tries to hide in the background, after having quietly taken* MICHAEL *back from* GRUSHA. *The* MOTHER-IN-LAW *waves him away.*]

THE MOTHER-IN-LAW. Who will be here any moment are the witnesses.

[GRUSHA *has bowed to the* MONK. *They go to the bed. The* MOTHER-IN-LAW *lifts the mosquito net. The* MONK *starts reeling off the marriage ceremony in Latin. Meanwhile, the* MOTHER-IN-LAW *beckons to* LAVRENTI *to get rid of the* CHILD, *but fearing that it will cry he draws its attention to the ceremony.* GRUSHA *glances once at the* CHILD, *and* LAVRENTI *waves the* CHILD'S *hand in a greeting.*]

THE MONK. Are you prepared to be a faithful, obedient, and good wife to this man, and to cleave to him until death you do part?

GRUSHA [*looking at the* CHILD]. I am.

THE MONK [*to the sick* PEASANT]. And are you prepared to be a good and loving husband to your wife until death you do part? [*As the sick* PEASANT *does not answer, the* MONK *looks inquiringly around.*]

THE MOTHER-IN-LAW. Of course he is! Didn't you hear him say yes?

THE MONK. All right. We declare the marriage contracted! How about extreme unction?

THE MOTHER-IN-LAW. Nothing doing! The wedding cost quite enough. Now I must take care of the mourners. [*To* LAVRENTI.] Did we say seven hundred?

LAVRENTI. Six hundred. [*He pays.*] Now I don't want to sit with the guests and get to know people. So farewell, Grusha, and if my widowed sister comes to visit me, she'll get a welcome from my wife, or I'll show my teeth. [*Nods, gives the* CHILD *to* GRUSHA, *and leaves. The* MOURNERS *glance after him without interest.*]

THE MONK. May one ask where this child comes from?

THE MOTHER-IN-LAW. Is there a child? I don't see a child. And you don't see a child either—you understand? Or it may turn out I saw all sorts of things in the tavern! Now come on.

[*After* GRUSHA *has put the* CHILD *down and told him to be quiet, they move over left;* GRUSHA *is introduced to the* NEIGHBORS.]

This is my daughter-in-law. She arrived just in time to find dear Jussup still alive.

ONE WOMAN. He's been ill now a whole year, hasn't he? When our Vassili was drafted he was there to say good-bye.

ANOTHER WOMAN. Such things are terrible for a farm. The corn all ripe and the farmer in bed! It'll really be a blessing if he doesn't suffer too long, I say.

THE FIRST WOMAN [*confidentially*]. You know why we thought he'd taken to his bed? Because of the draft! And now his end is come!

THE MOTHER-IN-LAW. Sit yourselves down, please! And have some cakes!

[*She beckons to* GRUSHA *and* BOTH WOMEN *go into the bedroom, where they pick up the cake pans off the floor. The* GUESTS, *among them the* MONK, *sit on the floor and begin conversing in subdued voices.*]

ONE PEASANT [*to whom the* MONK *has handed the bottle which he has taken from his soutane*]. There's a child, you say! How can that have happened to Jussup?

A WOMAN. She was certainly lucky to get herself hitched, with him so sick!

THE MOTHER-IN-LAW. They're gossiping already. And wolfing down the funeral cakes at the same time! If he doesn't die today, I'll have to bake some more tomorrow!

GRUSHA. I'll bake them for you.

THE MOTHER-IN-LAW. Yesterday some horsemen rode by, and I went out to see who it was. When I came in again he was lying there like a corpse! So I sent for you. It can't take much longer. [*She listens.*]

THE MONK. Dear wedding and funeral guests! Deeply touched, we stand before a bed of death and marriage. The bride gets a veil; the groom, a shroud: how varied, my children, are the fates of men! Alas! One man dies and has a roof over his head, and the other is married and the flesh turns to dust from which it was made. Amen.

THE MOTHER-IN-LAW. He's getting his own back. I shouldn't have hired such a cheap one. It's what you'd expect. A more expensive monk would behave himself. In Sura there's one with a real air of sanctity about him, but of course he charges a fortune. A fifty-piaster monk like that has no dignity, and as for piety, just fifty piasters' worth and no more! When I came to get him in the tavern he'd just made a speech, and he was shouting: "The war is over, beware of the peace!" We must go in.

GRUSHA [*giving* MICHAEL *a cake*]. Eat this cake, and keep nice and still, Michael.

[*The* TWO WOMEN *offer cakes to the* GUESTS. *The* DYING MAN *sits up in bed. He puts his head out from under the mosquito net, stares at the* TWO WOMEN, *then sinks back again. The* MONK *takes two bottles from his soutane and offers them to the* PEASANT *beside him. Enter* THREE MUSICIANS *who are greeted with a sly wink by the* MONK.]

THE MOTHER-IN-LAW [*to the* MUSICIANS]. What are you doing here? With instruments?

ONE MUSICIAN. Brother Anastasius here [*pointing at the* MONK] told us there was a wedding on.

THE MOTHER-IN-LAW. What? You brought them? Three more on my neck! Don't you know there's a dying man in the next room?

THE MONK. A very tempting assignment for a musician: something that could be either a subdued Wedding March or a spirited Funeral Dance.

THE MOTHER-IN-LAW. Well, you might as well play. Nobody can stop you eating in any case.

[*The* MUSICIANS *play a potpourri. The* WOMEN *serve cakes.*]

THE MONK. The trumpet sounds like a whining baby. And you, little drum, what have you got to tell the world?

THE DRUNKEN PEASANT [*beside the* MONK, *sings*].

> There was a young lady who said:
> I thought I'd be happier, wed;
> But my husband is old
> And remarkably cold;
> I make love to a candle instead.

[*The* MOTHER-IN-LAW *throws the* DRUNKEN PEASANT *out. The music stops. The* GUESTS *are embarrassed.*]

THE GUESTS [*loudly*]. Have you heard? The Grand Duke is back! But the Princes are against him.
—They say the Shah of Persia has lent him a great army to restore order in Grusinia.
—But how is that possible? The Shah of Persia is the enemy . . .
—The enemy of Grusinia, you donkey, not the enemy of the Grand Duke!
—In any case, the war's over, so our soldiers are coming back.

[GRUSHA *drops a cake pan.* GUESTS *help her pick up the cake.*]

AN OLD WOMAN [*to* GRUSHA]. Are you feeling bad? It's just excitement about dear Jussup. Sit down and rest a while, my dear.

[GRUSHA *staggers.*]

THE GUESTS. Now everything'll be the way it was. Only the taxes'll go up because now we'll have to pay for the war.

GRUSHA [*weakly*]. Did someone say the soldiers are back?

A MAN. I did.

GRUSHA. It can't be true.

THE FIRST MAN [*to a* WOMAN]. Show her the shawl. We bought it from a soldier. It's from Persia.

GRUSHA [*looking at the shawl*]. They are here. [*She gets up,*

*takes a step, kneels down in prayer, takes the silver cross
and chain out of her blouse, and kisses it.]*

THE MOTHER-IN-LAW [*while the* GUESTS *silently watch* GRU-
SHA]. What's the matter with you? Aren't you going to look
after our guests? What's all this city nonsense got to do
with us?

THE GUESTS [*resuming conversation while* GRUSHA *remains in
prayer.*]
—You can buy Persian saddles from the soldiers too.
Though many want crutches in exchange for them.
—The big shots on one side can win a war, the soldiers
on both sides lose it.
—Anyway, the war's over. It's something they can't draft
you any more.

[*The* DYING MAN *sits bolt upright in bed. He listens.*]

—What we need is two weeks of good weather.
—Our pear trees are hardly bearing a thing this year.

THE MOTHER-IN-LAW [*offering cakes*]. Have some more cakes
and welcome! There are more!

[*The* MOTHER-IN-LAW *goes to the bedroom with the empty
cake pans. Unaware of the* DYING MAN, *she is bending down
to pick up another tray when he begins to talk in a hoarse
voice.*]

THE PEASANT. How many more cakes are you going to stuff
down their throats? Think I'm a fucking gold mine?

[*The* MOTHER-IN-LAW *starts, stares at him aghast, while he
climbs out from behind the mosquito net.*]

THE FIRST WOMAN [*talking kindly to* GRUSHA *in the next
room*]. Has the young wife got someone at the front?

A MAN. It's good news that they're on their way home, huh?

THE PEASANT. Don't stare at me like that! Where's this wife
you've hung around my neck?

[*Receiving no answer, he climbs out of bed and in his night-
shirt staggers into the other room. Trembling, she follows
him with the cake pan.*]

THE GUESTS [*seeing him and shrieking*]. Good God! Jussup!

[*Everyone leaps up in alarm. The* WOMEN *rush to the door.*
GRUSHA, *still on her knees, turns round and stares at the
MAN.*]

THE PEASANT. A funeral supper! You'd enjoy that, wouldn't you? Get out before I throw you out! [*As the* GUESTS *stampede from the house, gloomily to* GRUSHA.] I've upset the apple cart, huh? [*Receiving no answer, he turns round and takes a cake from the pan which his mother is holding.*]

THE STORYTELLER.

O confusion! The wife discovers she has a husband.
By day there's the child, by night there's the husband.
The lover is on his way both day and night.
Husband and wife look at each other.
The bedroom is small.

[*Near the bed the* PEASANT *is sitting in a high wooden bathtub, naked, the* MOTHER-IN-LAW *is pouring water from a pitcher. Opposite,* GRUSHA *cowers with* MICHAEL, *who is playing at mending straw mats.*]

THE PEASANT [*to his* MOTHER]. That's her work, not yours. Where's she hiding out now?

THE MOTHER-IN-LAW [*calling*]. Grusha! The peasant wants you!

GRUSHA [*to* MICHAEL]. There are still two holes to mend.

THE PEASANT [*when* GRUSHA *approaches*]. Scrub my back!

GRUSHA. Can't the peasant do it himself?

THE PEASANT. "Can't the peasant do it himself?" Get the brush! To hell with you! Are you the wife here? Or are you a visitor? [*To the* MOTHER-IN-LAW.] It's too cold!

THE MOTHER-IN-LAW. I'll run for hot water.

GRUSHA. Let me go.

THE PEASANT. You stay here. [*The* MOTHER-IN-LAW *exits.*] Rub harder. And no shirking. You've seen a naked fellow before. That child didn't come out of thin air.

GRUSHA. The child was not conceived in joy, if that's what the peasant means.

THE PEASANT [*turning and grinning*]. You don't look the type.

[GRUSHA *stops scrubbing him, starts back. Enter the* MOTHER-IN-LAW.]

THE PEASANT. A nice thing you've hung around my neck! A simpleton for a wife!

THE MOTHER-IN-LAW. She just isn't cooperative.

THE PEASANT. Pour—but go easy! Ow! Go easy, I said. [*To* GRUSHA.] Maybe you did something wrong in the city . . .

I wouldn't be surprised. Why else should you be here? But I won't talk about that. I've not said a word about the illegitimate object you brought into my house either. But my patience has limits! It's against nature. [*To the* MOTHER-IN-LAW.] More! [*To* GRUSHA.] And even if your soldier does come back, you're married.

GRUSHA. Yes.

THE PEASANT. But your soldier won't come back. Don't you believe it.

GRUSHA. No.

THE PEASANT. You're cheating me. You're my wife and you're not my wife. Where you lie, nothing lies, and yet no other woman can lie there. When I go to work in the morning I'm tired—when I lie down at night I'm awake as the devil. God has given you sex—and what d'you do? I don't have ten piasters to buy myself a woman in the city. Besides, it's a long way. Woman weeds the fields and opens up her legs, that's what our calendar says. D'you hear?

GRUSHA [*quietly*]. Yes. I didn't mean to cheat you out of it.

THE PEASANT. She didn't mean to cheat me out of it! Pour some more water!

[*The* MOTHER-IN-LAW *pours*.]

THE STORYTELLER.

As she sat by the stream to wash the linen
She saw his image in the water
And his face grew dimmer with the passing moons.
As she raised herself to wring the linen
She heard his voice from the murmuring maple
And his voice grew fainter with the passing moons.
Evasions and sighs grew more numerous,
Tears and sweat flowed.
With the passing moons the child grew up.

[GRUSHA *sits by a stream, dipping linen into the water. In the rear, a few* CHILDREN *are standing*.]

GRUSHA [*to* MICHAEL]. You can play with them, Michael, but don't let them boss you around just because you're the littlest.

[MICHAEL *nods and joins the* CHILDREN. *They start playing*.]

THE BIGGEST BOY. Today it's the Heads-Off Game. [*To a* FAT BOY.] You're the Prince and you laugh. [*To* MICHAEL.]

You're the Governor. [*To a* GIRL.] You're the Governor's wife and you cry when his head's cut off. And I do the cutting. [*He shows his wooden sword.*] With this. First, they lead the Governor into the yard. The Prince walks in front. The Governor's wife comes last.

[*They form a procession. The* FAT BOY *is first and laughs. Then comes* MICHAEL, *then the* BIGGEST BOY, *and then the* GIRL, *who weeps.*]

MICHAEL [*standing still*]. Me cut off head!

THE BIGGEST BOY. That's my job. You're the littlest. The Governor's the easy part. All you do is kneel down and get your head cut off—simple.

MICHAEL. Me want sword!

THE BIGGEST BOY. It's mine! [*He gives him a kick.*]

THE GIRL [*shouting to* GRUSHA]. He won't play his part!

GRUSHA [*laughing*]. Even the little duck is a swimmer, they say.

THE BIGGEST BOY. You can be the Prince if you can laugh.

[MICHAEL *shakes his head.*]

THE FAT BOY. I laugh best. Let him cut off the head just once. Then you do it, then me.

[*Reluctantly, the* BIGGEST BOY *hands* MICHAEL *the wooden sword and kneels down. The* FAT BOY *sits down, slaps his thigh, and laughs with all his might. The* GIRL *weeps loudly.* MICHAEL *swings the big sword and "cuts off" the head. In doing so, he topples over.*]

THE BIGGEST BOY. Hey! I'll show you how to cut heads off!

[MICHAEL *runs away. The* CHILDREN *run after him.* GRUSHA *laughs, following them with her eyes. On looking back, she sees* SIMON SHASHAVA *standing on the opposite bank. He wears a shabby uniform.*]

GRUSHA. Simon!

SIMON. Is that Grusha Vashnadze?

GRUSHA. Simon!

SIMON [*formally*]. A good morning to the young lady. I hope she is well.

GRUSHA [*getting up gaily and bowing low*]. A good morning to the soldier. God be thanked he has returned in good health.

SIMON. They found better fish, so they didn't eat me, said the haddock.

GRUSHA. Courage, said the kitchen boy. Good luck, said the hero.

SIMON. How are things here? Was the winter bearable? The neighbor considerate?

GRUSHA. The winter was a trifle rough, the neighbor as usual, Simon.

SIMON. May one ask if a certain person still dips her toes in the water when rinsing the linen?

GRUSHA. The answer is no. Because of the eyes in the bushes.

SIMON. The young lady is speaking of soldiers. Here stands a paymaster.

GRUSHA. A job worth twenty piasters?

SIMON. And lodgings.

GRUSHA [with tears in her eyes]. Behind the barracks under the date trees.

SIMON. Yes, there. A certain person has kept her eyes open.

GRUSHA. She has, Simon.

SIMON. And has not forgotten? [GRUSHA shakes her head.] So the door is still on its hinges as they say? [GRUSHA looks at him in silence and shakes her head again.] What's this? Is something not as it should be?

GRUSHA. Simon Shashava, I can never return to Nuka. Something has happened.

SIMON. What can have happened?

GRUSHA. For one thing, I knocked an Ironshirt down.

SIMON. Grusha Vashnadze must have had her reasons for that.

GRUSHA. Simon Shashava, I am no longer called what I used to be called.

SIMON [after a pause]. I do not understand.

GRUSHA. When do women change their names, Simon? Let me explain. Nothing stands between us. Everything is just as it was. You must believe that.

SIMON. Nothing stands between us and yet there's something?

GRUSHA. How can I explain it so fast and with the stream between us? Couldn't you cross the bridge there?

SIMON. Maybe it's no longer necessary.

GRUSHA. It is very necessary. Come over on this side, Simon. Quick!

SIMON. Does the young lady wish to say someone has come too late?

[GRUSHA *looks up at him in despair, her face streaming with tears.* SIMON *stares before him. He picks up a piece of wood and starts cutting it.*]

THE STORYTELLER.

So many words are said, so many left unsaid.
The soldier has come.
Where he comes from, he does not say.
Hear what he thought and did not say:
"The battle began, gray at dawn, grew bloody at noon.
The first man fell in front of me, the second behind me, the third at my side.
I trod on the first, left the second behind, the third was run through by the captain.
One of my brothers died by steel, the other by smoke.
My neck caught fire, my hands froze in my gloves, my toes in my socks.
I fed on aspen buds, I drank maple juice, I slept on stone, in water."

SIMON. I see a cap in the grass. Is there a little one already?

GRUSHA. There is, Simon. How could I conceal the fact? But please don't worry, it is not mine.

SIMON. When the wind once starts to blow, they say, it blows through every cranny. The wife need say no more.

[GRUSHA *looks into her lap and is silent.*]

THE STORYTELLER.

There was yearning but there was no waiting.
The oath is broken. Neither could say why.
Hear what she thought but did not say:
"While you fought in the battle, soldier,
The bloody battle, the bitter battle
I found a helpless infant
I had not the heart to destroy him
I had to care for a creature that was lost
I had to stoop for bread crumbs on the floor
I had to break myself for that which was not mine
That which was other people's.
Someone must help!
For the little tree needs water
The lamb loses its way when the shepherd is asleep
And its cry is unheard!"

SIMON. Give me back the cross I gave you. Better still, throw it in the stream. [*He turns to go.*]

GRUSHA [*getting up*]. Simon Shashava, don't go away! He isn't mine! He isn't mine! [*She hears the* CHILDREN *calling.*] What's the matter, children?

VOICES. Soldiers! And they're taking Michael away!

[GRUSHA *stands aghast as* TWO IRONSHIRTS, *with* MICHAEL *between them, come toward her.*]

ONE OF THE IRONSHIRTS. Are you Grusha?

[*She nods.*]

Is this your child?

GRUSHA. Yes.

[SIMON *goes.*]

Simon!

THE IRONSHIRT. We have orders, in the name of the law, to take this child, found in your custody, back to the city. It is suspected that the child is Michael Abashwili, son and heir of the late Governor Georgi Abashwili, and his wife, Natella Abashwili. Here is the document and the seal. [*They lead the* CHILD *away.*]

GRUSHA [*running after them, shouting*]. Leave him here. Please! He's mine!

THE STORYTELLER.

The Ironshirts took the child, the beloved child.
The unhappy girl followed them to the city, the dreaded city.
She who had borne him demanded the child.
She who had raised him faced trial.
Who will decide the case?
To whom will the child be assigned?
Who will the judge be? A good judge? A bad?
The city was in flames.
In the judge's seat sat Azdak.[2]

[2] The name Azdak should be accented on the second syllable.

PART TWO

1

The Story of the Judge

THE STORYTELLER.

Hear the story of the judge
How he turned judge, how he passed judgment, what kind
  of judge he was.
On that Easter Sunday of the great revolt, when the Grand
  Duke was overthrown
And his Governor Abashwili, father of our child, lost his
  head
The Village Scrivener Azdak found a fugitive in the woods
  and hid him in his hut.

[AZDAK, *in rags and slightly drunk, is helping an* OLD BEGGAR
into his cottage.]

AZDAK. Stop snorting, you're not a horse, And it won't do you
  any good with the police to run like a snotty nose in April.
  Stand still, I say. [*He catches the* OLD MAN, *who has
  marched into the cottage as if he'd like to go through the
  walls.*] Sit down. Feed. Here's a hunk of cheese. [*From
  under some rags, in a chest, he fishes out some cheese, and
  the* OLD MAN *greedily begins to eat.*] Haven't eaten in a long
  time, huh?

[*The* OLD MAN *growls.*]

Why were you running like that, asshole? The cop wouldn't
  even have seen you.   — The grand duke
THE OLD MAN. Had to! Had to!
AZDAK. Blue funk?

[*The* OLD MAN *stares, uncomprehending.*]

Cold feet? Panic? Don't lick your chops like a Grand Duke.
  Or an old sow. I can't stand it. We have to accept respectable stinkers as God made them, but not you! I once heard
  of a senior judge who farted at a public dinner to show

[380]

an independent spirit! Watching you eat like that gives me
the most awful ideas. Why don't you say something?
[*Sharply.*] Show me your hand. Can't you hear?

[*The* OLD MAN *slowly puts out his hand.*]

White! So you're not a beggar at all! A fraud, a walking
swindle! And I'm hiding you from the cops as though you
were an honest man! Why were you running like that if
you're a landowner? For that's what you are. Don't deny
it! I see it in your guilty face! [*He gets up.*] Get out!

[*The* OLD MAN *looks at him uncertainly.*]

What are you waiting for, peasant flogger?

THE OLD MAN. Pursued. Need undivided attention. Make proposition . . .

AZDAK. Make what? A proposition? Well, if that isn't the
height of insolence. He's making me a proposition! The
bitten man scratches his fingers bloody, and the leech that's
biting him makes him a proposition! Get out, I tell you!

THE OLD MAN. Understand point of view! Persuasion! Pay
hundred thousand piasters one night! Yes?

AZDAK. What, you think you can buy me? For a hundred
thousand piasters? Let's say a hundred and fifty thousand.
Where are they?

THE OLD MAN. Have not them here. Of course. Will be sent.
Hope do not doubt.

AZDAK. Doubt very much. Get out!

[*The* OLD MAN *gets up, waddles to the door. A* VOICE *is heard
offstage.*]

A VOICE. Azdak!

[*The* OLD MAN *turns, waddles to the opposite corner, stands
still.*]

AZDAK [*calling out*]. I'm not in! [*He walks to door.*] So *you're*
sniffing around here again, Shauwa?

POLICEMAN SHAUWA [*reproachfully*]. You caught another
rabbit, Azdak. And you'd promised me it wouldn't happen
again!

AZDAK [*severely*]. Shauwa, don't talk about things you don't
understand. The rabbit is a dangerous and destructive beast.
It feeds on plants, especially on the species of plants knows
as weeds. It must therefore be exterminated.

SHAUWA. Azdak, don't be so hard on me. I'll lose my job if I don't arrest you. I know you have a good heart.

AZDAK. I do not have a good heart! How often must I tell you I'm a man of intellect?

SHAUWA [slyly]. I know, Azdak. You're a superior person. You say so yourself. I'm just a Christian and an ignoramus. So I ask you: When one of the Prince's rabbits is stolen, and I'm a policeman, what should I do with the offending party?

AZDAK. Shauwa, Shauwa, shame on you. You stand and ask me a question, than which nothing could be more seductive. It's like you were a woman—let's say that bad girl Nunowna, and you showed me your thigh—Nunowna's thigh, that would be—and asked me: "What shall I do with my thigh, it itches?" Is she as innocent as she pretends? Of course not. I catch a rabbit, but you catch a man. Man is made in God's image. Not so a rabbit, you know that. I'm a rabbit eater, but you're a man eater, Shauwa. And God will pass judgment on you. Shauwa, go home and repent. No, stop, there's something . . . [He looks at the OLD MAN who stands trembling in the corner.] No, it's nothing. Go home and repent. [He slams the door behind SHAUWA.] Now you're surprised, huh? Surprised I didn't hand you over? I couldn't hand over a bedbug to that animal. It goes against the grain. Now don't tremble because of a cop! So old and still so scared? Finish your cheese, but eat it like a poor man, or else they'll still catch you. Must I even explain how a poor man behaves? [He pushes him down, and then gives him back the cheese.] That box is the table. Lay your elbows on the table. Now, encircle the cheese on the plate like it might be snatched from you at any moment—what right have you to be safe, huh?—now, hold your knife like an undersized sickle, and give your cheese a troubled look because, like all beautiful things, it's already fading away. [AZDAK watches him.] They're after you, which speaks in your favor, but how can we be sure they're not mistaken about you? In Tiflis one time they hanged a landowner, a Turk, who could prove he quartered his peasants instead of merely cutting them in half, as is the custom, and he squeezed twice the usual amount of taxes out of them, his zeal was above suspicion. And yet they hanged him like a common criminal—because he was a Turk—a thing he couldn't do much about. What injustice!

He got onto the gallows by a sheer fluke. In short, I don't trust you.

THE STORYTELLER.

Thus Azdak gave the old beggar a bed,
And learned that old beggar was the old butcher, the Grand
    Duke himself,
And was ashamed.
He denounced himself and ordered the policeman to take
    him to Nuka, to court, to be judged.

[*In the court of justice* THREE IRONSHIRTS *sit drinking. From a beam hangs a man in judge's robes. Enter* AZDAK, *in chains, dragging* SHAUWA *behind him.*]

AZDAK [*shouting*]. I've helped the Grand Duke, the Grand Thief, the Grand Butcher, to escape! In the name of justice I ask to be severely judged in public trial!

THE FIRST IRONSHIRT. Who's this queer bird?

SHAUWA. That's our Village Scrivener, Azdak.

AZDAK. I am contemptible! I am a traitor! A branded criminal! Tell them, flatfoot, how I insisted on being chained up and brought to the capital. Because I sheltered the Grand Duke, The Grand Swindler, by mistake. And how I found out afterwards. See the marked man denounce himself! Tell them how I forced you to walk with me half the night to clear the whole thing up.

SHAUWA. And all by threats. That wasn't nice of you, Azdak.

AZDAK. Shut your mouth, Shauwa. You don't understand. A new age is upon us! It'll go thundering over you. You're finished. The police will be wiped out—poof! Everything will be gone into, everything will be brought into the open. The guilty will give themselves up. Why? They couldn't escape the people in any case. [*To* SHAUWA.] Tell them how I shouted all along Shoemaker Street [*with big gestures, looking at the* IRONSHIRTS]: "In my ignorance I let the Grand Swindler escape! So tear me to pieces, brothers!" I wanted to get it in first.

THE FIRST IRONSHIRT. And what did your brothers answer?

SHAUWA. They comforted him in Butcher Street, and they laughed themselves sick in Shoemaker Street. That's all.

AZDAK. But with you it's different. I can see you're men of iron. Brothers, where's the judge? I must be tried.

THE FIRST IRONSHIRT [*pointing at the hanged man*]. There's

the judge. And please stop "brothering" us. It's rather a sore spot this evening.

AZDAK. "There's the judge." An answer never heard in Grusinia before. Townsman, where's His Excellency the Governor? [*Pointing to the floor.*] There's His Excellency, stranger. Where's the Chief Tax Collector? Where's the official Recruiting Officer? The Patriarch? The Chief of Police? There, there, there—all there. Brothers, I expected no less of you.

THE SECOND IRONSHIRT. What? *What* was it you expected, funny man?

AZDAK. What happened in Persia, brother, what happened in Persia?

THE SECOND IRONSHIRT. What did happen in Persia?

AZDAK. Everybody was hanged. Viziers, tax collectors. Everybody. Forty years ago now. My grandfather, a remarkable man by the way, saw it all. For three whole days. Everywhere.

THE SECOND IRONSHIRT. And who ruled when the Vizier was hanged?

AZDAK. A peasant ruled when the Vizier was hanged.

THE SECOND IRONSHIRT. And who commanded the army?

AZDAK. A soldier, a soldier.

THE SECOND IRONSHIRT. And who paid the wages?

AZDAK. A dyer. A dyer paid the wages.

THE SECOND IRONSHIRT. Wasn't it a weaver, maybe?

THE FIRST IRONSHIRT. And why did all this happen, Persian?

AZDAK. Why did all this happen? Must there be a special reason? Why do you scratch yourself, brother? War! Too long a war! And no justice! My grandfather brought back a song that tells how it was. I will sing it for you. With my friend the policeman. [*To* SHAUWA.] And hold the rope tight. It's very suitable. [*He sings with* SHAUWA *holding the rope tight around him.*]

THE SONG OF INJUSTICE IN PERSIA

Why don't our sons bleed any more? Why don't our
   daughters weep?
Why do only the slaughterhouse cattle have blood
   in their veins?
Why do only the willows shed tears on Lake Urmia?
The king must have a new province, the peasant must
   give up his savings.

inevitable history

That the roof of the world might be conquered, the
  roof of the cottage is torn down.
Our men are carried to the ends of the earth, so
  that great ones can eat at home.
The soldiers kill each other, the marshals salute
  each other.
They bite the widow's tax money to see if it's good,
  their swords break.
The battle was lost, the helmets were paid for.
Refrain: Is it so? Is it so?

SHAUWA [*refrain*]. Yes, yes, yes, yes, yes it's so.
AZDAK. Do you want to hear the rest of it?

[THE FIRST IRONSHIRT *nods.*]

THE SECOND IRONSHIRT [*to* SHAUWA]. Did he teach you that
  song?
SHAUWA. Yes, only my voice isn't very good.
THE SECOND IRONSHIRT. No. [*To* AZDAK.] Go on singing.
AZDAK. The second verse is about the peace. [*He sings.*]

The offices are packed, the streets overflow with
  officials.
The rivers jump their banks and ravage the fields.
Those who cannot let down their own trousers rule
  countries.
They can't count up to four, but they devour eight
  courses.
The corn farmers, looking round for buyers, see only
  the starving.
The weavers go home from their looms in rags.
Refrain: Is it so? Is it so?

SHAUWA [*refrain*]. Yes, yes, yes, yes, yes it's so.
AZDAK.

That's why our sons don't bleed any more, that's why
  our daughters don't weep.
That's why only the slaughterhouse cattle have blood
  in their veins,
And only the willows shed tears by Lake Urmia toward
  morning.

THE FIRST IRONSHIRT. Are you going to sing that song here
  in town?

AZDAK. Sure. What's wrong with it?

THE FIRST IRONSHIRT. Have you noticed that the sky's getting red?

[*Turning round,* AZDAK *sees the sky red with fire.*]

It's the people's quarters on the outskirts of town. The carpet weavers have caught the "Persian Sickness," too. And they've been asking if Prince Kazbeki isn't eating too many courses. This morning they strung up the city judge. As for us, we beat them to pulp. We were paid one hundred piasters per man, you understand?

AZDAK [*after a pause*]. I understand. [*He glances shyly round and, creeping away, sits down in a corner, his head in his hands.*]

THE IRONSHIRTS [*to each other*]. If there ever was a trouble-maker it's him.

—He must've come to the capital to fish in the troubled waters.

SHAUWA. Oh, I don't think he's a really bad character, gentlemen. Steals a few chickens here and there. And maybe a rabbit.

THE SECOND IRONSHIRT [*approaching* AZDAK]. Came to fish in the troubled waters, huh?

AZDAK [*looking up*]. I don't know why I came.

THE SECOND IRONSHIRT. Are you in with the carpet weavers maybe?

[AZDAK *shakes his head.*]

How about that song?

AZDAK. From my grandfather. A silly and ignorant man.

THE SECOND IRONSHIRT. Right. And how about the dyer who paid the wages?

AZDAK [*muttering*]. That was in Persia.

THE FIRST IRONSHIRT. And this denouncing of yourself? Because you didn't hang the Grand Duke with your own hands?

AZDAK. Didn't I tell you I let him run? [*He creeps farther away and sits on the floor.*]

SHAUWA. I can swear to that: he let him run.

[*The* IRONSHIRTS *burst out laughing and slap* SHAUWA *on the back.* AZDAK *laughs loudest. They slap* AZDAK *too, and un-chain him. They all start drinking as the* FAT PRINCE *enters with a* YOUNG MAN.]

not heroic

THE FIRST IRONSHIRT [*to* AZDAK, *pointing at the* FAT PRINCE]. There's your "new age" for you! [*More laughter.*]

THE FAT PRINCE. Well, my friends, what is there to laugh about? Permit me a serious word. Yesterday morning the Princes of Grusinia overthrew the warmongering government of the Grand Duke and did away with his Governors. Unfortunately the Grand Duke himself escaped. In this fateful hour our carpet weavers, those eternal troublemakers, had the effrontery to stir up a rebellion and hang the universally loved city judge, our dear Illo Orbeliani. Ts—ts—ts. My friends, we need peace, peace, peace in Grusinia! And justice! So I've brought along my dear nephew Bizergan Kazbeki. He'll be the new judge, hm? A very gifted fellow. What do you say? I want your opinion. Let the people decide!

THE SECOND IRONSHIRT. Does this mean *we* elect the judge?

THE FAT PRINCE. Precisely. Let the people propose some very gifted fellow! Confer among yourselves, my friends.

[*The* IRONSHIRTS *confer.*]

Don't worry, my little fox. The job's yours. And when we catch the Grand Duke we won't have to kiss this rabble's ass any longer.

THE IRONSHIRTS [*among themselves*]. Very funny: they're wetting their pants because they haven't caught the Grand Duke.

—When the outlook isn't so bright, they say: "My friends!" and "Let the people decide!"

—Now he even wants justice for Grusinia! But fun is fun as long as it lasts! [*Pointing at* AZDAK.] *He* knows all about justice. Hey, rascal, would you like this nephew fellow to be the judge?

AZDAK. Are you asking me? You're not asking *me*?!

THE FIRST IRONSHIRT. Why not? Anything for a laugh!

AZDAK. You'd like to test him to the marrow, correct? Have you a criminal on hand? An experienced one? So the candidate can show what he knows?

THE SECOND IRONSHIRT. Let's see. We do have a couple of doctors downstairs. Let's use them.

AZDAK. Oh, no, that's no good, we can't take real criminals till we're sure the judge will be appointed. He may be dumb, but he must be appointed, or the law is violated. And the law is a sensitive organ. It's like the spleen, you mustn't hit it—that would be fatal. Of course you can hang those two without violating the law, because there was no judge in the vicinity. But judgment, when pronounced, must be pronounced with absolute gravity—it's all such nonsense. Suppose, for instance, a judge jails a woman— let's say she's stolen a corn cake to feed her child—and this judge isn't wearing his robes—or maybe he's scratching himself while passing sentence and half his body is uncovered—a man's thigh *will* itch once in a while—the sentence this judge passes is a disgrace and the law is violated. In short it would be easier for a judge's robe and a judge's hat to pass judgment than for a man with no robe and no hat. If you don't treat it with respect, the law just disappears on you. Now you don't try out a bottle of wine by offering it to a dog; you'd only lose your wine.

THE FIRST IRONSHIRT. Then what do you suggest, hairsplitter?

AZDAK. I'll be the defendant.

THE FIRST IRONSHIRT. You? [*He bursts out laughing.*]

THE FAT PRINCE. What have you decided?

THE FIRST IRONSHIRT. We've decided to stage a rehearsal. Our friend here will be the defendant. Let the candidate be the judge and sit there.

THE FAT PRINCE. It isn't customary, but why not? [*To the* NEPHEW.] A mere formality, my little fox. What have I taught you? Who got there first—the slow runner or the fast?

THE NEPHEW. The silent runner, Uncle Arsen.

[THE NEPHEW *takes the chair. The* IRONSHIRTS *and the* FAT PRINCE *sit on the steps. Enter* AZDAK, *mimicking the gait of the Grand Duke.*]

AZDAK [*in the Grand Duke's accent*]. Is any here knows me? Am Grand Duke.

THE IRONSHIRTS. *What* is he?
—The Grand Duke. He knows him, too.
—Fine. So get on with the trial.

AZDAK. Listen! Am accused instigating war? Ridiculous! Am saying ridiculous! That enough? If not, have brought lawyers, Believe five hundred. [*He points behind him, pretending to be surrounded by lawyers.*] Requisition all available seats for lawyers!

[*The* IRONSHIRTS *laugh; the* FAT PRINCE *joins in.*]

THE NEPHEW [*to the* IRONSHIRTS]. You really wish me to try

this case? I find it rather unusual. From the taste angle, I mean.

THE FIRST IRONSHIRT. Let's go!

THE FAT PRINCE [*smiling*]. Let him have it, my little fox!

THE NEPHEW. All right. People of Grusinia versus Grand Duke. Defendant, what have you got to say for yourself?

AZDAK. Plenty. Naturally, have read war lost. Only started on the advice of patriots. Like Uncle Arsen Kazbeki. Call Uncle Arsen as witness.

THE FAT PRINCE [*to the* IRONSHIRTS, *delightedly*]. What a screwball!

THE NEPHEW. Motion rejected. One cannot be arraigned for declaring a war, which every ruler has to do once in a while, but only for running a war badly.

AZDAK. Rubbish! Did not run it at all! Had it run! Had it run by Princes! Naturally, they messed it up.

THE NEPHEW. Do you by any chance deny having been commander-in-chief?

AZDAK. Not at all! Always *was* commander-in-chief. At birth shouted at wet nurse. Was trained drop turds in toilet, grew accustomed to command. Always commanded officials rob my cash box. Officers flog soldiers only on command. Landowners sleep with peasants' wives only on strictest command. Uncle Arsen here grew his belly at *my* command!

THE IRONSHIRTS [*clapping*]. He's good! Long live the Grand Duke!

THE FAT PRINCE. Answer him, my little fox. I'm with you.

THE NEPHEW. I shall answer him according to the dignity of the law. Defendant, preserve the dignity of the law!

AZDAK. Agreed. Command you proceed with trial!

THE NEPHEW. It is not your place to command me. You claim that the Princes forced you to declare war. How can you claim, then, that they—er—"messed it up"?

AZDAK. Did not send enough people. Embezzled funds. Sent sick horses. During attack, drinking in whorehouse. Call Uncle Arsen as witness.

THE NEPHEW. Are you making the outrageous suggestion that the Princes of this country did not fight?

AZDAK. No. Princes fought. Fought for war contracts.

THE FAT PRINCE [*jumping up*]. That's too much! This man talks like a carpet weaver!

AZDAK. Really? I told nothing but truth.

THE FAT PRINCE. Hang him! Hang him!

THE FIRST IRONSHIRT [*pulling the* PRINCE *down*]. Keep quiet! Go on, Excellency!

THE NEPHEW. Quiet! I now render a verdict: You must be hanged! By the neck! Having lost war!

AZDAK. Young man, seriously advise not fall publicly into jerky clipped manner of speech. Cannot be employed as watchdog if howl like wolf. Got it? If people realize Princes speak same language as Grand Duke, may hang Grand Duke *and Princes,* huh? By the way, must overrule verdict. Reason? War lost, but not for Princes. Princes won their war. Got 3,863,000 piasters for horses not delivered, 8,240,-000 piasters for food supplies not produced. Are therefore victors. War lost only for Grusinia, which as such is not present in this court.

THE FAT PRINCE. I think that will do, my friends. [*To* AZDAK.] You can withdraw, funny man. [*To the* IRONSHIRTS.] You may now ratify the new judge's appointment, my friends.

THE FIRST IRONSHIRT. Yes, we can. Take down the judge's gown.

[ONE IRONSHIRT *climbs on the back of the* OTHER, *pulls the gown off the hanged man.*]

[*To the* NEPHEW.] Now you run away so the right ass can get on the right chair. [*To* AZDAK.] Step forward! Go to the judge's seat! Now sit in it!

[AZDAK *steps up, bows, and sits down.*]

The judge was always a rascal! Now the rascal shall be a judge!

[*The judge's gown is placed round his shoulders, the hat on his head.*]

And what a judge!

THE STORYTELLER.

> And there was civil war in the land.
> The mighty were not safe.
> And Azdak was made a judge by the Ironshirts.
> And Azdak remained a judge for two years.

THE STORYTELLER AND CHORUS.

> When the towns were set afire
> And rivers of blood rose higher and higher,
> Cockroaches crawled out of every crack.

And the court was full of schemers
And the church of foul blasphemers.
In the judge's cassock sat Azdak.

[AZDAK *sits in the judge's chair, peeling an apple.* SHAUWA *is sweeping out the hall. On one side an* INVALID *in a wheelchair. Opposite, a* YOUNG MAN *accused of blackmail. An* IRONSHIRT *stands guard, holding the Ironshirts' banner.*]

AZDAK. In consideration of the large number of cases, the Court today will hear two cases at a time. Before I open the proceedings, a short announcement—I accept. [*He stretches out his hand. The* BLACKMAILER *is the only one to produce any money. He hands it to* AZDAK.] I reserve the right to punish one of the parties for contempt of court. [*He glances at the* INVALID.] You [*to the* DOCTOR] are a doctor, and you [*to the* INVALID] are bringing a complaint against him. Is the doctor responsible for your condition?

THE INVALID. Yes. I had a stroke on his account.

AZDAK. That would be professional negligence.

THE INVALID. Worse than negligence. I gave this man money for his studies. So far, he hasn't paid me back a cent. It was when I heard he was treating a patient free that I had my stroke.

AZDAK. Rightly. [*To a* LIMPING MAN.] And what are *you* doing here?

THE LIMPING MAN. I'm the patient, Your Honor.

AZDAK. He treated your leg for nothing?

THE LIMPING MAN. The wrong leg! My rheumatism was in the left leg, he operated on the right. That's why I limp.

AZDAK. And you were treated free?

THE INVALID. A five-hundred-piaster operation free! For nothing! For a God-bless-you! And I paid for this man's studies! [*To the* DOCTOR.] Did they teach you to operate free?

THE DOCTOR. Your Honor, it is actually the custom to demand the fee before the operation, as the patient is more willing to pay before an operation than after. Which is only human. In the case in question I was convinced, when I started the operation, that my servant had already received the fee. In this I was mistaken.

THE INVALID. He was mistaken! A good doctor doesn't make mistakes! He examines before he operates!

public prosecutor

AZDAK. That's right. [*To* SHAUWA.] Public Prosecutor, what's the other case about?

SHAUWA [*busily sweeping*]. Blackmail.

THE BLACKMAILER. High Court of Justice, I'm innocent. I only wanted to find out from the landowner concerned if he really *had* raped his niece. He informed me very politely that this was not the case, and gave me the money only so I could pay for my uncle's studies.

AZDAK. Hm. [*To the* DOCTOR.] You, on the other hand, can cite no extenuating circumstances for your offense, huh?

THE DOCTOR. Except that to err is human.

AZDAK. And you are aware that in money matters a good doctor is a highly responsible person? I once heard of a doctor who got a thousand piasters for a sprained finger by remarking that sprains have something to do with blood circulation, which after all a less good doctor might have overlooked, and who, on another occasion made a real gold mine out of a somewhat disordered gallbladder, he treated it with such loving care. You have no excuse, Doctor. The corn merchant Uxu had his son study medicine to get some knowledge of trade, our medical schools are so good. [*To the* BLACKMAILER.] What's the landowner's name?

SHAUWA. He doesn't want it mentioned.

AZDAK. In that case I will pass judgment. The Court considers the blackmail proved. And you [*to the* INVALID] are sentenced to a fine of one thousand piasters. If you have a second stroke, the doctor will have to treat you free. Even if he has to amputate. [*To the* LIMPING MAN.] As compensation, you will receive a bottle of rubbing alcohol. [*To the* BLACKMAILER.] You are sentenced to hand over half the proceeds of your deal to the Public Prosecutor to keep the landowner's name secret. You are advised, moreover, to study medicine—you seem well suited to that calling. [*To the* DOCTOR.] You have perpetrated an unpardonable error in the practice of your profession: you are acquitted. Next cases!

THE STORYTELLER AND CHORUS.

> Men won't do much for a shilling.
> For a pound they may be willing.
> For twenty pounds the verdict's in the sack.
> As for the many, all too many,
> Those who've only got a penny—
> They've one single, sole recourse: Azdak.

[*Enter* AZDAK *from the caravansary on the highroad, followed by an old bearded* INNKEEPER. *The judge's chair is carried by a* STABLEMAN *and* SHAUWA. *An* IRONSHIRT, *with a banner, takes up his position.*]

AZDAK. Put me down. Then we'll get some air, maybe even a good stiff breeze from the lemon grove there. It does justice good to be done in the open: the wind blows her skirts up and you can see what she's got. Shauwa, we've been eating too much. These official journeys are exhausting. [*To the* INNKEEPER.] It's a question of your daughter-in-law?

THE INNKEEPER. Your Worship, it's a question of the family honor. I wish to bring an action on behalf of my son, who's away on business on the other side the mountain. This is the offending stableman, and here's my daughter-in-law.

[*Enter the* DAUGHTER-IN-LAW, *a voluptuous wench. She is veiled.*]

AZDAK [*sitting down*]. I accept.

[*Sighing, the* INNKEEPER *hands him some money.*]

Good. Now the formalities are disposed of. This is a case of rape?

THE INNKEEPER. Your Honor, I caught the fellow in the act. Ludovica was in the straw on the stable floor.

AZDAK. Quite right, the stable. Lovely horses! I specially liked the little roan.

THE INNKEEPER. The first thing I did, of course, was to question Ludovica. On my son's behalf.

AZDAK [*seriously*]. I said I specially liked the little roan.

THE INNKEEPER [*coldly*]. Really? Ludovica confessed the stableman took her against her will.

AZDAK. Take your veil off, Ludovica.

[*She does so.*]

Ludovica, you please the Court. Tell us how it happened.

LUDOVICA [*well schooled*]. When I entered the stable to see the new foal the stableman said to me on his own accord: "It's hot today!" and laid his hand on my left breast. I said to him: "Don't do that!" But he continued to handle me indecently, which provoked my anger. Before I realized his sinful intentions, he got much closer. It was all over when my father-in-law entered and accidentally trod on me.

THE INNKEEPER [*explaining*]. On my son's behalf.

AZDAK [*to the* STABLEMAN]. You admit you started it?

THE STABLEMAN. Yes.

AZDAK. Ludovica, you like to eat sweet things?

LUDOVICA. Yes, sunflower seeds!

AZDAK. You like to lie a long time in the bathtub?

LUDOVICA. Half an hour or so.

AZDAK. Public Prosecutor, drop your knife—there—on the
ground.

[SHAUWA *does so.*]

Ludovica, pick up that knife.

[LUDOVICA, *swaying her hips, does so.*]

See that? [*He points at her.*] The way it moves? The rape
is now proven. By eating too much—sweet things especially—by lying too long in warm water, by laziness and
too soft a skin, you have raped that unfortunate man. Think
you can run around with a behind like that and get away
with it in court? This is a case of intentional assault with a
dangerous weapon! You are sentenced to hand over to the
Court the little roan which your father liked to ride "on
his son's behalf." And now, come with me to the stables,
so the Court can inspect the scene of the crime, Ludovica.

THE STORYTELLER AND CHORUS.

> When the sharks the sharks devour
> Little fishes have their hour.
> For the while the load is off their back.
> On Grusinia's highways faring
> Fixed-up scales of justice bearing
> Strode the poor man's magistrate: Azdak.
>
> And he gave to the forsaken
> All that from the rich he'd taken.
> And a bodyguard of roughnecks was Azdak's.
> And our good and evil man, he
> Smiled upon Grusinia's Granny.
> His emblem was a tear in sealing wax.
>
> All mankind should love each other
> But when visiting your brother
> Take an ax along and hold it fast.
> Not in theory but in practice
> Miracles are wrought with axes
> And the age of miracles is not past.

[AZDAK's *judges chair is in a tavern.* THREE RICH FARMERS *stand before* AZDAK. SHAUWA *brings him wine. In a corner stands an* OLD PEASANT WOMAN. *In the open doorway, and outside, stand* VILLGERS *looking on. An* IRONSHIRT *stands guard with a banner.*]

AZDAK. The Public Prosecutor has the floor.

SHAUWA. It concerns a cow. For five weeks the defendant has had a cow in her stable, the property of the farmer Suru. She was also found to be in possession of a stolen ham, and a number of cows belonging to Shutoff were killed after he asked the defendant to pay the rent on a piece of land.

THE FARMERS. It's a matter of my ham, Your Honor.
—It's a matter of my cow, Your Honor.
—It's a matter of my land, Your Honor.

AZDAK. Well, Granny, what have *you* got to say to all this?

THE OLD WOMAN. Your Honor, one night toward morning, five weeks ago, there was a knock at my door, and outside stood a bearded man with a cow. "My dear woman," he said, "I am the miracle-working Saint Banditus and because your son has been killed in the war, I bring you this cow as a souvenir. Take good care of it."

THE FARMERS. The robber, Irakli, Your Honor!
—Her brother-in-law, Your Honor!
—The cow-thief!
—The incendiary!
—He must be beheaded!

[*Outside, a woman screams. The* CROWD *grows restless, retreats. Enter* THE BANDIT *Irakli with a huge ax.*]

THE BANDIT. A very good evening, dear friends! A glass of vodka!

THE FARMERS [*crossing themselves*]. Irakli!

AZDAK. Public Prosecutor, a glass of vodka for our guest. And who are you?

THE BANDIT. I'm a wandering hermit, Your Honor. Thanks for the gracious gift. [*He empties the glass which* SHAUWA *has brought.*] Another!

AZDAK. I am Azdak. [*He gets up and bows. The* BANDIT *also bows.*] The Court welcomes the foreign hermit. Go on with your story, Granny.

THE OLD WOMAN. Your Honor, that first night I didn't yet know Saint Banditus could work miracles, it was only the cow. But one night, a few days later, the farmer's servants came to take the cow away again. Then they turned round in front of my door and went off without the cow. And bumps as big as a fist sprouted on their heads. So I knew that Saint Banditus had changed their hearts and turned them into friendly people.

[*The* BANDIT *roars with laughter.*]

THE FIRST FARMER. I know what changed them.

AZDAK. That's fine. You can tell us later. Continue.

THE OLD WOMAN. Your Honor, the next one to become a good man was the farmer Shutoff—a devil, as everyone knows. But Saint Banditus arranged it so he let me off the rent on the little piece of land.

THE SECOND FARMER. Because my cows were killed in the field.

[*The* BANDIT *laughs.*]

THE OLD WOMAN [*answering* AZDAK's *sign to continue*]. Then one morning the ham came flying in at my window. It hit me in the small of the back. I'm still lame, Your Honor, look. [*She limps a few steps. The* BANDIT *laughs.*] Your Honor, was there ever a time when a poor old woman could get a ham *without* a miracle?

[*The* BANDIT *starts sobbing.*]

AZDAK [*rising from his chair*]. Granny, that's a question that strikes straight at the Court's heart. Be so kind as to sit here.

[*The* OLD WOMAN, *hesitating, sits in the judge's chair.*]

AZDAK [*sits on the floor, glass in hand, reciting*].

> Granny
> We could almost call you Granny Grusinia
> The Woebegone
> The Bereaved Mother
> Whose sons have gone to war
> Receiving the present of a cow
> She bursts out crying.
> When she is beaten
> She remains hopeful.
> When she's not beaten
> She's surprised.
> On us
> Who are already damned

May you render a merciful verdict
Granny Grusinia!

[*Bellowing at the* FARMERS.] Admit you don't believe in miracles, you atheists! Each of you is sentenced to pay five hundred piasters! For godlessness! Get out!

[*The* FARMERS *slink out.*]

And you Granny, and you [*to the* BANDIT] pious man, empty a pitcher of wine with the Public Prosecutor and Azdak!

THE STORYTELLER AND CHORUS.

And he broke the rules to save them.
Broken law like bread he gave them,
Brought them to shore upon his crooked back:
At long last the poor and lowly
Had someone who was not too holy
To be bribed by empty hands: Azdak.
For two years it was his pleasure
To give the beasts of prey short measure:
He became a wolf to fight the pack.
From All Hallows to All Hallows
On his chair beside the gallows
Dispensing justice in his fashion sat Azdak.

THE STORYTELLER.

But the era of disorder came to an end.
The Grand Duke returned.
The Governor's wife returned.
A trial was held.
Many died.
The people's quarters burned anew.
And fear seized Azdak.

[AZDAK's judge's chair stands again in the court of justice. AZDAK *sits on the floor, shaving and talking to* SHAUWA. *Noises outside. In the rear the* FAT PRINCE's *head is carried by on a lance.*]

AZDAK. Shauwa, the days of your slavery are numbered, maybe even the minutes. For a long time now I have held you in the iron curb of reason, and it has torn your mouth till it bleeds. I have lashed you with reasonable arguments, I have manhandled you with logic. You are by nature a weak

man, and if one slyly throws an argument in your path,
you *have* to snap it up, you can't resist. It is your nature
to lick the hand of some superior being. But superior beings
can be of very different kinds. And now, with your libera-
tion, you will soon be able to follow your natural inclina-
tions, which are low. You will be able to follow your
infallible instinct, which teaches you to plant your fat heel
on the faces of men. Gone is the era of confusion and
disorder, which I find described in the Song of Chaos. Let
us now sing that song together in memory of those terrible
days. Sit down and don't do violence to the music. Don't
be afraid. It sounds all right. And it has a fine refrain. [*He
sings.*]

THE SONG OF CHAOS

Sister, hide your face! Brother, take your knife!
The times are out of joint!
Big men are full of complaint
And small men full of joy.
The city says:
"Let us drive the mighty from our midst!"
Offices are raided. Lists of serfs are destroyed.
They have set Master's nose to the grindstone.
They who lived in the dark have seen the light.
The ebony poor box is broken.
Sesnem wood is sawed up for beds.
Who had no bread have barns full.
Who begged for alms of corn now mete it out.

SHAUWA [*refrain*]. Oh, oh, oh, oh.
AZDAK. [*refrain*].

Where are you, General, where are you?
Please, please, please, restore order!

The nobleman's son can no longer be recognized;
The lady's child becomes the son of her slave girl.
The councilors meet in a shed.
Once, this man was barely allowed to sleep on the wall;
Now, he stretches his limbs in a bed.
Once, this man rowed a boat; now, he owns ships.
Their owner looks for them, but they're his no longer.
Five men are sent on a journey by their master.
"Go yourself," they say, "we have arrived."

SHAUWA [*refrain*]. Oh, oh, oh, oh.
AZDAK [*refrain*].

> Where are you, General, where are you?
> Please, please, please, restore order!

Yes, so it might have been, had order been neglected much longer. But now the Grand Duke has returned to the capital, and the Persians have lent him an army to restore order with. The people's quarters are already aflame. Go and get me the big book I always sit on.

[SHAUWA *brings the big book from the judge's chair.* AZDAK *opens it.*]

This is the Statute Book and I've always used it, as you can testify. Now I'd better look in this book and see what they can do to me. I've let the down-and-outs get away with murder, and I'll have to pay for it. I helped poverty onto its skinny legs, so they'll hang me for drunkenness. I peeped into the rich man's pocket, which is bad taste. And I can't hide anywhere—everybody knows me because I've helped everybody.

SHAUWA. Someone's coming!

AZDAK [*in panic, he walks trembling to the chair*]. It's the end. And how they'd enjoy seeing what a Great Man I am! I'll deprive them of that pleasure. I'll beg on my knees for mercy. Spittle will slobber down my chin. The fear of death is in me.

[*Enter Natella Abashwili, the* GOVERNOR'S WIFE, *followed by the* ADJUTANT *and an* IRONSHIRT.]

THE GOVERNOR'S WIFE. What sort of a creature is that, Shalva?

AZDAK. A willing one, Your Highness, a man ready to oblige.

THE ADJUTANT. Natella Abashwili, wife of the late Governor, has just returned. She is looking for her two-year-old son, Michael. She has been informed that the child was carried off to the mountains by a former servant.

AZDAK. The child will be brought back, Your Highness, at your service.

THE ADJUTANT. They say that the person in question is passing it off as her own.

AZDAK. She will be beheaded, Your Highness, at your service.

THE ADJUTANT. That is all.

THE GOVERNOR'S WIFE [*leaving*]. I don't like that man.

AZDAK [*following her to door, bowing*]. At your service, Your Highness, it will all be arranged.

2

The Chalk Circle

THE STORYTELLER.

> Hear now the story of the trial
> Concerning Governor Abashwili's child
> And the determination of the true mother
> By the famous test of the Chalk Circle.

[*The court of justice in Nuka.* IRONSHIRTS *lead* MICHAEL *across stage and out at the back.* IRONSHIRTS *hold* GRUSHA *back with their lances under the gateway until the* CHILD *has been led through. Then she is admitted. She is accompanied by the former Governor's* COOK. *Distant noises and a fire-red sky.*]

GRUSHA [*trying to hide*]. He's brave, he can wash himself now.

THE COOK. You're lucky. It's not a real judge. It's Azdak, a drunk who doesn't know what he's doing. The biggest thieves have got by through him. Because he gets everything all mixed up and the rich never offer him big enough bribes, the likes of us sometimes do pretty well.

GRUSHA. I *need* luck right now.

THE COOK. Touch wood. [*She crosses herself.*] I'd better offer up another prayer that the judge may be drunk. [*She prays with motionless lips, while* GRUSHA *looks around, in vain, for the child.*] Why must you hold on to it at any price if it isn't yours? In days like these?

GRUSHA. He's mine. I brought him up.

THE COOK. Have you never thought what'd happen when she came back?

GRUSHA. At first I thought I'd give him to her. Then I thought she wouldn't come back.

THE COOK. And even a borrowed coat keeps a man warm, hm?

[GRUSHA *nods.*]

> I'll swear to anything for you. You're a decent girl. [*She sees the soldier* SIMON SHASHAVA *approaching.*] You've done

wrong by Simon, though. I've been talking with him. He
just can't understand.

GRUSHA [*unaware of* SIMON's *presence*]. Right now I can't be
bothered whether he understands or not!

THE COOK. He knows the child isn't yours, but you married
and not free "till death you do part"—he can't understand
that.

[GRUSHA *sees* SIMON *and greets him.*]

SIMON [*gloomily*]. I wish the lady to know I will swear I am
the father of the child.

GRUSHA [*low*]. Thank you, Simon.

SIMON. At the same time I wish the lady to know my hands
are not tied—nor are hers.

THE COOK. You needn't have said that. You know she's
married.

SIMON. And it needs no rubbing in.

[*Enter an* IRONSHIRT.]

THE IRONSHIRT. Where's the judge? Has anyone seen the judge?

ANOTHER IRONSHIRT [*stepping forward*]. The judge isn't here
yet. Nothing but a bed and a pitcher in the whole house!

[*Exeunt* IRONSHIRTS.]

THE COOK. I hope nothing has happened to him. With any
other judge you'd have as much chance as a chicken has
teeth.

GRUSHA [*who has turned away and covered her face*]. Stand
in front of me. I shouldn't have come to Nuka. If I run into
the Ironshirt, the one I hit over the head . . .

[*She screams. An* IRONSHIRT *had stopped and, turning his
back, had been listening to her. He now wheels around. It
is the* CORPORAL, *and he has a huge scar across his face.*]

THE IRONSHIRT [*in the gateway*]. What's the matter? Shotta?
Do you know her?

THE CORPORAL [*after staring for some time*]. No.

THE IRONSHIRT. She's the one who stole the Abashwili child,
or so they say. If you know anything about it you can make
some money, Shotta.

[*Exit the* CORPORAL, *cursing.*]

THE COOK. Was it him?

[GRUSHA *nods.*]

I think he'll keep his mouth shut, or he'd be admitting he was after the child.

GRUSHA. I'd almost forgotten him.

[*Enter the* GOVERNOR'S WIFE, *followed by the* ADJUTANT *and* TWO LAWYERS.]

THE GOVERNOR'S WIFE. At least there are no common people here, thank God. I can't stand their smell. It always gives me migraine.

THE FIRST LAWYER. Madam, I must ask you to be careful what you say until we have another judge.

THE GOVERNOR'S WIFE. But I didn't say anything, Illo Shuboladze. I love the people with their simple straightforward minds. It's only that their smell brings on my migraine.

THE SECOND LAWYER. There won't be many spectators. The whole population is sitting at home behind locked doors because of the riots in the people's quarters.

THE GOVERNOR'S WIFE [*looking at* GRUSHA]. Is that the creature?

THE FIRST LAWYER. Please, most gracious Natella Abashwili, abstain from invective until it is certain the Grand Duke has appointed a new judge and we're rid of the present one, who's about the lowest fellow ever seen in judge's gown. Things are all set to move, you see.

[*Enter* IRONSHIRTS *from the courtyard.*]

THE COOK. Her Grace would pull your hair out on the spot if she didn't know Azdak is for the poor. He goes by the face.

[IRONSHIRTS *begin fastening a rope to a beam.* AZDAK, *in chains, is led in, followed by* SHAUWA, *also in chains. The* THREE FARMERS *bring up the rear.*].

AN IRONSHIRT. Trying to run away, were you? [*He strikes* AZDAK.]

ONE FARMER. Off with his judge's gown before we string him up!

[IRONSHIRTS *and* FARMERS *tear off* AZDAK'S *gown. His torn underwear is visible. Then someone kicks him.*]

AN IRONSHIRT [*pushing him into someone else*]. Want a heap of justice? Here it is!

[*Accompanied by shouts of* "You take it!" *and* "Let me have him, brother!" *they throw* AZDAK *back and forth until he collapses. Then he is lifted up and dragged under the noose.*]

THE GOVERNOR'S WIFE [*who, during this "ball game," has clapped her hands hysterically*]. I disliked that man from the moment I first saw him.

AZDAK [*covered with blood, panting*]. I can't see. Give me a rag.

AN IRONSHIRT. What is it you want to see?

AZDAK. You, you dogs! [*He wipes the blood out of his eyes with his shirt.*] Good morning, dogs! How goes it, dogs! How's the dog world? Does it smell good? Got another boot for me to lick? Are you back at each other's throats, dogs?

[*Accompanied by a* CORPORAL, *a dust-covered* RIDER *enters. He takes some documents from a leather case, looks at them, then interrupts.*]

THE RIDER. Stop! I bring a dispatch from the Grand Duke, containing the latest appointments.

THE CORPORAL [*bellowing*]. Atten—shun!

THE RIDER. Of the new judge it says: "We appoint a man whom we have to thank for saving a life indispensable to the country's welfare—a certain Azdak of Nuka." Which is he?

SHAUWA [*pointing*]. That's him, Your Excellency.

THE CORPORAL [*bellowing*]. What's going on here?

AN IRONSHIRT. I beg to report that His Honor Azdak was already His Honor Azdak, but on these farmers' denunciation was pronounced the Grand Duke's enemy.

THE CORPORAL [*pointing at the* FARMERS]. March them off!

[*They are marched off. They bow all the time.*]
See to it that His Honor Azdak is exposed to no more violence.

[*Exeunt* RIDER *and* CORPORAL.]

THE COOK [*to* SHAUWA]. She clapped her hands! I hope he saw it!

THE FIRST LAWYER. It's a catastrophe.

[AZDAK *has fainted. Coming to, he is dressed again in judge's robes. He walks, swaying, toward the* IRONSHIRTS.]

AN IRONSHIRT. What does Your Honor desire?

AZDAK. Nothing, fellow dogs, or just an occasional boot to lick. [*To* SHAUWA.] I pardon you.

[*He is unchained.*]

Get me some red wine, the sweet kind.

[SHAUWA *stumbles off.*]

Get out of here, I've got to judge a case.

[*Exeunt* IRONSHIRTS. SHAUWA *returns with a pitcher of wine.* AZDAK *gulps it down.*]

Something for my backside.

[SHAUWA *brings the Statute Book, puts it on the judge's chair.* AZDAK *sits on it.*]

I accept.

[*The* PROSECUTORS, *among whom a worried council has been held, smile with relief. They whisper.*]

THE COOK. Oh dear!

SIMON. A well can't be filled with dew, they say.

THE LAWYERS [*approaching* AZDAK, *who stands up, expectantly*]. A quite ridiculous case, Your Honor. The accused has abducted a child and refuses to hand it over.

AZDAK [*stretching out his hand, glancing at* GRUSHA]. A most attractive person. [*He fingers the money, then sits down, satisfied.*] I declare the proceedings open and demand the whole truth. [*To* GRUSHA.] Especially from you.

THE FIRST LAWYER. High Court of Justice! Blood, as the popular saying goes, is thicker than water. This old adage . . .

AZDAK [*interrupting*]. The Court wants to know the lawyers' fee.

THE FIRST LAWYER [*surprised*]. I beg your pardon?

[AZDAK, *smiling, rubs his thumb and index finger.*]

Oh, I see. Five hundred piasters, Your Honor, to answer the Court's somewhat unusual question.

AZDAK. Did you hear? The question is unusual. I ask it because I listen in quite a different way when I know you're good.

THE FIRST LAWYER [*bowing*]. Thank you, Your Honor. High

Court of Justice, of all ties the ties of blood are strongest.
Mother and child—is there a more intimate relationship?
Can one tear a child from its mother? High Court of Justice,
she has conceived it in the holy ecstasies of love. She has
carried it in her womb. She has fed it with her blood. She
has borne it with pain. High Court of Justice, it has been
observed that even the wild tigress, robbed of her young,
roams restless through the mountains, shrunk to a shadow.
Nature herself . . .

AZDAK [*interrupting, to* GRUSHA]. What's you answer to all this
and anything else that lawyer might have to say?

GRUSHA. He's mine.

AZDAK. Is that all? I hope you can prove it. Why should I
assign the child to you in any case?

GRUSHA. I brought him up like the priest says "according to my
best knowledge and conscience." I always found him something to eat. Most of the time he had a roof over his head.
And I went to such trouble for him. I had expenses too. I
didn't look out for my own comfort. I brought the child
up to be friendly with everyone, and from the beginning
taught him to work. As well as he could, that is. He's still
very little.

THE FIRST LAWYER. Your Honor, it is significant that the girl
herself doesn't claim any tie of blood between her and the
child.

AZDAK. The Court takes note of that.

THE FIRST LAWYER. Thank you, Your Honor. And now permit
a woman bowed in sorrow—who has already lost her
husband and now has also to fear the loss of her child—
to address a few words to you. The gracious Natella Abashwili is . . .

THE GOVERNOR'S WIFE [*quietly*]. A most cruel fate, sir, forces
me to describe to you the tortures of a bereaved mother's
soul, the anxiety, the sleepless nights, the . . .

THE SECOND LAWYER [*bursting out*]. It's outrageous the way
this woman is being treated! Her own husband's palace is
closed to her! The revenue of her estates is blocked, and
she is cold-bloodedly told that it's tied to the heir. She can't
do anything without that child. She can't even pay her
lawyers!! [*To the* FIRST LAWYER, *who, desperate about this
outburst, makes frantic gestures to keep him from speaking.*] Dear Illo Shuboladze, surely it can be divulged now
that the Abashwili estates are at stake?

THE FIRST LAWYER. Please, Honored Sandro Oboladze! We agreed . . . [*To* AZDAK.] Of course it is correct that the trial will also decide if our noble client can take over the Abashwili estates, which are rather extensive. I say "also" advisedly, for in the foreground stands the human tragedy of a mother, as Natella Abashwili very properly explained in the first words of her moving statement. Even if Michael Abashwili were not heir to the estates, he would still be the dearly beloved child of my client.

AZDAK. Stop! The Court is touched by the mention of estates. It's a proof of human feeling.

THE SECOND LAWYER. Thanks, Your Honor. Dear Illo Shuboladze, we can prove in any case that the woman who took the child is not the child's mother. Permit me to lay before the Court the bare facts. High Court of Justice, by an unfortunate chain of circumstances, Michael Abashwili was left behind on that Easter Sunday while his mother was making her escape. Grusha, a palace kitchen maid, was seen with the baby . . .

THE COOK. All her mistress was thinking of was what dresses she'd take along!

THE SECOND LAWYER [*unmoved*]. Nearly a year later Grusha turned up in a mountain village with a baby and there entered into the state of matrimony with . . .

AZDAK. How'd you get to that mountain village?

GRUSHA. On foot, Your Honor. And it was mine.

SIMON. I'm the father, Your Honor.

THE COOK. I used to look after it for them, Your Honor. For five piasters.

THE SECOND LAWYER. This man is engaged to Grusha, High Court of Justice: his testimony is not trustworthy.

AZDAK. Are you the man she married in the mountain village?

SIMON. No, Your Honor, she married a peasant.

AZDAK [*to* GRUSHA]. Why? [*Pointing at* SIMON.] Is he no good in bed? Tell the truth.

GRUSHA. We didn't get that far. I married because of the baby. So he'd have a roof over his head. [*Pointing at* SIMON.] He was in the war, Your Honor.

AZDAK. And now he wants you back again, huh?

SIMON. I wish to state in evidence . . .

GRUSHA [*angrily*]. I am no longer free, Your Honor.

AZDAK. And the child, you claim, comes from whoring?

[GRUSHA *doesn't answer.*]

I'm going to ask you a question: What kind of child is he? A ragged little bastard? Or from a well-to-do family?

GRUSHA [*angrily*]. He's an ordinary child.

AZDAK. I mean—did he have refined features from the beginning?

GRUSHA. He had a nose on his face.

AZDAK. A very significant comment! It has been said of me that I went out one time and sniffed at a rosebush before rendering a verdict—tricks like that are needed nowadays. Well, I'll make it short, and not listen to any more lies. [*To* GRUSHA.] Especially not yours. [*To all the accused.*] I can imagine what you've cooked up to cheat me! I know you people. You're swindlers.

GRUSHA [*suddenly*]. I can understand you wanting to cut it short, now I've seen what you accepted!

AZDAK. Shut up! Did I accept anything from you?

GRUSHA [*while the* COOK *tries to restrain her*]. I haven't got anything.

AZDAK. True. Quite true. From starvelings I never get a thing. I might just as well starve, myself. You want justice, but do you want to pay for it, hm? When you go to a butcher you know you have to pay, but you people go to a judge as if you were off to a funeral supper.

SIMON [*loudly*]. When the horse was shod, the horsefly held out its leg, as the saying is.

AZDAK [*eagerly accepting the challenge*]. Better a treasure in manure than a stone in a mountain stream.

SIMON. A fine day. Let's go fishing, said the angler to the worm.

AZDAK. I'm my own master, said the servant, and cut off his foot.

SIMON. I love you as a father, said the Czar to the peasants, and had the Czarevitch's head chopped off.

AZDAK. A fool's worst enemy is himself.

SIMON. However, a fart has no nose.

AZDAK. Fined ten piasters for indecent language in court! That'll teach you what justice is.

GRUSHA [*furiously*]. A fine kind of justice! You play fast and loose with us because we don't talk as refined as that crowd with their lawyers!

AZDAK. That's true. You people are too dumb. It's only right you should get it in the neck.

GRUSHA. You want to hand the child over to her, and she wouldn't even know how to keep it dry, she's so "refined"! You know about as much about justice as I do!

AZDAK. There's something in that. I'm an ignorant man. Haven't even a decent pair of pants on under this gown. Look! With me, everything goes for food and drink—I was educated in a convent. Incidentally, I'll fine you ten piasters for contempt of court. And you're a very silly girl, to turn me against you, instead of making eyes at me and wiggling your backside a little to keep me in good temper. Twenty piasters!

GRUSHA. Even if it was thirty, I'd tell you what I think of your justice, you drunken onion! [*Incoherently.*] How dare you talk to me like the cracked Isaiah on the church window? As if you were somebody? For you weren't born to this. You weren't born to rap your own mother on the knuckles if she swipes a little bowl of salt someplace. Aren't you ashamed of yourself when you see how I tremble before you? You've made yourself their servant so no one will take their houses from them—houses they had stolen! Since when have houses belonged to the bedbugs? But you're on the watch, or they couldn't drag our men into their wars! You bribe taker!

[AZDAK *half gets up, starts beaming. With his little hammer he halfheartedly knocks on the table as if to get silence. As* GRUSHA's *scolding continues, he only beats time with his hammer.*]

I've no respect for you. No more than a thief or a bandit with a knife! You can do what you want. You can take the child away from me, a hundred against one, but I tell you one thing: only extortioners should be chosen for a profession like yours, and men who rape children! As punishment! Yes, let *them* sit in judgment on their fellow creatures. It is worse than to hang from the gallows.

AZDAK [*sitting down*]. Now it'll be thirty! And I won't go on squabbling with you—we're not in a tavern. What'd happen to my dignity as a judge? Anyway, I've lost interest in your case. Where's the couple who wanted a divorce? [*To* SHAUWA.] Bring 'em in. This case is adjourned for fifteen minutes.

THE FIRST LAWYER [*to the* GOVERNOR'S WIFE]. Even without using the rest of the evidence, Madam, we have the verdict in the bag.

THE COOK [*to* GRUSHA]. You've gone and spoiled your chances with him. You won't get the child now.

THE GOVERNOR'S WIFE. Shalva, my smelling salts!

[*Enter a* VERY OLD COUPLE.]

AZDAK. I accept.

[*The* OLD COUPLE *don't understand.*]

   I hear you want to be divorced. How long have you been together?

THE OLD WOMAN. Forty years, Your Honor.

AZDAK. And why do you want a divorce?

THE OLD MAN. We don't like each other, Your Honor.

AZDAK. Since when?

THE OLD WOMAN. Oh, from the very beginning, Your Honor.

AZDAK. I'll think about your request and render my verdict when I'm through with the other case.

[SHAUWA *leads them back.*]

   I need the child. [*He beckons* GRUSHA *to him and bends not unkindly toward her.*] I've noticed you have a soft spot for justice. I don't believe he's your child, but if he *were* yours, woman, wouldn't you want him to be rich? You'd only have to say he wasn't yours, and he'd have a palace and many horses in his stables and many beggars on his doorstep and many soldiers in his service and many petitioners in his courtyard, wouldn't he? What do you say— don't you want him to be rich?

[GRUSHA *is silent.*]

THE STORYTELLER.
   Hear now what the angry girl thought but did not say:

> Had he golden shoes to wear
> He'd be cruel as a bear.
> Evil would his life disgrace.
> He'd laugh in my face.
>
> Carrying a heart of flint
> Is too troublesome a stint.
> Being powerful and bad
> Is hard on a lad.

Then let hunger be his foe!
Hungry men and women, no.
Let him fear the darksome night
But not daylight!

AZDAK. I think I understand you, woman.
GRUSHA [*suddenly and loudly*]. I won't give him up. I've raised him, and he knows me.

[*Enter* SHAUWA *with the* CHILD.]

THE GOVERNOR'S WIFE. It's in rags!
GRUSHA. That's not true. But I wasn't given time to put his good shirt on.
THE GOVERNOR'S WIFE. It must have been in a pigsty.
GRUSHA [*furiously*]. I'm not a pig, but there are some who are! Where did you leave your baby?
THE GOVERNOR'S WIFE. I'll show you, you vulgar creature! [*She is about to throw herself on* GRUSHA, *but is restrained by her* LAWYERS.] She's a criminal, she must be whipped. Immediately!
THE SECOND LAWYER [*holding his hand over her mouth*]. Natella Abashwili, you promised . . . Your Honor, the plaintiff's nerves . . .
AZDAK. Plaintiff and defendant! The Court has listened to your case, and has come to no decision as to who the real mother is; therefore, I, the judge, am obliged to *choose* a mother for the child. I'll make a test. Shauwa, get a piece of chalk and draw a circle on the floor.

[SHAUWA *does so*.]

Now place the child in the center.

[SHAUWA *puts* MICHAEL, *who smiles at* GRUSHA, *in the center of the circle*.]

Stand near the circle, both of you.

[*The* GOVERNOR'S WIFE *and* GRUSHA *step up to the circle*.]

Now each of you take the child by one hand.

[*They do so*.]

The true mother is she who can pull the child out of the circle.
THE SECOND LAWYER [*quickly*]. High Court of Justice, I

object! The fate of the great Abashwili estates, which are tied to the child, as the heir, should not be made dependent on such a doubtful duel. In addition, my client does not command the strength of this person, who is accustomed to physical work.

AZDAK. She looks pretty well fed to me. Pull!

[*The* GOVERNOR'S WIFE *pulls the* CHILD *out of the circle on her side;* GRUSHA *has let go and stands aghast.*]

What's the matter with you? You didn't pull!

GRUSHA. I didn't hold on to him.

THE FIRST LAWYER [*congratulating the* GOVERNOR'S WIFE]. What did I say! The ties of blood!

GRUSHA [*running to* AZDAK]. Your Honor, I take back everything I said against you. I ask your forgiveness. But could I keep him till he can speak all the words? He knows a few.

AZDAK. Don't influence the Court. I bet you only know about twenty words yourself. All right, I'll make the test once more, just to be certain. [*The* TWO WOMEN *take up their positions again.*] Pull! [*Again* GRUSHA *lets go of the* CHILD.]

GRUSHA [*in despair*]. I brought him up! Shall I also tear him to pieces? I can't!

AZDAK [*rising*]. And in this manner the Court has determined the true mother. [*To* GRUSHA.] Take your child and be off. I advise you not to stay in the city with him. [*To the* GOVERNOR'S WIFE.] And you disappear before I fine you for fraud. Your estates fall to the city. They'll be converted into a playground for the children. They need one, and I've decided it'll be called after me: Azdak's Garden.

[*The* GOVERNOR'S WIFE *has fainted and is carried out by the* LAWYERS *and the* ADJUTANT. GRUSHA *stands motionless.* SHAUWA *leads the* CHILD *toward her.*]

Now I'll take off this judge's gown—it has grown too hot for me. I'm not cut out for a hero. In token of farewell I invite you all to a little dance outside on the meadow. Oh, I'd almost forgotten something in my excitement . . . to sign the divorce decree. [*Using the judge's chair as a table, he writes something on a piece of paper, and prepares to leave. Dance music has started.*]

SHAUWA [*having read what is on the paper*]. But that's not right. You've not divorced the old couple. You've divorced Grusha!

AZDAK. Have I divorced the wrong couple? What a pity! And I never retract! If I did, how could we keep order in the land? [*To the* OLD COUPLE.] I'll invite you to my party instead. You don't mind dancing with each other, do you? [*To* GRUSHA *and* SIMON.] I've got forty piasters coming from you.

SIMON [*pulling out his purse*]. Cheap at the price, Your Honor. And many thanks.

AZDAK [*pocketing the cash*]. I'll need this.

GRUSHA [*to* MICHAEL]. So we'd better leave the city tonight, Michael? [*To* SIMON.] You like him?

SIMON. With my respects, I like him.

GRUSHA. Now I can tell you: I took him because on that Easter Sunday I got engaged to you. So he's a child of love. Michael, let's dance.

[*She dances with* MICHAEL, SIMON *dances with the* COOK, *the* OLD COUPLE *with each other.* AZDAK *stands lost in thought. The dancers soon hide him from view. Occasionally he is seen, but less and less as* MORE COUPLES *join in the dance.*]

THE STORYTELLER.

And after that evening Azdak vanished and was never seen again.

The people of Grusinia did not forget him but long remembered

The period of his judging as a brief golden age,

Almost an age of justice.

[ALL THE COUPLES *dance off.* AZDAK *has disappeared.*]

But you, you who have listened to the Story of the Chalk Circle,

Take note what men of old concluded:

That what there is shall go to those who are good for it,

Children to the motherly, that they prosper,

Carts to good drivers, that they be driven well,

The valley to the waterers, that it yield fruit.

THE WRITERS AND THEIR PLAYS

BUECHNER, GEORG—1813–1837 (completion dates).
Danton's Death, 1835; Lenz, 1836; Leone and Lena, 1836; Woyzeck, 1836.

HEBBEL, FRIEDRICH—1813–1863 (publication dates).
Judith, 1841; Genoveva, 1843; Maria Magdalena, 1844; Der Diamant, 1847; Herod and Mariamne, 1850; Der Rubin, 1851; Ein Trauerspiel in Sicilien, 1851; Julia, 1851; Michel Angelo, 1855; Agnes Bernauer, 1855; Gyges and His Ring, 1856; Die Nibelungen, 1862; Demetrius, 1864 (unfinished).

HAUPTMANN, GERHARDT—1862–1946 (publication dates).
Before Sunrise, 1889; The Festival of Peace; 1890; Lonely Lives, 1891; Colleague Crampton, 1892; The Weavers, 1892; The Beaver Coat, 1893; The Assumption of Hannele, 1893; Florian Geyer, 1894; Helios, 1896; The Sunken Bell, 1896; Elga, 1898; Pastoral, 1898; Drayman Henschel, 1898; Michael Kramer, 1900; The Conflagration (The Red Cock), 1901; Poor Heinrich, 1902; Rose Bernd, 1903; And Pippa Dances, 1906; The Maidens of Bishofsberg, 1907; Charlemagne's Hostage, 1908; Griselda, 1909; The Rats, 1911; Gabriel Schilling's Flight, 1912; The Festival Play, 1913; The Bow of Odysseus, 1914; Winter Ballad, 1917; The White Savior, 1920; Indipohdi, 1920; Peter Brauer, 1921; Veland, 1925; Dorothea Angermann, 1926; Witches' Ride, 1930; The Black Mask, 1930; Before Sunset, 1932; The Golden Harp, 1933; Hamlet at Wittenberg, 1935; Die Finsternisse, 1937; Ulrich of Lichtenstein, 1939; The Daughter of the Cathedral, 1939; Iphigenia in Delphi, 1941; Iphigenia in Aulis, 1944; Agamemnon's Death and Electra, 1948.

WEDEKIND, FRANK—1864–1918 (publication dates).
Der Schnellmaler, oder Kunst und Mammon, 1887; Rie junge, Welt oder Kinder und Narren, 1889; The Awakening of Spring, 1891; Fritz Schwigerling, 1892; The Earth Spirit, 1895; The Tenor, 1897; The Marquis of Keith, 1900; Such Is Life, 1902; Pandora's Box, 1904; Hidalla, 1904; Damnation, 1905; Music, 1906; Zensur, 1908; Der Stein der Weisen, 1909; Oaha (Till Eulenspiegel), 1909; Schloss Wetterstein, 1910; Franzisca, 1912;

Simson, 1914; Bismarck, 1915; Herakles, 1919; The Solar Spectrum, 1921.

BRECHT, BERTOLT—1898-56 (approximate completion dates).
Baal, 1918; Drums in the Night, 1918; The Wedding, 1919; The Beggar, or The Dead Dog, 1919; He Exorcises a Devil, 1919; Light in Darkness, 1919; In the Jungle of Cities, 1923; Life of Edward II of England (with Lion Feuchtwanger), 1924; Calcutta, May 4 (with Lion Feuchtwanger), 1925; A Man's a Man, 1925; The Baby Elephant, 1925; The Threepenny Opera, 1928; Happy End (written with Elisabeth Hauptmann), 1929; The Flight of the Lindberghs, 1929; Downfall of the Egoist Johann Fatzer (unfinished), 1930; Rise and Fall of the City of Mahagonny, 1929; The Didactic Play of Baden: On Consent, 1929; He Who Says Yes, 1930; He Who Says No, 1930; The Bread Shop, 1930; St. Joan of the Stockyards, 1930; The Measures Taken, 1930; The Exception and the Rule, 1930; The Mother: Life of the Revolutionary Pelageya Vlasova from Tver, 1932; The Roundheads and the Peakheads, 1934; The Seven Deadly Sins of the Petty Bourgeois (Anna Anna), 1933; The Horatians and the Curiatians, 1934; Senora Carrar's Rifles, 1937; Fear and Misery of the Third Reich (also known as The Private Life of the Master Race), 1938; Mother Courage and Her Children, 1939; The Trial of Lucullus, 1939; Galileo, 1939; The Good Woman of Setzuan, 1940; Mr. Puntila and His Hired Man, Matti, 1941; The Resistible Rise of Arturo Ui, 1941; The Visions of Simone Machard (with Lion Feuchtwanger), 1942; Schweik in the Second World War, 1944; Life of Confucius, 1944; The Caucasian Chalk Circle, 1945; The Antigone of Sophocles, 1948; The Days of the Commune, 1949; The Private Tutor, 1950; Report on Herrnburg, 1951; The Trial of Joan of Arc of Roven, 1431, 1952; Don Juan, 1952; Coriolan, 1953; Turandot, or the Congress of Whitewashers (unfinished), 1955; Trumpets and Drums (with Elisabeth Hauptmann and Benno Besson), 1955.

SELECTED BIBLIOGRAPHY

General

BENTLEY, ERIC. *The Playwright As Thinker*. New York, 1946; revised 1955.

BRUSTEIN, ROBERT. *The Theatre of Revolt*. New York, 1964.

CORRIGAN, ROBERT W. *The Theatre in the 20th Century*. New York, 1963.

GARTEN, H. F. *Modern German Drama*. Fairlawn, N. J., 1959.

SHAW, LEROY R. *German Theatre Today*. Austin, Texas, 1964.

Buechner

BAXANDALL, LEE. Introduction to *Woyzeck* and *Leone and Lena* (Tr. by Carl Richard Mueller), Chandler Editions in Drama. San Francisco, 1962.

————. "Buechner's *Danton's Death*," *Tulane Drama Review*. March, 1962.

HOFFMAN, THEODORE. Introduction to *Danton's Death* (Tr. by James Maxwell), Chandler Editions in Drama. San Francisco, 1961.

KNIGHT, A. J. H. *George Buechner*. Oxford, 1951.

PEACOCK, RONALD. *The Poet in the Theatre*. New York, 1960.

VIETOR, KARL. "Georg Buechner," *New Directions* vol. 1, no. 12, New York, 1950.

Hebbel

ALLEN, L. H. Introduction to *Herod and Other Plays*, New York, 1914.

MUELLER, CARL RICHARD. Introduction to *Maria Magdalena* (Tr. by Carl Richard Mueller), Chandler Editions in Drama. San Francisco, 1962.

PEACOCK, RONALD. *op. cit.*, New York, 1960.

Hauptmann

GARTEN, H. F. *Gerhart Hauptmann*, New Haven, 1954.

SINDEN, MARGARET. *Gerhart Hauptmann: The Prose Plays*. Toronto, 1957.

Wedekind

FEUCHTWANGER, LEON. Introduction to *Five Tragedies of Sex.* New York, 1952.
SOKEL, WALTER. *The Writer in Extremis.* Stanford, 1959.

Brecht

DEMETZ, PETER. *Brecht* (Twentieth Century Views Series). Englewood Cliffs, 1962.
ESSLIN, MARTIN. *Brecht: The Man and His Work.* Garden City, 1960.
GRAY, RONALD. *Bertolt Brecht.* New York, 1961.
Tulane Drama Review: Brecht Issue. September, 1961.
WEIDELI, WALTER. *The Art of Bertolt Brecht.* New York, 1963.
WILLETT, JOHN. *The Theatre of Bertolt Brecht.* London, 1959.